Democratic Governance
in Latin America

WITHDRAWN
UTSA LIBRARIES

Democratic Governance
in Latin America

Edited by
Scott Mainwaring and Timothy R. Scully

STANFORD UNIVERSITY PRESS
STANFORD, CALIFORNIA

Stanford University Press
Stanford, California

This book has been published with the assistance of the
University of Notre Dame.

Printed in the United States of America on acid-free, archival-quality paper

Library of Congress Cataloging-in-Publication Data

Democratic governance in Latin America / edited by Scott Mainwaring and
Timothy R. Scully.
p. cm.
Includes bibliographical references and index.
ISBN 978-0-8047-6084-3 (cloth : alk. paper)—ISBN 978-0-8047-6085-0
(pbk. : alk. paper)
1. Democracy—Latin America.   2. Latin America—Politics and
government—1980–   3. Latin America—Economic conditions—1982–
I. Mainwaring, Scott, 1954–   II. Scully, Timothy.
JL966.D4575 2009
321.8098—dc22   2009027001

Typeset by Publishers' Design and Production Service, Inc. in 10/12 Sabon

Contents

Tables and Figures

Acknowledgments

We undertook this book because of a normative concern about the quality of democratic governance in much of contemporary Latin America, a conviction that improving democratic governance is the single greatest challenge facing Latin America today, and a desire to contribute toward scholarly understanding of ways to improve democratic governance. Much of the scholarship on contemporary Latin America has justifiably emphasized the shortcomings of democratic governance. With this volume, we wanted to also call attention to the possibilities of success and the conditions that might foster it.

Most of the chapters for this volume were presented at an eponymous conference at the Kellogg Institute for International Studies at the University of Notre Dame, October 7–8, 2005. We are grateful to the Coca-Cola Company for a generous grant that helped support the conference, the last of many that this grant helped to underwrite. The Provost Office of the University of Notre Dame provided additional support for the project. Comments by Wendy Hunter, Jaime Ros, Eugenio Tironi, Constantino Urcuyo, Samuel Valenzuela, and Jorge Vargas Cullell enriched the conference held at Notre Dame. Joan Nelson also participated in and enhanced the conference. The staff of the Kellogg Institute provided capable support in organizing the conference.

The Kellogg Institute has been a great intellectual home for both of us. Our colleagues Michael Coppedge, Robert Fishman, Frances Hagopian, Guillermo O'Donnell, and Samuel Valenzuela have enriched our understanding of the issues we analyze in this volume. Seven of the authors who contributed to this volume have been Visiting Fellows at the Kellogg Institute, and another, Alejandro Foxley, was a faculty colleague at Kellogg. We also thank the staff members of the Kellogg Institute for organizing the conference, and our assistants, Peg Hartman and Terri Prister, for help with many details.

Ignacio Walker, who coauthored a chapter in this volume, was a key part of the conversations and brainstorming that led to this project.

Several of the papers were also presented at a conference on democratic governance organized by CIEPLAN in Santiago, Chile, in January 2006. We thank our friends at CIEPLAN for organizing the Santiago conference, which was cosponsored by the Kellogg Institute.

Dana Bell, Drew Clary, María Victoria De Negri, and Emily Wauford provided invaluable assistance putting the book together.

Both of us have long valued the support Stanford University Press has offered us. We are especially grateful to our editor, Norris Pope. Both of us worked with Norris on our first books, and it was a particular pleasure having the opportunity to work with him on this project many years later. We also appreciated the assistance of Emily Smith of Stanford University Press and of Denise Botelho, our very capable project manager.

Contributors

Alan Angell is Emeritus Fellow of Saint Antony's College, Oxford University where he was University Lecturer in Latin American Politics and Fellow of St. Antony's College, Oxford University. Angell also served as director of the Latin American Centre at Oxford (2002–2004). His major interests are in the politics of Chile, the politics of the Left in Latin America, social policies, and the relationship between law and politics in the process of democratic transition. His recent publications include, with Rosemary Thorp and Pamela Lowden, *Decentralising Development: the Political Economy of Institutional Change in Colombia and Chile* (Oxford University Press, 2001), and *Democracy after Pinochet: Politics, Parties and Elections in Chile* (Institute for the Study of the Americas, London, 2006)

Daniel M. Brinks is Associate Professor of Political Science at the University of Notre Dame. His research focuses on the role of the law and courts in supporting democratic citizenship, with a primary regional interest in Latin America. His most recent projects address the judicial response to police violence in South America and the enforcement of social and economic rights around the world. He recently published *The Judicial Response to Police Killings in Latin America: Inequality and the Rule of Law* (Cambridge, 2008) and *Courting Social Justice: Judicial Enforcement of Social and Economic Rights in the Developing World* (Cambridge, 2008) (coedited with V. Gauris). He holds a PhD in Political Science from the University of Notre Dame and a JD from the University of Michigan Law School.

Fernando Henrique Cardoso served as President of Brazil for two terms (1995–2003). His pathbreaking scholarship on political and economic development shaped a generation of thought in Latin America. He established the Brazilian Center for Analysis and Research (CEBRAP), which became an influential think tank both in Brazil and internationally. He served as Senator of São Paulo, Minister of Foreign Relations, and Minister of Finance before serving as Brazil's President. Among many honors and awards, he received the Notre Dame Prize for Distinguished Public Service in Latin America in 2003. He is currently the President of the Fernando Henrique Cardoso Institute in Brazil.

Alejandro Foxley is a Senior Associate at the Carnegie Endowment in Washington and President of CIEPLAN in Santiago, Chile. He served as the Foreign Minister of Chile from 2006–2009. Previously, he served in the Chilean Senate from 1998 until 2006, where he was Chairman of the Finance Committee of the Senate. He was Minister of Finance under President Patricio Aylwin, 1990–1994, and later was President of the Christian Democratic Party. He has been a Senior Fellow at the Helen Kellogg Institute for International Studies and Helen Kellogg Professor of Economics at the University of Notre Dame. He is a member of the Growth and Development Commission of the World Bank and has been a member of the International Advisory Board of the Council on Foreign Relations, New York, and a member of the Board of the Inter-American Dialogue, Washington. He is the founding president of CIEPLAN. He holds a PhD in Economics from the University of Wisconsin.

José De Gregorio has been Governor of the Central Bank of Chile since 2007. He was Vice-President of the Bank from 2003–2007, and he has been a member of its Governing Board since June 2001. Previously, he simultaneously occupied three cabinet positions as Minister of Economy, Mining, and Energy (2000–2001). In these positions he was also chairman of the Board of CODELCO, Chile's publicly owned mining companies. From 1997–2000 he served as head of postgraduate programs and professor at the Center of Applied Economics at the University of Chile, where he taught macroeconomics and international economics. De Gregorio was also director of Economic Policy at the Ministry of Finance, Chile (1994–1997) and worked as an economist at the International Monetary Fund (1990–1994). He has published widely in international academic journals and books on issues including macroeconomic policies, exchange rates, and economic growth. He holds a PhD in economics from MIT.

Evelyne Huber is Morehead Alumni Professor of Political Science at the University of North Carolina, Chapel Hill. She is the author of *The Politics of Workers' Participation: The Peruvian Approach in Comparative Perspective* (1980), coauthor of *Democratic Socialism in Jamaica* (with John D. Stephens, 1986), coauthor of *Capitalist Development and Democracy* (with Dietrich Rueschemeyer and John D. Stephens, 1992;

co-winner of the Outstanding Book Award 1991–1992 from the American Sociological Association, Political Sociology Section), and coauthor of *Development and Crisis of the Welfare State* (with John D. Stephens, 2001; winner of the Best Book Award 2001 from the American Political Science Association, Political Economy Section).

José Miguel Insulza was elected Secretary General of the Organization of American States in 2005. Until 1973, he was Professor of Political Theory at the University of Chile and of Political Science at Chile's Catholic University. While in exile during Pinochet's rule, he was a researcher and Director of the United States Studies Institute in the Center for Economic Research and Teaching. He taught at Mexico's National Autonomous University, the Ibero-American University, and the Diplomatic Studies Institute. Since returning to Chile, Insulza has served as Minister of Foreign Affairs, Minister and Secretary General of the Office of the President, and President Ricardo Lagos's Minister of the Interior and Vice President of the Republic. He holds a law degree from the University of Chile and a MA in Political Science from the University of Michigan.

Scott Mainwaring is Eugene Conley Professor of Political Science at the University of Notre Dame and Director of the Helen Kellogg Institute for International Studies. His recent books include *The Crisis of Democratic Representation in the Andes* (Stanford University Press, 2006, coedited), *The Third Wave of Democratization in Latin America: Advances and Setbacks* (Cambridge University Press, 2005, coedited), *Democratic Accountability in Latin America* (Oxford University Press, 2003, coedited), and *Christian Democracy in Latin America* (Stanford University Press, 2003, coedited).

Juliana Martínez Franzoni investigates at the Institute of Social Research and teaches at the School of Political Science, both at the University of Costa Rica. Her research revolves around relations between markets, states and families. Recent publications include *Domesticar la incertidumbre en América Latina: mercado laboral, política social y familias* (San José: Editorial de la Universidad de Costa Rica, 2008); "Welfare Regimes in Latin America: Capturing Constellations of Markets, Families and Policies" (*Latin American Politics and Society*, Summer 2008); and "Costa Rica's Pension Reform: A Decade of Negotiated Incremental Change" (in *Lessons from Pension Reform in the Americas*, edited by Stephen J. Kay and Tapen Sinha, New York: Oxford University Press, 2008). She holds a PhD from the University of Pittsburgh.

Patricio Navia teaches in the General Studies Program and is an adjunct assistant professor in the Center for Latin American and Caribbean

Studies at New York University. He is also a researcher and professor at the Instituto de Investigación en Ciencias Sociales at Universidad Diego Portales in Chile. He has published articles and book chapters on democratization, electoral rules, and democratic institutions in Latin America. His books include *Las grandes alamedas: El Chile post Pinochet* (2004) and *Que gane el más mejor. Mérito y Competencia en el Chile de hoy* (coauthored with Eduardo Engel, 2006). He holds a PhD in Politics from New York University.

Francisco Rodríguez is Head of Research at the Human Development Report Office. He has taught at the University of Maryland, College Park, the Instituto de Estudios Superiores de Administración in Caracas, and Wesleyan University. From 2000–2004, he served as Chief Economist to the Venezuelan National Assembly. His publications include "Trade Policy and Economic Growth: A Skeptic's Guide to the Cross-National Evidence" (with Dani Rodrik, *2000 NBER Macroeconomics Annual*), "Why Do Resource-Abundant Economies Grow More Slowly?" (with Jeffrey Sachs, *Journal of Economic Growth*, September 1999), and "An Empty Revolution: The Unfulfilled Promises of Hugo Chávez" (*Foreign Affairs*, March/April 2008). He holds a PhD in Economics from Harvard University.

Timothy R. Scully is Professor of Political Science, Fellow of the Kellogg Institute for International Studies, and Director of the Institute for Educational Initiatives at the University of Notre Dame. He has held research grants from the Social Science Research Council and the Fulbright Commission, as well as the Woodrow Wilson Center for International Scholars. He is the author of numerous articles and books, including *Rethinking the Center: Party Evolution in Nineteenth and Twentieth Century Chile* (Stanford University Press, 1992), and coauthor of *Christian Democracy in Latin America: Electoral Competition and Regime Conflict* (Stanford University Press, 2003, coedited), *Building Democratic Institutions: Party Systems in Latin America* (Stanford University Press, 1995, coedited), *Vínculos, creencias e ilusiones. La cohesión social de los latinoamericanos* (Uqbar editors, 2008, coedited), *El eslabón perdido. Familia, bienestar y modernización en Chile* (Taurus, 2006, coedited).

Mitchell A. Seligson is Centennial Professor of Political Science and Professor of Sociology at Vanderbilt University and Director of the Latin American Public Opinion Project (LAPOP). He previously held the Daniel H. Wallace Chair of Political Science at the University of Pittsburgh, where he also served as Director of the Center for Latin American Studies. His current work involves directing the AmericasBarometer, which surveys over twenty countries in the hemisphere. He has held grants and fellowships from the Rockefeller Foundation, the Ford Foundation, the National Science Foundation, Fulbright, USAID and others; he has published over 140 articles and more than a 20 books and monographs. His most recent book, coauthored with John Booth is *The Legitimacy Puzzle in Latin America: Political Support and Democracy in Eight Nations* (Cambridge University Press, 2009).

John D. Stephens is Gerhard E. Lenski, Jr., Distinguished Professor of Political Science and Sociology at the University of North Carolina, Chapel Hill. He is the author or coauthor of four books including *Capitalist Development and Democracy* (with Evelyne Huber and Dietrich Rueschemeyer, 1992; winner, best book in political sociology), and *Development and Crisis of the Welfare State* (with Evelyne Huber, 2001; winner, best book in political economy) and numerous journal articles.

Jorge Vargas Cullell is Deputy Director of the Costa Rica-based State of the Nation Program. His current research involves citizen support for democracy and risks of political instability. He has served as a consultant for the United Nations Development Program (UNDP), the Swedish Agency for International Development Cooperation (SIDA), the United States Agency for International Development (USAID), and the Inter-American Development Bank (IDB). He has coauthored recent publications such as *The Political Culture of Democracy in Costa Rica* (2007) and *The Quality of Democracy: Theory and Applications* (2004). Vargas holds a PhD in Political Science from the University of Notre Dame.

Ignacio Walker is a research fellow of CIEPLAN, a widely respected research center in Santiago where, until 2008, he served as President. He is the author or editor of numerous books and articles including *Socialismo y Democracia (Chile y Europa en Perspectiva Comparada)* (CIEPLAN/ Hachette, Santiago, 1990) and *El Futuro de la Democracia Cristiana* (Ediciones B, Grupo Zeta, Santiago, 1999). Under the Pinochet dictatorship he served as a human rights lawyer at the Vicariate of Solidarity and Research Fellow of CIEPLAN. Following the return to democracy, Walker served as Director of Political Relations at the Ministerio Secretaría General de la Presidencia (1990–1994), Member of Congress (1994–2002), and Minister of Foreign Affairs of Chile (2004–2006). He holds a PhD in Politics from Princeton University and a law degree from the University of Chile.

Democratic Governance
in Latin America

Introduction

SCOTT MAINWARING AND
TIMOTHY R. SCULLY

This book examines democratic governance in Latin America in the post-1990 period. Constructing more effective democratic governance is the greatest challenge that faces most Latin American countries today. It entails governing both democratically and effectively. Successful democratic governance is successful governance within a democracy; it refers to the government's and state's ability to deliver goods and guarantee rights that are important for citizen well-being, within the rules and institutions of a democracy. Successful democratic governance means that governments succeed in maintaining a reasonably high quality of democratic practice, protect citizen rights, help their countries advance economically, provide citizen security, and help address the serious social problems (poverty, income inequalities, poor social services) that afflict, albeit to very different degrees, Latin American countries.

As a region, Latin America has made tremendous gains since 1978 in terms of governing democratically. However, only a few countries in the region, Chile and Costa Rica, and to a lesser degree Uruguay and Panama, have with a minimum degree of consistency met the challenge of governing both democratically and effectively since the early 1990s.

We map the variance in Latin America in how successful countries have been in democratic governance and attempt to advance understanding of why some policies and countries have been more successful in democratic governance than others in this period. We seek to understand differences in the success of democratic governance in three crucial policy areas—economic policy, social policy, and state capacity to provide citizen security—and across different countries. We chose these three policy areas because of their profound impact on individual life opportunities and on questions such as regime legitimacy.

Successful democratic governance is different from two related issues: the quality of democracy and the quality of governance. Successful democratic governance as we understand it is not the same as the quality of democracy. Democratic governance is mostly a top down phenomenon; it refers to how well democratic governments and states are functioning. In contrast, for most scholars, the quality of democracy refers to the "democraticness" of the political regime, that is, to how democratic the regime is. Most analyses of the quality of democracy have focused exclusively on democracy's procedural aspects (see Chapter 1 for an extended discussion). As we conceive it, good democratic governance also entails looking at policy results. It means not only governing democratically, but also governing effectively. Our project also differs from analyses of effective governance (Kaufmann, Kraay, and Mastruzzi 2006) because we focus specifically on democratic governance.

Identifying conditions that account for successful democratic governance is important for both scholars and practitioners. The literatures that address discrete pieces of this research puzzle are extensive. For example, considerable literature analyzes the factors that promote economic growth (see the chapters by De Gregorio, Rodríguez, and Foxley in this volume). The literature on social policy is also prolific (see the chapter by Huber and Stephens). Yet little has been written on successful democratic governance as a whole.[1] There are good reasons to focus most research on narrower and more easily specifiable dependent variables than we do in this volume. Nevertheless, it is also important on occasion to undertake broad integrative purviews. Sometimes they suggest connections that are less apparent through less panoramic lenses, and they usefully call attention to big questions that do not always come to the fore with more delimited projects.

We undertake a panoramic, interdisciplinary project because effective democratic governance involves formulating and implementing policies in a way that cuts across disciplines. Policy formulation and implementation under democracy is not a matter of technocrats devising an ideal policy. Rather, it involves complex interactions between governments' policy ideals and political negotiations and conflicts. These interactions can best be illuminated through an interdisciplinary dialogue. The potential for a fruitful interdisciplinary dialogue seemed propitious in this case. As we note in Chapter 1, many economists have called attention to the importance of institutions in promoting economic growth. Usually, however, economists have been vague in specifying which institutions are important in fostering growth.[2] Because political scientists and sociologists traditionally paid more attention to institutions than economists, it seemed possible that a multidisciplinary exchange on this issue might be fruitful. Economists have been attentive in recent years to the importance of "the politics of policies," to borrow the title of a recent publication by the Inter-American Development Bank (2005), and on this point, too, a dialogue across disciplines seemed potentially fruitful, because political scientists have devoted more attention to this issue than economists. Economists, sociologists, and political scientists grapple with the important yet difficult question of the generalizability of knowledge, and we saw potential for a meaningful exchange and mutual learning on this point. Moreover, economists can help inform the debate among the political scientists about what policies are more likely to promote success. Finally, we hoped that cutting across important policy areas and combining them with three country studies could generate synergy in understanding what policies and institutions have favored success in contemporary Latin America.

DEFICIENT DEMOCRACIES

Beginning with transitions to democracy in the Dominican Republic (1978), Ecuador (1979), and Peru (1980), Latin America experienced a burst of democratization from 1978 until 1992. A region that previously had always been predominantly authoritarian became predominantly democratic. Whereas in the past democratic breakdowns had been common, in the post-1978 period they have been rare.

Yet since the late 1990s, frustration with deficiencies in many of these competitive regimes has grown (Mainwaring 2006; O'Donnell 1993, 1999, 2003; UNDP 2005). Many regimes in Latin America are semi-democratic rather than full democracies because of limits to freedom, poor ability to protect human rights, or lack of civilian control of the military. The economic performance of most Latin American countries languished from the great debt crisis of the early 1980s until 2003 (De Gregorio, Chapter 2). Per capita income in much of the region fell between 1998 and 2003, leaving a majority of Latin Americans poorer than they were in 1996. Most countries experienced tepid progress in reducing poverty between 1982 and 2003.

In recent years, this frustration has culminated in the forced ousters of many democratically elected presidents and the revitalization of the left. Angry demonstrations by Bolivia's poverty-stricken indigenous population forced presidents to resign in 2003 and 2005. In this decade, two other South American presidents were forced from office by discontented, mobilized citizens (Pérez-Liñán 2007).[3] Venezuela remains deeply polarized between supporters and opponents of President Hugo Chávez.

The rule of law is precarious in most countries (O'Donnell 1999; Brinks 2004, 2008). An ineffective judiciary and incompetent and frequently corrupt police forces have failed to protect citizen security and citizen rights. According to the 2008 Latinobarómetro survey carried out in 18 Latin American countries, only 57% of respondents agreed that "Democracy is preferable to any other kind of government."

In two ways, this disappointment and frustration with the low quality of democracy in many countries provide the context for this book. First, the book attempts to contribute to thinking about ways to improve democracy in Latin America. Second, sometimes lost in the disappointment and frustration with poor performance in most countries is the fact that performance has varied markedly across countries. This variance provides one of the main themes of this book.

Because the shortcomings of most democratic governments in Latin America since 1990 have been so conspicuous, most scholarship has focused on these deficiencies. This scholarship has illuminated important issues. But success is possible, and examining variance in success is important for both intellectual and political reasons. Intellectually, there has been little systematic interdisciplinary exploration of what makes for successful democratic governance. The relatively successful cases might provide valuable lessons for the rest of the region. Politically, as Navia and Walker point out in this volume, if frustration about the limited capacity of most Latin American democratic governments to deliver policy goods deepens, it is likely to pave the way for populist leaders (e.g., Presidents Hugo Chávez of Venezuela, 1999–present; Evo Morales of Bolivia, 2006–present; Rafael Correa of Ecuador, 2007–present). These populist leaders tend to implement policies detrimental to the future of their countries, frequently have tenuous commitments to democracy, and sometimes exacerbate tensions in the inter-American system. If citizens believe that democracy is not satisfying their needs, there are likely to be more electorally successful populist and nondemocratic (as well as often antimarket) politicians who offer no sustainable hope for their countries. For this reason, one message of this project is that democracy in Latin America can succeed.[4]

ORGANIZATION OF THE VOLUME

The book is structured around three sets of essays. In Chapter 1, we propose a way to measure success in democratic governance in Latin America, and we compare 20 Latin American cases according to the dimensions we outline.

Six chapters examine keys to promoting economic growth, reducing poverty, and building democracy from cross-national perspectives. José De Gregorio, Francisco Rodríguez, and Alejandro Foxley analyze economic development under democracy. What have we learned about how to effectively promote economic development under democracy? Evelyne Huber and John Stephens discuss social policy. What approaches are more likely to reduce poverty, address inequalities, and improve the public provision of education and health? Daniel Brinks examines one of Latin America's thorny problems related to democratic governance: the difficulty in establishing equal rights for citizens related specifically to police killings. How can Latin American countries simultaneously improve public security and promote equal rights for citizens? Patricio Navia and Ignacio Walker call attention to the importance of building strong institutions in creating the conditions for successful democratic governance and avoiding the perils of populism.

We complement these thematic chapters with three country cases: by Alan Angell on Chile, Fernando Henrique Cardoso on Brazil, and Mitchell Seligson and Juliana Martínez on Costa Rica. Our idea was that it could be useful to examine variance in success in democratic governance by looking at some relatively successful countries in addition to looking at thematic issues. In the indicators of successful democratic governance that we employ in Chapter 1, Chile and Costa Rica stand out as the two most successful countries in post-1990 Latin America. If any Latin American countries offer lessons for successful democratic governance, these two are the most likely contenders. We therefore asked Angell and Seligson and Martínez to explain why Chile and Costa Rica have been more successful in many respects than the rest of Latin America, and to address whether Chile and Costa Rica offer policy lessons for other countries. In his chapter, Cardoso reflects on his experience over the course of a decade as Brazil's Finance Minister (1993–1994), and subsequently as President (1995–2003). His essay offers insights into what transformed Brazil from a country that performed poorly on a wide array of critical dimensions (inflation, poverty reduction, international credibility) between 1985 and 1993 into a moderate success story since then.

Our conclusion pulls together lessons from this volume and beyond about democratic governance in Latin America, focusing primarily on the political aspects of democratic governance. The post-1990 period has generated new perspectives on a range of issues related to democratic governance. These new perspectives, however, have not often been systematized.

José Miguel Insulza closes the book with reflections based on his experience as Secretary General of the Organization of American States and the longest serving cabinet member in Chile's history. His reflection, originally delivered as the keynote address for our conference and subsequently updated for this book, underscores some of the salient challenges and successes in democratic governance in contemporary Latin America.

The project brought together political scientists and economists from Latin America, the United States, and the UK, and six distinguished Latin American leaders who also have impeccable academic credentials (Fernando Henrique Cardoso, Alejandro Foxley, José De Gregorio, José Miguel Insulza, Francisco Rodríguez, and Ignacio Walker).[5] Cardoso was President of Brazil from 1995 to 2003, and he earlier served as Senator and Finance Minister. Before that, he was one of Latin America's most distinguished sociologists and the founder of a major research center, CEBRAP. Foxley has served as Finance Minister, Senator, and Minister of Foreign Affairs in Chile. He enjoyed a distinguished career as an economist before entering public service. Insulza has served as a Minister, Ambassador, Vice President, and Secretary General of the Organization of American States, and he also worked as a researcher and professor in Mexico. De Gregorio is Director of the Central Bank in Chile, and he has also worked in the academic world. Rodríguez was chief economist for the Venezuelan National Assembly; he is now Director of Research at the Human Development Report Office. Walker has served as a federal deputy, ambassador, and Minister of Foreign Affairs for Chile, with stints in the world of research and teaching. Their high level public service and their outstanding intellectual skills give these individuals a distinctive perspective for understanding and articulating the salient challenges of democratic governance in contemporary Latin America.

These individuals with leadership experience in public life enrich the variety of voices that contributed to our enterprise. More important, they ensure that we did not engage in academic work disconnected from the realities experienced by leaders who try to improve democratic governance. We aspired to produce a book that makes a scholarly contribution to understanding problems of great importance, in a manner that illuminates policy debates about these issues, and that appeals to a public beyond the academic world that both of us inhabit and cherish.

Notes

1. Domínguez and Shifter (2003) address related themes and provide a good overview of themes and countries, but without the sustained focus on successful democratic governance.

2. We do not definitively resolve which institutions are important for growth, but several authors in this volume underscore the importance of state institutions and party system institutionalization in fostering successful democratic governance.

3. Fernando de la Rua of Argentina in 2001 and Lucio Gutíerrez of Ecuador in 2005. In addition, Peruvian President Alberto Fujimori was forced to resign in 2000 only months after his election. Popular mobilization was less important in his resignation.

4. Along related lines, see Grindle's (2004) plea for more attention to developmental successes. Grindle notes that most of the literature focuses on failures.

5. All but Insulza have PhDs from renowned universities: the University of São Paulo, Wisconsin, MIT, Harvard, and Princeton, respectively. Insulza has an MA degree and taught at one of Mexico's best universities.

References

Brinks, Daniel M. 2004. Informal Institutions and the Rule of Law: The Judicial Response to State Killings in Buenos Aires and São Paulo in the 1990s. Comparative Politics 36(1): 1–19.

———. 2008. The Judicial Response to Police Killings in Latin America: Inequality and the Rule of Law. Cambridge: Cambridge University Press.

Dominguez, Jorge I., and Michael Shifter, eds. 2003. Constructing Democratic Governance in Latin America. Baltimore, MD: Johns Hopkins University Press.

Grindle, Merilee S. 2004. Good Enough Governance: Poverty Reduction and Reform in Developing Countries. Governance 17(4): 525–48.

Inter-American Development Bank. 2005. The Politics of Policies. Washington, DC: Inter-American Development Bank.

Kaufmann, Daniel, Aart Kraay, and Massimo Mastruzzi. 2006. Governance Matters V: Aggregate and Individual Governance Indicators for 1996–2005. The World Bank, Policy Research Paper 4012 (September). Available at http://econ.worldbank.org.

Mainwaring, Scott. 2006. State Deficiencies, Party Competition, and Confidence in Democratic Representation in the Andes. In The Crisis of Democratic Representation in the Andes, ed. Scott Mainwaring, Ana María Bejarano, and Eduardo Pizarro, 295–345. Stanford, CA: Stanford University Press.

O'Donnell, Guillermo. 1993. On the State, Democratization, and Some Conceptual Problems: A Latin American View with Glances at Some Post-Communist Countries. World Development 21(8): 1345–69.

———. 1999. Poliarchies and the (Un)Rule of Law in Latin America: A Partial Conclusion. In The (Un)Rule of Law and the Underprivileged in Latin America, ed. Juan E. Méndez, Guillermo O'Donnell, and Paulo Sérgio Pinheiro, 303–37. Notre Dame, IN: University of Notre Dame Press.

———. 2003. Democracia, Desarrollo Humano y Derechos Humanos. In Democracia, Desarrollo Humano y Ciudadanía, ed. Guillermo O'Donnell,

Osvaldo Iazzetta, Jorge Vargas Cullell, 25–147. Rosario, Argentina: Homo Sapiens Ediciones.

Pérez-Liñán, Aníbal. 2007. Presidential Impeachment and the New Political Instability in Latin America. Cambridge: Cambridge University Press.

UNDP (United Nations Development Programme). 2005. Democracy in Latin America: Towards a Citizens' Democracy. New York: United Nations Development Programme.

PART ONE

Variance in Success: Economics,
Social Policy, and the State

CHAPTER ONE

Measuring Success in
Democratic Governance

SCOTT MAINWARING, TIMOTHY R. SCULLY,
AND JORGE VARGAS CULLELL

☾

In this chapter, we present measures of democratic governance to give a
sense of how Latin American countries have fared since the early 1990s.
The rest of the book discusses reasons for success and failure in democratic governance, but first it is necessary to provide a descriptive map of
which countries have been more or less successful on which dimensions
of democratic governance. Our evaluation is concerned with the extent to
which democracies enhance citizen well-being and protect citizen rights.
We provide an empirical mapping of how Latin American countries have
fared since the early 1990s on a wide array of governance issues that are
infrequently brought together to provide a medium time perspective.

In addition to providing this descriptive map, we hope to stimulate
thinking about how to conceptualize and measure democratic governance. The closest existing measures are of effective governance in general (e.g., Kaufmann, Kraay, and Mastruzzi 2003, 2005, 2006, 2007,
2008) rather than specifically democratic governance, and of the quality of democracy based on its procedural ideals (Diamond and Morlino
2005; Levine and Molina 2006). Our enterprise is different, and we believe it merits an effort to create a systematic approach to measurement.
A measurement of democratic governance allows researchers and policy
makers to chart change over time in a given country and to compare
across countries with some precision. It enables us to move from impres-
sionistic assessments to more careful measurement.

We measure performance in nine dimensions of democratic governance: the level of democracy, ensuring respect for the rule of law, control of corruption, promoting economic growth, maintaining inflation under a reasonable level, reducing poverty, job creation, improving education, and providing citizen security. The basic assumptions underlying the analysis are twofold; that

1. these outcomes profoundly influence citizens' and societies' present and future well-being, and
2. governments and states significantly influence these outcomes.

We do not test these commonly held assumptions but rather provide a descriptive map to capture variance in the quality of democratic governance for twenty Latin American countries for the post-1990 period. Contrary to analyses that lump Latin America together as a more or less undifferentiated region with converging trends, we highlight differences across countries.

In recent years, there has been a proliferation of different indices to measure the quality of governance and the "democraticness" (i.e., the level of democracy) of a political regime. In relation to the existing literature on these subjects, we hope to make four contributions. First, we measure success in democratic governance. This endeavor is new and, we believe, worth undertaking. The most significant effort to measure good governance focuses on perceptions about the quality of policy and policy implementation (Kaufmann et al. 2003, 2005, 2006, 2007, 2008). In contrast, we believe that success in governance is best measured by actual results. We do not examine the relationship between the quality of policies or institutions and outcomes, but we assume that in the medium to long term, good outcomes result to a significant degree from good policies and/or institutions. The work on quality of democracy is valuable, but because of its focus on procedural aspects of democracy, it is narrower than our purview.

Second, we incorporate more objective indicators about government performance and outcomes than most existing works on related subjects. Because we focus on success in democratic governance, primary attention to outcomes is in order, since they affect citizens the most.

Third, because citizenship is core to democracy, we focus on aspects of democratic governance that have a great impact on citizens. This is not a focal point of Kaufmann et al.'s work on good governance or of the work on quality of democracy. Finally, we focus on results over the medium term, which we operationalize as fifteen years. Year-to-year assessments of Latin America can be valuable, but sometimes the medium term perspective gets lost in the sea of immediate, short-term analyses.

Many analysts have based their expectations about future performance on recent past performance, leading to exaggerated optimism or pessimism, depending on the case and year, and to dubious analytic framing of questions and answers.

CASE SELECTION OF COUNTRIES

Although the way we assess the quality of democratic governance might be useful for other regions of the world, we limit our selection of countries to Latin America. We include the twenty countries of the western hemisphere in which Spanish, Portuguese, or Creole is the official language or one of the official languages: Argentina, Bolivia, Brazil, Chile, Colombia, Costa Rica, Cuba, the Dominican Republic, Ecuador, El Salvador, Guatemala, Haiti, Honduras, Mexico, Nicaragua, Panama, Paraguay, Peru, Uruguay, and Venezuela.

Among the 20 Latin American countries, two have consistently (Cuba) or usually (Haiti) had authoritarian regimes since 1990. We include them for purposes of comparison, but we do not regard them as cases of democratic or even semi-democratic governance. Therefore, we include 20 countries in the tables in this chapter, but we have 18 cases of democratic or semi-democratic governance.

NINE DIMENSIONS OF DEMOCRATIC GOVERNANCE

Democratic governance refers to the capacity of democratic governments to implement policies that enhance citizen well-being and rights. In turn, a *democracy* is a regime 1) that sponsors free and fair competitive elections for the legislature and executive; 2) that allows for inclusive adult citizenship; 3) that protects civil liberties and political rights; and 4) in which the elected governments really govern, the military is under civilian control, and other armed actors do not dictate policy.

The nine dimensions of democratic governance that we examine are:

1. the level of democracy
2. rule of law
3. control of corruption
4. economic growth
5. inflation
6. job creation

7. poverty
8. education
9. citizen security

We chose these nine dimensions because citizens, social scientists, international institutions, politicians, and policy makers widely view them as very important. Our intention is not to be exhaustive, but rather to capture multiple important aspects of democratic governance. Because we wanted parsimony, it was important to select dimensions that were theoretically discrete. Of course, it is essential to focus on policy outcomes that are significantly affected by government and state policies and actions.

We focus on issues that citizens have identified as salient in public opinion surveys and those that have a profound impact on citizen well-being. This focus on citizen opinion and well-being is in order because more than their nondemocratic counterparts, democracies have obligations toward their citizens. According to democratic theory, the *"demos"*—the people—is the source of legitimacy for the regime (Sartori 1987). Stated in terms of principal/agent theory, the citizenry is the principal that elects public officials as its agents to carry out public responsibilities on its behalf.

The list of issues that one could include under the rubric of effective democratic governance is endless. We limit our attention to a few of the most important among them. We concentrate on policy outcomes more than policy processes. This decision enables us to exclude a wide array of issues and to concentrate on the ability of political systems to enhance citizen well-being and rights. Although processes are important in democratic life, citizen well-being is most affected by outcomes.

Following the distinction of Foweraker and Krznaric (2000), the first of these nine dimensions—how democratic the regime is—is *intrinsic* to the procedural ideals of liberal democracy. The second dimension, rule of law, is both intrinsic and partly extrinsic to democratic governance. Some nondemocratic regimes have well-functioning institutions of the rule of law, and in this sense, both democratic and nondemocratic governments can observe the rule of law. In a democracy, however, ensuring respect for the rule of law entails two distinctive tasks without which a democratic regime is severely hampered. The legal order must uphold the rights of citizens and noncitizens, and it must ensure that power holders are subject to the law (O'Donnell 2004). The other seven dimensions are *extrinsic* to democracy as a political regime. They refer to outcomes of all governments, whether or not they are democratic.

Although these measures could be used for shorter time periods, we are interested in how countries have fared over an extended period. For most dimensions, we therefore constructed country-level measures for a fifteen-year period since the early 1990s. We look at the medium term because it takes an extended period of time for governments to address most pressing issues. In addition, for some dimensions of governance, especially economic growth, there is a lot of "noise" in short-term performance.

The fifteen-year period has three advantages. Most important, it is long enough that the "noise" of short term economic fluctuations caused by idiosyncratic factors is considerably reduced. Second, in several countries (Chile, Haiti, and Panama), new and more democratic political regimes came into existence around 1990. Given our concern with *democratic* governance, we wanted to begin the analysis at a time when most regimes in Latin America were competitively elected even if not fully democratic. Third, by the early 1990s, market-oriented economic reforms were taking hold in most of Latin America. We measure democratic governance in the aftermath of the emergence of the "Washington Consensus." Otherwise, initial differences in economic policy attributable to antecedent authoritarian regimes could explain differences in performance.

Because there are solid existing indicators that effectively measure performance for these nine dimensions, and because of the advantages of comparability across research projects that accrue from using the same indicators, we rely on a new combination of existing measures rather than building new ones. Where possible, our measures focus on political, economic, and social outcomes rather than perceptions of the quality of government policies or institutions.[1] This focus represents a departure from Kaufmann et al.'s (2003, 2005, 2006, 2007, 2008) governance indicators, which measure perceptions about government performance. Both approaches are useful, though for different purposes. As noted, the rationale for focusing on outcomes is that we are measuring success, not the perceived quality of policies. In addition, citizens care deeply about results and understand democracy partly in terms of substantive outcome (Camp 2001; Vargas Cullell 2004, 113–29).

IDENTIFYING CRITICAL DIMENSIONS: CITIZEN VIEWS

Citizen viewpoints were one consideration in selecting the nine dimensions. Table 1.1 presents survey data on what citizens identify as the most pressing problems in contemporary Latin America.

The seven surveys in Table 1.1 register some change over time, yet also show some consistency in citizen perceptions of their countries' most

TABLE 1.1

Citizen Opinions about Their Countries' Most Important Problem
(Percentage who identified each issue as most important)

	2003 Latinobarómetro	2004 LAPOP	2005 Latinobarómetro	2006 LAPOP	2006 Latinobarómetro	2007 Latinobarómetro	2008 Latinobarómetro
Unemployment	29	28	30	19	24	18	15
Economic problems		18		12		11	
Low wages	11						
Poverty	10	17		11			
Corruption	10	7		5		11	
Crime	8	17	14	26	16	17	17
Job instability	5						
Inflation, high prices		5	9	2		3	
Political problems			9				

Sources: Corporación Latinobarómetro 2003:48; Corporación Latinobarómetro 2005:70–71; Corporación Latinobarómetro 2006:39–40; LAPOP 2004; LAPOP 2006; Corporación Latinobarómetro 2007:20–22; Corporación Latinobarómetro 2008:23.

important problem. Unemployment, crime, poverty, economic problems, corruption, and inflation have consistently topped the list of citizen concerns. Corruption has become more salient over time as inflation has decreased in salience. Our nine dimensions cover all of these problems.

Three of these nine dimensions do not appear high on the list of citizen concerns: the level of democracy, the rule of law, and education. Most citizens weight the level of democracy and rule of law less significantly than substantive outcomes, but they are crucial in an assessment of democratic governance. Education provides citizens with greater economic, social, and cultural opportunities, and high levels of education position societies well for today's global economy.

THE LEVEL OF DEMOCRACY

A high level of democracy is an important dimension of successful democratic governance. Through their policies and practices, governments and states help produce the level of democraticness of the political regime. Government action impinges on the degree to which political regimes meet the four defining criteria of democracy. Governments and states obstruct or facilitate the holding of free and fair elections. They make it easier or harder for citizens to exercise their right to vote. They hinder or promote freedom of the press, freedom of expression, freedom of assembly, and the preservation and development of civil and political rights and liberties. Finally, governments affect the degree to which they have control over the military and other nonelected potential veto players. Some governments vigorously pursue greater control over these actors; others willingly cede more power to them.

To measure the level of democracy, we use mean Freedom House scores from 1994 to 2008. So that a high score registers a high level of democracy and vice versa, we inverted the scores by subtracting the combined Freedom House score from 14. With this inverted scale, 12 is the maximum possible value, and 0 is the lowest possible value. Table 1.2 shows the scores for twenty Latin American countries for our first four dimensions. The second column reports mean Freedom House scores for 1994 to 2008. The level of democracy has varied considerably across countries. According to Freedom House, Uruguay (11.5), Costa Rica (11.3), and Chile (10.8) have had the highest levels of democracy, followed at some distance by Panama (10.3), Argentina (9.3), and the Dominican Republic (9.1). In recent years, Chile (since 2003), Costa Rica (since 2004), and Uruguay (since 2000) have consistently had the best possible scores for both civil liberties and political rights, indicating a

TABLE 1.2
Measures of Democratic Governance in Latin America

	Mean Freedom House scores, 1994–2008[a]	Kaufmann et al. rule of law, 2007	Our score for Kaufmann et al. rule of law	Kaufmann et al. control of corruption, 2007	Our score for Kaufmann et al. control of corruption	Annual per capita GDP growth, 1991–2006	Mean annual change in consumer price index, 1992–2006
Argentina	9.3	-0.52	-0.63	-0.45	-0.63	2.3%	7%
Bolivia	8.7	-0.96	-1.63	-0.49	0.06	1.3%	6%
Brazil	8.5	-0.44	-0.65	-0.24	-0.30	1.3%	92%
Chile	10.8	1.17	1.12	1.35	1.41	4.0%	6%
Colombia	6.6	-0.57	-0.47	-0.28	-0.04	1.3%	14%
Costa Rica	11.3	0.44	0.31	0.39	0.05	2.9%	13%
Cuba	0.1	-0.79	-0.59	-0.21	-0.23	nd	nd
Dominican Rep.	9.1	-0.55	-0.54	-0.65	-0.93	4.0%	11%
Ecuador	8.3	-1.04	-1.66	-0.87	-0.91	1.3%	28%
El Salvador	8.8	-0.68	-0.45	-0.13	0.58	2.1%	6%
Guatemala	6.3	-1.11	-1.30	-0.75	-0.47	1.2%	8%
Haiti	3.2	-1.42	-1.41	-1.28	-1.52	-3.0%	20%
Honduras	8.1	-0.86	-0.97	-0.69	-0.35	1.3%	13%
Mexico	8.5	-0.58	-0.65	-0.35	-0.31	1.5%	12%
Nicaragua	7.7	-0.84	-1.35	-0.78	-1.35	1.8%	10%
Panama	10.3	-0.20	-0.25	-0.34	-0.16	2.7%	1%
Paraguay	7.4	-0.97	-1.48	-0.96	-1.40	-0.0%	11%
Peru	7.5	-0.71	-0.84	-0.38	-0.62	2.9%	12%
Uruguay	11.5	0.49	0.42	0.96	1.49	2.1%	26%
Venezuela	7.1	-1.47	-2.26	-1.04	-1.25	0.3%	34%

Sources: Freedom House scores: www.freedomhouse.org

Kaufmann et al. (2008:91–93) rule of law

Kaufmann et al. (2008:94–96) control of corruption

Annual per capita GDP growth: Calculated from data in the World Bank, *WDI World Development Indicators.* 2008: The World Bank Group. Calculated in 2005 constant dollars in purchasing parity power.

Change in consumer price index: World Bank, *2008 World Development Indicators*

[a]Freedom House scores are inverted. The inverted score = 14 − (Political Liberties + Civil Liberties)

high quality democracy. In contrast, Haiti (even when it has had a competitive regime), Guatemala, and several other countries have had serious deficiencies in democratic practice. And Cuba, of course, remains steadfastly authoritarian.

The Latin American countries cover almost the entire range of the inverted Freedom House scores (from 0 to 12). Although there is much room for improvement in the level of democracy in many countries in the region, the period since 1990 has been by far the most democratic in the history of Latin America.

Freedom House scores are one of three exceptions to our preference for objective measures; they are based on expert assessments. They provide a better measure of democracy than assessments that rely exclusively on conventional objective data such as electoral turnout, electoral results, and turnover in office. Democracy also requires protection of civil and political rights, as well as the control of democratically elected officials over the military.

RULE OF LAW

Effective democratic governance entails effective rule of law. Without effective rule of law, citizen rights cannot be ensured (O'Donnell 1999, 2005), and citizen rights are integral to democracy. Some aspects of the rule of law are especially important for poor citizens because otherwise they cannot exercise their legal rights. Effective rule of law also entails holding elected officials accountable for transgressions of the law. In a region where corruption has had corrosive effects on democracy, this is important. In addition, without effective rule of law, patrimonial practices more easily permeate the state bureaucracy, thwarting efforts at universalism and undermining meritocracy and efficiency. Finally, effective rule of law is important to counter authoritarian moves by elected presidents because it implies the exercise of constitutional review by an independent judiciary.

For this dimension, we use Kaufmann et al.'s (2003, 2005, 2006, 2007, 2008) indicator for rule of law. It is a sophisticated composite indicator that in 2007 was based on an aggregation of 75 survey and expert opinion questions taken from 26 organizations. We use this subjective measure because of the great difficulty in obtaining valid objective measures for a large number of countries. Their indicator is the best available measure that covers a wide range of countries. Kaufmann et al. (2008, 76–77) detail the sources and the specific survey questions for the rule of law dimension.

The score for a given country is equal to the number of standard deviations it is away from the mean score for all countries in a given year. A positive score indicates that a country in a given year ranked above the world mean; a negative score indicates a ranking worse than the world mean. Kaufmann et al. (2008) have calculated scores for eight years: 1996, 1998, 2000, 2002, 2003, 2004, 2005, 2006, and 2007.

For this indicator and our other five indicators in which radical change from one year to the next is all but impossible, we added the absolute level for the final year for which we have data (2007 in this case) and the change from the first year (1996 in this case) to the last.[2] It is essential to consider both how countries fare relative to one another, and how they fare relative to their own past. This method inherently advantages neither countries that start off with a high level, nor those that start off with a low level.[3] In principle, this combined approach weights both the initial starting point and the amount of change equally.[4]

One of the great deficiencies in democratic governance in most of Latin America has been establishing effective rule of law. The Kaufmann et al. indicator underscores this point. In 2007, seventeen of twenty Latin American countries on average scored below the world mean for rule of law. It also underscores the wide range in Latin America in terms of the rule of law. Scores ranged from an abysmal −1.42 for Haiti, one of the worst scores in the world, to 1.17 for Chile. There was a substantial gap between Chile, Uruguay (0.49), and Costa Rica (0.44), on the one hand, and the rest of the countries. Brinks's chapter in this volume provides empirical evidence to support the claim of a large gap between Uruguay, on the one hand, and Brazil and Argentina, on the other, even though Brazil and Argentina are roughly in the middle of the Kaufmann et al. scores for Latin America.

Our scores for rule of law range from −2.26 (Venezuela) to 1.12 (Chile).

CONTROL OF CORRUPTION

Corruption has come to the fore in public opinion as one of the most important problems confronting democracy in contemporary Latin America (Seligson 2002, 2006; Weyland 1998). It appears high on the list of problems identified by citizens as the most pressing in their countries (see Table 1.1).

Public sector corruption is inimical to democracy. Goods, services, and policies that should benefit the public are instead appropriated for narrow private benefit. According to existing scholarship, public sector corruption has a corrosive effect on state effectiveness and economic performance generally (Krueger 1974; Mauro 1995) and on democratic legitimacy in Latin America (Seligson 2002, 2006). Della Porta (2000) argued that corruption worsens government performance and reduces confidence in government in Western Europe, and Pharr (2000) showed that corruption had a strong impact on confidence in government in Japan.

As is the case with our first two dimensions, for control of corruption, there are no valid cross-national objective data that cover most of our countries.[5] Given this data problem, we added Kaufmann et al.'s (2008) measure of control of corruption for 2007 to the change in this measure between 1996 and 2007. It is the best available indicator of corruption for the twenty countries analyzed here.[6]

Kaufmann et al.'s scores for control of corruption suggest the same two conclusions as their scores for rule of law: first, that Latin America as a region fares relatively poorly; second, that there are great differences across countries within Latin America, making any sweeping generalization problematic. Chile stood out as far more successful than any other Latin American countries, with a score of 1.35 standard deviations above the world mean in 2007. Uruguay (0.96) and Costa Rica (0.39) again scored above the world mean, while the remaining seventeen countries scored below the world mean. Haiti's score of −1.28 was among the worst in the world.

Our scores adding level and change in control of corruption range from −1.52 for Haiti to 1.49 for Uruguay.

ECONOMIC GROWTH

We include economic performance in this assessment of the success of democratic governance for two reasons. First, economists have established that governments and states affect economic growth. Good governance is a major factor in economic growth in the medium to long term (Glaeser et al. 2004; Hall and Jones 1999; Kaufmann et al. 2005).

Second, especially in a region with great poverty, citizens have material needs. Citizens expect governments to address their most pressing problems, and in contemporary Latin America, large numbers of citizens identify economic issues as the most salient problems confronting their countries (see Table 1.1). Many citizens indicate in public opinion surveys that they would be willing to sacrifice democracy if a nondemocratic regime would resolve the economic problems. In the 2004 Latinobarómetro survey, 55 percent of respondents stated that it would be acceptable to have a nondemocratic regime if it resolved their country's economic problems (Latinobarómetro 2004). In this context—a high salience of economic problems coupled with a citizen willingness to support nondemocratic regimes if they could solve such problems—democratic regimes can suffer if governments fail to stimulate economic growth and well-being.

To measure growth, we take the annual change in per capita GDP in constant 2005 dollars, measured in purchasing parity power, from 1991 to 2006 according to the World Bank's *World Development Indicators*. Column 7 of Table 1.2 shows the growth performance of Latin American countries for this period. Consistent with conventional wisdom, the median performance in Latin America in these years was mediocre, notwithstanding sustained growth in most of the region from 2003 to 2008. Only eight countries had an average increase in per capita GDP of at least 2 percent per year.

Consistent with our emphasis on the wide variance within Latin America, the dispersion in growth performance has been great. With an annual average per capita growth of 4.0% over these fifteen years, Chile and the Dominican Republic easily eclipsed the rest of Latin America. Per capita GDP increased by 80% in Chile and 79% in the Dominican Republic between 1991 and 2006. Costa Rica (2.9%), Peru (2.9%), Panama (2.7%), Argentina (2.3%), Uruguay (2.1%), and El Salvador (2.1%) experienced moderate growth. Growth performance in the remaining countries ranged from anemic to dreadful. Two countries (Paraguay and Haiti) suffered regressions in per capita income, very slight in Paraguay (–1% cumulatively) and steep (–36% cumulatively) in Haiti.

Although the common observation that region-wide growth performance in the 1990s was disappointing is true, it could obscure these large differences. Haiti's per capita GDP fell from $1848 in 1991 to $1186 in 2006, a decline of 36%. The income gap between Chile and Haiti increased from 3.8:1 in 1991 to 10.6:1 in 2006. If in this fifteen-year period Chile's economy had declined as much as Haiti's and Haiti's had grown as much as Chile's, Haiti would have reached 74% of Chile's per capita GDP in 2006.

INFLATION

Inflation is an important measure of success in democratic governance. As Fernando Henrique Cardoso emphasizes in his chapter in this book, high inflation strongly affects the well-being of citizens. In the 1980s and early 1990s, when many Latin American countries experienced three or four digit inflation rates, this problem had an extremely deleterious impact on citizens, particularly the poor, who usually bore the brunt of the impact because they could not protect their revenues as effectively as the wealthy. Moreover, as José De Gregorio argues in his chapter in this book, inflationary crises affect other aspects of economic performance including growth.

We measure inflation with the mean annual change in consumer prices, 1992 to 2006, according to the *World Development Indicators.*[7] Because of persistent extremely high inflation during the early part (1992 to 1994) of this fifteen-year period, Brazil had an average annual inflation rate much higher than any other Latin American country (92%). The figure for Brazil will diminish substantially as the very high inflation years of 1992 to 1994 drop out of the revolving fifteen-year period. Venezuela (34%), Ecuador (28%), Uruguay (26%), and Haiti (20%) have had recurrent problems with inflation. Panama (1%), El Salvador (6%), Bolivia (6%), and Chile (6%) are on the low end.

Control of inflation has been one of the achievements of democratic governance in Latin America since the early 1990s. Inflation (measured by the consumer price index according to the *World Development Indicators*) peaked at 3080% in Argentina in 1989, 11,750% in Bolivia in 1985, 2948% in Brazil in 1990, and 7482% in Peru in 1990. In contrast, in 2007, for the nineteen countries with competitive regimes in Latin America, the highest inflation rate was 14%.

JOB CREATION

Jobs are crucial for citizen well-being. For most people, insertion in the labor market is an indispensable means to generate the income they require to live decently. When large segments of the population lack decent jobs, widespread poverty, inequality, and looming social problems follow because people do not have enough money to buy food or services and because the state has no tax base to fund social services. Unfortunately, in Latin America, large segments of the citizenry do not have access to good quality jobs. Precarious and informal insertion in the labor market prevails,[8] and only a minority have well-paid jobs with social security and labor rights (CEPAL 2005; Tokman 2001).

Government policies and institutions affect the behavior of economic agents in ways that influence employment. Economic policies, education policies and training of the labor force, and the enforcement of rights and social security all affect job creation. In Latin America, in recent decades, job creation has varied independently of economic growth in many cases; hence, we include it as a separate dimension.

Not all jobs promote citizen well-being, though. We are interested in what the International Labour Organization terms decent work, or "productive work in which rights are protected, which generates an adequate income, with adequate social protection" (ILO 2005).

As a proxy for decent work in Latin America we use the share of the active labor force (employed or unemployed individuals who are seeking jobs) that is employed in the formal sector. The rationale for using this proxy in the absence of a direct measure of decent work is that overall, formal sector workers enjoy better working conditions than their informal counterparts. We multiplied the percentage of the active labor force that was employed times by the percentage among the employed who were in the formal sector. Merely using the unemployment rate for Latin America would be inadequate because it disguises underemployment and informal work, both of which are central features of labor markets in the region (Tokman 2001).

Most Latin American countries have not generated sufficient formal sector jobs since the early 1980s. In thirteen of the seventeen Latin American countries for which there are data, formal sector employment comprises less than half of the labor market that is employed or seeking employment (column 5 of Table 1.3). The region's poor countries have a low percentage of the labor force employed in the formal sector: Bolivia (29.9%), Colombia (35.5%) although it is not among the poor countries, Paraguay (35.8%), Ecuador (37.7%), Nicaragua (38.3%). At the high end are Chile (62.7%), Costa Rica (56.0%), Panama (54.8%), and Mexico (54.7%). Most countries experienced a deterioration of formal sector employment between 1990 and 2005 (column 6).

Our gauge of performance adds the absolute level of formal work (as a percentage of the active labor force) and its change over time (also as a percentage) by adding columns 5 and 6. It is essential to consider the level of formal sector employment. A government that registers a modest improvement in job generation, from the worst in the world to only marginally better, does not deserve an average ranking just because of the improvement. It is equally essential to take into consideration whether the situation is improving. We reproduce this mixed method (level + change over time) for the remaining three dimensions of democratic governance. Theoretically, the scores can range from −100 (an initial level of formal sector employment of 100% that declines to 0%) to 200 (an initial percentage of formal sector employment of 0% that increases to 100%). Table 1.3 shows the results.

TABLE 1.3
Generation of Formal Sector Jobs, 1990–2005

	Beginning and end year for employment rate	Beginning and end year for % employed in formal sector	Employment rate × % employed in formal sector circa 1990	Employment rate × % employed in formal sector circa 2005	Percent change circa 1990 to circa 2005	Column 5 + Column 6
Argentina	1990–2005	1996–2005	46.6	49.9	3.3	53.2
Bolivia	1990–2003	1996–2002	37.0	29.9	−7.1	22.8
Brazil	1990–2005	1990–2005	55.7	45.9	−9.8	36.1
Chile	1990–2005	1990–2003	56.8	62.7	5.9	68.6
Colombia	1990–2005	2000–2005	39.8	35.5	−4.3	31.2
Costa Rica	1990–2005	1990–2005	62.9	56.0	−6.1	49.9
Dominican Republic	1995–2005	2000–2004	45.5	41.9	−3.6	38.3
Ecuador	1990–2005	1990–2005	41.9	37.7	−4.2	33.5
El Salvador	1990–2005	1990–2005	41.1	40.8	−0.3	40.5
Honduras	1990–2005	1990–2001	43.5	46.9	3.4	50.3
Mexico	1990–2005	1990–2005	59.5	54.7	−4.8	49.9
Nicaragua	1990–2005	1993–2005	43.7	38.3	−5.4	32.9
Panama	1990–2005	1991–2005	55.4	54.8	−0.6	54.2
Paraguay	1990–2005	1995–2005	39.1	35.8	−3.3	32.5
Peru	1990–2005	1990–2005	36.5	40.8	4.3	45.1
Uruguay	1990–2005	1997–2005	55.1	48.6	−6.9	41.7
Venezuela	1990–2005	1995–2005	46.5	43.9	−2.6	41.3

Source: International Labour Organization, *Panorama Laboral 2006: América Latina y el Caribe*, Tables 1-A and 6-A.

By an ample margin, Chile had the best performance in job generation for the 1990 to 2005 period. In 1990, Costa Rica had the highest percentage (62.9%) of jobs in the formal sector, followed by Mexico (59.5%), Chile (56.8%), Brazil (55.7%), Panama (55.4%), and Uruguay (55.1%), with all other countries in the region considerably lower. By 2005, Chile had the highest percentage of jobs in the formal sector, and it also showed the largest increase between 1990 and 2005. Bolivia anchors the very low end of the spectrum, with the lowest percentage of workers in the formal sector (29.9% in 2002) and a significant decrease between 1990 and 2002.

POVERTY

Our seventh criterion of success is reduction of poverty over time. In a region characterized by widespread poverty, the ability to reduce poverty over time is crucial. If a democratic regime does not reduce poverty, it fails on an important social dimension that has a huge direct impact on human well-being (see Huber and Stephens, Chapter 5 in this volume). Moreover, as De Gregorio argues in this volume, poverty and/or high inequalities can adversely affect economic growth (see also Birdsall and de la Torre 2001, 9–12; Engerman and Sokoloff 1997).

We use CEPAL (2005, 2006, 2007, 2008) data for poverty rates in the region. These are the best available data that cover the region for an extended time span. Unfortunately, data are not exactly comparable for all countries; the poverty line is not the same across countries. Nevertheless, the data are consistent in ordinal terms with World Bank data that uses $1 or $2 per capita per household as the indicator of extreme poverty and poverty, respectively.[9]

The four countries that Huber and Stephens (in this volume) identify as having the most successful social policies have much lower rates of poverty than the others (column 3 of Table 1.4). According to recent estimates, Chile has a poverty rate of 13.7% of the population; Uruguay, 18.1%; Costa Rica, 18.6%; and Argentina, 21.0%. Once again, variance across Latin America is considerable. The traditional bastions of poverty are Honduras (68.9%), Nicaragua (61.9%), Paraguay (60.5%), Guatemala (54.8%), and Bolivia (54.0%), all of which are substantially higher than the next countries.

We base our measure for poverty on a combination of the level of poverty circa 2007 and change between circa 1991 and circa 2007. Column 4 of Table 1.4 provides the data. A low score represents a good performance with poverty and vice versa. Scores theoretically range from –100 (best) to 200 (worst).

During this period, several countries achieved sharp reductions in the rate of poverty mostly in the years since 2002. Chile's success in attacking poverty has been steady and dramatic: a decline from 38.6% of the population in 1990 to 13.7% in 2006. Based on urban data, Ecuador is a surprising success story in poverty reduction, with a decline from 62.1% of the population in 1990 to 38.8% in 2007. Panama, Brazil, Mexico, and Peru also experienced sharp reductions in poverty. In contrast, two countries showed a slight deterioration in the rate of poverty during these approximately fifteen years: Argentina (16.1% to 21.0%), and Uruguay (17.9% to 18.1%).

By virtue of having a moderate level of poverty in 2005 and of its great success in reducing poverty between 1990 and 2006, Chile has by far the best score (–11.2) for this dimension of democratic governance, followed at a considerable distance by Panama (9.3), Costa Rica (10.9), Brazil (12.0), Ecuador (15.5) (whose low score is in part an artifact of using urban data only), Mexico (15.7), and Uruguay (18.3). While Chile succeeded in greatly reducing poverty, the Dominican Republic, with the same increase in per capita GDP from 1991 to 2006, barely reduced poverty. At the poorly performing end of the spectrum is a cluster of countries with high poverty levels and modest success in reducing poverty over the fifteen-year period: Paraguay (60.4), Honduras (57.0), Nicaragua (50.2), Bolivia (45.0), El Salvador (40.8), and Guatemala (40.2).

EDUCATION

In reasonably open economies as is now the case throughout Latin America, education is a crucial asset in enabling individual achievement (Birdsall 1999; Birdsall and Székely 2003; CEPAL 1998, 65–83). At the macro level, higher levels of education usually help reduce poverty and income inequalities. Education is a crucial asset for societies in this era of globalization and the growth of "the knowledge economy" (Wolff and Castro 2003). For this reason, high levels of education also foster economic growth (Birdsall 1999; Glaeser et al. 2004). Innovation and scientific advances depend crucially on the skills of the population, as Alejandro Foxley argues in his chapter in this volume. These are among the reasons education is one of our nine dimensions for evaluating the success of democratic governance.

TABLE 1.4

Change in Percentage of Population below the Poverty Line, 1991–2007

	Percentage below the poverty line circa 1991	Percentage below the poverty line circa 2007	Percentage poverty circa 2007 + change (2007–1991)
Argentina	16.1 (1994)	21.0 (2006)	25.9
Bolivia[a]	63.0 (1989)	54.0 (2007)	45.0
Brazil	48.0 (1990)	30.0 (2007)	12.0
Chile	38.6 (1990)	13.7 (2006)	−11.2
Colombia	56.1 (1991)	46.8 (2005)	37.5
Costa Rica	26.3 (1990)	18.6 (2007)	10.9
Cuba	nd	nd	
Dominican Republic	46.9 (2000)	44.5 (2007)	42.1
Ecuador	62.1 (1990)	38.8 (2007)	15.5
El Salvador	54.2 (1995)	47.5 (2004)	40.8
Guatemala	69.4 (1989)	54.8 (2006)	40.2
Haiti	nd	nd	
Honduras	80.8 (1990)	68.9 (2007)	57.0
Mexico	47.7 (1989)	31.7 (2006)	15.7
Nicaragua	73.6 (1993)	61.9 (2005)	50.2
Panama[b]	48.7 (1991)	29.0 (2007)	9.3
Paraguay	60.6 (1999)	60.5 (2007)	60.4
Peru	54.1 (2001)	39.3 (2007)	24.5
Uruguay	17.9 (1990)	18.1 (2007)	18.3
Venezuela	39.8 (1990)	28.5 (2007)	17.2

Source: CEPAL, *Panorama Social de América Latina 2005* (2005):317–18; ECLAC, *Social Panorama of Latin America 2006* (Preliminary Version); ECLAC, *Social Panorama of Latin America 2007* (Preliminary Version):11; ECLAC, *Social Panorama of Latin America 2008*, Briefing Paper: 11.

Data for Argentina, Ecuador, and Uruguay are for urban areas.

[a]Bolivia 1989 is our estimate for the country as a whole based on CEPAL's figure of a 52.6% poverty rate for urban areas in 1989 and on a poverty rate that was on average 10.4% higher in the country as a whole than in urban areas only in 1997, 1999, and 2000 (the three years for which CEPAL has estimates for both the country as a whole and for urban areas only). We added 52.6% + 10.4% to produce the estimate of 63.0% for 1989. The estimation procedure for 1989 enabled us to develop a longer time series.

[b]Panama 1991 is our estimate for the country as a whole based on CEPAL's figure of a 39.9% poverty rate for urban areas in 1991 and on a poverty rate that was on average 8.8% higher in the country as a whole than in urban areas only for 2002, 2005, and 2006. These are the three years for which CEPAL has estimates for both the country as a whole and for urban areas only. We added 39.9% + 8.8% to produce the estimate of 48.7% for 1991. The estimation procedure for 1991 enabled us to develop a longer time series.

We measure success in education by adding the absolute level and the improvement in the percentage of fifteen- to nineteen-year-olds who are in school or who have graduated. Ideally, measures of quality would supplement this measure of access to education, but we could not obtain valid time series measures of quality for enough countries. The available data indicate problems of quality of education throughout Latin America.

Table 1.5 reports the data on access to secondary education. Columns 2 and 3 give the raw data on the percentage of fifteen- to nineteen-year-olds who were enrolled or had graduated for circa 1990 and circa 2005.[10] Chile (88%), the Dominican Republic (surprisingly high at 83%), and Argentina (82%) led the region in the share of fifteen- to nineteen-year-olds who are enrolled in school or finished high school. The modest rates for Uruguay (70%) and Costa Rica (69%) are surprising in light of the fact that these two countries consistently score toward the top of the region on most other social indicators. The countries that fare worst, Guatemala (42%), Honduras (48%), and Nicaragua (53%) score poorly on most social indicators.

Several countries achieved major improvements in access to secondary education between 1990 and 2005. Brazil led the way with an increase of 23%, which reduced by 50% (from 46% to 23%) the percentage of fifteen- to nineteen-year-olds who are neither high school graduates nor enrolled. Costa Rica (with an increase of 22%), Argentina and Venezuela (18%), Chile and Colombia (15%), and Bolivia and Honduras (14%) also experienced double digit increases in the percentage of fifteen- to nineteen-year-olds who are graduates or enrolled. Only one country, Nicaragua, experienced a decline (from 56% to 53%). Far more Latin Americans are gaining access to secondary education today than in the past.

We scored education by combining the percentage of those enrolled or graduated circa 2005 with the improvement between circa 1990 and circa 2005. Once again, the variance across Latin American countries is great. Chile (103), Brazil (100), Argentina (100), Venezuela (96), Costa Rica (91), the Dominican Republic (89), and Colombia (88) are at the high end of the spectrum. With the lowest rate of access to secondary education in the region (excepting presumably Haiti, for which there is no data) and a record of almost no change between 1990 and 2005, Guatemala anchors the low end (43).

CITIZEN SECURITY

In Thomas Hobbes's classic work, *Leviathan*, the state's primary function is to protect citizens. In Hobbes's view, without the state's capacity

TABLE 1.5
Improvement in Access to Secondary Education in Latin America, 1990–2005

	Percentage enrolled or graduated, 15- to 19-year-olds, circa 1990	Percentage enrolled or graduated, 15- to 19-year-olds, circa 2005	Score for percentage enrolled or graduated, 15- to 19-year-olds
Argentina	64	82	100
Bolivia	49	63	77
Brazil	54	77	100
Chile	73	88	103
Colombia	58	73	88
Costa Rica	47	69	91
Cuba	—	—	—
Dominican Republic	77	83	89
Ecuador	—	68	69
El Salvador	55	61	67
Guatemala	41	42	43
Haiti	—	—	—
Honduras	34	48	62
Mexico	55	61	67
Nicaragua	56	53	50
Panama	65	73	81
Paraguay	—	67	76
Peru	60	68	76
Uruguay	63	70	77
Venezuela	60	78	96

Sources: CEPAL, *Panorama Social de América Latina 2007*, Cuadros 36 and 37 (online); CEPAL, *Panorama Social de América Latina 2006*, Cuadros 36 and 37:398–401; CEPAL, *Panorama Social de América Latina 2005*, Cuadros 36 and 39:406–407, 412–413. The data for Argentina and Uruguay are urban only. The national data for Ecuador and Paraguay are available for 2005/06 but not for the early 1990s. The urban data for Ecuador show an increase of 1% over this time (76% in 1990 and 77% in 2006), so we assumed the same 1% increase for the national data. The urban only data for Paraguay show an increase of 12%, from 66% in 1994 to 78% in 2006. We assumed the same increase of 12% for the country as a whole. This might be a conservative estimate of the national increase for Paraguay but we had no grounds for any other means of calculating change over time. The original sources give the precise years for the data.

to impose law and order, ruthlessness and violence would prevail. This view of the state's most primordial function has much to say for it. Citizens need a state that will protect them from violence.

Unfortunately, in much of Latin America, the state has failed at this basic function, with pernicious consequences for citizens and for democracy. Violence escalated in recent decades as the ranks of the urban young and unemployed swelled and as drug trafficking and organized crime took hold in most large Latin American cities. Citizens view crime as one of the most important problems in contemporary Latin America (refer back to Table 1.1). In seven of the eight countries in the 2004 LAPOP surveys, crime victimization lowered mass support for democracy (Seligson 2004), so there is a direct connection between high crime and diminished support for democracy. The 2006 LAPOP confirmed this connection.

To assess government performance in citizen security, we primarily used the Pan American Health Organization's data on homicides.[11] Data on other kinds of crime are less comparable across national borders and are more difficult to obtain, especially for a time series. Moreover, high homicide rates affect the quality of life more than other forms of crime. Homicide rates measure one of the most important elements of citizen security, and it is likely that homicide rates are correlated with other forms of crime.

Columns 2 and 3 of Table 1.6 show the homicide rate in the 1990s and this decade. Homicide rates vary widely across Latin America. According to relatively recent data, Peru, Uruguay, Argentina, Chile, Cuba, and Costa Rica had between 4.5 and 8.0 homicides per 100,000 people. (The data on Peru, however, seem quite underreported.) With one of the highest homicide rates in the world, 61.3 homicides per 100,000 people, El Salvador was eight to fourteen times above the level of these other countries. Colombia (52.5 per 100,000), Honduras (46.0), and Guatemala (45.2) were about ten times higher than the countries with lowest homicide rates. For purposes of comparison, the United States has a homicide rate of about 6 per 100,000 inhabitants per year.

High homicide rates have pernicious effects on the quality of every day life, and they reflect differences in the state's ability to protect citizens from other citizens (and in today's world, from organized gangs). These differences in homicide rates antedate the democratic and semidemocratic regimes, but in the countries with very high crime and homicide rates, these problems have gotten worse since the transitions to competitive regimes.

We measure state performance in protecting citizens from homicide by adding the most recent level and change over time. El Salvador (72.4),

TABLE 1.6
Homicides per 100,000 People in Nineteen Latin American Countries

	1990s	2000s	Change in homicide rate (Column 3 – Column 2)	Score (Column 3 + Column 4)
Argentina	4.9 (1995)	5.0 (2006)	0.1	5.1
Brazil	26.6 (1995)	29.2 (2005)	2.6	31.8
Chile	2.9 (1991)	5.8 (2005)	2.9	8.7
Colombia	79.3 (1991)	52.5 (2005)	−26.8	25.7
Costa Rica	5.4 (1995)	8.0 (2006)	2.6	10.6
Cuba	6.1 (1995)	6.5 (2004)	0.4	6.9
Dominican Republic	12.4 (1991)	10.7 (2004)	−1.7	9.0
Ecuador	10.8 (1991)	18.4 (2005)	7.6	26.0
El Salvador	51.2 (1995)	61.3 (2005)	10.1	72.4
Guatemala	21.6 (1995)	45.2 (2005)	23.6	68.8
Haiti	—	18.6 (2002)	—	18.6
Honduras	33.8 (1999)	46.0 (2005)	12.2	58.2
Mexico	16.7 (1991)	11.3 (2003)	−5.4	5.9
Nicaragua	11.3 (1995)	17.5 (2005)	6.2	23.7
Panama	11.1 (1995)	12.4 (2004)	1.3	13.7
Paraguay	15.6 (1995)	20.3 (2004)	4.7	25.0
Peru	6.2 (1995)	4.5 (2002)	−1.7	2.8
Uruguay	4.8 (1995)	4.6 (2004)	−0.2	4.4
Venezuela	12.5 (1991)	32.5 (2004)	20.0	52.5

Note: For Haiti, 2002 is the only year reported. For Honduras, 1999 is the only year reported.

Sources: For recent data for most countries: Pan American Health Organization (PAHO), Health Analysis and Information Systems Area. Regional Core Health Data Initiative, Technical Health Information Systems, Washington, DC, 2005; PAHO, Health Analysis and Statistics Unit, Regional Core Health Data Initiative, Technical Health Information Systems, Washington, DC, 2007. Available at www.paho.org. For 1991 for several countries: Pan American Health Organization, "Statistics on Homicides, Suicides, Accidents, Injuries, and Attitudes towards Violence," online at www.paho.org/English/AD/DPC/NC/violence-graphs.

For the Dominican Republic in 1991, Mayra Brea de Cabral and Edylberto Cabral, "La violencia y los factores socioeconómicos de riesgo en la República Dominicana." At www.psicologiacientifica.com/bv/psicologia-150-1-la-violencia-y-los-factores-socioeconomicos-de-riesgo-en-la-.html. For Guatemala and Honduras 2005, Freedom House, Freedom in the World 2007. For Honduras 1999, www.paho.org/Spanish/DD/PUB/Causas_externas.pdf.

Guatemala (68.8), Honduras (58.2), and Venezuela (52.5) have the worst scores. Although Colombia maintained the second highest homicide rate, a steep decline in relation to the 1990s gave it a better score than El Salvador, Guatemala, Honduras, and Venezuela. Peru (where the data are of dubious validity), Uruguay, Argentina, Mexico (another case of dubious validity), Cuba, Chile, and Costa Rica cluster closely at the low end.

CORRELATIONS AMONG DIMENSIONS

To provide a first indication of how performance is related across these nine dimensions, Table 1.7 shows the Pearson bivariate correlations among the dimensions. To facilitate ease of interpretation, we reversed the coefficients for inflation, poverty, and homicides so that in all cases a positive coefficient in Table 1.7 means that a good performance on one dimension is correlated positively with a good dimension on the other.

The table indicates that good results have tended to bundle together in contemporary Latin America. Except for inflation, good performance in one dimension has been related to good performance in others. Virtuous cycles have prevailed in some countries and vicious ones have prevailed in others.

Eight of the nine dimensions have some statistically significant correlations with other dimensions; the only exception is inflation. Of the 36 cells in Table 1.7, 19 are statistically significant with a p value of .10 or less (thirteen have a p value of .05 or less). With all 19 of the statistically significant correlations, good scores on one dimension are correlated with good scores on the other. Excluding inflation, 19 of the 28 correlations are statistically significant at $p < .10$. Of the 36 correlations in the table, 34 have a positive coefficient. The two exceptions (inflation with poverty and access to secondary education) have very low coefficients and are nowhere close to being statistically significant.

Many of the significant correlations in Table 1.7 mesh with theoretical and comparative expectations based on prior work. Level of democracy, rule of law, and control of corruption are highly correlated. Although positive correlations between the level of democracy and rule of law seem intuitively sensible, this finding is still somewhat notable because the level of democracy is measured as a mean score for fifteen years while rule of law is measured as the 2007 level added to change from 1996 to 2007. The common methodology and common sources for rule of law and control of corruption help explain the high (.80) correlation.

The correlation (.56) between per capita growth and generation of formal sector jobs is consistent with expectations, as is the correlation

TABLE 1.7
Correlations among Indicators of Democratic Governance in Latin America

	Freedom House	Rule of law	Control of corruption	Growth	Inflation (natural log)	Generation of jobs	Poverty	Enrollment + graduates	Homicide rate
Freedom House	1.00	.46**	.47**	.80***	.25	.54**	.56**	.42*	.11
Rule of law		1.00	.80***	.63***	.25	.65***	.53**	.37	.43*
Control of corruption			1.00	.53**	.18	.41	.47*	.22	.10
Growth				1.00	.35	.56**	.44*	.31	.29
Inflation (log)					1.00	.34	-.06	-.18	.08
Generation of jobs						1.00	.61**	.34	.27
Poverty							1.00	.56**	.43*
Enrollment + graduates								1.00	.44*
Homicide rate									1.00

*Correlation is significant at .10 (2-tailed).

** Correlation is significant at .05 (2-tailed).

***Correlation is significant at .01 (2-tailed).

Note: Due to missing information for some of the variables, the number of cases in the cells is not always the same. The same correlation has different p values depending on the number of cases.

(.44) between growth and poverty (higher growth is associated with a better score for poverty). These results, however, are still notable because per capita growth measures change while the variables for generation of jobs and poverty measure a combination of the level and change. This asymmetry in measurement is likely to lower the correlations, making the strength of the correlations notable.

More striking are the high correlations between level of democracy, rule of law, and control of corruption on one hand, and economic growth, generation of formal sector jobs, and poverty, on the other. Freedom House scores are correlated at .80 with per capita GDP growth. In the post-1990 period, Latin American countries that have been more democratic have had better performances in economic growth, generating formal sector jobs, and curbing poverty. Based on prominent work in comparative politics (e.g., Przeworski et al. 2000), there is no reason to expect that countries with a higher level of democracy would also perform better in economic growth. This result would not hold up for some other regions or for Latin America in other times.

Somewhat surprisingly, the log of inflation is not correlated with any of the other measures; the same result obtains with the raw (i.e., not logged) numbers for inflation. This reflects (among other things) the fact that several countries with low inflation have otherwise not been success cases. For example, Bolivia, El Salvador, and Guatemala are among the six countries with average annual inflation rates in the single digits for 1992 to 2006.

COMMENSURABILITY ACROSS DIMENSIONS

Each of these nine dimensions uses different units and has a different scale. The level of democracy is measured in inverted Freedom House scores; economic growth is measured in annual change in per capita GDP growth; and so forth. To create commensurability among measures, we rescaled all dimensions into a scale that runs from 0 (the worst performance in the world) to 100 (the best performance in the world). Except for inflation, all other scores are transformed in linear fashion. For example, the worst (0) and best (12) Freedom House scores are transformed into 0 and 100, respectively, on our index. All other Freedom House scores are transformed in linear fashion.

Table 1.8 indicates the best and worst performances in the world on these nine dimensions. Using the range of performances in the world ensures that we do not artificially truncate scales by limiting the comparisons to Latin American experience. At the same time, it ensures that we establish standards of excellence and failure that are actually attained.

To determine a given country's indexed score on a given dimension, we took its score, subtracted the score of the worst performing country, divided by the range of scores (best score minus worst score) for that dimension, and multiplied by 100. For example, to determine Costa Rica's indexed Freedom House score, we took its inverted mean score (11.3), subtracted the score of the worst performing country on that dimension (0), divided by the range of scores (best score minus worst score) and multiplied by 100, producing an indexed score of 94.25.

For per capita GDP growth, we used the country with the second best performance in the world, China (9.3% per capita per year), rather than Equatorial Guinea, which was an extreme outlier with an 18.4% per capita per year growth rate. The rapid growth in Equatorial Guinea resulted from the discovery and rapid exploitation of petroleum wealth in a small country (the population is about 504,000). Including Equatorial Guinea makes very large differences in growth performance seem small. On the other eight dimensions, no country was such an extreme outlier.

For inflation, we constructed the index with the natural logarithm of the annual increase in consumer prices because the expected impact of increases in prices on citizens and economic agents is nonlinear. An increase in the inflation rate of 0 to 25% usually has a far greater impact than in increase from 400 to 425%. For inflation rates lower than 1%, we used a logged value of 0.

Among the 177 countries for which we have data for inflation for 1992 to 2006, the Democratic Republic of Congo had the highest average increase in consumer prices at 401.1% per year.[12] Among countries that had data for at least twelve years, Japan was lowest at 0.2% per year. With the logged transformations of the original inflation values, a score of 1.5013[13] (equivalent to an annual inflation of 20%) produces the median indexed score of 50.

Systematic time series data for the world on employment and informal employment are difficult to find. For this reason, we base the best and worst case performances on level only, without also including data about change over time. We surveyed the available ILO information (2002, 2004, 2006) to set benchmarks for the worst and best cases. The best record in formal employment was Canada, where about 92% of the labor force was in the formal sector. Canada's unemployment level was around 7%. Multiplying the percentage employed by the percentage of those employed who have formal jobs (.92 · .93) produces a score of 85.6% on our measure. Based on crossectional ILO data, no country scored worse than Bolivia, so we used its score as the worst in the world.

TABLE 1.8
Best and Worst Performances in the World on Nine Dimensions of Democratic Governance

	Best in world	Score	Worst in world	Score
Freedom House scores	Many countries	12.0	Many countries	0.0
Rule of law	Bhutan	2.32	Somalia	-3.18
Control of corruption	Iceland	3.38	North Korea	-3.05
GDP per capita growth	Equatorial Guinea	18.4%	Democratic Republic of Congo	-4.6%
Inflation	Japan	0.2%	Dem. Rep. of Congo	401.1%
Generation of jobs	Canada	85.6	Bolivia	22.8
Poverty	Chile	-11.2	Paraguay	60.4
Net secondary enrollment	Chile	103	Mozambique	7
Homicides	Israel	0.5/100,000	El Salvador	72.4/100,000

Sources:

Freedom House scores: www.freedomhouse.org.

Rule of law: Kaufmann et al. (2007:88–90).

Control of corruption: Kaufmann et al. (2007:91–93).

GDP per capita growth (annual): Calculated from the World Bank, *WDI World Development Indicators*. Calculated in 2005 constant dollars in purchasing parity power. Equatorial Guinea had the highest per capita annual growth but was an extraordinary outlier.

Inflation (annual percentage change in consumer price index): World Bank, *World Development Indicators*.

Generation of jobs: International Labour Organization, *Panorama Laboral de América Latina*.

Poverty: Best and worst are based on Latin American data only. From: CEPAL, *Panorama Social de América Latina 2005* (2005):317–18; ECLAC, *Social Panorama of Latin America 2006* (Preliminary Version).

Net secondary enrollment: World Bank, EdStats, at http://devdata.worldbank.org/edstats/indicators.html.

Homicides: World Health Organization, *World Report on Violence and Health* (2002).

For poverty, we could not find reliable data for a large sample of countries in the world, so we indexed the scores with our Latin American sample.

For education, we used ECLAC data in Table 1.5, because it seemed more valid than the World Bank's EdStats data. For the world's low score, we used the World Bank's EdStats using the same mixed method as in Table 1.5 (combining current level of net secondary enrollment plus change from circa 1990 to circa 2005). With this mixed method, Mozambique had the lowest score in the world for net secondary enrollment (7), and Brazil had the highest score. To be consistent with Table 1.5, we counted Chile's score of 103, which was the highest according to ECLAC data, as the highest in the world. Most Latin American countries had scores above 50, reflecting large gains in access to secondary education in the 1990s and 2000s.

For homicides per 100,000 inhabitants, to establish the best and worst performances, we used the *World Report on Violence and Health*, published in 2002 by the World Health Organization. We did not attempt to construct a time series for the best and worst in the world because of large gaps in data. According to the *World Report on Violence and Health*, Colombia had the highest homicide rate in the world (61.6 homicides per 100,000 inhabitants); Israel had the lowest (0.5). However, because Colombia registered a substantial reduction in homicide in our time series, the Latin American country with the worst score in Table 1.6 above is El Salvador (72.4). Accordingly, we use its score as the worst in the world. We take Israel's 0.5 per 100,000 homicide rate as its score for public security.

Table 1.9 gives the indexed scores for the nine dimensions. Because of the bundling of good and poor performances across different arenas, a few countries stand out generally as cases of successful democratic governance while others are marked by failure in many ways. Chile has high scores on all nine dimensions, consistent with the common view that it has been the great success case in the post-1990 period. Chile has built a robust democracy, fostered rapid economic growth, and dramatically reduced poverty. On most dimensions of democratic governance, Costa Rica, Panama, and Uruguay have also fared well. A few countries' performance varied considerably across different dimensions. For example, Argentina did very well on education and public security but poorly on control of corruption.

The indexed scores help identify nine countries that have been stuck in vicious cycles: low quality democracy (or semi-democracy), poor rule of law, poor control of corruption, poor growth, and poor performance in reduction of poverty. For 1991 to 2006, Bolivia, Colombia, Ecuador, Guatemala, Haiti, Honduras, Nicaragua, Paraguay, and Venezuela fit

TABLE 1.9

Indexed and Composite Scores of Democratic Governance in Latin America

	Freedom House scores[a]	Rule of law	Control of corruption	GDP growth, 1991–2006	Inflation, 1992–2006	Jobs in formal sector	Poverty	Education	Homicides	Composite score
Argentina	78	46	38	50	67	48	48	97	93	69
Bolivia	73	28	48	43	70	0	22	73	—	54
Brazil	71	46	43	43	25	21	68	97	56	60
Chile	90	78	69	63	70	73	100	100	89	85
Colombia	55	49	47	43	56	13	32	84	65	52
Costa Rica	95	63	48	55	57	43	69	87	86	78
Cuba	1	47	44	—	—	—	84	—	91	8
Dominican Republic	76	48	33	63	60	25	26	85	88	64
Ecuador	69	28	33	43	44	17	63	64	64	55
El Salvador	73	50	56	49	70	28	27	62	0	56
Guatemala	53	34	40	42	65	—	28	37	5	44
Haiti	27	32	24	12	50	—	—	—	75	32
Honduras	68	40	42	43	57	44	5	57	20	51
Mexico	71	46	43	45	59	43	62	62	92	63
Nicaragua	64	33	26	47	62	16	14	44	68	50
Panama	86	53	45	53	100	50	71	77	82	76
Paraguay	62	31	26	34	60	15	0	72	66	49
Peru	63	43	38	55	59	36	50	72	97	60
Uruguay	96	65	71	49	46	30	59	73	95	77
Venezuela	59	17	28	36	41	30	60	93	28	50

[a]Freedom House scores are inverted [14 − (Political Liberties + Civil Liberties)]

The composite index for Bolivia, Cuba, Guatemala, and Haiti is based on eight, five, eight, and six, columns, respectively.

this description. All of these countries scored poorly for Kaufmann et al.'s score for rule of law, and all but Bolivia and Colombia also did for control of corruption. They also all experienced anemic per capita GDP growth. Only two countries of the nine, Ecuador and Venezuela, performed above the regional mean in reducing poverty. Colombia and Venezuela are relative newcomers to this category of low performers, having experienced an erosion of democracy and of government performance since the 1980s. Colombia has fared better in most dimensions in recent years than in the 1990s.

If Chile anchors the very successful end of the Latin American spectrum, Haiti anchors the low end among the nineteen countries that have experimented with competitive political regimes. In Haiti, two attempted transitions to competitive regimes were short lived and resulted in a coup in 1991 and a rebellion in 2004, both leading to the overthrow of a democratically elected president. The congress has been closed twice (in 1999 and 2004), two international interventions took place (in 1994 and 2004), and the state at times tottered on the brink of collapse.

A COMPOSITE INDEX OF DEMOCRATIC GOVERNANCE

One can build a reasonable argument for or against aggregating different dimensions of democratic governance into a composite score. The case for a composite score is that highly aggregated information can provide a useful synthesis. The widespread dissemination of the Human Development Index illustrates the advantages of a composite score; it provides a useful summary snapshot of average human well-being in about 175 countries. In recent years, the Commitment of Development Index (Roodman 2006) provides an example of a useful summary of how much wealthy countries support development efforts in the Third World. The arguments against a composite score are that variance across dimensions can be lost, that in most cases there is no ideal way to aggregate across dimensions to create the single score, and that the composite can be misleading for these and other reasons.

Aggregating the nine dimensions into one composite score loses valuable information, but it offers a highly synthetic sense of how different countries compare. All nine dimensions reflect government performance and outcomes, so a composite score might generate useful summary information about success in democratic governance. Accordingly, we created a composite score although our primary focus is on the nine underlying dimensions.

We opted for a multiplicative approach that recognizes the special importance of the level of democracy in a composite score of democratic governance. We took the simple indexed mean for the other eight dimensions and multiplied it by the indexed Freedom House score, then took the square root. Scores could range from 0 to 100. With the exception of the Freedom House scores, rather than undertaking a complex weighting scheme, we followed Roodman's (2006) logic that it is reasonable to take a simple mean of dimensions when there is no clear criterion for weighting. Following this method, the final column of Table 1.9 presents a composite index for democratic governance for our twenty countries, with the caveat that Cuba is not a case of *democratic* governance, and that Haiti usually has not been.

This aggregation method rests on the implicit assumption that the other eight dimensions should have equal weight under conditions of relatively democratic government. It is difficult to defend an absolute version of this assumption, but all eight dimensions are highly important.

The composite scores reinforce three conclusions of this chapter. First, the outcomes of democratic governance have varied greatly across countries; the composite scores properly reflect huge differences.[14] Second, Chile (85) has been the most successful case of democratic governance in contemporary Latin America, followed at some distance by Costa Rica (78), Uruguay (77), and Panama (76). After this, there is another substantial drop to Argentina (69), the Dominican Republic (64), and Mexico (63), followed by another substantial gap. Third, at the opposite end of the spectrum, the composite index shows the very poor scores for Cuba (8) and Haiti (32), and the deficient overall performance in democratic governance of Guatemala (44), Paraguay (49), Venezuela (50), Nicaragua (50), Honduras (51), Colombia (52), Bolivia (54), and Ecuador (55). In the last several years, Colombia has improved its record in democratic governance relative to the 1990s, but it remains in the group of poor performers because of the results of the period before Alvaro Uribe assumed the presidency. In our judgment, the composite index performs well in identifying the relatively successful cases and the poor performers for this period of fifteen years.

PRIOR WORKS ON EFFECTIVE GOVERNANCE

Our reason for building a new measure of democratic governance is that no measure closely resembles what we have undertaken here.[15] In the next sections of this chapter, we develop this point by comparing our index to the most prominent existing works on effective governance, the quality of democracy, and democratic performance. Our point is not that our measure is better than these alternatives, but rather that it is different and that it captures an important phenomenon.

Successful democratic governance has much in common with successful governance, except that it occurs under conditions of democracy. Whether they are democratic or not, governments that succeed at governing must ensure citizen security and promote human well-being. For this reason, our project has some elements in common with Kaufmann et al.'s (2003, 2005, 2006, 2007, 2008) governance indicators. They include six important dimensions of governance: voice and accountability, political stability and absence of violence, government effectiveness, regulatory quality, rule of law, and control of corruption. They provide solid empirical measures for the dimensions, and their methodology is sophisticated.

Our project differs from Kaufmann et al.'s governance indicators in six respects. First, they attempt to measure how effective governance is; we attempt to measure how successful it is. All of their indicators are subjective whereas six of our dimensions are objective and are based on outcomes. We prefer some objective data about outcomes because of their greater reliability and validity.

Second, we focus on governance under competitive political regimes. There is much common ground between successful *democratic* governance (our enterprise) and effective governance (Kaufmann et al.), but governing under democracy presents distinctive challenges and advantages. The pursuit of efficiency is bounded by democratic checks and balances and by electoral competition; political goals are established through a competitive process. Only one of Kaufmann et al.'s indicators, voice and accountability, taps the democratic character of the political regime.[16]

Third, Kaufmann et al.'s indicators compare countries in a given year, but they have no validity for temporal comparisons. (The same is true for our indexed scores and composite score). If there is a general trend in the world, Kaufmann et al.'s indicators fail to register this change. Seven of our nine dimensions measure change over time, not merely change relative to the world average in a given year. For the rule of law and control of corruption indicators, we are not able to track change over time because we rely on Kaufmann et al.

Fourth, for our purposes, Kaufmann et al. overweight perceptions by business groups (Arndt and Oman 2006, 69–71; Kurtz and Shrank 2007). Seventeen of the thirty-one organizations that provide the basis for Kaufmann et al.'s measures (2005, appendix A, 62–100, 108–109) are business oriented. The individual questions from surveys and expert opinion polls also disproportionately—for our purposes—reflect business perspectives and concerns. The fact that business interests have a favorable opinion of governance does not always mean that democratic governance is effective. We are especially concerned with aspects of government performance that have a deep impact on citizens.

Fifth, the Kaufmann et al. measures are based on the idea that a large amount of information (the surveys and expert opinion questions) presented in a highly synthetic manner (the number of standard deviations from the mean) is optimal. Without dismissing the merits of their approach, our index is predicated on different assumptions. We opted for relative parsimony by choosing only nine dimensions, eight of which are built from only one form of data. One advantage of our approach is greater intuitive comprehensibility. The mean inverted Freedom House scores of 11.3 for Costa Rica and 6.3 for Guatemala are meaningful to the sizable number of scholars who have worked with Freedom House measures. The fact that Costa Rica was 0.44 standard deviations about the mean for Kaufmann et al.'s rule of law in 2007 is useful information, but the deeper meaning of this fact requires examining the survey and expert opinion questions that underlie the index. Kaufmann et al.'s scores are technically sophisticated but they do not produce an intuitively obvious substantive meaning. In opting for parsimony and simplicity, our approach differs.

Finally, whereas Kaufmann et al. give annual scores, our measure tracks performance over a longer period of time. Our measures could in principle assess performance in a particular year. However, objective data such as per capita growth that can oscillate sharply from one year to the next are not good measures of success. High growth in a single year can reflect a strong recovery from a recession, a good harvest, a favorable change in the terms of international trade, etc.

Another well-known measure of governance is Putnam (1993, 63–82), who devised twelve measures of the effectiveness of Italy's regional governments.[17] His measures might be appropriate for assessing the quality of regional governments, but national governments have different responsibilities (e.g., macroeconomic policy and management) than regional governments. For an assessment of government performance at the national level, our measures are more suitable.

OUR MEASURE COMPARED TO MEASURES OF
THE QUALITY OF DEMOCRACY

Most measures of the quality of democracy focus exclusively or largely on procedural issues (Altman and Pérez-Liñán 2002; Diamond and Morlino 2005; Levine and Molina 2006; Lijphart 1999, 275–300). In contrast, our assessment of democratic governance also focuses significantly on policy results.

As conceptualized by Diamond and Morlino (2005) and Levine and Molina (2006), the quality of democracy refers to the extent to which democracies live up to a procedural liberal understanding of democracy. Both sets of authors exclude policy results from their purview. Our enterprise is different because we evaluate not only democratic procedures, but also the governance results of democratic governments.

Because we include the results of democratic governance from the standpoint of citizen well-being, our measures are generally broader than the procedural measures. We also exclude some issues that some measures of the democraticness of the political regime include. For example, Foweraker and Krznaric (2000) include the level of electoral disproportionality (the difference between parties' vote and seat shares) and the size of the legislature divided by the number of seats of the largest party in their measure of the quality of democracy.

Our project also differs from the Programa Estado de la Nación (PEN)/UNDP citizen audit of the quality of democracy in Costa Rica (Vargas Cullell 2004). The PEN/UNDP defined quality of democracy as "the extent to which political life and institutional performance in a country...with a democratic regime coincides with the democratic aspirations of its people" (Vargas Cullell 2004, 96). The citizen audit thus depends on citizen aspirations and beliefs about what a democracy should be. Our project differs in three ways. First, we employ criteria for measuring success that we determined in consultation with other scholars. Even though our criteria were influenced by public opinion surveys regarding what citizens value in a democracy, our endeavor is different from one that begins with citizen aspirations. Second, we focus partly on objective performance. Third, we use a more bounded procedural definition of democracy that is consistent with most contemporary scholarly definitions, whereas the PEN-UNDP assessed the quality of democracy based a broad understanding of democracy including non-regime dimensions.

CONCLUSION

We hope to make three main contributions with this chapter. First, we believe that charting how Latin American countries have performed on some of the issues that are critical to citizen well-being over the past fifteen years is useful. To the best of our knowledge, no previous work has examined the sweep of dimensions that we have here for all of Latin America over the medium term.

Second, social scientists should develop tools for assessing and measuring success in democratic governance. Existing measures focus on other issues. They are useful, but it is also important to be able to measure success in democratic governance. We hope to stimulate thinking about ways to do so.

Third, the chapter underscores the wide variance in success in democratic governance in contemporary Latin America. There are meaningful ways in which it is useful to think about Latin America as a region (Mainwaring and Pérez-Liñán 2007). However, this fact should not obscure the important differences within this diverse region.

Notes

We are grateful to Daniel Brinks, David Collier, Tasha Fairfield, Daniel Levine, James McGuire, Irma Méndez, Gerardo Munck, Aníbal Pérez-Liñán, Kurt Weyland, one anonymous reviewer, and colleagues at the Kellogg Institute for International Studies for comments. We thank Carol Hendrickson and Kate Schuenke for research assistance.

1. Gerring et al. (2005) also focus partly on outcomes in their measure of good democratic governance.

2. Perceptions about the efficacy of rule of law tend to be remarkably stable over time. For the twenty Latin American countries, the 2006 scores are correlated with the 2005 scores at 0.99 and with the 1996 scores at 0.93.

3. Some methods that examine only change would disadvantage countries that start off in a good position. For example, if we measured the percentage of change relative to the starting point, $(V_{t+15} - V_t)/V_t$, where V_{t+15} is the value at year t+15 and V_t is the value at year t, countries that started off with a high value on this variable would be at a disadvantage. V_{t+15} can increase relative to V_t more easily if V_t is low. Using this method, an increase from 6 to 10 yields a better score (an increase of 66.7%) than an increase from 40 to 65 (an increase of 62.5%). Likewise, an increase from 29 to 30 produces a better score than a constant level of 60. Methods that examine only change relative to how much improvement is theoretically possible are flawed when a country that starts off at a high level slips slightly, while a country that starts off at a low level increases slightly. Assume that 100 is the maximum value for a dimension and that we calculated performance as $(V_{t+15} - V_t)/(100 - V_t)$. With this method, country A, which slips from 96 to 95 over fifteen years, would appear to perform worse (with a score of −.25) than country B, which improved from 40 to 41 (with a score of .025). With most issues, however, it would be very misleading to conclude that B was more successful than A.

4. Whether it does so in practice depends on the dispersion of the values for the initial level and the amount of change.

5. Olken (2006) and Seligson (2002, 2006) developed innovative approaches to measuring corruption. However, cross-national time series data that measure

corruption in these ways are not yet available for all twenty Latin American countries.

6. Kaufmann et al. incorporated more sources of information and more countries than Transparency International. We prefer Kaufmann et al. for these reasons, among others.

7. We calculated the geometric annual mean, that is, the cumulative increase over fifteen years, then the fifteenth root of this figure.

8. The concept and measurement of informal work is highly contested (Husmmanns 2004). We adopt the ILO's definition: Informal work "includes all remunerative work (i.e. both self-employment and wage employment), that is not registered, regulated or protected by existing legal or regulatory frameworks, as well as non-remunerative work undertaken in an income-producing enterprise. Informal workers do not have secure employment contracts, workers' benefits, social protection or workers' representation" (ILO 2005).

9. For debates about the virtues and shortcomings of different measures of poverty, see Székely et al. (2000) and Gruben and McLeod (2003).

10. We used CEPAL's data rather than the World Bank's EdStats data on net secondary enrollment because of doubts about the validity of the latter. For example, the World Bank shows Costa Rica as having the third lowest net secondary enrollment in Latin America in 2005 at 41%, a figure far below that for Bolivia (73%), to take just one example.

11. The data on homicides have some inconsistencies and shortcomings. In some countries, the data underreport homicides. The Pan American Health Organization (PAHO 2006, 6) stated that the data are particularly unreliable for Guatemala and Honduras. The PAHO (2006, 7) reports that in the 1980s, homicides were 11% of all deaths in Guatemala, compared to 0.03% in England; that is, homicides as a share of all deaths were more than 360 greater in Guatemala than in England. The homicide data for Peru also seem to be considerably understated. In 2006, Peru was the country (among those in the 2006 LAPOP survey) with the highest rate of crime victimization in Latin America, and Peruvians exhibited the highest rate of personal insecurity in the region (Carrión, Zárate, and Seligson 2006). For Argentina, according to a report of the Ministry of Justice, the actual rate of homicides exceeded the reported rate by 80% in 1997 (8.8 per 100,000 population rather than 4.9).

For most countries the cross-national patterns in the data are consistent across sources and over time.

12. This is based on fourteen years, 1992–2005, because of a lack of availability of data for 2006.

13. This is the mean of the logged values for the average inflation rate in the Democratic Republic of Congo (6.00) and Japan (0).

14. Even so, these differences are almost certainly understated because of missing data. We do not have data for Haiti for formal sector jobs, poverty, or education. In all three areas, Haiti fares disastrously, and it seems probable that the official data understate homicides.

15. The Indice de Desarrollo Democrático (www.idd-lat.org) comes closer than other measures to focusing on success in democratic governance. We do

not discuss it in the text because it has been less influential than the measures we analyze. Our measures are constructed in very different ways than those of the Indice de Desarrollo Democrático.

16. If there were no other differences between our vision of successful democratic governance and Kaufmann et al.'s indicators of successful governance, we could have imposed a minimum threshold on their voice and accountability indicator (or used Freedom House scores to establish a minimum threshold), discarded the cases that failed to meet this threshold, and used their indicators to compare the level of success among democratic cases. However, our project differs in other ways, so this threshold approach would not accomplish our purpose.

17. Cabinet stability, budget promptness, quality of statistical services, quality of legislative output as judged by experts, legislative innovation, the number of day care centers, the number of family clinics, government spending on agriculture, expenditures on local health units, government spending on housing and urban development, and bureaucratic responsiveness. Several of these measures are biased toward social democratic governments.

References

Altman, David, and Aníbal Pérez-Liñán. 2002. Assessing the Quality of Democracy: Freedom, Competitiveness, and Participation in Eighteen Latin American Countries. *Democratization* 9(2):85–100.

Arndt, Christiane, and Charles Oman. 2006. Uses and Abuses of Governance Indicators. Development Centre Studies, Organisation for Economic Co-Operation and Development.

Birdsall, Nancy. 1999. Education: The People's Asset. Center on Social and Economic Dynamics, Working Paper No. 5. (September).

Birdsall, Nancy, and Augusto de la Torre. 2001. *Washington Contentious: Economic Policies for Social Equity in Latin America*. Washington, DC: Carnegie Endowment for International Peace and Inter-American Dialogue.

Birdsall, Nancy, and Miguel Székely. 2003. Bootstraps, not Band-Aids: Poverty, Equity, and Social Policy. In *After the Washington Consensus: Restarting Growth and Reform in Latin America*, ed. Pedro-Pablo Kuczynski and John Williamson, 49–73. Washington, DC: Institute for International Economics.

Camp, Roderic Ai. 2001. Democracy through Latin American Lenses: An Appraisal. In *Citizen Views of Democracy in Latin America*, ed. Roderic Ai Camp. Pittsburgh: University of Pittsburgh Press.

Carrión, Julio F., Patricia Zárate, and Mitchell A. Seligson. 2006. The Political Culture of Democracy in Peru. Unpublished mimeo.

CEPAL (Comisión Económica para América Latina y el Caribe). 1998. *Panorama Social de América Latina 1997*. Santiago: United Nations, CEPAL.

———. 2005. *Panorama Social de América Latina 2005*. New York: United Nations, CEPAL.

———. 2006. *Panorama Social de América Latina 2006*. New York: United Nations, CEPAL.

———. 2007. *Panorama Social de América Latina 2007.* New York: United Nations, CEPAL.

———. 2008. *Panorama Social de América Latina 2008.* Available at www. eclac.org.

CEPAL (Comisión Económica para América Latina y el Caribe), and the Centro de las Naciones Unidas para los Asentamientos Humanos (Habitat). 2001. *El espacio regional: Hacia la consolidación de los asentamientos humanos en América Latina y el Caribe.* Santiago, Chile: CEPAL.

della Porta, Donatella. 2000. Social Capital, Beliefs in Government, and Political Corruption. In *Disaffected Democracies: What's Troubling the Trilateral Countries?*, ed. Susan J. Pharr and Robert D. Putnam, 202–28. Princeton, NJ: Princeton University Press.

Diamond, Larry, and Leonardo Morlino. 2005. Introduction. In *Assessing the Quality of Democracy,* ed. Larry Diamond and Leonardo Morlino, ix–xliii. Baltimore, MD: Johns Hopkins University Press.

Engerman, Stanley L., and Kenneth L. Sokoloff. 1997. Factor Endowments, Institutions, and Differential Paths of Growth Among New World Economies. In *How Latin America Fell Behind: Essays on the Economic Histories of Brazil and Mexico,* ed. Stephen Haber, 260–304. Stanford, CA: Stanford University Press.

Foweraker, Joe, and Roman Krznaric. 2000. Measuring Liberal Democratic Performance: An Empirical and Conceptual Critique. *Political Studies* 48:759–87.

Freedom House. 2005. Available at: www.freedomhouse.org/template. cfm?page=35&year=2005.

Gerring, John, Strom C. Thacker, and Carola Moreno. 2005. Centripetal Democratic Governance: A Theory and Global Inquiry. *American Political Science Review* 99(4): 567–81.

Glaeser, Edward L., Rafael La Porta, Florencio Lopez-de-Silanes, and Andrei Shleifer. 2004. Do Institutions Cause Growth? *Journal of Economic Growth* 9 (3) (September): 271–303.

Gruben, William, and Darryl McLeod. 2003. Choosing Among Rival Poverty Rates: Some Tests for Latin America. Available at www.dallasfed.org/research/claepapers/2003/lawp0301.pdf.

Hall, Robert E., and Charles I. Jones. 1999. Why Do Some Countries Produce So Much More Output per Worker than Others? *The Quarterly Journal of Economics* 114(1):83–116.

Husmmanns, Ralf. 2004. Measuring the informal sector: from employment in the informal sector to informal employment. Geneva: ILO Working Paper 53, December.

International Labour Organization (ILO). 2002. Stat Working Paper No. 1. Geneva. Available at: www.ilo.org/public/english/bureau/stat/download/comp5a. pdf. Access date: 06 June 2007.

———. 2004. Women and Men in the Informal Sector: A Statistical Picture. Geneva, ILO.

———. 2005. *ILO Thesaurus 2005*. Available at www.ilo.org/public/Libdoc/ ILO_Thesaurus/english/index.html.

———. 2006. Global Employment Trends Brief, January. Geneva, ILO.

Kaufmann, Daniel, Aart Kraay, and Massimo Mastruzzi. 2003. Governance Matters III: Governance Indicators for 1996–2002. The World Bank, Policy Research Paper 3106 (August). Available at http://econ.worldbank.org.

———. 2005. Governance Matters IV: Governance Indicators for 1996–2004. The World Bank, Policy Research Paper 3630 (June). Available at http://econ. worldbank.org.

———. 2006. Governance Matters V: Aggregate and Individual Governance Indicators for 1996–2005. The World Bank, Policy Research Paper 4012 (September). Available at http://econ.worldbank.org.

———. 2007. Governance Matters VI: Aggregate and Individual Governance Indicators for 1996–2006. The World Bank, Policy Research Paper 4280 (July). Available at http://econ.worldbank.org.

———. 2008. Governance Matters VII: Aggregate and Individual Governance Indicators for 1996–2007. Available at http://econ.worldbank.org.

Kreuger, Anne O. 1974. The Political Economy of the Rent-Seeking Society. *American Economic Review* 64(3):291–303.

Kurtz, Marcus J., and Andrew Schrank. 2007. Growth and Governance: Models, Measures, and Mechanisms. *The Journal of Politics* 69 (May): 538–54.

Latinobarómetro (Corporación Latinobarómetro). 2003. Informe-Resumen. La Democracia y la Economía. Latinobarómetro 2003. Available at www.latinobarometro.org.

———. 2004. Informe Resumen Latinobarómetro 2004. Available at www. latinobarometro.org.

———. 2005. Informe Latinobarómetro 2005. Available at www.latinobarometro .org.

———. 2006. Informe Latinobarómetro 2006. Available at www.latinobarometro .org.

———. 2007. Latinobarómetro Report 2007. Available at www.latinobarometro .org.

———. 2008. Latinobarómetro Informe 2008. Available at www.latinobarometro .org.

Levine, Daniel H., and José Molina. 2006. The Quality of Democracy in Latin America: Another View. Paper for the international conference of the Latin American Studies Association, San Juan, Puerto Rico, March 15–18.

Lijphart, Arend. 1999. *Patterns of Democracy: Government Forms and Performance in Thirty-Six Countries*. New Haven, CT: Yale University Press.

Mainwaring, Scott, and Aníbal Pérez-Liñán. 2007. Why Regions of the World are Important: Regional Specificities and Region-Wide Diffusion of Democracy. In *Regimes and Democracy in Latin America: Theories and Methods*, ed. Gerardo Munck, 199–229. Oxford: Oxford University Press.

Mauro, Paulo. 1995. Corruption and Growth. *The Quarterly Journal of Economics* (August): 681–712.

Observatorio de los Derechos Humanos en Colombia. 2004. Vicepresidencia de la República, Programa Presidencial de los Derechos Humanos y Derecho Internacional Humanitario.

O'Donnell, Guillermo. 1999. Poliarchies and the (Un)Rule of Law in Latin America: A Partial Conclusion. In *The (Un)Rule of Law and the Underprivileged in Latin America*, ed. Juan E. Méndez, Guillermo O'Donnell, and Paulo Sérgio Pinheiro, 303–37. Notre Dame, IN: University of Notre Dame Press.

———. 2004. Human Development, Human Rights, and Democracy. In *The Quality of Democracy: Theory and Applications*, ed. Guillermo O'Donnell, Osvaldo Iazzetta, and Jorge Vargas-Cullell, 9–92. Notre Dame, IN: University of Notre Dame Press.

———. 2005. Why the Rule of Law Matters. In *Assessing the Quality of Democracy*, ed. Larry Diamond and Leonardo Morlino, 3–17. Baltimore, MD: Johns Hopkins University Press.

Olken, Benjamin R. 2006. Corruption Perceptions vs. Corruption Reality. National Bureau of Economic Research Working Paper #12428 (August). Available at http://papers.nber.org/papers/w12428.

PAHO (Pan American Health Organization). 2005. Health Analysis and Information Systems Area. Regional Core Health Data Initiative, Technical Health Information System. Washington, DC. Available at www.paho.org/English/SHA/coredata/tabulator.

———. 2006. Guidelines for the Design, Implementation, and Evaluation of Epidemiological Surveillance Systems on Violence and Injuries. Available at www.paho.org/.

Pharr, Susan J. 2000. Officials' Misconduct and Public Trust: Japan and the Trilateral Democracies. In *Disaffected Democracies: What's Troubling the Trilateral Countries?*, ed. Susan J. Pharr and Robert D. Putnam, 173–201. Princeton, NJ: Princeton University Press.

Przeworski, Adam, Michael E. Alvarez, José Antonio Cheibub, and Fernando Limongi. 2000. *Democracy and Development: Political Institutions and Well-Being in the World, 1950–1990*. Cambridge: Cambridge University Press.

Putnam, Robert D. 1993. *Making Democracy Work: Civic Traditions in Modern Italy*. Princeton, NJ: Princeton University Press.

Roodman, David. 2006. The Commitment to Development Index: 2006 Edition. Center for Global Development. Available at www.cgdev.org.

Sartori, Giovanni. 1987. *The Theory of Democracy Revisited*. Chatham, NJ: Chatham House.

Seligson, Mitchell. 2002. The Impact of Corruption on Regime Legitimacy. *The Journal of Politics* 64(2):408–33.

———. 2004. *The Political Culture of Democracy in Mexico, Central America, and Colombia*. Nashville, TN: ARD-Vanderbilt University-USAID.

———. 2006. The Measurement and Impact of Corruption Victimization: Survey Evidence from Latin America. *World Development* 34(2):381–404.

Székely, Miguel, Nora Lustig, Martín Cumpa, and José Antonio Mejía. 2000. Do We Know How Much Poverty There Is? Research Department and the

Poverty and Inequality Advisory Unit, Inter-American Development Bank. Available at www.iadb.org/Publications/index.cfm?language=english.

Tokman, Victor. 2001. De la informalidad a la modernidad. Lima: OIT. Boletin Cinterfor #155. Available at www.ilo.org/dyn/infoecon/docs/486/F1558379.

Vargas Cullell, Jorge. 2004. Democracy and the Quality of Democracy: Empirical Findings and Methodological and Theoretical Issues Drawn from the Citizen Audit of the Quality of Democracy in Costa Rica. In *The Quality of Democracy: Theory and Applications*, ed. Guillermo O'Donnell, Osvaldo Iazzetta, and Jorge Vargas-Cullell, 93–162. Notre Dame, IN: University of Notre Dame Press.

Weyland, Kurt. 1998. The Politics of Corruption in Latin America. *The Journal of Democracy* 2:108–21.

Wolff, Laurence, and Claudio de Moura Castro. 2003. Education and Training: The Task Ahead. In *After the Washington Consensus: Restarting Growth and Reform in Latin America*, ed. John Williamson and Pedro-Pablo Kucyznski. Washington, DC: Institute for International Economics.

World Bank. 2008. *World Development Indicators*. Available at www.worldbank. org.

World Health Organization. 2002. *World Report on Violence and Health*. Available at www.who.int/publications/en/.

CHAPTER TWO

Economic Growth in Latin America: From the Disappointment of the Twentieth Century to the Challenges of the Twenty-First

JOSÉ DE GREGORIO

☽

INTRODUCTION

Any volume that analyzes the lessons of democratic governance must give considerable weight to *economic growth*. Economic growth creates new wealth and new opportunities for citizens. No democracy can provide citizens with their needs without stimulating economic growth. And economic performance is likely to affect democratic legitimacy and perhaps even durability. This chapter therefore revisits some major issues regarding economic growth in Latin America.

Latin America experienced disappointing economic results during the twentieth century. Although there were many spurts of growth, they usually ended in a crisis and a long period of slow growth. The 1960s and 1970s—particularly the former—are remembered as periods of high growth, but in those days Latin American growth was slower than in the world at large and in many other regions (Table 2.1). Perhaps the most important feature of the 1960s was that growth variability across countries in the region was very low. In contrast, during the 1990s, with the world growing much less, some Latin American economies managed to grow strongly, at much higher rates than the rest of the world. But a number of those countries came to a sharp stop. Few have been able to cope with scarce capital inflows and an unstable international environment for emerging markets. More recently, the external atmosphere has been positive for emerging markets, but the issue in many Latin American countries is how to resume, or in many cases start, a process of sustained growth.

During the approximately two decades covered by this volume, social scientists and policy makers have learned a lot about how we are more likely to promote economic growth. I argue that currency crises are damaging to economic growth, and that in turn the likelihood and severity of currency crises depend on sound fiscal management. Trade openness tends to be favorable to growth, and it is especially favorable under conditions of strong institutions. Trade openness also indirectly supports growth by encouraging improvement in institutions; institutions in turn play a key role in fostering trade. High inequalities are bad for growth, mainly because they encourage poor policies, but governments can use social policy to partially offset some of the damaging consequences for growth. I argue that secure property rights and an adequate incentive structure provide the basic underpinnings of economic growth.

GROWTH PERFORMANCE AND INCOME GAPS

The growth performance of a number of Latin American countries since 1960 has been volatile and modest (see Table 2.1).[1] Volatility was particularly high toward the end of the century. In contrast, the 1960s are usually remembered as a period of high and stable growth. Even the 1970s look reasonably dynamic despite the oil shock. However, as Table 2.1 shows, the 1960s were years of strong growth all around the world. For this reason, a better assessment can be made by looking at the income gap between Latin America and the developed world. This allows us to see whether the region has been catching up with the advanced economies.

A long-term view, using Maddison's (2001) data, is presented in Figure 2.1, which compares Latin American per-capita GDP to that of the U.S. and the advanced economies. Panel (a) shows the simple average of per-capita GDP, while panel (b) weights by GDP of each country. Alternatively, the weights could have been based on population, but the figure looks the same. Latin America grew mildly with respect to the U.S. in the first forty years of the twentieth century. Latin America did not grow during the Great Depression, but the decline was somewhat milder. In contrast, in the second half of the century Latin America steadily lost

TABLE 2.1
Latin American Countries' Annual Growth in Per Capita GDP (%)

	1960–1970	1970–1980	1980–1990	1990–2000	1960–2000	1970–2000
LATIN AMERICA						
Argentina	2.29	1.38	−3.87	4.22	1.00	0.57
Bolivia	0.60	2.01	−2.22	1.08	0.37	0.29
Brazil	4.23	5.67	−0.26	1.46	2.77	2.29
Chile	2.19	1.22	1.28	4.79	2.37	2.43
Colombia	2.23	3.11	1.35	0.87	1.89	1.78
Costa Rica	1.85	2.59	−0.94	1.75	1.31	1.13
Ecuador	1.35	6.16	−1.17	−0.85	1.37	1.38
El Salvador	2.24	0.05	−1.66	2.30	0.73	0.23
Guatemala	2.44	3.05	−1.21	0.84	1.28	0.90
Jamaica	3.43	−1.14	1.72	−1.05	0.74	−0.16
Mexico	3.28	3.27	−0.43	1.78	1.97	1.54
Nicaragua	3.25	−2.70	−3.00	−2.42	−1.22	−2.71
Panama	4.98	3.35	−0.69	1.96	2.40	1.54
Paraguay	1.70	4.46	1.01	−0.58	1.64	1.63
Peru	3.73	0.45	−3.13	2.47	0.88	−0.07
Uruguay	0.43	2.70	−1.00	2.81	1.23	1.50
Venezuela	2.95	−2.79	−1.36	−0.80	−0.50	−1.65
Average	*2.05*	*1.56*	*−0.74*	*0.98*	*0.96*	*0.60*
REFERENCE						
Japan	9.27	3.09	3.53	1.05	4.23	2.55
USA	2.87	2.66	2.16	2.30	2.50	2.37
East Asia (9)	4.69	5.36	4.45	3.95	4.61	4.58
World	2.53	1.99	0.98	1.32	1.70	1.43

Source: Heston, Summers, and Aten (2002)

ground with respect to the advanced world. During the 1940s each Latin American country sharply narrowed its gap with respect to the U.S. and then broadened it due, largely, to abrupt increases in output in the developed world.

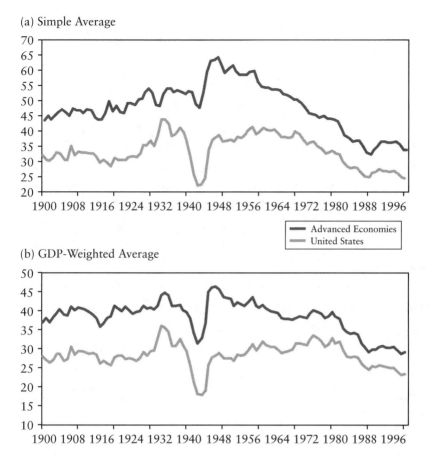

(a) Simple Average

(b) GDP-Weighted Average

FIGURE 2.1 Latin America's Relative Per Capita GDP (%)
Source: Maddison (1995) and Heston, Summers, and Aten (2002)

The evolution of the output gap with respect to the U.S. for individual countries during the twentieth century is presented in Table 2.2. Argentina and Uruguay were relatively high-income countries, as was to a lower extent, Chile. The post 1950 decline affected almost all of the countries with the exception of Mexico and, most importantly, Brazil, which grew quickly during the Brazilian "miracle" of the 1960s and 1970s. Brazil is the only country in Table 2.2 whose gap with respect to the U.S. was smaller in 2000 than in 1970. Latin America's decline was sharper during the 1980s, the so-called lost decade. As Table 2.1 shows, the 1990s saw greater stability despite low growth, although a decline

TABLE 2.2

Latin American Countries' Per Capita GDP as Ratio of GDP Per Capita
of the United States

	1900	1913	1950	1960	1970	1980	1990	2000
Argentina	0.67	0.72	0.52	0.49	0.49	0.44	0.28	0.30
Bolivia	n/a	n/a	0.20	0.14	0.14	0.14	0.09	0.09
Brazil	0.17	0.15	0.17	0.21	0.20	0.28	0.21	0.20
Colombia	0.24	0.23	0.23	0.22	0.21	0.23	0.21	0.18
Chile	0.48	0.50	0.40	0.38	0.35	0.31	0.28	0.35
Ecuador	n/a	n/a	0.19	0.20	0.19	0.22	0.17	0.11
Mexico	0.33	0.33	0.25	0.28	0.29	0.34	0.26	0.26
Paraguay	n/a	n/a	0.17	0.14	0.12	0.18	0.14	0.11
Peru	0.20	0.20	0.24	0.27	0.25	0.23	0.13	0.13
Uruguay	0.54	0.62	0.49	0.44	0.34	0.35	0.28	0.28
Venezuela	0.20	0.21	0.78	0.85	0.71	0.55	0.36	0.30
Latin America	*0.32*	*0.29*	*0.31*	*0.35*	*0.33*	*0.32*	*0.22*	*0.22*
East Asia (9)	*0.16*	*0.18*	*0.13*	*0.14*	*0.17*	*0.24*	*0.29*	*0.33*
Asian-4	*n/a*	*0.19*	*0.16*	*0.18*	*0.25*	*0.40*	*0.54*	*0.66*

Source: Maddison (2001)
n/a = not available

took place during the last years of the century. Looking across decades,
the two most important examples of catching up with the U.S. were Brazil in the 1970s and Chile in the 1990s.[2]

Having shown some basic facts for the output gap between Latin
American and developed economies, it is possible to decompose this
gap in a similar way to traditional growth decompositions. Traditional
growth decompositions compute the relative contribution of productive
factor accumulation and total factor productivity to economic growth.
I decompose the output gap into factor and productivity gaps, which is
more consistent with the predictions of the neoclassical growth model
since it explains income differentials rather than growth differentials. In
this decomposition I explicitly consider human capital. This is relevant
because comparing levels of income is important in controlling for differences in the quality of the labor force across countries. I compare the

income per capita of some Latin American countries and other regions with that of the United States (as is usually done in the literature), and then decompose the difference between them into a productivity gap, a capital-output ratio gap, and a human capital gap. I follow the decomposition suggested by Klenow and Rodríguez-Clare (1997) and Hall and Jones (1999).

Consider a Cobb-Douglas production function at time t for country j:

$$Y_{jt} = A_{jt}K_{jt}^{\alpha}H_{jt}^{1-\alpha}. \tag{1}$$

where A is total factor productivity (TFP), K is physical capital, and H is labor adjusted for human capital. The last of these can be rewritten as Lh, where L is employment and h is a measure of human capital per worker. Using lowercase letters for per capita (or, more properly, per worker) variables, and omitting the time index, we have:

$$y_j = A_j k_j^{\alpha} h_j^{1-\alpha}. \tag{2}$$

Now we can compare the levels of income per capita of two countries, j and i, as

$$\frac{y_j}{y_i} = \frac{A_j}{A_i}\left(\frac{k_j}{k_i}\right)^{\alpha}\left(\frac{h_j}{h_i}\right)^{1-\alpha}. \tag{3}$$

We could simply use this decomposition, but, as we know from growth theory, if a productivity shock hits (that is, if A rises), it will lead to an increase in the capital-labor ratio in the steady state, and therefore the increase in productivity will be wrongly attributed to an increase in the capital-labor ratio. However, what remains invariant to a productivity increase in the steady state is the capital-output ratio, which depends on the investment rate, which in turn depends on the saving rate. Therefore, an increase in investment will lead to an increase in the capital-output ratio, but an increase in productivity will not.[3]

Rewriting equation (2) in terms of the capital-output ratio—that is, dividing and multiplying the right-hand side by y^{α}—and rearranging, we have

$$y_j = A_j^{1/(1-\alpha)}\left(\frac{k_j}{y_j}\right)^{\alpha/(1-\alpha)} h_j. \tag{4}$$

Finally, we can consider two countries and decompose the output gap between them as

$$\frac{y_j}{y_i} = \left(\frac{A_j}{A_i}\right)^{1/(1-\alpha)} \left(\frac{k_j/y_j}{k_i/y_i}\right)^{\alpha/(1-\alpha)} \frac{h_j}{h_i}. \tag{5}$$

The comparisons here are done with respect to the United States (country i). Therefore, if output per capita turns out to be Z percent of that of the United States, Z_a percent can be explained by productivity differentials, measured as the first term on the right-hand side of equation (5), Z_{ky} percent by differences in the capital-output ratio, and Z_h percent by differences in human capital. By construction, then, $(1 + Z) = (1 + Z_a)(1 + Z_{ky})(1 + Z_h)$.[4]

Finally, to measure human capital I use the traditional specification based on the returns to education per year of schooling:

$$h = e^{\varphi E}, \tag{6}$$

where E represents years of education and φ the returns on schooling, which can be estimated using Mincer equations.[5] Following Hall and Jones (1999), the exponent in equation (6) is assumed to be piecewise linear. For the first four years of schooling I use a return of 13.4 percent, which is the return to education in Africa. For the next four years I use a return of 10.1 percent, and for years beyond I use the return on schooling in OECD countries, which is 6.8 percent.

The rest of the data are constructed in the same way as for the Solow decomposition discussed previously. For the national accounts I use the Penn World Tables version 6.1 from Heston, Summers, and Aten (2002), in order to have internationally comparable data. The results are presented in Table 2.3. Latin America's per-capita GDP was only 21 percent that of the United States when measured at purchasing power parity (PPP).[6] The capital-output ratio in Latin America was only 27 percent lower than that in the United States, and human capital was 42 percent lower. The largest difference appeared for TFP, which was 57 percent lower than that of the United States. Therefore, the most important factor explaining the differences with the United States is TFP, followed by human capital.[7] If the TFP gap were eliminated, the output gap between Latin America and the U.S. would be 42 percent. In contrast, closing the capital-output ratio gap would increase the regional income with respect to the U.S. from 21 percent to 25 percent.

For all countries in the table, the most important gap is the TFP gap. Chile and Mexico are the countries where this gap is the narrowest within Latin America, and is similar to that of human capital. The human capital gap is not corrected by quality and, as was mentioned before, there is strong evidence that quality of education in the region

TABLE 2.3
Level Decomposition, GDP Per Capita, 2000

	Per capita GDP	Capital-output ratio	Human capital	Productivity
Argentina	0.398	0.921 [0.432]	0.943 [0.422]	0.458 [0.868]
Chile	0.389	0.863 [0.450]	0.694 [0.560]	0.649 [0.599]
Colombia	0.178	0.701 [0.254]	0.629 [0.283]	0.403 [0.441]
Mexico	0.381	0.922 [0.413]	0.684 [0.557]	0.604 [0.631]
Peru	0.156	1.006 [0.155]	0.695 [0.225]	0.224 [0.699]
Venezuela	0.275	0.936 [0.294]	0.666 [0.413]	0.441 [0.624]
Korea	0.571	1.185 [0.482]	0.977 [0.584]	0.493 [1.158]
Greece	0.546	1.127 [0.485]	0.940 [0.581]	0.515 [1.060]
Israel	0.675	1.114 [0.605]	0.955 [0.706]	0.634 [1.065]
Asia-4	0.670	1.089 [0.640]	0.885 [0.788]	0.724 [0.963]
Latin America	0.225	0.816 [0.301]	0.648 [0.379]	0.464 [0.529]

Each figure represents the ratio between that country or region with respect to the United States. The product of capital, human capital, and producivity equals the output gap, except for averages. The figures in square brackets are the values that would take the ratio of income with respect to the United States if that specific gap would be zero.
Source: Author's calculation is based on Heston, Summers, and Aten (2002).

is relatively poor, which may indicate that the human capital gap in Table 2.3 could be underestimated. The countries from other regions in the table also show that the largest gap is the one on TFP. This feature is common around the world with only a few exceptions (Parente and Prescott 2002).

Hence, the largest gains in terms of closing the income gap could be obtained by closing the productivity gap—that is, by increasing efficiency in the use of existing factors of production, in order to produce more with the same inputs. The table also shows that the Asian "miracle" has been more the result of capital deepening than of productivity enhancement, a point originally raised by Young (1995).

A REVIEW OF EMPIRICAL EVIDENCE
ON GROWTH DETERMINANTS

A huge amount of research has been done in the last fifteen years attempting to determine the main factors that underlie economic growth. In this section, I summarize some of the findings of De Gregorio and Lee (2004). In a five-year panel data covering from 1970 to 2000, per-capita growth (GROWTH) is regressed on a number of variables. The regression controls for initial per-capita GDP in each period (Yo) in order to take into account conditional convergence. The regression also includes the investment (I) and fertility rates (F). The neoclassical growth model predicts that high savings (foreign and domestic) speed up the transition and lead to a higher level of steady-state income. In contrast, a high rate of population growth leads to a lower level of steady-state income.

Both quantity and the quality of resources matters; to control for the quality of human resources, the explanatory variables include the average years of schooling for males aged 25 and over (SCH), available from Barro and Lee (2001), and life expectancy at birth (LIFE). The latter variable is considered another important component of human capital stock. A longer life expectancy tends to indicate a healthier, more productive labor force. As explained before, there are not enough data on quality of education to correct the measures of educational quality. However, the existing scattered evidence does indeed show that education is mediocre in Latin America. We included a number of standard institutional and policy variables: government expenditure (G), rule of law (RL), inflation (INF), and openness (OPE).

Finally, a dummy variable to measure whether or not a country experienced a currency crisis in a five-year period was included (CRISIS) and, in order to control for the external environment, the growth rate of the terms of trade (TOT) was used. The results of this regression are shown here[8]:

Growth = −0.023 Log(Y0) + 0.0442 I − 0.0157 Log(F) + 0.0020 SCH
          (0.0036)   (0.0283)   (0.0061)   (0.0018)

$$+ 0.0686 \text{ Log(LIFE)} - 0.0651 \text{ G} + 0.0158 \text{ RL} - 0.0157 \text{ INF}$$
$$(0.0222) \qquad (0.0250) \quad (0.0077) \qquad (0.0100)$$

$$+ 0.0092 \text{ OP} + 0.0287 \text{ TOT} - 0.0176 \text{ CRISIS}$$
$$(0.0044) \qquad (0.024) \qquad (0.00056)$$

No. of countries: 85, obs: 464.

The results are quite standard, although it is important to note some particularities. As usual, after controlling for factors determining long-run income, conditional convergence is obtained. Inflation, one of the most recurrent economic problems in Latin America, loses some significance when the currency crisis variable is included. The reason is the co-linearity between currency crisis and inflation; currency crisis occurs more in countries that have high inflation during the five-year period. However, it is not possible to establish causality between a currency crisis and inflation, and most likely both are determined jointly by bad macroeconomic management.

In his Chapter 3, Rodríguez argues that cross-country regressions are not robust when taking into account all possible interactions among explanatory variables, and any result could be obtained. This view would apply to almost all empirical work using cross-country data. However, there is ample evidence beyond econometrics to confirm many results, and the regressions help to quantify the magnitude of the effects. No small country has developed without being open to trade or with high inflation. Although terms of trade are important determinants of economic performance, the evidence shows that they have not been a relevant factor in explaining why Latin America has grown less than the world or even less than East Asia, if its countries are supposed to have experienced the largest increases in terms of trade. Econometric results will always lack full robustness, but taking them as indicative, rather than as definitive, of broad correlations is very useful. Most of the time, the effects of some variable depend on the presence of other conditions, but this does not imply that any combination of good and bad policies can succeed.[9]

Bearing this criticism in mind, the regression presented above is used to compare growth performance between Latin American countries and the world average. The benchmark of comparison is the entire world, although comparing the results with regions whose economies have been more successful in terms of growth might be more instructive. That exercise is done in De Gregorio and Lee (2004), which compares Latin America with East Asia, in which case there are some differences, in particular regarding the role of openness. The results of the comparison with the world are presented in Table 2.4. The first column presents the

TABLE 2.4
Differentials of Latin American Countries Relative to World Average, 1970–2000*

| Country | Difference in | | Contributing Factors | | | | | | | | | | |
	Actual growth	Predicted growth	Initial income	Investment	Fertility	Human resource	Total	Government consumption	Rule of law	Inflation	Openness	Terms of trade shock	Balance of payments
Argentina	-1.5	-2.9	-1.2	0.0	0.0	0.3	-1.4	0.1	-0.1	-1.1	-0.3	-0.1	-0.5
Bolivia	-1.8	-1.4	1.7	-0.3	-1.0	-1.0	-0.4	-0.1	-0.1	0.0	-0.2	0.0	-0.3
Brazil	.02	-3.2	0.0	0.1	-0.2	-0.3	-2.0	-0.5	-0.1	-1.3	-0.1	-0.1	-0.7
Chile	0.3	-0.8	0.0	-0.1	0.1	0.3	-0.5	-0.2	0.2	-0.3	-0.1	-0.2	-0.5
Colombia	-0.3	-0.7	0.6	-0.3	-0.2	-0.1	-1.0	-0.1	-0.6	-0.1	-0.2	-0.1	0.3
Mexico	-0.6	-1.6	-0.5	0.0	-0.5	0.1	-0.2	0.2	-0.1	-0.2	-0.1	-0.1	-0.5
Paraguay	-0.5	0.9	0.7	-0.2	-0.7	0.1	-0.6	0.0	-0.4	0.0	-0.3	0.0	0.0
Peru	-2.2	-1.3	0.5	0.0	-0.3	-0.3	-0.8	0.2	-0.1	-0.7	-0.2	0.0	-0.3
Uruguay	-0.6	-2.0	-0.6	-0.2	0.2	0.5	-1.2	-0.2	-0.2	-0.4	-0.4	-0.1	-0.5
Venezuela	-3.8	-1.1	-0.8	0.0	-0.4	0.2	0.1	0.3	0.0	-0.1	-0.1	0.1	-0.2
Latin 21 Average	-1.2	-1.2	0.6	-0.2	-0.4	-0.2	-0.8	-0.1	-0.2	-0.2	-0.2	-0.1	-0.2
World Average**	2.1	3.0											

*Author's calculation. Human resources include life expectancy variable.

**The figures are actual and predicted growth, used to compute the differences reported for each country.

difference between actual growth in the region and in the world. The second column shows the predicted difference according to the regression and is then decomposed in the rest of the columns into the different explanatory factors used in the regression. The bottom row presents the average rate of actual and predicted growth for the world. Actual growth during 1970 to 2000 was 2.1 percent a year per capita, while the predicted yearly rate of growth is 3 percent. This implies that Latin America grew on average 0.9 percent (1.2 percentage points below the world), and the prediction is 1.8 percent (1.2 percentage points below the prediction for the world). Initial income, due to convergence, would have implied more growth for the region, except for the four countries that started above the world average: Argentina, Mexico, Uruguay, and Venezuela. Low investment, high fertility, and poor human resources (i.e., schooling and life expectancy) retarded growth with respect to the world. Institutional factors explain an important part of the lower growth in the region. High government consumption, weak rule of law, high inflation, and a low degree of openness had a negative impact on growth, and they account for almost three-quarters of Latin America's growth lag. This has been particularly important in countries with high inflation, such as Argentina and Brazil. Openness played a less important role; however, as discussed below, using the world as a benchmark could be misleading. Countries with high instability, measured by the number of currency crises, also suffered from slower growth. Argentina, Brazil, Chile, Mexico, and Venezuela are in this group. The absence of crisis played a positive role only in Colombia.

Terms of trade shocks played a small part (0.110 per capita growth per year) in explaining the poor growth performance of the region. Therefore, the old idea that supported the import-substitution strategy in Latin America during the 1960s, which held that opening to trade would result in developing countries producing "bad goods"—mostly commodities, whose terms of trade would decline—has been proven wrong. Countries that face unfavorable terms of trade do grow less rapidly, but there has not been such a deterioration in the terms of trade in Latin America.[10]

Finally, comparing with the world average could give a partial view about the region's strengths and weaknesses, as the world is not necessarily the best control group. In De Gregorio and Lee (2004), we compare growth performance between Latin America and a group of high growth East Asian economies. That exercise revealed that the two most important factors to explain the 3-percentage-point difference in growth performance are low investment and low openness in the region. Both account separately for 0.6 percentage point of lower growth in Latin America with respect to East Asia.

In the following sections I will discuss in greater detail some of the issues raised in the empirical discussion presented in this section.[11]

OPENNESS, REGIONAL TRADE,

AND INSTITUTIONS

As discussed, openness is good for growth, and here I discuss issues regarding openness, regional trade, and their interplay with institutions. Most empirical research on economic growth has supported this finding. This result enjoys broad (but by no means total) consensus. In sum, more open economies tend to grow faster than closed ones.[12] This is particularly significant in periods of trade liberalization. Of course, we can add many caveats to the strategy of opening up; the institutional framework in which opening up takes place, etc. However, it is a proven fact that more open economies grow faster than closed ones. This lesson is especially valid for small economies. I have been unable to find an example of a relatively high-income small economy that is not integrated with the rest of the world, or that has managed to grow being isolated from the world. Although openness plays a small role in explaining GDP growth of Latin America vis-à-vis the rest of the world, it is an important factor in explaining differences with high growth economies of East Asia (De Gregorio and Lee, 2004).

In a detailed review of the evidence, Winters, McCulluch, and McKay (2004) find that openness is associated with poverty reduction in the long run, and this association probably holds in the short run as well. Of course, trade liberalization may also work with other policies to alleviate poverty. Therefore, trade liberalization is good for the economy, and it is advisable to undertake it right away. (The same cannot be said of other areas, such as financial liberalization.)

Unilateral trade liberalization has already occurred in most of Latin America, most intensely during the 1990s. Argentina, Bolivia, Brazil, Chile, Colombia, Costa Rica, Dominican Republic, Ecuador, El Salvador, Guatemala, Honduras, Mexico, Nicaragua, Paraguay, Peru, Uruguay, and Venezuela, i.e. most of Latin America, were classified as closed in the period 1970–89 according to Wacziarg and Welch (2003), and as open economies in the period 1990–99.

Although tariffs have been reduced and non-tariff barriers have been removed, Latin America still has small trade coefficients (i.e., trade divided by gross domestic product). Most Asian countries have substantially more trade than Latin American countries (Figure 2.2). Only China is below three Latin American countries in the sample, but after

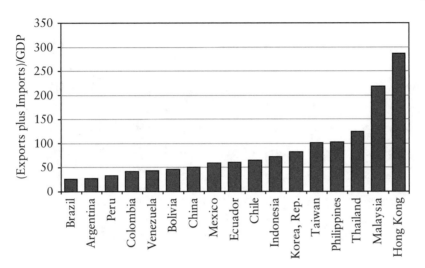

FIGURE 2.2 Trade as Percentage of GDP, 2000–2002
Source: World development indicators, Department of Statistics of Taiwan, Singapore Statistics. (All figures are expressed in dollars of each year.)

correcting trade by size, China is much more open than Latin America. This raises the question of how to increase integration and gain access to new markets, given that tariffs and most barriers to trade have been substantially reduced. Policymakers may feel frustrated when they liberalize trade, only to find that it takes time for trade to increase.

Intraregional trade in Latin America is low compared to other regions of the world (Figure 2.3). It was low in the 1960s, at about 10 percent of total trade, and although it has shown some increase in recent years, it remains comparatively low. Trade among South American countries is 24 percent of their total trade, and trade among all Latin American countries is 17 percent, the lowest among the regions shown in the figure. The same pattern of low integration emerges for other country groupings such as Mercosur or Aladi (not shown). These findings stand in sharp contrast to the dynamic intraregional trade among the East Asian countries: Already in the 1960s, about 26 percent of these countries' trade was with each other, and that number has increased to 50 percent in recent years. Trade among the industrialized countries has long been an important share of their total trade.

Institutions play a key role in fostering trade. I use institutions in the definition of Douglass North as the formal and informal rules that constrain human economic behavior. However, my discussion focuses more

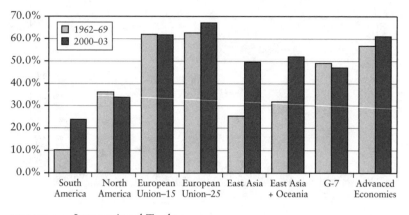

FIGURE 2.3 Intraregional Trade
Source: Comtrade Database, United Nations

on formal rules, for which we have some indicators to measure quality—
such as the rule of law—in cross-country regressions.

For countries to develop deep and extensive trade relations, each must
demonstrate at home the ability to enforce contracts, to maintain the
rule of law, and to establish enduring trade relations. The existence of
a stable macroeconomic environment is also important, because it reduces uncertainty among trade participants. Yet Latin America has weak
institutions and is subject to recurrent macroeconomic crises, and this
impedes the growth of trade linkages. Recent trade disputes—such as the
problems over natural gas between Argentina, Bolivia, and Chile—bear
witness to these obstacles.

As previously shown, the indicators of institutional quality, such as
the rule of law index, are correlated with economic growth. Latin America has weak institutions. Figure 2.4 presents additional evidence, showing the Transparency International index of corruption in 2003. The
index ranges from 0, the most corrupt, to 10, the least corrupt. Latin
American countries are depicted with dark bars, and all of them with
the sole exception of Chile, followed by Costa Rica, are on the high-
corruption side.

The next questions to ask is how to proceed, and what do we know
about institutional building, especially from the standpoint of fostering
trade. Strong institutions are needed for trade liberalization to be effective
in promoting growth. This is particularly important in countries rich in
natural resources, where the possibility of rent seeking and voracity effects is high. This does not imply that strong institutions are a prerequisite
for successful trade liberalization, but building strong institutions helps

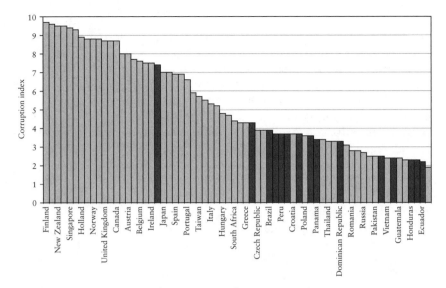

FIGURE 2.4 Corruption Index, 2003. (Index range: 0 = most corrupt,
10 = least corrupt.)
Source: Transparency International
For the purpose of graphic clarity, only every other country is named.

to maximize the benefits from reforms. Indeed, in Rodríguez's argument
(this volume) about massive interactions among growth determinants, perhaps one of the most important candidates is the quality of institutions.
For example, privatization works only when it is appropriately done and
not used as a vehicle to assault the state. Privatization is unlikely to work
in a corrupt state. In recent work, Prasad et al. (2003) show that only
countries with strong institutions benefit from financial liberalization.

Recent research at the IMF (IMF 2005) sheds more light on policies
that can help to improve institutions. Institutions are slow to adjust, and
some major changes involve constitutional and political reforms. However, many countries have gone through institutional transitions during
the last thirty years.[13] IMF (2005) reports empirical evidence on the determinants of the probability of having an institutional transition and on
the quality of institutions. Openness, measured by an index that takes a
value of 0 prior to liberalization and 1 thereafter, increases the probability of having an institutional transition and the quality of institutions.
Hence, openness not only has direct effects on growth, but it also helps
to strengthen institutions.

In the regressions reported in IMF (2005), other variables were significant determinants of the probability of having an institutional transition and quality of institutions.[14] This is the case of accountability and

freedom of the press. High levels of education and strong institutions in neighboring countries also increase the probability of having a transition, but their effects on the quality of institutions are weak. As expected, countries with high income are less likely to have an institutional transition, but their institutions are of better quality. Foreign aid reduces the probability of having a transition, but has little relation with quality. The greater the dependence on natural resources, the weaker the institutions, although the effect on the probability of transition is insignificant. These findings help to explain why some research has found a negative effect between economic growth and natural resource abundance.

Overall, the evidence not only points to the importance of openness on economic growth, but also on its impact on the quality of institutions and on the probability of improving them.

MACROECONOMIC STABILITY AND CRISIS PREVENTION

When thinking about Latin American economies, observers would point first to macroeconomic instability such as high inflation, hyperinflation, currency crisis, and weak fiscal polices. Moreover, as shown in previous sections, these problems have been important deterrents of economic growth. Macroeconomic instability hampers growth through many channels. It distorts the allocation of talents because it rewards speculation and instability-protection rather than productivity and innovation. Financial markets work less efficiently. Finally, macroeconomic instability signals incompetent policymakers and a weak institutional framework.

Clearly, on the macro front one size does not fit all. The exchange rate regime, integration to international financial markets, and other policy choices do not have a unique answer. However, the recurrent crises in the region suggest some general policy principles. But before discussing them briefly, I must clarify that a crisis is not a purely random phenomenon. Good policy can shield countries from crisis and contagion while enjoying the benefits of integration and financial development. Recent literature, particularly after the Asian crisis of 1997 to 1998, has modeled crisis as a self-fulfilling phenomenon, many times unrelated to economic fundamentals. I do not believe this is the case since there are always policy distortions at the macro or financial level. Crises may be triggered by external developments, but the economies affected are never entirely innocent because crises do not occur at random. Contagion and frantic financial markets may make a bad situation worse, but there is no substitute for sound domestic policy. Therefore, I do not share the view that crises can be bad outcomes of otherwise sound economies. Crises happen because of mismanagement.

First, fiscal discipline is crucial. Most crises in Latin America have been associated with fiscal imbalances. Countries that recovered strongly from their difficulties—such as Chile in 1982 and Mexico in 1994, and also most Asian countries in 1997 to 1998—had a strong fiscal position before the crisis hit. Despite some mild deterioration in the fiscal position on the eve of these crises, there is no evidence that expansionary fiscal policy was central to the recovery (Céspedes and De Gregorio 2005). Therefore, not only are countries with a weak fiscal position more vulnerable to a crisis, those that have solid public finances recover more quickly.

Regarding inflation, a low rate indicates credible monetary policy and sound monetary institutions. Rather than discussing details of monetary policy, stable low inflation is a summary statistic for a good macroeconomic environment, which also is the basis for strong institutions at the macro level. It is desirable to have an independent central bank, but it is also necessary to implement good policies. For example, a stable macroeconomic environment allows implementing a flexible exchange rate regime and using monetary policy as the instrument for stabilization, which is the most effective way to achieve macroeconomic stability.

Perhaps the Achilles heel during crises in emerging markets is their weak financial sectors. Liability dollarization, mismatched currencies and maturities, implicit guarantees, and related lending are among the factors that lead to financial crisis when there are significant corrections in relative prices or a curtailment of capital inflows. Prudent regulation and strong institutions are important to take full advantage of financial development. Unlike trade opening, financial liberalization can be the source of problems in a weak institutional setup. The Chilean economy learned this lesson the hard way, with a huge financial crisis in the early eighties.

One of the most relevant vulnerabilities of financial systems is dollarization. It happens when trust in the domestic currency is lost. This in general is the result of rising inflation and sudden and sharp devaluations. Dollarization is many times irreversible. After the economy and the value of the currency stabilize, the de-dollarization process may never take place. Chile went a different route, minimizing the risk of permanent dollarization. After the 1982 crisis, instead of going into the dollar, most financial contracts were linked to the indexed currency (on a daily basis to the previous month's Consumer Price Index) known as the UF (Unidad de Fomento). Deposits and loans denominated in UFs in the banking system increased significantly.[15] As the inflation rate declined, the economy has actually "de-UFized," and currently the peso is the main unit to denominate financial contracts. This has been achieved in part by the policy decision to base monetary policy on a nominal interest rate. The composition of public debt has shifted from UFs to pesos. Therefore, financial indexation helped in the transition, but it is no panacea. The unit in which contracts are written is not the only relevant consideration for avoiding dollarization; the ability to enforce and honor financial contracts is also key. The dollar is always a superior instrument when the enforcement of contracts is weak.

Currency crises are costly. Empirical estimations indicate that a country that suffers a currency crisis has a cost of about 8 percent in terms of lost GDP. This cost is doubled when accompanied by a banking crisis (De Gregorio and Lee 2004). Of course these are averages across countries, and there are many examples in the region where the costs have been much higher.

A much debated proposal to avoid crises is capital controls. An example of successful capital controls is the Chilean experience during the nineties. Chile was the country that suffered the least with the crisis of emerging markets in the late 1990s. In my view, capital controls did not introduce severe costs to the Chilean economy, nor were they responsible for the success of the nineties. Capital controls did not prevent contagion from the Asian crisis and did not impede the appreciation of the real exchange rate during the decade. They were quite ineffective. Their main effect was to tilt loan maturity from short-term to long-term. Although this was a good thing, the orders of magnitude involved in this shift were fairly small. Moreover, what was at the center of the recession in 1999 and also in part the massive inflows in the nineties were the rigidities of the exchange rate. In recent years, the economy has absorbed a very volatile international environment with a flexible exchange rate and without capital controls. Today the Chilean economy is no longer booming, as it was in the past with an international environment similar to the current one, but it is better prepared to face adverse external conditions. Prudent fiscal policy based on a rule for the cyclically adjusted budget deficit and a flexible exchange rate as part of an inflation target regime for monetary policy provide more resilience to the Chilean economy to face external shocks.[16]

One of the most persuasive demonstrations that capital controls were not central to Chile's success was that in 1982, Chile had stricter capital controls than in the late 1990s. Borrowing for less than two years was not allowed, and a reserve requirement (*encaje*) was in place for all remaining borrowing up to sixty-five months. Furthermore, the banking sector was fully currency-matched in its assets and liabilities. The crisis struck hardest in the corporate sector that was severely mismatched. A large proportion of loans in foreign currency was lent to non-tradable sectors. The lack of adequate financial regulation governing related to lending, and a fixed-exchange-rate regime that provided insurance to those that borrowed abroad, explain the depth of the Chilean currency-financial crisis of 1982. Capital controls did not shield the economy from these effects.

In contrast to the Chilean case, capital controls have been used as a substitute for sound financial policies in many countries. Authorities may think—wrongly, of course—that instead of undertaking serious and necessary adjustments in the fiscal and financial fronts, they can get away with overspending by imposing capital controls. They give the wrong impression that the economy is well sheltered to face external shocks, and they delay necessary reforms to strengthen macroeconomic institutions. Macroeconomic institutions, not capital controls, were the pillars of the Chilean economic success.

INEQUALITY, DISTORTIONS, AND GROWTH

One of the most notorious characteristics of Latin American countries is their high level of inequality (Figure 2.5). Some people might be inclined to attribute most of the region's economic problems to the severe

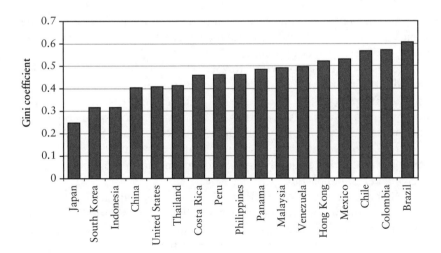

FIGURE 2.5 Income Distribution in the 1990s
Source: World Bank

disparities in income distribution. But Chile, with inequality at the same levels as some of its neighbors, has overcome the distortions caused by high inequality.

Theoretical and empirical evidence suggests that unequal income distribution is bad for growth, although some recent research has challenged this view. The theoretical literature emphasizes that inequality can lead to inefficient policies that harm growth in an attempt to compensate for severe inequality. The classic case is the introduction of inefficient taxation for purposes of redistribution. Inequality hampers economic growth primarily due to its impact on the quality of economic policy provoked by social conflicts. In the cross-section regression discussed earlier in this chapter, inequality did not have a statistically significant effect on growth. De Gregorio and Lee (2004) show that inequality deteriorates the factors and policies that foster growth.

After adjusting for the level of development, countries with more unequal income distributions, as measured by the Gini coefficient, are more likely to have characteristics and policies that are bad for growth. For example, they have lower school enrollment rates, probably because after controlling for average income, a larger fraction of their population cannot afford to go to school. In addition, countries with greater inequality have higher fertility rates, larger governments, lower educational attainment, and weaker institutions.

Two issues are relevant in this discussion. First, we know little about policies that can reduce inequality of income in a short period of time. Income distribution changes very slowly, and we do not know what its main determinants are. The relationship between inequality and income is unclear. Education helps[17]; increasing educational achievement for the underprivileged reduces inequality, but it takes a long time to improve income distribution. Improving education today will have effects on income distribution many years later, when more educated people become a significant part of the labor force. This should not discourage educational reform, however, since it has an immediate effect on income mobility and the intertemporal distribution of income. Therefore, education contributes to equalizing opportunities faster than it affects actual income. Welfare is more equally distributed when children of poor families receive a better education.

A second issue that is also relevant in economies with high inequality is how to avoid its negative effects on policies and, through them, on economic growth. A stable unequal income distribution in a country that is experiencing growth is very different from high inequality in another where the economy is stagnant. Although growth may have only modest effects on inequality, growth is essential for poverty alleviation.

Good social policies, which can partly compensate for inequalities and are growth-enhancing, must be a priority. Strengthening institutions is particularly necessary in countries where inequality may be the source of corruption and other institutional distortions.

Chile is a good example of a country that has done well despite high inequalities. Despite its high inequality, its institutions and policies have not deteriorated, and the economy has grown, which in turn has reduced social conflict and focused policies on growth and helping the poor. Fast growth has perhaps been the most important factor alleviating tensions from inequality and lending broad support to economic policies since the 1990s. It has also improved the living conditions of the whole population. Income distribution has been roughly constant since 1990, and hence the whole population has seen its income increased at the rate of aggregate per-capita growth.

As mentioned earlier, countries with pronounced inequality face worse economic conditions to foster growth. In Chile, these factors have been offset by policies. The levels of respect for rule of law and secondary school enrollment are greater than would be predicted by Chile's levels of inequality and income. Similarly, the fertility rate is lower than what would be predicted by income and inequality. Therefore, Chile has overcome, through institutions and public policy, the growth problems that tend to come with inequality.

Since income distribution changes slowly and there are no clear prescriptions to alter it in the short run, one may wonder what can be done to avoid the noxious effects of inequality on policies. The clearest instrument policymakers have at their disposal is fiscal policy, in particular the allocation of public spending. We can take a closer look at inequality in Latin America and the role of fiscal policy using the data in de Ferranti et al. (2003), which include information on the provision of government spending across income quintiles. Figure 2.6 shows the distribution among quintiles of transfers excluding social security (de Ferranti et al. 2003). Among the countries in the table, Chile is the only one where transfers are disproportionately allocated to the poorest (quintile 1). Since these transfers are about 1 percent of GDP, a relatively small amount of total government expenditure, it is important to look at other components of government expenditure, especially education and health.

Figure 2.7 shows income distribution measured by the Gini coefficient (the scale on the right), represented by the dots. The left scale shows the average gross national income per capita of the country and the average gross national income for the first quintile, using income data for 2003. The countries are presented from the highest income of the first quintile to the lowest quintile. We see a high correlation between per

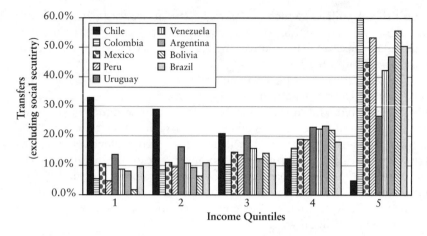

FIGURE 2.6 Distribution of Transfers
Source: de Ferranti et al. (2003)

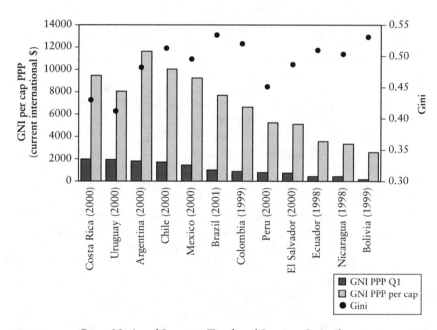

FIGURE 2.7 Gross National Income, Total and Poorest Quintile, 2003
Source: de Ferranti et al. (2003)

capita income and the income of the poorest quintile. This implies that, for most countries, the income of the poor is highest in the countries with the highest income per capita. Gini coefficients are very volatile, but the relevant range for Latin America cannot by itself change significantly the overall ranking of income and the ranking of the first quintile. The notable exceptions are the most egalitarian countries in the region: Costa Rica and Uruguay. Despite not having the highest per capita income, the income of the poorest quintile is the highest in the region.[18]

Although I already showed evidence on the distribution of transfers and highlighted the importance of focusing these expenditures on the poor, the expenditure allocated to the poor is much larger than transfers. Although transfers are the most direct form of helping the poor, its weight is low in total social expenditure. I use World Bank data to compute, in the same sample of Latin American countries of Figure 2.7, the impact in reducing inequality of social expenditure once allocated. In particular, I use the distribution of education and health expenditures and add these expenditures to gross national income to recompute the Gini coefficients. These computations are presented in Figure 2.8. The black dots depict the gross national income per capita of the poorest

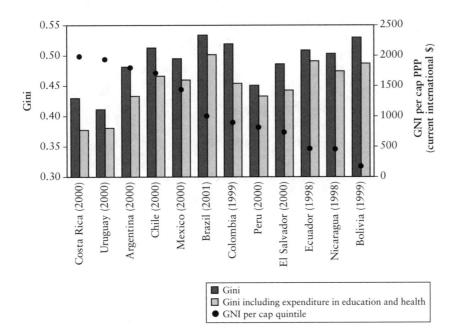

FIGURE 2.8 Social Expenditure Impact on Gini
Source: de Ferranti et al. (2003)

quintile; the scale is on the right axis. For all the countries the Gini coefficient declines, and therefore, as expected, inequality declines as a result of social expenditure. Fiscal policy plays an important role in reducing income inequality at the expenditure level.

The reduction in the Gini coefficient and the differences across countries presented in Figure 2.8 are the combined result of two factors. The first is the level of education and health expenditure, and the second is the form in which these expenditures are allocated across different income brackets. This decomposition is presented in Figure 2.9. The dark column shows the percentage change in the Gini coefficient as a result of government expenditure (based on data in Figure 2.8). The gray column shows the level of education and health expenditure as percentage of GDP. The largest level of social expenditure as percentage of GDP is in Colombia, where the decline in the Gini is the largest. Using these data, we can compute the efficiency of social expenditure in terms of the changes in the Gini per unit of social expenditure. This is presented as dots in the figure and measured on the right axis of Figure 2.9. This

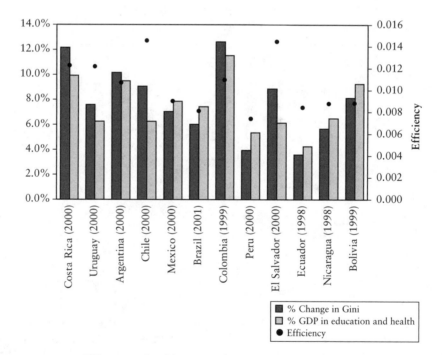

FIGURE 2.9 Efficiency of Public Expenditure
Source: de Ferranti et al. (2003)

measure is constructed by dividing the percentage change in the Gini by the level of government expenditure. Chile and El Salvador are the countries with the most efficient social expenditure from the point of view of reducing inequality, but their social expenditure is relatively low.[19] This evidence suggests that as social expenditure increases, its focalization declines, as illustrated by the contrast between Chile and El Salvador with Colombia and Costa Rica. Therefore, according to these figures, there are limits to the efficacy with which social expenditure can improve income distribution.

Latin America has very unequal income distribution and this is an important handicap for growth. High inequality deteriorates the quality of economic policies and reduces growth potential. High inequality tends to induce policies that generate significant distortions and hamper economic growth. The quest to reduce inequality may induce inefficiencies. Classical examples are minimum wages and labor market regulations. A more effective and direct way to ameliorate the problems inequality generates is through social expenditure, which provides income to the poor. However, as illustrated here, the effectiveness of social expenditure also has limits. In addition, issues such as financing of the budget may tilt the balance enough to introduce distortions because of inability to obtain all the required revenues. Finally, good institutional and policy frameworks are important in order for policies for the poor to succeed.

ON GROWTH FUNDAMENTALS: INSTITUTIONS, COMPETITION, AND MOBILITY

We could list many areas where improvement is possible and would foster growth. But ultimately the question we would like to answer is, *What are the main foundations that support the accumulation of human and physical capital and improvements in productivity—in short, that determine economic growth?* Growth occurs when incentives encourage people and firms to spend their talents in growth-enhancing activities, as opposed, for example, to rent seeking or political capture. In my view, two basic principles underlie growth:

- *Secure property rights.* When people invest in their own human capital, or when entrepreneurs invest in plant and equipment or in new techniques to increase productivity, they must be certain that the benefits of these investments will not be taken away from them. For this to happen, property rights need to be clearly defined and respected.

- *Adequate structure of rewards.* Investment and effort must be properly rewarded. This is essential to encourage creativity, entrepreneurship, and a growth-promoting allocation of talent.

In terms of policy, securing property rights implies setting clear rules of the game. It is inevitable that some policies, or changes in policies, will have redistributive effects. Modifying tax policies, for example, changes the profitability of investment in physical and human capital, in effect reducing or increasing the value of that capital. Improving regulation, too, often changes profitability. A firm that has become a monopoly may be obliged to take steps to reduce its monopolistic power and cut down its profits. In short, redistribution happens. In other cases, property rights are not clearly defined. This is typical of environmental conflicts, for example between the agricultural sector and industrial development that causes pollution. Property rights have their limits and there are conflicts as well as gray areas. The important thing is to be clear on those limits and the mechanisms to resolve disputes. To achieve this, countries must have strong institutions and clear rules to define and delimit property rights, as well as mechanisms for fair compensation when changes in policy have redistributive effects.

In a democracy, taxes are generally decided upon by the legislature, and no one should be surprised, although some may not like it, when changes in taxes occur. Of course, a sound constitution and good laws will prevent arbitrary enforcement of the tax laws and outright expropriation. The lesson here is again on the need to have strong institutions, and these institutions must have a clear orientation toward protecting property rights.

A stable macroeconomic environment is also an important part of securing property rights. High and unstable inflation also redistributes income, usually from savers to borrowers, and this discourages saving. By in effect liquidating nominal public debt through sharp price increases, inflation also redistributes wealth from bondholders to governments. The same is true of freezes on deposits during banking crises and of other confiscatory policies. Macroeconomic stability thus promotes growth by providing a safe environment in which to invest, allowing entrepreneurs to focus on the usual and unavoidable risks of business, rather than protecting themselves from macroeconomic instability.

The second principle—an adequate reward structure—is also important and necessary for growth. One can imagine a country where property rights are secure and immutable but the business sector consists of monopolists who enjoy significant barriers to entry. No one will then have any incentive to invest or to compete: the established monopolists have no need to do so, and potential new entrants encounter clear disadvantages. Therefore, although it is necessary, it is not enough to protect property rights. The means to establish this second principle in the economic arena is full and strong competition that allows markets to operate efficiently. Openness and free trade, in turn, are essential to ensure and increase competition, especially in a small economy. Under these conditions, in order to compete and succeed, firms need to operate efficiently and creatively. Absent any competitive threat to established business, there will be no incentive for these businesses to be efficient.

Regulating and fostering competition has implications regarding the protection of property rights and also providing adequate rewards to effort and entrepreneurship. Many countries are discussing regulatory reforms to spur growth, and this is good. But in my view, the most important institutional basis is to define how conflicts are resolved, who is responsible for setting regulations, and who is charged with administering those regulations. Granting independence to and requiring accountability from regulators, and defining independent panels to settle disputes (including interpretation of the law) are the most important reforms that ensuring stability and fair rules of the game may provide for encouraging investment and productivity. However, it is important to foster accountability, which is particularly necessary for independent institutions.

The second principle also has implications for social policy. It is important that workers, as well as businesses, receive rewards appropriate to their effort. A natural aspiration of parents, especially among the poor, is that their children enjoy more prosperous lives than they did. For this they need opportunities. A person's income from labor depends on the productivity of that labor, and so the goal of educational policy must be to transfer useful knowledge and thus transform people into more productive workers. Stated more generally, this second principle translates into social mobility, or equal opportunity, on the social front.

We can better understand difficulties in Latin America in the light of these two principles. In many Latin American countries, institutions are weak, the macroeconomic environment is unstable, and therefore property rights are not properly safeguarded. In addition, trade is still very low, and hence the scope for competition is limited. Therefore, investors are not always well rewarded. The quality of education must be improved, and efforts to reduce inequality through social policies aimed at improving the living conditions of the poor and creating conditions for greater social mobility must be reinforced. From the point of view of government activities, it is important to focus on how to foster growth and help the poor and the disadvantaged, while minimizing policy distortions. This is not a trivial challenge, but as long as growth can be sustained, the task is easier, because populist temptations are then reduced, although never eliminated.

FINAL REMARKS: THE MOOD, THE FACTS,
AND THE PROSPECTS

There is a lot of uncertainty and skepticism about Latin America's prospects. Certainly this skepticism is well grounded in a history of deception, recurrent crisis, and inability to sustain economic progress. Latin America has been perhaps the most fertile ground for proposing ideologies and "new" ways to face development, but they have not succeeded. There is also skepticism about whether reforms and the "Washington Consensus," or some new incarnation of it, is the way to go. I have argued that one size does not fit all, and not only the reform package, but also the timing, political legitimacy, and delivery are critical. However, some basic principles such as protecting property rights and encouraging competition and openness must be at the basis of policy. In this final section I want to summarize the current mood, what the facts are, and what we can conclude about prospects for economic progress.

The Mood

The mood is gloomy. There is uncertainty and some disappointment. Perhaps the 1990s were good years for some, but they did not succeed at promoting growth. For others, reforms were incomplete or plainly wrong, so disappointing results came as no surprise. The lack of results from reforms, together with much more political uncertainty today, has generated pessimism. Corruption scandals, not only the recent ones, but also past experiences, add to the pessimism, or at least skepticism. Recent macroeconomic crises have placed reforms, especially institutional and microeconomic ones, on the back burner. However, I will argue that although there could be reasons for moderate skepticism, the region is in a position where it could (finally?) start sustainable growth.

The Facts

Recent data as well as short-term forecasts on macroeconomic performance are presented in Tables 2.5 and 2.6. In terms of growth, the region has moved closer to the world average. The region has done much better this decade than in the 1990s. Although the ten years up to 2002

TABLE 2.5
Recent Macroeconomic Indicators

	GDP growth (%)				Inflation (%)				Current account (% GDP)			
	1993–2002	2002–2006 (f)	2005	2006 (f)	1993–2002	2002–2006 (f)	2005	2006 (f)	1993–2002	2002–2006 (f)	2005	2006 (f)
World	3.5	4.4	4.8	4.9	2.1	2.0	2.3	2.3				
Argentina	0.7	4.7	9.2	7.3	4.2	13.2	9.6	12.9	-2.2	4.1	1.8	1.2
Bolivia	3.5	3.4	3.9	4.1	6.1	3.5	5.4	3.4	-5.4	0.8	2.6	1.7
Brazil	3.0	2.6	2.3	3.5	412.3	8.3	6.9	4.9	-2.9	0.8	1.8	1.0
Chile	5.0	4.8	6.3	5.5	6.4	2.7	3.1	3.8	-2.7	-0.4	-0.4	0.5
Colombia	2.4	4.0	5.1	4.5	15.9	5.8	5.0	4.7	-2.9	-1.4	-1.7	1.6
Ecuador	2.2	3.8	3.3	3.0	38.4	5.8	2.4	3.4	-2.4	-1.7	-0.9	0.2
El Salvador	3.9	2.4	2.8	3.5	6.4	3.7	4.0	4.0	-1.6	-3.8	-4.0	-4.0
Guatemala	3.7	2.9	3.2	4.1	8.8	7.5	9.1	6.9	-5.0	-4.5	-4.5	-4.2
Mexico	2.8	2.6	3.0	3.5	16.0	4.3	4.0	3.5	-3.1	-1.2	-0.7	-0.6
Peru	4.4	5.1	6.7	5.0	12.0	2.1	1.6	2.7	-5.0	-0.2	1.3	1.4
Uruguay	0.5	2.7	6.0	4.0	22.9	11.0	5.9	5.5	-1.5	-1.2	-2.4	-5.8
Venezuela	0.1	3.3	9.3	6.0	41.9	20.6	15.9	11.7	3.8	13.5	19.1	14.1
Average	2.7	3.5	5.1	4.5	49.3	7.4	6.1	5.6	-2.6	0.4	1.0	0.6

(f): Forecast.

Source: World Economic Outlook, April 2006. For inflation, the average is for advanced economies.

TABLE 2.6
General Government Fiscal Balance

	Primary balance			Overall balance		
	1997–2002	2002–2005 (f)	2005 (f)	1997–2002	2002–2005 (f)	2005 (f)
Argentina	0.8	2.3	3.1	−2.0	0.3	1.0
Bolivia	−3.5	−4.4	−2.3	−5.2	−7.0	−5.2
Brazil	2.3	3.6	3.9	−5.0	−5.8	−5.5
Chile (*)	0.9	1.5	2.3	0.0	0.5	1.3
Colombia	−0.8	0.9	1.6	−4.6	−3.8	−3.4
Ecuador (*)	3.2	1.9	1.6	−1.6	−1.2	−1.3
El Salvador	−1.2	0.4	1.2	−2.9	−3.3	−2.8
Guatemala (*)	−0.6	−0.4	−0.3	−1.8	−1.5	−1.4
Mexico	1.8	1.4	1.6	−1.1	−0.9	−0.5
Peru	0.2	0.6	1.0	−2.0	−1.6	−1.1
Uruguay (*)	−1.6	2.2	4.4	−4.2	−2.7	−0.4
Venezuela (*)	0.1	0.7	0.8	−2.0	−3.9	−3.7
Average	0.1	0.9	1.6	−2.7	−2.6	−1.9

(f): Forecast.
(*): Central government.
Source: Moody's

experienced some crises that reduced average growth, since then Latin America in general has recovered at a reasonable pace. The largest economies, Brazil and Mexico, are growing below the simple regional average, and of course improving their performance should spill over to the rest of the region.

The chronic malaise, inflation, is historically low. Of the countries represented in Table 2.5, only Argentina and Venezuela have two-digit inflation, something that was very common until as recently as the nineties. This is a very important achievement, which could in part be due to the slack of economic activity, but no measure of output gap will suffice to explain the large decline in inflation since the nineties. Most likely, this is a durable achievement. On the external front, the data show that the region is not relying too heavily on foreign financing in this phase of the cycle.

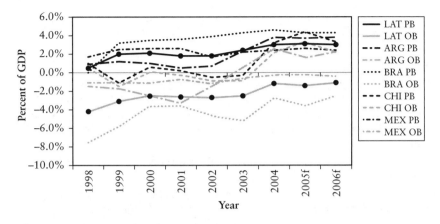

FIGURE 2.10 Fiscal Balance in Latin America
(*OB*): overall balance; (*PB*): primary balance.
Source: UBS (November 2005)

Regarding fiscal performance, there has also been an improvement (Table 2.6). Some of this improved performance may be due to high commodity prices. But taking into account the fact that in general Latin American economies are not in a boom and that inflation is still contained, it is very likely that this improved performance is more structural than simply a result of good conditions for high revenues. Further evidence is shown in Figure 2.10, which presents the evolution of the primary fiscal balance (PB) and the overall fiscal balance (OB) for Argentina, Brazil, Chile, Mexico, and the average of Latin American countries as reported by UBS. Latin America has had an improvement between 2.5 and 3 percentage points of GDP since 1998. This is major progress and has been achieved in governments of different political stripes.

Overall, at least on the macro front, Latin America is in good standing. Whether this is the result of a good external environment and a favorable cyclical position is open to discussion. However, progress on the fiscal side as well as in lowering inflation indicates that the region has good initial conditions to resume growth, and the challenge is to consolidate stability.

The Prospects
Macroeconomic stability, an open economy, institutions oriented to the protection of property rights and the rule of law, and good human resources, among others, are key to growth. One can add caveats about

timing, intensity, and deepness of reforms, but there are no shortcuts to basic principles. Inability to sustain growth in the region has been the result of failure to deliver.

It is necessary to build support for reforms, assuring that their benefits reach all of the population. Reforms and transformation have their costs. They must be perceived as fair. Some people cannot always bear the costs while those who enjoy the benefits are always the same minority. Policies that promote competition and openness bring better living conditions across the whole population.

As I have argued, the recent crises in emerging countries have brought better macroeconomic management. It is essential to maintain it during good times and to increase the economies' resilience to external shocks to be better prepared for bad times. All things being equal, the region will still grow modestly. Progress in reforms is necessary to speed up growth, and perhaps one primary factor to sustain reforms and growth is to build support for growth-oriented economic policies. In the successful case of Chile, despite large unsatisfied needs and deep inequalities, the benefits of growth have been widespread. This has helped build strong support for macroeconomic stability, market oriented reforms, and strong social policies.

Notes

I am very grateful to María Cristina Betancour, Scott Mainwaring, Jaime Ros, and Tim Scully for very useful comments. I have also benefited from previous discussions at presentations at the University of Southern California, Yale University, and Expansiva. I am grateful to Christopher Neilson and Marco Nuñez for excellent research assistance. All views expressed here are my own.

1. For Tables 2.1 and 2.2 the sample consists of 21 countries: Argentina, Bolivia, Brazil, Chile, Colombia, Costa Rica, Dominican Republic, Ecuador, El Salvador, Guatemala, Haiti, Honduras, Jamaica, Mexico, Nicaragua, Panama, Paraguay, Trinidad and Tobago, Uruguay, and Venezuela. These tables compare these 21 countries with the East Asian countries that are listed in Table 2.1.

2. For further details on the Chilean experience, see De Gregorio (2004).

3. For further justification, see Cole et al. (2005). For a skeptical view of this approach, see Bosworth and Collins (2003), who argue that not all increases in the capital-labor ratio are the result of increases in total factor productivity.

4. The decompositions are constructed on a country-by-country basis, so if averages are taken across countries, this identity may not hold.

5. We have $(1/h)(dh/dE) = \varphi$, which is the return to schooling.

6. This is a simple average of the Latin American countries for which data were available in 2000.

7. The data on human capital are based exclusively on measures of the educational attainment of the labor force and are not adjusted for quality. This is the

implicit assumption when using the same return for education across countries. As will be discussed later, there is evidence of low relative quality of education in Chile, which would increase the human capital gap.

8. The system has six equations corresponding to the periods 1970–75, 1975–80, 1980–85, 1985–90, 1990–95, and 1995–2000. The dependent variable is the growth rate of per capita GDP. Data on GDP are from Penn-World Tables version 6.1. The log of per capita GDP, the average years of male secondary and higher schooling, and the log of life expectancy at age one are measured at the beginning of each period. The ratios of government consumption and investment to GDP, the inflation rate, the total fertility rate and the growth rate of the terms of trade are period averages. The rule-of-law index is the earliest value available (for 1982 or 1985). The openness variable is the period average. Estimation is by three-stage least squares. Instruments are the actual values of the variables for schooling, life expectancy, openness, and the terms of trade; dummy variables for Spanish or Portuguese colonies and other colonies (which have substantial explanatory power for inflation); lagged values of the log of per capita GDP, the government consumption ratio, and the investment ratio; and the initial values for each period of the rule-of-law index and democracy index. The instrument for the rule-of-law indicator is its value for 1982 or 1985. The initial values of foreign reserve-import ratio are used as an instrument for balance-of-payments crisis. Individual constants (not shown) are included for each period. Standard errors of the coefficient estimates are shown in parentheses. For further details and additional estimations, see De Gregorio and Lee (2004).

9. Ros (2006) argues that the way I measure openness in this paper, trade corrected by size, includes an implicit interaction effect between size and openness, which is the one theory would suggest.

10. Meller (2002) provides a clear illustration of this claim for the Chilean case. He says that in 1980 two tons of copper were needed to buy one personal computer, while in 2000 one ton could buy two personal computers. In 2005 the price of copper was double that of 2000, and in 2006 it rose further.

11. Loayza, Fajnzylber, and Calderón (2004) present some additional and detailed empirical evidence on growth in Latin America.

12. See also Edwards (1998) and Dollar and Kraay (2002). For a more skeptical view, see Rodríguez and Rodrik (2001).

13. The definition of institutional transition is based on indices of political score (Polity index) and economic freedom score (Cato index) and involves three characteristics: (i) they must result in a minimum level of institutional quality, (ii) significant increase in quality, and (iii) they endure. In Latin America the transitions are: Argentina 1991, Brazil 1999, Chile 1976, Costa Rica 2000, Dominican Republic 1996, Ecuador 2000, El Salvador 1994, Guatemala 1994, Honduras 2003, Mexico 1991, Panama 2000, Paraguay 2004, and Peru 2003.

14. In the regressions for quality of institutions this variable is measured with indices of governance, corruption, and economic freedom.

15. See Herrera and Valdés (2004) for further details.

16. Analyzing the effects of capital controls, Cowan and De Gregorio (2005) argue that the key to explaining capital inflows, financial vulnerability,

and currency crises is the exchange rate regime in place, rather than capital controls.

17. In some recent studies on the determinants of income distribution, education appears to be an important factor in reducing inequality. However, it takes time to reduce inequality via education. Other recent papers have emphasized the role of financial development in reducing inequality. See Li, Squire, and Zou (1998) and Beck, Dermigüc-Kunt, and Levine (2004).

18. Data on income distribution of Argentina and Uruguay are taken a year before the sharp crisis they had with the collapse of convertibility in late 2001.

19. These figures are illustrative and present broad trends, but there are always measurement problems, first due to the traditional problem of coverage, which is different across countries, and second due to the forms in which expenditure is made.

References

Barro, Robert, and Jong-Wha Lee. 2001. International Data on Educational Attainment: Updates and Implications. *Oxford Economic Papers* 53(3).

Beck, Thorsten, Asli Dermigüc-Kunt, and Ross Levine. 2004. Finance, Inequality and Poverty: Cross-Country Evidence. World Bank Policy Research Working Paper No. 3338 (June).

Bosworth, Barry, and Susan Collins. 2003. The Empirics of Growth: An Update. *Brookings Papers on Economic Activity* 2:113–79.

Céspedes, Luis Felipe, and José De Gregorio. 2005. Recuperaciones cíclicas: Evidencia internacional. Mimeo, Central Bank of Chile.

Cole, Harold, Lee Ohanina, Alvaro Riascos, and James Schmitz. 2005. Latin America in the Rearview Mirror. *Journal of Monetary Economics* 52:69–107.

Cowan, Kevin, and José De Gregorio. 2005. International Borrowing, Capital Controls and the Exchange Rate: Lessons from Chile. Mimeo, Central Bank of Chile.

de Ferranti, David, Guillermo Perry, Francisco Ferreira, and Michael Walton. 2003. *Inequality in Latin America and the Caribbean: Breaking with History?* Washington, DC: World Bank.

De Gregorio, José. 2004. Economic Growth in Chile: Evidence, Sources and Prospects. Working Paper No. 298 (December), Central Bank of Chile.

De Gregorio, José, and Jong-Wha Lee. 2004. Economic Growth and Adjustment in East Asia and Latin America. *Economia* 5(1). (Previous version, Working Paper No. 245, Central Bank of Chile).

Dollar, David, and Aart Kraay. 2002. Institutions, Trade and Growth. *Journal of Monetary Economics* 50(1):133–62.

Edwards, Sebastian. 1998. Openness, Productivity and Growth: What Do We Really Know? *The Economic Journal* 108(447):680–702.

Hall, Robert, and Charles Jones. 1999. Why Do Some Countries Produce So Much More Output Per Worker Than Others? *Quarterly Journal of Economics* 114(1):83–116.

Herrera, Luis Oscar, and Rodrigo Valdés. 2004. Dedollarization, Indexation and Nominalization: The Chilean Experience. *Economic and Social Study Series*, IADB.

Heston, Alan, Robert Summers, and Bettina Aten. 2002. Penn World Table Version 6.0. Center for International Comparisons at the University of Pennsylvania (CICUP), October.

International Monetary Fund (IMF). 2005. *World Economic Outlook*. Washington, DC: International Monetary Fund.

Klenow, Peter, and Andrés Rodríguez-Clare. 1997. The Neoclassical Revival in Growth Economics: Has It Gone Too Far? *NBER Macroeconomics Annual 1997*.

Li, Hongyi, Lyn Squire, and Heng-fu Zou. 1998. Explaining International and Intertemporal Variations in Income Inequality. *The Economic Journal* 108(447):26–43.

Loayza, Norman, Pablo Fajnzylber, and César Calderón. 2004. Economic Growth in Latin America and the Caribbean: Stylized Facts, Explanations, and Forecasts. Working Paper No. 264 (June), Central Bank of Chile.

Maddison, Angus. 1995. *Monitoring the World Economy*. Paris: OECD.

———. 2001. *The World Economy: A Millennial Perspective*. Paris: OECD.

Meller, Patricio. 2002. El Cobre Chileno y la política minera. In *Dilemas y debates en torno al cobre*, ed. Patricio Meller. Santiago: Ediciones Dolmen.

Parente, Stephen, and Edward Prescott. 2002. *Barriers to Riches*. Cambridge, MA: MIT Press.

Prasad, Eswar, Kenneth Rogoff, Shang-Jin Wei, and M. Ayhan Kose. 2003. Effects of Financial Globalization on Developing Countries: Some Empirical Evidence. Occasional Paper No. 220, Washington, DC, International Monetary Fund.

Rodríguez, Francisco, and Dani Rodrik. 2001. Trade Policies and Economics Growth: A Skeptic's Guide to the Cross-national Evidence. *NBER Macroeconomics Annual 2000*: 261–325.

Ros, Jaime. 2006. Comments. Presented at the Conference on Democratic Governability in Latin America held at the Kellogg Institute, University of Notre Dame.

Wacziarg, Romain, and Karen Horn Welch. 2003. Trade Liberalization and Growth: New Evidence. NBER (National Bureau of Economic Research) Working Paper No. 10152.

Winters, L. Alan, Neil McCulloch, and Andrew McKay. 2004. Trade Liberalization and Poverty: The Evidence So Far. *Journal of Economic Literature* 52(1):72–115.

Young, Alwyn. 1995. The Tyranny of Numbers: Confronting the Statistical Realities of the East Asian Growth Experience. *Quarterly Journal of Economics* 110(3):641–80.

CHAPTER THREE

Does One Size Fit All in Policy Reform?
Cross-National Evidence and
Its Implications for Latin America

FRANCISCO RODRÍGUEZ

INTRODUCTION

In an oft-cited article published in 1990, John Williamson (1990) coined the term *Washington Consensus* to refer to the lowest common denominator of policy advice being offered by the Washington-based institutions to Latin American countries at the end of the nineties. The list summarized ten propositions that, Williamson argued, most of official Washington (a group in which he evidently includes himself) thought would be good for Latin America.[1]

Williamson's article accurately reflected the state of thinking about development policy in the late eighties and early nineties, a period during which almost all Latin American nations embarked on a process of market-oriented economic reforms. The implementation of these reforms came to be seen as the central component of a strategy for reestablishing economic growth and making the region's turn to democracy sustainable. It would be fair to say that the overwhelming majority of policymakers in Latin America felt at that time that they knew what policies had to be enacted in order to make their economies succeed, and that whether they were able to achieve growth or not would depend essentially on their ability to overcome the political constraints to the adoption of these policies. To borrow from the language used by Mainwaring and Scully in the introduction to this volume, one vital part of the democratic governance problem—how to implement effective policies for a country's political, economic, and social welfare—appeared to have been solved, while the other part—how to do this in a democracy—was the one that policymakers had to turn their attention to.

Both academic observers and policymakers are by now much less sanguine about the capacity of free market reforms—at least as originally conceived—to deliver rapid economic growth. There is an emerging consensus that the results of Washington Consensus reforms have, at best, been much weaker than expected (Loayza, Fajnzylber, and Calderón 2005; Ocampo 2004). The failure of the region to attain solid growth outcomes in the 1990s has coincided with growing difficulties in the consolidation and institutionalization of democratic regimes in the region. The high levels of political instability and fragility of countries like Bolivia, Ecuador, and Venezuela are the most extreme examples of the way in which economic failures go hand in hand with political failures. Understanding the reasons for the disappointing performance of countries that followed Washington Consensus growth strategies is thus a fundamental ingredient of any attempt to understand how the region can retake a path of consolidation of stable democratic institutions.

As scholars have reevaluated the economic effects of Washington Consensus reforms, a new debate has emerged on the merits of potential alternatives to it. Discussions have centered upon what should be included or excluded from this list, both as a description of what Washington thinks as well as a normative statement regarding what countries should do. Critics such as Stiglitz (1999) have argued that the evidence of the nineties reveals a failure of the Washington Consensus and advocated drawing up a new list altogether, focusing on objectives of sustainable, egalitarian, and democratic development and including concrete policies such as sound financial regulation. Williamson himself (2000) has expressed doubts about the role of interest rate liberalization and argued for a much more comprehensive view of financial liberalization. Naím (2000) has gone as far as to say that disagreements are so prevalent among economists and Washington institutions over issues such as the effectiveness of open trade policies and the need for an international financial architecture that no such consensus actually exists.

Behind much of the discussion on the Washington Consensus there appears to be implicit agreement that such a list should exist, in the sense that there is a set of policy prescriptions that, if applied in any Latin American country, would generate at the very least the basic conditions necessary for sustained economic growth. Williamson has captured appropriately the state of thinking about policy reforms when he stated that "in practice there would probably not have been a lot of difference if I had undertaken a similar exercise for Africa or Asia" (2000, 255). In other words, underlying the discussion about the Washington Consensus versus new or alternative "consensuses" there is a coincidence on the idea that there is sufficient similarity between all developing economies so as to permit applying the same thought exercise to all of them when thinking about development policies.

This state of thinking contrasts starkly with the view of development economics shared by the structuralist and dependency schools (Prebisch 1962; Furtado 1961; Myrdal 1957). These authors argued for the specificity of the experience of developing countries at different stages of development and explicitly opposed attempts to use the same theories to think about broadly distinct institutional and structural settings. In this view of development, the effects of economic policies depended on historical and structural forces, so that policies that worked adequately in some settings would fail to do so in others.

Although many have by now forgotten the structuralist and dependency schools, there has been a recent rebirth of sorts of their basic ideas in thinking about economic policies. Critical analysis of the growth experience of the 1990s has produced numerous observations of economies that have implemented different sets of policies and have shown widely divergent growth experiences. Although some of the highest growing countries in the world during the 1990s, such as Chile and Korea, whose growth rates of per capita GDP over the 1990 to 2003 period were respectively 3.7 and 4.7%, had relatively open free market economies, others, such as Lebanon and Lesotho (growth rates of 6.1% and 4.8% over the same period), clearly did not. According to the Heritage Foundation (2005), Botswana and Mongolia had similar levels of economic freedom in the mid-nineties; the former grew at an average rate of 2.8% during the 1990 to 2003 period; the latter at −3.0% (Rodríguez 2006). Deeper analysis of development experiences has led to the identification of country cases—such as that of El Salvador (Hausmann and Rodrik 2005)—that have "done everything right" in terms of following the Washington Consensus, yet have not seen payoffs in terms of economic growth. In a recent comprehensive appraisal of the results of a decade of economic reforms published by the World Bank, the role of interactions between policies, institutions, and economic structure is not only recognized but made to play a central role. In their words:

> To sustain growth requires key functions to be fulfilled, but there is no unique combination of policies and institutions for fulfilling them...different polices can yield the same result, and the same policy can yield different results, depending

on country institutional contexts and underlying growth strategies....Countries with remarkably different policy and institutional frameworks—Bangladesh, Botswana, Chile, China, Egypt, India, Lao PDR, Mauritius, Sri Lanka, Tunisia and Vietnam—have all sustained growth in GDP per capita incomes above the U.S. long-term growth rate of close to 2 percent a year. (World Bank 2005b, 12)

The theoretical literature has also seen renewed interest in understanding why similar economic policies appear to work differently in different countries. The importance of interactions among different dimensions of potential regressors has become the focus of recent attention in the academic literature. In a recent paper, Hausmann, Rodrik, and Velasco (2004) point out that the Theorem of the Second Best would lead us to expect that the reduction of a particular distortion may have very different effects on welfare (and growth) depending on the initial levels of other distortions. Their theoretical examples illustrate the potentially complex interactions that can arise even in relatively simple models. They also present a discussion of a number of cases in which similar policies appear to have had very different growth effects and suggest that they may be due to the fact that the countries faced different binding constraints on economic growth.

This new (or renewed) vision of economic growth contrasts with the methodological tools currently used by growth economists to understand the effect of policies in developing countries. The standard empirical workhorse model of economic growth (the linear regression of growth on its determinants) assumes that the effect of a change in a policy is the same in all countries regardless of their structural or institutional characteristics. These growth regressions have become a ubiquitous form of policy analysis. Empirical work in this literature is often geared towards reaching (or rebutting) a conclusion that a certain variable of interest—say a particular economic policy or one of a variety of institutional arrangements—is harmful or beneficial for growth. It is not uncommon for research in this area to conclude with phrases such as "the evidence indicates that the growth rate of real per capita GDP is enhanced by better maintenance of the rule of law, smaller government consumption, and lower inflation."[2] Even the widespread practice of inspection of partial scatter plots and correlations between growth and policies is, in essence, the use of a growth regression framework.

Such a vision rules out the existence of strong interactions between policies, institutions, and economic structure. When such interactions are considered in the literature, it is common to explore nonlinearities with respect to the variable of interest, assuming linearity in the remaining regressors. The most frequent approach is to introduce a quadratic or multiplicative interaction term, assuming that all remaining variables enter linearly. Regrettably, as we discuss in detail later, there is little reason to think that this approach will give unbiased estimators of the underlying effects if reality is characterized by complex interactions between different variables.

This chapter steps into the debate by asking how we should use the cross-country data while at the same time allowing for complex interactions between different potential determinants of economic growth that seriously take into account the idea that the effects of policies may be critically dependent on a nation's structural and institutional characteristics. We will make three basic points: (i) that the empirical estimates of growth effects of policies are severely biased if nonlinearities are ignored; (ii) that there is strong evidence that these nonlinearities are important in the data; and (iii) that appropriate nonparametric tests on the cross-country data are often inconclusive with respect to the effect of Washington Consensus policies on economic growth.

These conclusions are highly relevant for policy analysis. They imply that development thinking should be much more specific to a country's institutional and structural characteristics and that thinking about a "list" of policy prescriptions to apply to a broad group of developing economies is methodologically erroneous. They also suggest the need to rely on local, case-specific knowledge for designing growth strategies. One size does not fit all in terms of policy reform, and not recognizing this is likely to lead to frequent missteps in the search for economic growth.

Our results suggest that the idea of thinking about what the "new consensus" should be to replace the Washington Consensus may be ultimately misguided. If the effectiveness of policies is context dependent and it is difficult to ascertain the direction of these interactions based on cross-national data, then the question of what policies all developing countries should follow makes as much sense as the question of what subject all undergraduates should major in. Rather, development thinking should be oriented at finding the appropriate combinations of policies that may work under particular institutional and structural configurations. The first leg of the democratic governance problem—finding effective policies for social and economic development—needs to receive as much attention as the second one—making these policies feasible in a democracy.

The rest of the chapter proceeds as follows. The next section takes a first look at the data from Latin America as well as from a broader cross-section of countries and argues that there exist substantial differences in growth performances between countries that implemented similar policies. The following section lays the theoretical groundwork, discussing the theoretical underpinnings of the linear growth regression and the econometric effects of failure of these assumptions. Then, we shift to empirical analysis, presenting the results of our empirical analysis. The final section presents some reflections.

DOES ONE SIZE FIT ALL? A FIRST LOOK
AT THE DATA

In many dimensions, Ecuador and Perú look remarkably alike. As shown in Table 3.1, both countries produce roughly one tenth of their value added in agriculture, three-tenths in industry, and six-tenths in services. Both countries have a savings rate near 20 percent, and about two-thirds of their populations live in cities. Their debt service amounts to approximately one-fourth of their exports, and they devote roughly 10 percent of GDP to government consumption. During the nineties, both countries made ultimately successful efforts to stabilize their inflation rates: Perú through a monetary adjustment program in the early nineties, Ecuador through its dollarization. Both countries belong to the Andean Community and have similar trade policies: their average tariff

TABLE 3.1
A Tale of Two Countries

	Ecuador	Perú
Agriculture/GDP	7.7	10.3
Industry/GDP	28.7	29.3
Services/GDP	63.6	60.4
Savings/GNP	23.7	17.5
Urbanization rate	64	74
Inflation	7.9	2.3
Average tariff	11.29	11.23
Fuel and mining exports/Total exports	40.67	48.1
Current account surplus/Deficit	−1.75	−1.67
Government consumption/GDP	9.5	10.1
Fiscal surplus/GDP	1.9	−1.8
Growth rate, 1990–2003	−0.13	1.92

Source: World Bank (2005a). All data from 2005 except for the urbanization rate, which reflects the earliest available, and the growth rate, which is for 1990–2003.

rate weighted by imports is approximately 11 percent. They are heavily dependent on natural resource exports, with fuel and mining exports making up four-tenths of their total exports. They have moderate current account deficits roughly under 2 percent of GDP.

Perú and Ecuador, however, are not similar in their economic performance. Since 1990, Perú has experienced a moderately high growth rate of 1.9 percent in its per capita GDP. Ecuador, in contrast, has stagnated and experienced a negative growth rate of −0.13 percent of GDP.

The comparison between Perú and Ecuador highlights an interesting pattern about economic growth both within the Latin America and Caribbean region and among developing countries: a very broad dispersion among the economic performances of countries that carried out similar economic policies, as well as broad variation in the economic policies that led to high levels of economic growth. These points are illustrated with the simple comparisons set out in Tables 3.2 and 3.3, which show the growth behavior and tariff rates for two sets of Latin American countries. While tariff rates are just one indicator of policy, and countries can differ substantially in other policy dimensions, they provide a useful starting point as they tend to be a reasonable indicator of how much governments are willing to intervene in their economies.

TABLE 3.2

Countries Exceeding 2 Percent Annual Growth in the Region, 1990–2003

Rank	Country	Growth rate	Average tariff rate
1	Chile	3.9%	11.1%*
2	St. Kitts and Nevis	3.6%	14.8%
3	Belize	3.6%	17.5%
4	Dominican Republic	3.5%	13.3%
5	Trinidad and Tobago	2.9%	4.5%
6	Panama	2.8%	3.1%
7	Costa Rica	2.6%	5.1%
8	Grenada	2.3%	7.4%
	Region average	1.2%	7.2%

Source: World Bank (2005a)

*MFN tariff in 1997–1997 WTO Trade Policy Review (WTO 1997). Averages of tariff rates are over all available years in the 1990–2003 period. Growth rates are the log-difference between the most recent observation for growth and its 1990 value, divided by the number of years.

TABLE 3.3
Growth Performance of Ten Most Liberalized Economies in the Region
(Tariff Criteria), 1990–2003

Rank	Country	Growth rate	Average tariff rate
1	El Salvador	1.7%	0.3%
2	Panama	2.8%	3.1%
3	Bolivia	1.1%	3.1%
4	Mexico	1.1%	3.4%
5	Trinidad and Tobago	2.9%	4.5%
6	Paraguay	−0.5%	4.6%
7	Jamaica	0.0%	4.7%
8	Colombia	0.5%	4.8%
9	Costa Rica	2.6%	5.1%
10	Nicaragua	0.3%	5.4%
	Region average	1.33%	6.28%

Source: World Bank (2005a)

Averages of tariff rates are over all available years in the 1990–2003 period. Growth rates are the log-difference between the most recent observation for growth and its 1990 value, divided by the number of years.

Certainly, countries that differ in their trade policy would appear to be more likely to differ in other policy dimensions. Table 3.2 shows the trade policies and growth rates of the eight economies in the region that had an annual per capita growth rate in excess of 2%. What is striking is that there is such dispersion in the economic policies that were compatible with high growth. For example, the three Caribbean island economies in this group, St. Kitts and Nevis, Trinidad and Tobago, and Grenada all achieved per capita growth rates in excess of 2%, but ranged from having tariff rates of 4.5% in the case of Trinidad and Tobago, substantially below the region (and the world) average, to 14.8% in the case of St. Kitts and Nevis, more than twice the region average.

Table 3.3 makes this point in another way: countries that shared the same policy strategy (in the dimension of trade policy) experienced very different growth performances, ranging from Paraguay's −0.5% average annual growth rate to Trinidad and Tobago's 2.9% annual rate. It appears that having similar policies is not a precondition for having similar growth experiences.

The comparisons that I have just presented are obviously extremely simplified. There are many policies other than trade policies. There are also structural and institutional factors that can account for differences in growth. One would expect that, after controlling for these factors, one would find that countries that adopt similar policies have similar growth performances.

In order to take these factors into account, Figures 3.1 and 3.2 and Table 3.4 display the results of a more complex exercise, in which I attempt to measure how similar countries are in terms of economic policies through the use of four indicators that are broadly available and that thus allow us to carry out cross-country comparisons using a large number of countries. These are the log of the black market premium (*bmp*), the log of 1 plus the inflation rate (*inf*), the ratio of government consumption to GDP (*govc*), and the average tariff rate (*tar*). We are interested in testing the hypothesis that countries with similar policies have similar growth outcomes. We can get at this issue by building all pair wise comparisons of countries and looking at how they differ in policies and how they differ in economic growth. More concretely, I estimate the relationship:

$$\left\| \gamma_i - \gamma_j \right\| = f\left(\left\| p_i - p_j \right\| \right) + \varepsilon_{ij} \qquad (1)$$

Where γ_i is country i's growth rate, $p_i = (bmp, inf, govc, tar)$ is our vector of policies and ε_{ij} is a random error term. We expect $f(.)$ to be a monotonically increasing function. In other words, if two countries have very different policies then we would expect them to have different growth rates, but if they have similar policies we would expect them to have similar growth rates. Equation (1) thus provides a first way to test whether one size fits all in terms of policy formulation. It tests whether all countries can be seen as operating within the same model, so that the effects of policies are broadly similar for all of them.

Table 3.4 shows a first look at this data. In it we report the differences in the mean growth rates between pairs of countries split by two groups: those that have similar policies and those that have different policies. Our criterion for classifying two countries as similar is that the Euclidean distance between their policy vectors be less than the median of the sample. We present for the whole world sample as well as restricting to the Latin American countries. We also present a specification where we use the residuals of growth on a previous regression on initial GDP, total years of schooling, the rule of law, and the growth rate of population. From a statistical point of view, the results appear to confirm the idea that similar countries have similar growth rates: differences in growth

TABLE 3.4

Mean Absolute Value of Differences in Growth Performances between Pairs of Economies

		Euclidean Distance between Policy Vectors				
		Below median	Above median	Difference	T scores	n
World	No controls	1.98%	2.35%	0.36%	7.75**	7306
	With controls	1.85%	2.30%	0.45%	7.67**	4028
Latin America	No controls	1.40%	1.75%	0.35%	2.50*	238
	With controls	1.39%	1.55%	0.16%	1.09	208

*p < .01

**p < .001

rates are indeed systematically higher in all cases, and three out of four of them are statistically significant. But from an economic point of view, what is striking is how small the differences in growth rates are. They imply that changing from having very similar policies to having very different policies will cause a difference of between 0.16% and 0.45% in the average growth rate.

Figures 3.1 and 3.2 show the scatter plots of the relationship between the absolute differences in growth rates and the absolute distance between policy vectors for Latin America. In what will serve as a useful introduction to some of the discussion about formal treatment of nonlinearities that we take on below, we present both a linear estimate of the relationship (Figure 3.1) and a nonparametric estimate that can flexibly accommodate any functional form (Figure 3.2). In the next section, we will explain the reasons why the nonparametric estimate is strictly preferable to the linear estimate when the functional form is unknown. Note that the nonparametric estimate in Figure 3.2 is strictly decreasing for low values of the distance between policies $\|p_i - p_j\|$, flat for intermediate values, and increasing only for very high values. In other words, there are large numbers of countries for which similar policies are not associated with similar economic performances. Note also that the difference between the linear estimate and the nonparametric estimate is striking. If we were to look only at the linear estimate, we would conclude that

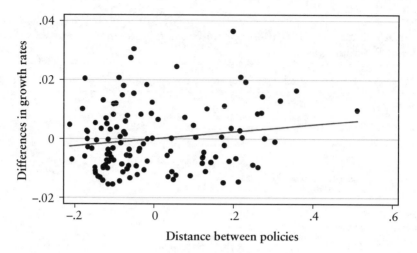

FIGURE 3.1 Linear OLS Estimates, No Controls: Latin America, 1990–2003
coef = 0.1191172, se = .0046997, t = 2.53

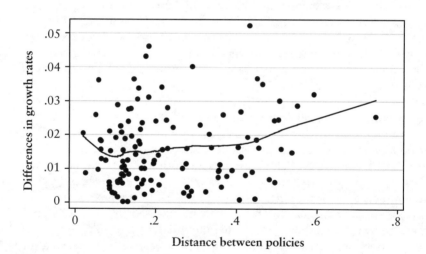

FIGURE 3.2 Nonparametric Estimates, No Controls: Latin America, 1990–2003
bandwidth = .8

countries that are farther apart in terms of policies have dissimilar economic performances. The nonparametric estimate shows that this conclusion is highly misguided for most countries in the sample.

Figures 3.3 and 3.4 repeat this exercise after having purged the differences in growth rates from the effect of other potential structural determinants of economic growth. The dependent variable here is the residual of a regression of the growth rate on the log of initial GDP, total years of schooling, a rule of law indicator, and population growth rates. Note that now both the linear and nonlinear estimate are generally decreasing. It thus appears that, within Latin America, countries that follow similar policies don't have similar economic performances, even after controlling for some of their structural characteristics.

Figures 3.1 to 3.4 also show that there exists broad variation in growth performances for countries with similar policies. Many pairs of countries appear to have similar policies and substantial differences in their growth rates, while a substantial number of countries have similar growth performances despite having different policies.

There are a number of possible explanations for these results. In the first place, it could be that policies have none or little effect on growth. If policies were irrelevant for growth, then the slope of the function in (1) would be zero and one would expect to see no clear pattern arising from fitting such an equation. Granted that the slope of the estimated

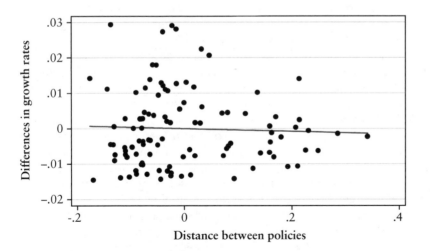

FIGURE 3.3 Linear OLS Estimates, with Controls: Latin America, 1990–2003
coef = −.00385333, se = .00642872, t = −.6

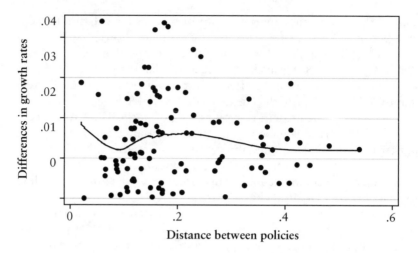

FIGURE 3.4 Nonparametric Estimates, with Controls: Latin America, 1990–2003
bandwidth = .8

functions is not zero, but it is small when measured according to its economic significance. Another possibility is that the pattern of use of different policies served to systematically offset their differences. For example, if policy A is good for growth but policy B is bad for growth, then a country with high A and high B would have a similar growth performance to one with low A and low B, despite having very different policies. The problem with that argument is that it would require a special configuration of policy patterns, in which there are few countries with low A and high B or high A and low B in the sample.

A third explanation is that this pattern could be due to nonlinearities in the growth relationship. There are two ways in which a nonlinear growth function could explain the behavior of the data. On the one hand, a nonlinear function could imply that growth is a nonmonotonic function of policies, so that different values of policies are compatible with the same growth outcome (Figure 3.5). Alternatively, nonlinearities could imply the existence of relevant interactions, so that the marginal effect of policies on growth may depend on the values of other variables (Figure 3.6).

In the rest of the chapter, I will explore the case for nonlinearities. I will show that the theoretical case for linearity of the growth function is tenuous and will argue that ignoring it can have damaging consequences. I then go on to show that the cross-country evidence shows strong evi-

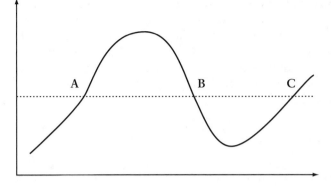

FIGURE 3.5 Nonlinear Example 1

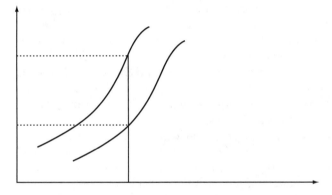

FIGURE 3.6 Nonlinear Example 2

dence of nonlinearities in the growth function. These sections present a nontechnical summary of the results of these exercises; readers interested in exploring the full technical nuances behind this work are referred to Rodríguez (2007).

THEORETICAL FRAMEWORK

Where Does the Linear Growth Regression Come From?
In this section, I discuss the theoretical basis for the linear growth regression. This regression, often referred to as a *Barro* regression because of the deep influence of Robert Barro's 1991 *Quarterly Journal of Economics*

article, was proposed almost simultaneously by several other authors including Mankiw, Romer, and Weil (1992) and Sala-i-Martin (1991). It consists of a growth regression that is linear in the log of initial GDP, some measures of investment or the stock of human capital, population growth, and a set of "production function shifters" that commonly includes policy, institutional, and structural controls. Formally, the specification often looks like:

$$\gamma_Y = \alpha_0 + \alpha_1 \ln y_{t-1} + \alpha_2 s_k + \alpha_3 H + \alpha_4 n + \beta Z \qquad (2)$$

where γ_Y is the rate of per capita GDP growth, y_{t-1} is initial GDP, s_k refers to the savings rate, H is the stock of human capital, n is the rate of population growth and Z is a vector of potential production function shifters.

Given the ease of running this regression with readily available data sets and the obvious interest of exploring whether a particular set of policies, institutions, or structural variables is harmful or beneficial for growth, the proliferation of applied work using equation (2) is not surprising. For obvious reasons, I will not discuss this voluminous literature here; the reader is referred to Aghion and Howitt (1998) and Temple (1999) as well as the articles in the recent *Handbook of Economic Growth* (Aghion and Durlauf 2005) for exhaustive surveys. It suffices to note for our purposes that this analysis tends to take the form of varying the subset of variables included in Z and using conventional significance tests to evaluate the effect of potential determinants on economic growth.

Equation (2) is not a purely *ad-hoc* specification. Its analytical foundations were elaborated early on in the literature and, to my knowledge, were first presented systematically in Mankiw, Romer, and Weil's (1992) augmented Solow model. These authors started out from a simple aggregate economy production function in which output Y_t was a multiplicative function of human and physical capital H_t and K_t as well as productivity A_t with constant exponents on the first two:

$$Y_t = A_t K_t^{\alpha} H_t^{\beta} \qquad (3)$$

This is the functional form known as the Cobb-Douglas production function because of the empirical estimation of it carried out by Charles Cobb and Paul Douglas (1928).[3] It is useful to stop a minute to consider the implications of this equation. Production functions are, of course, a common staple of economics. At the firm level they can be thought of as a technological relationship between physical and human capital inputs on the one hand and output on the other hand. Even at the firm level, though, a production function is much more than a mathematical description of the production technology. A firm can derive less outputs, given a certain quantity of inputs, for a plethora of reasons ranging from high levels of worker conflict, low employee morale, poor management, lack of effective planning, and supply disruptions. All of these factors will be subsumed in the "technology" term A_t. Some of these reasons are so clearly *not* technological that many economists prefer to use the more general and inclusive term "productivity."

What is true at the firm level is even truer at the aggregate economy-wide level. The reasons why a society may be able to produce much less output per worker than other societies, given the amount of inputs that it utilizes, can range from the quality of its institutions and its dependence on volatile primary goods industries to the stability of its macroeconomic policies, to name just a few. Indeed, many economists believe that A_t—and not K_t or H_t—is the fundamental source of cross-national differences in output per worker (Hall and Jones 1999; Parente and Prescott 2000).

The second set of assumptions of the Mankiw-Romer-Weil setup simply describes the evolution of the stocks of human and physical capital by the accumulation equations:

$$\frac{dK_t}{dt} = s_k Y_t - \delta K_t \tag{4}$$

$$\frac{dH_t}{dt} = s_h Y_t - \delta H_t \tag{5}$$

where s_k and s_h respectively denote the fractions of income devoted to savings in the form of physical and human capital and δ is the common depreciation rate for physical and human capital. In other words, both human and physical capital grow on net by the difference between the resources devoted to their accumulation and their depreciation. What Mankiw, Romer and Weil showed is that out of this extremely simple setup you could derive the following equation to describe the growth rate of the economy near its long-run equilibrium[4]:

$$\gamma_t = \frac{d\left(Y_t / L_t\right)}{Y_t / L_t}$$

$$= \beta_0 + \beta_1 \ln\frac{Y_0}{L_0} + \beta_2 \ln s_k + \beta_3 \ln\frac{H_t}{L_t} + \beta_4 \ln(n+g+\delta) + \beta_6 \ln A_0 + \lambda_{it}. \tag{6}$$

where γ_t denotes the proportional growth rate of per capita GDP. The latter is defined simply as the ratio between output Y_t and the labor force L_t. n is the growth rate of population $\frac{1}{L}\frac{dL_t}{dt}$ and g is the growth rate of technology $\frac{1}{A}\frac{dA_t}{dt}$. Recall that A_t denotes the level of productivity, so that A_0 would be the level of productivity at the initial time period. λ_i is a country specific random effect.

There is a key additional assumption that Mankiw, Romer and Weil (1992) make that allows them to turn (6) into an equation that can be estimated econometrically. That is to assume that cross-national differences in the initial level of technology vary randomly according to:

$$\ln(A_0) = \ln(A) + \varepsilon_i \tag{7}$$

with ε_i representing a country-specific random term. This is evidently an extremely simplifying assumption. Obviously we would expect cross-national differences in productivity to depend on cross-national differences in institutions, policies, and economic structure—precisely the terms that growth empirics often studies and that we have grouped under the vector **Z**. We will return to this briefly. Substituting (7) in (6) gives us the linear regression:

$$\gamma_t = B_0 + \beta_1 \ln\frac{Y_0}{L_0} + \beta_2 \ln s_k + \beta_3 \ln\frac{H_t}{L_t} + \beta_4 \ln(n+g+\delta) + \eta_{it}. \tag{8}$$

where $B_0 = \beta_0 + \beta_6 \ln(A)$, which can be treated as a constant term, and $\eta_{it} = \lambda_{it} + \beta_6\varepsilon_i$, which can be dealt with as a compound disturbance term. In other words, equation (8) can be estimated as a simple linear regression. As long as we can ensure that η_{it} is uncorrelated with the rest of the independent variables in equation (8), it can be estimated by ordinary least squares; if we cannot make that assumption about the distribution of η_{it}, other methods such as instrumental variables techniques may be adequate.

Equation (8) gives us a well-defined theoretical prediction linking economic growth to specific observables—namely initial income, the savings rate, the stock of human capital per worker, and population growth. Indeed, Mankiw, Romer and Weil center on estimating precisely this equation. As we have seen, however, this approach sweeps under the rug one of the most interesting potential sources of variation in per capita income and growth: the effect that changes in variables like institutions, economic structure, and economic policies may have on economic growth through the aggregate productivity term A_t.

Equation (8) is not, however, the equation used by most researchers. The bulk of the literature on cross-national growth empirics uses some version of equation (2). There are two distinctions between (8) and (2). One is that (2) uses n as a control instead of $\ln(n + g + \delta)$. This flaw can be—and often is—easily corrected.[5] The other, more serious, problem is that (8) does not (yet) depend on Z, the vector of policies, institutions, and structural variables that may affect the economy's aggregate productivity.

There are at least two important reasons to take Z into account when estimating a regression like (8). One is econometric. If differences across countries in the determinants of productivity are not simply randomly distributed, but rather ε_i is correlated with any of the regressors in (8), its omission would lead to omitted variable bias in our coefficient estimates of that regression. The other reason is more basic. Potentially the most important reason why we are interested in the empirical study of economic growth is because we care about how policy decisions, institutional reforms, and structural economic changes can affect long-run growth, all of which we have characterized as belonging in Z. The effect that theses variables in Z may have on economic growth is potentially much more relevant than that of initial income, savings rates, or population growth, all of which may be very difficult to change.

How do we go about putting variables like policies, institutions, and structure in this framework? The most logical way would be by seeing their effect as affecting the efficiency with which society converts inputs like human and physical capital into outputs, that is, as affecting our productivity term A_t. That is precisely why a broad—as opposed to a strictly technological—concept of productivity is necessary to think about A_t. In that case equation (7) would need to be replaced with:

$$\ln(A_t) = h(Z_t) + \varepsilon_{it} \tag{9}$$

which leads us to derive the following estimation form in place of equation (8):

$$\gamma_t = \beta_0 + \beta_1 \ln\frac{Y_0}{L_0} + \beta_2 \ln s_k + \beta_3 \ln\frac{H_t}{L_t} + \beta_4 \ln(n + g + \delta) + \beta_6 h(Z) + \eta_{it}. \tag{10}$$

What we wish to point to is that there are two key characteristics of (10) in which it is distinguished from (8). One is that it is an inherently non-linear function of Z, as can be clearly seen from the nonlinear term $h(Z)$. The second one is that even if we assume that the log of productivity is a linear function of Z, say:

$$\ln(A_t) = \sum_i \gamma_i Z_i \tag{11}$$

then equation (10) becomes:

$$\gamma_t = \beta_0 + \beta_1 \ln\frac{Y_0}{L_0} + \beta_2 \ln s_k + \beta_3 \ln\frac{H_t}{L_t} + \beta_4 \ln(n+g+\delta) + \sum_i \beta_{6i} Z_i + \eta_{it}, \quad (12)$$

where we have denoted $\beta_{6i} = \beta_6\gamma_i$. This is *still* a nonlinear function of Z since the growth rate of technology g that forms part of the nonlinear term $\ln(n + g + \delta)$ is:

$$g = \frac{1}{A}\frac{dA_t}{dt} = \sum_i \gamma \frac{dZ_i}{dt}. \quad (13)$$

In other words, there is what we can call an *inescapable nonlinearity* in the growth function. Even if we assume that the effect of policies, institutions, and structure on productivity is linear, it will still be the case that growth will be a nonlinear function of these variables because it depends on them both through their direct effect through productivity and through their indirect effect that works through the $\ln(n + g + \delta)$ term.

An alternative way of putting this is by thinking about the conditions that would be necessary for growth to be a linear function of the variables in Z. Since $\ln(n + g + \delta)$ is a nonlinear function of Z, the only way for (12) to become linear is for g to be the same for all countries. In other words, we do not only need variables like institutions, structure, and policies to affect productivity linearly, we also need them to do it in such a way that the growth rate of productivity will be the same in all countries. This will be possible only in very peculiar cases (e.g., if all countries in the world have the same exact pace of economic reform).

While some of the assumptions of the Mankiw, Romer and Weil model have received considerable attention, the inescapable nonlinearity in production function shifters has been almost completely ignored in the applied literature.[6] One possible line of defense, taken by Mankiw, Romer and Weil (1992), is to see g as capturing only the effects of technological change, which is assumed to be public and available to all countries, while $A(Z_0)$ is held to be fixed at its initial level. Research exploring the failure of this hypothesis often looks at varying rates of diffusion of technologies across countries (Coe and Helpman 1995; Coe, Helpman, and Hoffmaister 1997). This leaves unanswered the questions raised by the terms of Z that have no relation to technological diffusion. While the assumption that they are time-invariant may be adequate for thinking about some production function shifters such as economic geography and perhaps institutions, it is much less useful if one wants to understand the effect of variables like economic policies, institutional reform, or structural change.

This chapter will concentrate on empirically analyzing the validity of equation (11). I know of no systematic treatment of the effects of failure of the assumption that technology is a linear function of its determinants embodied in this equation. This is surprising, given that, unlike the other assumptions of the Mankiw-Romer-Weil model, this assumption is almost completely atheoretical. There is no reason why one would expect variables as diverse as economic policies, institutions, and structural characteristics to have separable, linear effects on the log of the production function. Indeed, to the extent that one sees the "production-shifting" effect of the Z variables on the production function as reflecting the efficiency effects of relaxing different distortions, basic economic theory as captured by the Theorem of the Second Best tells us that there is no reason to expect that relaxing one distortion would lead to an increase in efficiency when another distortion is present; in other words, it tells us that the effects of distortions on efficiency are unlikely to be separable.

Economics is, of course, full of simplifying assumptions, and there is by now a broad methodological consensus—at least among neoclassical economists—on some version of Milton Friedman's (1953) methodological postulate that an assumption should not be judged by its realism or lack of it but rather by its capacity to help explain reality. It is thus possible to develop a line of defense of the linearity hypothesis using this argument if we could show that the cross-country data is consistent with the predictions that emerge out of a model characterized by a linear growth function. In a later section, we turn to the discussion of how well the linearity hypothesis fares when posed against the data. Before that, however, it is useful to turn to an analysis of the consequences of erroneously assuming that the growth function is linear when it is not.

What Can the Data Say?

The Dangers of Running a Misspecified Regression   If our key contention is correct, then empirical work on economic growth has consistently attempted estimating a nonlinear relationship through the use of linear methods. In slightly more technical jargon, they have estimated misspecified models. What types of problems arise from doing this?

The key problem arising from estimation of a misspecified regression is that it is unclear that the resulting coefficients can be given any meaningful interpretation. The reason is that estimating a nonlinear regression through linear techniques is the same thing as omitting the nonlinear term from the regression, and thus generates a bias which is formally identical to omitted variable bias.

In order to fix ideas, let us think about a simple univariate nonlinear function:

$$y = f(x) + \varepsilon_i \tag{14}$$

It is straightforward to rewrite this equation in order to split $f(x)$ into its linear and nonlinear components:

$$y = Ax + h(x) + \varepsilon_i \tag{15}$$

where $h(x) = f(x) - Ax$. Suppose then that we estimate the linear regression:

$$y = \alpha x + \eta_i \tag{16}$$

Estimating (16) when (15) is true is the same thing as throwing $h(x)$ in the disturbance term, that is, omitting it from the regression. Recall that omitted variable bias affects coefficient estimates of the included variables whenever the is a correlation between the disturbance term and the right-hand side variables in the regression. In most cases it is very hard to know whether omitted variable bias is a serious problem unless we know whether the right-hand side variables in our regression are correlated with the excluded, often unobservable variables. In this case, in contrast, $h(x)$ is by definition a function of our right-hand side variable x, and thus will generally be correlated with it.[7]

The crux of this is that $\hat{\alpha}$ will generally be a biased estimate of A. It is impossible to predict the sign of this bias unless we know the sign of the correlation of $h(x)$ and x. We will generally not know this unless we know the functional form of $h(.)$, which, of course, we don't. Thus $\hat{\alpha}$ will not be an adequate estimator of the linear component of $f(x)$.

Is there a meaningful interpretation to the linear estimator? Some authors (see, for example, Helpman 2004, 73) have suggested that the linear estimator of a growth regression gives us the average effect of changing the explanatory variable over the sample of countries. If this were true, it would imply that the linear estimator may not be a poor guide to evaluating the expected effects of changes in policies or institutional and structural reforms: even if we cannot recover the expected effect of these changes for a given country, we may still be able to inform the policymaker of the expected effect of making such a change over all countries.

Regrettably, this interpretation is not correct. In Rodríguez (2007), I establish the necessary conditions for a linear estimator to give us an unbiased estimate of the average partial derivative of a nonlinear function.

The conditions are highly restrictive, and require, among other things, that the explanatory variables be distributed normally. However, normality tests carried out on a standard list of regressors in cross-national data show that these variables almost invariably fail to meet this basic condition.

Much of the recent literature in empirical growth analysis has been concerned with finding solutions for another type of misspecification problem: that of endogeneity or reverse causation. The state of the art for tackling endogeneity problems is the use of instrumental variables estimators. The basic intuition behind these is simple. Suppose that we are worried that reverse causation is contaminating the estimate of our variable of interest on growth. For concreteness, suppose we are attempting to estimate the effect of institutions on growth but think that part of the positive correlation displayed by the data comes from the fact that richer countries tend to develop better institutions. A simple solution would be to find a subset of events in which institutions changed for reasons that had nothing to do with growth. In a statistician's ideal world, we would have controlled experiments in which we could be sure that institutions had varied randomly, much as explanatory variables change in real laboratory settings. It is not clear that such an experiment is feasible or desirable for anyone except those completely obsessed with growth econometrics. However, there may be cases in which history or nature is able to give us this type of exogenous variation, so that there is a source of change in our variable of interest which is so clearly exogenous to the process under consideration that if we do observe that it is associated with changes in growth, those cannot reflect a process of reverse causation.

Some of the most relevant recent contributions in growth empirics are indeed ingenious applications of instrumental variables techniques to the study of the determinants of growth (see, for example, Frankel and Romer 1999 or Acemoglu, Johnson, and Robinson 2001). Regrettably, instrumental variables estimators are ill-equipped to handle the issue of nonlinearities. The reason is that in order for the estimates derived from the use of instrumental variables to be unbiased, three key conditions have to be satisfied: (i) the instrument has to be exogenous; (ii) it has to be correlated with the potentially endogenous variable; and (iii) it has to be uncorrelated with the error term in the equation of interest. When there is an omitted nonlinearity, conditions (ii) and (iii) cannot be simultaneously satisfied: if an instrument is correlated with the variable x in equation (16), it will also be correlated with the nonlinear term $h(x)$ which is treated as part of the error term.

Making Inferences in a Complex World   What then is the appropriate method to estimate an inherently nonlinear function like (14)? The answer to this question depends on whether we believe that we know enough about the functional form of this equation so as to estimate it parametrically or nonparametrically. If we were to have sufficient information about the functional form of the growth function so as to be able to postulate a particular functional form, then the adequate approach would be to estimate such functional form through a nonlinear technique such as nonlinear least squares.

Regrettably, it is hard to argue that we have such knowledge. Indeed, the prevalence of the use of the linearity assumption is in itself a manifestation of the lack of generally accepted theories about the functional form that the effect of the production function shifters that we have grouped in Z has on productivity. Therefore it seems appropriate to use methods that do not make *a priori* assumptions about functional forms. Nonparametric methods would appear to be appropriate in this case.

Regardless of whether we use parametric or nonparametric methods, estimating a nonlinear function is always much more demanding in terms of data than estimating a linear function, because we must sample it at many more points to be certain of its shape. In the parametric case, if there were no sampling error, we would need only two observations to fit a linear function $y = \beta_0 + \beta_1 x$ to the data. However, if the function is a nonlinear function of the form $f(x, \beta)$ with β a k-dimensional vector, then even in the absence of sampling error we will need at least k points to infer β.

In the nonparametric case this problem is exacerbated. If the function is unknown, then we will need much more information to sample it at many points if we want to keep the approximation error within reasonable bounds. Even more important is the fact that this problem becomes much greater when the dimensionality of the function grows. As shown by Yatchew (2003), if we sample a function at n equidistant points then the magnitude of the error of approximation will be proportional to the n-th root of the number of observations. In other words, having 100 observations to estimate a one-dimensional relationship is tantamount to having 10 observations ($100^{1/2}$) to estimate a two-dimensional specification and to having 4.64 observations ($100^{1/3}$) to estimate a three-dimensional specification. To be consistent, a researcher should place the same faith on a regression estimate of a general nonlinear function in three dimensions that is run with 100 observations that she should put on a correctly specified linear regression that was run with five observations. This result is known as the *curse of dimensionality* in the literature on nonparametric econometrics and it underlines the difficulty in making appropriate inferences about unknown nonlinear functions with few observations.[8]

One implication of the curse of dimensionality is that the confidence that we may have in the inferences that can be derived from nonparametric estimation will depend not so much on whether the function is nonlinear but on whether it is separable or not. In other words, what is key is our ability to write:

$$y = f(x_1, \ldots x_n) = f_1(x_1) + \ldots + f_n(x_n) \tag{17}$$

In which case we say that $f(.)$ is additively separable. If this is the case, then the curse of dimensionality is not a problem because each of the subfunctions $f_i(.)$ varies along just one dimension.[9] Whether the curse becomes an obstacle to estimation will thus depend on whether we expect the effects of production-function shifters such as institutions, policies, and economic structure to be independent of each other. To use a simple example, consider the effect of trade policy on growth. If we think that an increase of a certain magnitude—say 10 percentage points—in tariffs has the same marginal effect on growth regardless of the initial level of tariffs, then we believe that the relationship between tariffs and growth is linear. If we believe that this effect varies with the initial level of tariffs—such that, for example, they are much larger for an increase from 0 to 10% than from 90, to 100%, then we say that it is nonlinear. If we believe that it depends on the value of another variable—such that the effect of increasing tariffs will not be the same in a country with solid institutions as in one with rampant corruption, then we say that it is not separable. Estimation of the growth function through nonparametric techniques may be feasible if the curse of dimensionality is held in check by separability.

However, it is important to keep in perspective what the actual implications of the curse of dimensionality are. The result states that we cannot estimate the growth function with any reasonable degree of precision unless the effects of the potential determinants of growth are additively separable. But estimating an unknown nonlinear function with a certain degree of precision means ascertaining the value of growth that should correspond to *any* potential combination of growth determinants. In other words, what we are unlikely to be able to do is to infer what level of growth we can expect for, say, a country that has high tariffs, is moderately dependent on natural resources, and has low levels of corruption (note that the linear approach does give an answer to this question, which is restricted by assumption to be the same as that for a country with any other characteristics). But what we may be able to do is to infer certain characteristics of the relationship between growth and its underlying determinants—for example, whether we can reject the hypothesis that there are some countries for which an increase in tariffs can increase growth. Thus, the growth data may enable us to answer some interesting, policy-relevant questions about the relationship between growth and policies, even if they are not the type of questions that we are used to asking of the data.

EMPIRICAL EVIDENCE

Until now, I have argued that the theoretical basis for the standard linear "kitchen sink" regression commonly used in cross-national growth analysis is tenuous. Contrary to common opinion, this form does not naturally emerge from a simplified version of standard growth theory, but is actually extremely hard to derive without very stringent assumptions that are themselves at odds with the type of variations that we are commonly interested in studying for the purposes of policy analysis. I have also argued that the real risk to the cross-country empirical project comes not only from failure of linearity but from the potential failure of separability: if the effects of potential production function shifters such as policies, institutions, and economic structure are not separable from each other, then the amount of information often found in cross-national data sets may be insufficient to estimate the growth function with any degree of confidence.

Whether nonlinearities or nonseparabilities are an empirical characteristic of the growth data is a question whose answer ultimately lies with the data itself. In this section I will present a brief summary of the empirical evidence regarding the issue of generalized nonlinearities and nonseparabilities in the growth data. We will concentrate on testing the assumption that production function shifters have a linear effect on productivity as captured by equation (11). As we have argued above, (11) is a necessary condition for linearity of the growth function. If we were to find evidence invalidating it, our results would shed doubts on the validity of the whole linear approach.[10]

The bulk of the tests discussed in what follows rely on nonparametric or semiparametric methods of estimation. The basic intuition behind these methods is that they do not make strong assumptions about the functional form underlying the estimated function but rather maintain sufficient flexibility so as to estimate any functional form. As explained above, this is the correct approach to take unless we are willing to make strong *a priori* assumptions about the underlying functional form of the growth function.

For the analysis that follows, I will use a cross-sectional data set of economy-wide measures of growth and its potential determinants for the 1975 to 2003 period. The cross-sectional approach is the hallmark of the empirical growth literature and has dominated cross-country growth analysis since the early nineties. Despite the recent interest in the use of panel data techniques, the cross-sectional approach is still broadly used and characterizes some of the most relevant recent contributions.[11] Furthermore, relevant methodological questions remain about the applicability of the panel data approach to study questions of long-term economic growth. For example, it is not clear that segmenting the data into ten- or five-year intervals is appropriate when the phenomenon of interest is long-run growth, and most methods used require the introduction of fixed effects, impeding the analysis of the effect of potential growth determinants, such as institutions or geography, which exhibit little or no variation over time.[12] A natural extension of the work considered here, however, would explore its application in a panel data setting.

I use the World Bank's (2005a) PPP-adjusted per capita GDP Growth Rates for the 1975 to 2000 period as the dependent variables As right-hand side indicators of the potential production-function shifters Z, I use twelve variables commonly used in empirical growth analysis as well as three summary indicators made up of subgroups of these. The sample attempts to cover the three key dimensions that have played relevant roles in the analysis of growth empirics: policies, institutions, and economic structure. To measure policy distortions, I use government consumption as a percent of GDP, the average tax on imports and exports, the log of one plus the inflation rate, and the log of the black market premium. To capture the role of institutions, I introduce four commonly used indicators: a measure of the rule of law, a measure of political instability, an index of economic freedom, and an index of the effectiveness of government spending. In the list of structural measures of the level of social development and economic modernization of nations, I use the share of primary exports in GDP in 1975, the rate of urbanization, the ratio of liquid liabilities to GDP, and the average years of life expectancy. I also use three summary indicators of each of these three dimensions, made up by simple normalized averages of the relevant indicators. A full description of the variables is provided in Table 3.5.

Estimation starts out from the semi-linear growth equation in (10):

$$\gamma_t = \beta_0 + \beta_1 \ln\frac{Y_0}{L_0} + \beta_2 \ln s_k + \beta_3 \ln\frac{H_t}{L_t} + \beta_4 \ln(n+g+\delta) + \beta_6 h(\mathbf{Z}) + \eta_{it}. \quad (10)$$

TABLE 3.5
Variable Descriptions

Policy Indicators

1. Trade policy openness	$(1 + t_m)(1 + t_e) - 1$, with t_m (t_e) the ratio of import (export) tax revenue in total imports (exports); Data from World Bank (2005a)
2. Log of black market Premiump	Dollar and Kraay (2002)
3. Government consumption as a percentage of GDP	World Bank (2005a)
4. Log of (1 + inflation rate)	World Bank (2005a)
5. Summary policy indicator	Sum of 1–4, normalized over the unit interval

Institutional Indicators

6. Rule of law	Dollar and Kraay (2002)
7. Political instability	Average Variation in POLITY variable, Polity IV Data Set.
8. Effectiveness of government spending	Glaeser et al. (2004)
9. Economic Freedom Index	Heritage Foundation (2005)
10. Summary Institutions indicator	Sum of 6–9, normalized over the unit interval

Economic Structure Indicators

11. Share of primary exports in total exports	World Bank (2005a)
12. Urbanization rate	World Bank (2005a)
13. Share of liquid liabilities in GDP	International Monetary Fund (2005)
14. Life expectancy	World Bank (2005a)
15. Summary structure indicator	Sum of 10–14, normalized over the unit interval

---

Our basic idea is to test the model embodied in equation (10) against two alternative models. One is the fully linear model of equation (12):

$$\gamma_t = \beta_0 + \beta_1 \ln\frac{Y_0}{L_0} + \beta_2 \ln s_k + \beta_3 \ln\frac{H_t}{L_t} + \beta_4 \ln(n+g+\delta) + \sum_i \beta_{6i} Z_i + \eta_{it}. \quad (12)$$

The second one is an intermediate additively separable model in which the effect of each of the production function shifters, while nonlinear, is independent from each other. As noted above, this specification, were it to be valid, could considerably attenuate the effects of the curse of dimensionality:

$$\gamma_t = \beta_0 + \beta_1 \ln\frac{Y_0}{L_0} + \beta_2 \ln s_k + \beta_3 \ln\frac{H_t}{L_t} + \beta_4 \ln(n + g + \delta) + \sum_i f_i(Z_i) + \eta_{it}. \quad (18)$$

The first column of Table 3.6 shows the results of evaluating the linearity hypothesis—that is, testing (12) against (10)—by testing for the joint significance of added nonlinear terms in a third-order Taylor expansion. In order to make sure that our results are not driven by the specific choice of explanatory variables, we reran each specification using all possible combinations of our indicators of institutions, policies, and economic structure in which one variable from each group was included. This gives 125 (5^3) specifications. Table 3.6 reports the median F-statistic and the median p-value for the test of the null hypothesis of linearity. It also reports the number of regressions in which the test rejected the null hypothesis at a 5% level of significance. We see that in 119 of the 125 specifications (95.2%) the linearity hypothesis was rejected. This very high rejection rate indicates that the failure of linearity is not due to a specific variable or interaction but is rather a generalized phenomenon that turns up in many alternative specifications that use different indicators.

The second column of Table 3.6 reports the results of carrying out a similar set of tests in order to evaluate the separability hypothesis. In this case, we test whether the nonseparable terms of the Taylor expansion (those involving only cross-products of different variables) are jointly equal to zero. This test is thus similar to the linearity test, but in contrast we now test for the joint significance only of the terms in the polynomial that contain interactions between the variables (e.g., tariffs^2 × primary exports). Since this is a subset of all the nonlinear terms, the results will

TABLE 3.6
Taylor Polynomial Tests of Linearity and Separability,
Penn World Tables, 1975–2003

Equation	Linearity	Separability
Median F-statistic	4.97	3.13
Median P-value	0.00	0.00
Number significant (/125)	119	95
	95.2%	76.0%

obviously be somewhat weaker than those of the previous test where we evaluated the excludability of *all* the nonlinear terms. Nevertheless, our results indicate that in 95 out of 125 specifications (76%), these higher-order interaction terms cannot be excluded. In other words, the data points to evidence for strongly significant nonseparabilities, shedding doubt on the sense of attempting to estimate the growth function with any reasonable degree of precision.[13]

The results just shown suggest that the cross-country data appear to be characterized by high-dimensional nonlinearities. Our discussion of underlying growth theory has highlighted the fact that theory is not much of a guide as to the way in which these variables may affect the growth function; our review of the empirical evidence has shown that neither is the empirical evidence.

These results contrast with the widespread use of empirical growth analysis to derive strong normative recommendations. Is there a way in which we can reconcile these two visions? In this section, we will use nonparametric tests to attempt to uncover the normative content of the cross-country data as regards the implications that can be drawn for the purposes of policy, institutional, and structural reforms.

Within the linear cross-country empirical growth framework, it is common to use the results of conventional significance tests in order to draw policy implications. Therefore, the result that higher protection of property rights is associated with higher growth is often used to advocate recommendations for institutional reforms leading to greater protection of property rights. A logical question is what the counterpart of this type of analysis is in the nonlinear setting. In other words, what type of evidence would be necessary to find in the growth data to support a blanket recommendation to all countries to follow a specific course in terms of, for example, institutional reform?

We suggest that the appropriate concept in the nonlinear case is that of *monotonicity*. That is, a policy recommendation to follow a certain course of action should only be given if our evidence says that the growth function is monotonically increasing in the suggested course of action. An implication of this principle is that one should not recommend a policy if one knows that it may be damaging to the growth prospects of a country.

The monotonicity criterion may justly be perceived to be excessively restrictive, as it would imply that we should not recommend a policy if it were to harm just one country. An alternative possibility would be to adopt the criterion that one should not recommend a policy that is monotonically harmful for growth. In other words, if we find that the cross-country evidence shows that a policy hurts *all* countries, then we could not in good faith recommend such a policy.

For simplicity, assume that $h(\mathbf{Z})$ is a continuously differentiable function.[14] Estimation is based again on equation (10):

$$\gamma_t = \beta_0 + \beta_1 \ln\frac{Y_0}{L_0} + \beta_2 \ln s_k + \beta_3 \ln\frac{H_t}{L_t} + \beta_4 \ln(n + g + \delta) + \beta_6 h(\mathbf{Z}) + \eta_{it}. \quad (10)$$

We will test (10) against two restrictive hypotheses. The first one is that growth is monotonically increasing in variable Z_i. This is the same as estimating (10) subject to the restriction that, for all possible values of the vector $\mathbf{Z}$, the first derivative of the growth function with respect to $\mathbf{Z}$ is positive:

$$R_1 : \frac{\partial h(\mathbf{Z})}{\partial Z_i} > 0 \forall Z \quad (19)$$

while the second one asserts that that derivative is negative (that the policy is harmful for growth):

$$R_2 : \frac{\partial h(\mathbf{Z})}{\partial Z_i} < 0 \forall Z \quad (20)$$

Table 3.7 illustrates the possible configurations of results that could be obtained from these tests. For example, it is possible that the tests reject R_1 but do not reject R_2 (upper right corner). This evidence would be consistent with the idea that growth is monotonically decreasing in this

TABLE 3.7
Possible Results of Monotonicity Tests and Implications

	Reject R_2	Cannot Reject R_2
Reject R_1	• Nonlinear function that has both increasing and decreasing segments. • No general policy recommendations can be given.	• Evidence is consistent with Z_i being harmful for growth. • Recommendation of increasing Z_i can be given.
Cannot Reject R_1	• Evidence is consistent with Z_i being beneficial for growth. • Recommendation of decreasing Z_i can be given.	• Evidence is uninformative about the form of the growth function. • No general policy recommendations can be given.

variable, while at the same time rejecting the idea that the variable could be uniformly good for growth. The evidence would thus seem to give tentative support to a policy recommendation to decrease Z_i. Likewise, it is possible for us to reject R_2 but be unable to reject R_1 (lower left corner). This would imply that we have found no evidence that the policy can be uniformly bad for growth but rather we have found support for the idea that it is conducive to higher growth. A policy recommendation to increase values of this variable would find support in the data.[15]

The other two cases are trickier. Suppose we reject both hypotheses (upper left corner). Then the data would be telling us that growth is sometimes an increasing function and sometimes a decreasing function of policy Z_i. It would thus be difficult to give concrete policy recommendations because we are unsure of whether the policy will harm a country or not, as the data tell us that it is likely to harm some countries and not others. Alternatively, suppose we are in the lower right corner of Table 3.7. Here we find that the data can reject neither the positive monotonicity hypothesis nor the negative monotonicity hypothesis. Here the test is telling us that there is too little information in our data set to assert that either the variable is good for growth or bad for growth. In contrast to the upper left corner—where we know that the variable is good for growth in some countries and is bad for growth in others—here we cannot know whether it is uniformly good for growth, uniformly bad for growth, or neither.

The tests of the monotonicity hypothesis are shown in Table 3.8. These results show the outcome of tests carried out using Fourier expansions. Forurier expansions are a more general version of Taylor expansions which use linear combinations of trigonometric terms. There is an extensive econometric literature studying the properties of these estimators (Gallant 1982, 1987; Geman and Hwang 1982). The basic benefit of a Fourier approximation is the greater flexibility of the trigonometric expansion to approximate highly nonlinear functions. We have coded the variables so that the positive monotonicity result (R_1) will always correspond to the "conventional wisdom" view. We refer to the conventional wisdom as that which is associated with Washington Consensus recommendations: that openness is good for growth, black market premia are harmful, protection of the rule of law is beneficial, etc. We present the results of these tests for our indicators of economic policies, institutions, and economic structure.[16]

Our results give some interesting indications about the forms of the underlying nonlinearities in the growth data. In terms of the quadrants outlined in Table 3.7, three variables fall in the upper left quadrant, none in the upper right quadrant, six in the lower left quadrant, and six

TABLE 3.8
Monotonicity Tests, Fourier Series Estimators

	Hong-White Fourier Series Test	
	Conventional wisdom	Anti-conventional wisdom
Null hypothesis	Decreasing	Increasing
Inflation	0.97	0.55
Log (black market premium)	0.32	0.27
Government consumption	0.63	0.31
Tariffs	0.04	0.02
Combined policy index	0.49	0.15
Null hypothesis	Increasing	Decreasing
Rule of law	0.30	0.10
Political instability	0.24	0.10
Effectiveness of government spending	0.02	0.05
Index of economic freedom	0.06	0.00
Combined institutions index	0.54	0.00
Null hypothesis	Increasing	Decreasing
Primary exports	0.37	0.09
Urbanization	0.48	0.06
Life expectancy	0.54	0.00
Financial development	0.11	0.01
Combined structure index	0.58	0.00

Table reports p-values for the null hypothesis of monotonicity. Hong-White tests are based on estimation of the HW statistic. Confidence intervals built using bootstrapped test statistics with residual sampling and 100 observations. HW tests use $J = 1$ and $K^* = 2$.

in the lower right quadrant. In the case of those that fall in the lower left quadrant, the data is telling us that the evidence is not consistent with the idea that they are always harmful for growth and is consistent with the idea that they are always beneficial for growth. A recommendation to improve general measures of institutions, lower primary export dependence, increase urbanization, increase life expectancy, and increase financial development could thus be argued to count with tentative support from the data, in the limited sense outlined above. One could even take the argument further and state that the data gives support to the conventional wisdom view as in none of the fifteen cases do we find evidence rejecting it.

Note, however, that these conclusions change significantly once we center on only the policy variables. Indeed, none of the policy variables fall in the off-diagonal quadrants of Table 3.7. Four of them fall in the upper-left quadrant—indicating that the evidence can neither refute the hypothesis that they are always harmful for growth nor the hypothesis that they are always beneficial—while one (tariffs) falls in the lower-left quadrant—indicating that they are growth-enhancing in some countries and growth-reducing in other countries. To the extent that *policy reforms* form the core of the Washington Consensus, our results argue that the cross-national data can really give very little evidence in favor of it. The data is either inconclusive with respect to the effects of policies on growth, or, where it is conclusive, it clearly rejects the idea that the same direction of change in policies could be expected to be good for growth in all countries.

It is also interesting to note that our results seem to provide stronger evidence of the effect of institutional and structural variables on growth than of the effect of policies. This result is confirmed in more complex exercises presented in Rodríguez (2007). The results can be interpreted as suggesting that the primary emphasis of reforms should be in the institutional and structural rather than the policy aspects. In this sense, the results of accurately taking into account the complexities inherent in the data would seem to turn the conventional wisdom on its head in that it appears to support the idea of the primacy of "second generation" reforms.

CONCLUDING COMMENTS

It is useful to offer a brief summary of what our empirical analysis has—and has not—done. First, it has shown that there is decisive evidence against a linear view of the growth process. The data consistently reject linear specifications in favor of more general, nonlinear ones. Second, it has shown that there is also strong evidence against a view of the world in which interactions between different growth determinants are absent. Specifications that allow for these interactions perform much more strongly and a preponderance of tests prefer these complex specifications to the simpler, separable ones.

The third important result that emerges from our empirical analysis is that there are strong limitations on what the cross-national growth data can tell us about the effect of potential determinants on economic growth. This appears to be particularly marked in the case of economic policies such as reducing tariffs, reducing the scope of black markets, lowering inflation, or reducing government consumption. In these cases, the curse of dimensionality conspires to make it very difficult for us to reject even extreme, unconventional visions of the growth process.

If the results of this chapter are correct, they have strong implications for the Washington Consensus approach to thinking about policies. Strong nonlinearities in the growth process imply that it makes little sense to think about policy reforms abstracting from an economy's structural or institutional characteristics. The reforms that will work for a country may not work for others. Policy thinking should start from considering the country-specific characteristics that are likely to make certain policies work rather than trying to draw lists of reforms to be applied to large groups of countries.

Our results also suggest that serious attempts at improving democratic governance in the region must shed aside the idea that there is a well-established consensus on what countries must do in order to achieve economic growth. The key implication arising out of the inconclusiveness of many of our exercises is that the cross-national experience is consistent with different interpretations of what generates economic growth, and that the correct interpretation may vary significantly depending on a country's institutional and structural characteristics. If it is difficult for state-of-the-art econometrics to identify what policies are good for growth, then it makes little sense to label governments as good or bad according to whether they follow a set of pre-specified policies. Rather, our discussion of democratic governance must start out from the recognition that governments are continuously searching for policies that can generate sustainable and equitable development in a context of radical uncertainty about the very complex interactions that plague the reform process.

These conclusions can appear nihilistic. If we can't say anything about the effect of policies on growth, the reader may ask, then what is the use of this analysis? Is there any value of looking at the cross-country data? Or should we be resigned to the idea that we live in a world that we cannot understand?

I believe that a close reading of the results presented in this chapter suggests a different interpretation. The results of the linearity and separability tests reported in Table 3.6, for example, are decisive in their rejection of these visions of the growth process. In other words, the data is telling us that we do not live in a simple world, where the effects of policies are approximately constant or can be separated from the values of other determinants of the growth process. The data has thus allowed us to distinguish between two competing visions of the world: one in which the growth process is approximately similar in the bulk of the world's countries, and another one where it is not. A nihilistic approach would not have been able to choose between these two visions; our approach has. The results of Table 3.8 have given support to the idea that the conventional wisdom has much more of a basis in reality when it comes to structural and institutional determinants than when it comes to policy variables. I believe that further research along these lines may be able to uncover other interesting characteristics of the growth process that will be useful in the design of growth strategies.

The main lesson that emerges from the exercise carried out in this chapter is that growth empirics—particularly in the dimension of economic policies—may have been asking the wrong set of questions. Growth empirics has attempted to garner evidence that can support policy recommendations that can be given to all developing countries. In this sense, it has acted as the academic counterpart of the "one size fits all" approach to policy design. The reason that the data is unable to come up with adequate answers to the questions posed by this paradigm is that in a world characterized by complexities and high-dimensional nonlinearities in the growth process, these questions stop making much sense. Once we recognize that the growth effects of a policy will depend on a country's structural and institutional characteristics, asking whether openness is good for growth makes as little sense as asking whether all undergraduates should major in physics or in history.

A complex vision of the growth process is necessary for us to make sense of the wide divergences that exist in the growth performances of countries that have carried out similar policies. It is also a vital part of understanding the phenomenon of countries that have found alternative pathways to high growth. I have argued that these varied experiences can be understood in the context of the existence of strong nonlinearities and interactions in the growth process. Different policies can bring the same outcome because growth can be increasing in that policy over certain ranges but decreasing over others. Countries may experience few growth effects of a policy reform because they don't have in place the institutional or structural conditions necessary to implement them.[17]

The results of this chapter may be of particular interest to those involved in quantitative research in other social sciences. The problem of choosing a functional form to estimate the effect of potential determinants on, for example, political outcomes, is subject to the same type of problems faced by the determination of how potential production function shifters affect aggregate productivity and economic growth. Political theory can seldom provide concrete guidance as to the functional form that should be used to capture complex social processes. The adoption of linear specifications is a convenient expedient, but, as we have pointed out in this chapter, erroneously adopting a linear specification can often lead to significantly distorted results. A logical step to take in this type of research would be to evaluate whether existing specifications are able to pass the type of linearity and separability tests that we propose in this paper. If they cannot, this result would invite deeper thinking about the feasibility of answering the type of questions that are commonly posed to this data.

Recognizing the true informational limitations of cross-national data sets to handle the study of complex social processes is likely to lead us to a reevaluation of the use of country-level evidence. There is a wealth of methods that can be used to attempt to understand the growth process at the level of specific economies. Detailed microeconomic studies can exploit the availability of information in labor and industrial surveys to help us understand the causes of productivity and human capital accumulation. Time-series studies of macroeconomic interactions can help us make sense of an economy's reaction to monetary and fiscal policy shocks. Historical and institutional analyses can help us understand the complex links between political alliances and economic policy design.

It is regrettably rare to see serious attempts at putting these different pieces of a country's growth puzzle together. In contrast, many fields of economics have developed methodologies to test hypotheses about aggregate economic performance at the country level. To take an example, the broad literature on the effects of trade on income inequality in the United States has relied almost completely on the application of methods that combine the use of theoretical knowledge with the analysis of country level evidence.[18] My hope is that this example can be followed within the field of empirical growth analysis in a way that allows us to evaluate competing hypotheses in a rigorous manner. The development of a *within-country growth empirics* that can help answer some of the questions that cross-country growth empirics have been unable to do represents one of the most exciting research projects in the study of economic development.[19]

Notes

The author thanks William López for his research assistance. Extremely valuable comments were received from José De Gregorio, Scott Mainwaring, Jaime Ros, Tim Scully, and Eduardo Zambrano, as well as by participants in the

Notre Dame and CIEPLAN conferences. All errors remain the author's pure responsibility.

1. The list consisted of: fiscal discipline, a redirection of public expenditure toward fields offering high economic returns and the potential to improve income distribution, tax reform, interest rate liberalization, a competitive exchange rate, trade liberalization, liberalization of inflows of foreign direct investment, privatization, deregulation, and secure property rights.

2. This particular phrase is taken from Barro (1997).

3. Although equation (3) may appear to be a somewhat arbitrary specification, many economists have thought that it is necessary to explain long-run trends in a number of macroeconomic aggregates, such as the apparent constancy over time and across countries of capital shares of GDP (Gollin 2002). This evidence has recently been questioned by Ortega and Rodríguez (2006).

4. In order to derive this equation, Mankiw, Romer, and Weil (2002) approximate the differential equation for growth near the steady state (or long-run equilibrium). An implication of this is that another reason for the possible failure of this specification is that countries are far from their steady states. Dowrick (2004) analyzes this subject in detail.

5. Since g and δ are by assumption constant in this model it is simply a matter of estimating these and calculating $\ln(n + g + \delta)$ as a control. We do not emphasize this flaw because, even though it is common, it is not difficult to handle, and in practice many researchers do use the correct functional form.

6. Durlauf, Johnson, and Temple's (2005) recent comprehensive survey of the empirical growth literature concurs with this assertion: "As far as we know, empirical work universally ignores the fact that $\log(n_i + g + \delta)$ should also be replaced with $\log(n_i + g_i + \delta)$" (2005, 580).

7. One can come up with examples of nonlinear functions that are not correlated with linear functions of their arguments, but this will only be true in very special cases.

8. The result can be slightly attenuated if the optimal nonparametric estimator (which is not always easy to find) is used (Stone 1980), but is still a significant impediment to making inferences with small data sets.

9. This result was first established by Hastie and Tibshirani (1990).

10. Recall that constancy of g is also necessary for linearity. Since failure of (11) is sufficient to invalidate linearity, we will not deal with this other assumption in detail. Were we to find confirmatory evidence of linearity—which we don't—it would also become necessary to evaluate this additional assumption.

11. Some examples are Frankel and Romer (1999), Acemoglu, Johnson, and Robinson (2001), and Sala-i-Martin, Doppelhoffer, and Miller (2004). The first two articles use a levels specification, whereas the third uses the growth specification that we reproduce here. For a recent critique of the levels approach, see Sachs (2005).

12. Standard random effects estimators require the random effect to be uncorrelated with the residual, which is by construction not the case in a growth regression. See Durlauf, Johnson, and Temple (2005) for a discussion.

13. A broader set of results, including tests of the nonlinear Mankiw, Romer,

and Weil (1992) specification as well as use of other nonparametric methods, is presented in Rodríguez (2007). While some nonparametric specifications deliver lower rejection rates of the nonseparability hypothesis, these are still higher than what one would expect if a linear specification were adequate.

14. See Rodríguez (2007) for a more general setup.

15. Of course in neither of these cases has the possibility that the variable in question be good for growth in some cases and bad in others been rejected. Thus it can be argued that even when a variable falls into the off-diagonal quadrants the data is giving only very weak support to a specific policy recommendation—in the sense of showing that that recommendation is not always wrong. For this reason we emphasize that these results could only give *tentative* support to these policy recommendations.

16. In this case, we introduce each variable separately into the regression together with the combined indicators from the other two dimensions. See Rodríguez (2007) for a more in-depth discussion as well as variation on this methodology.

17. One possible criticism of our analysis is that it subjects the field of growth empirics to an unfairly high standard. As pointed out by Jaime Ros in his comments to the conference version of this paper, linear specifications are prevalent in economics and in other social sciences. Thus it is possible that many other fields would be open to the same criticism that we have leveled.

While it is true that linear specifications are common in some fields of economics, it is also true that there are many other fields of the discipline where that is not the case. Many of the tests used in this paper as well as in Rodríguez (2007) were in fact developed in the field of production function estimation, where considerable attention has been paid to the issue of functional form and where tests for misspecification and omitted nonlinearities are common. My main contention is not that linear specifications are inadequate, but that they should be tested. The tests presented in this paper were able to reject the hypothesis of linearity decisively. This may or may not be the result of applying similar tests to other results in our discipline. What is certain is that we will never know this until we carry out the tests.

18. See, for example, Katz and Autor (1999), Freeman (1995), and Feenstra and Hanson (2003).

19. For a tentative attempt to develop and implement this type of analysis, see Hausmann and Rodríguez (2006).

References

Acemoglu, Daron, Simon Johnson, and James A. Robinson. 2001. The Colonial Origins of Comparative Development: An Empirical Investigation. *American Economic Review* 91(5):1369–1401.

Aghion, Philipe, and Steven Durlauf, eds. 2005. *Handbook of Economic Growth*. Amsterdam: North-Holland.

Aghion, Phillipe, and Peter Howitt. 1998. *Endogenous Growth Theory*. Cambridge, MA: MIT Press.

Barro, Robert. 1991. Economic Growth in a Cross-Section of Countries. *Quarterly Journal of Economics* 106(2):407–443.

———. 1997. *Determinants of Economic Growth.* Cambridge, MA: MIT Press.

Cobb, C. W., and P. H. Douglas. 1928. A Theory of Production. *American Economic Review* 18(Supplement):139–65.

Coe, David T., and Elhanan Helpman. 1995. International R&D Spillovers. *European Economic Review* 39(5):859–87.

Coe, David T., Elhanan Helpman, and Alexander W. Hoffmaister. 1997. North-South R&D Spillovers. *Economic Journal* 107:134–49.

Dollar, David, and Aart Kraay. 2002. Growth Is Good for the Poor. *Journal of Economic Growth* (Springer Netherlands) 7(3):195–225.

Dowrick, Steve. 2004. Delinearizing the Neoclassical Convergence Model. In *Economic Growth and Macroeconomic Dynamics: Recent Developments in Economic Theory*, ed. Steve Dowrick, Rohan Pitchford, and Stephen J. Turnovsky, 83–94. New York and Cambridge: Cambridge University Press.

Durlauf, Steven N., Paul A. Johnson, and Jonathan R. W. Temple. 2005. Growth Econometrics. In *Handbook of Economic Growth*, Vol. 1, ed. Philippe Aghion and Steven Durlauf, 555–677. Amsterdam: North-Holland.

Feenstra, Robert C., and Gordon Hanson. 2003. Global Production Sharing and Rising Inequality: A Survey of Trade and Wages. In *Handbook of International Trade*, ed. E. Kwan Choi and James Harrigan. Oxford: Blackwell.

Frankel, Jeffrey, and David Romer. 1999. Does Trade Cause Growth? *American Economic Review* 89(3):379–99.

Freeman, Richard B. 1995. Are Your Wages Set in Beijing? *Journal of Economic Perspectives* 9:15–32.

Friedman, Milton. 1953. The Methodology of Positive Economics. In *Essays in Positive Economics*. Chicago: University of Chicago Press.

Furtado, Celso. 1961. *Desarrollo y subdesarrollo [Desenvolvimento e subdesenvolvimento]*, 9th ed. Buenos Aires: Editorial Universitaria de Buenos Aires.

Gallant, A. Ronald. 1982. Unbiased Determination of Production Technologies. *Journal of Econometrics* 20:285–323.

———. 1987. Identification and Consistency in Seminonparametric Regression. In *Advances in Econometrics, Fifth World Congress*, Vol 1, ed. Truman F. Bewley, 145–70. New York: Cambridge University Press.

Geman, Stuart, and Hwang, Chii-Ruey. 1982. Nonparametric Maximum Likelihood Estimation By the Method of Sieves. *Annals of Statistics* 10:401–14.

Glaeser, Edward L, Rafael LaPorta, Florencio Lopes-de-Silanes, and Andrei Shleifer. 2004. Do Institutions Cause Growth? *Journal of Economic Growth* 9(3):271–303.

Gollin, Douglas. 2002. Getting Income Shares Right. *Journal of Political Economy* 90:458–74.

Hall, Robert, and Charles I. Jones. 1999. Why Do Some Countries Produce So Much More Output Per Worker Than Others? *The Quarterly Journal of Economics* 114(1):83–116.

Hastie, T.J, and R.J. Tibshirani. 1990. *Generalized Additive Models*. London: Chapman and Hall.

Hausmann, Ricardo, and Francisco Rodríguez, eds. 2006. Venezuelan Economic Growth: 1970–2005. Unpublished: Harvard University.

Hausmann, Ricardo, and Dani Rodrik. 2005. Self Discovery in a Development Strategy for El Salvador. *Economía* 6(1):43–101.

Hausmann, Ricardo, Dani Rodrik, and Andrés Velasco. 2004. *Growth Diagnostics*. Reproduced, Harvard University.

Helpman, Elhanan. 2004. *The Mystery of Economic Growth*. Cambridge, MA: Harvard University Press.

Heritage Foundation. 2005. *2005 Index of Economic Freedom*. Washington, DC: The Heritage Foundation.

IMF (International Monetary Fund). 2005. *International Financial Statistics*. Washington, DC: International Monetary Fund. Electronic database.

Katz, Lawrence F., and David Autor. 1999. Changes in the Wage Structure and Earnings Inequality. In *Handbook of Labor Economics*, Vol. 3A, ed. Orley Ashenfelter and David Card. Amsterdam: Elsevier.

Loayza, Norman, Pablo Fajnzylber, and César Calderon. 2005. *Economic Growth in Latin America: Stylized Facts, Explanations, Forecasts*. World Bank Latin American and Caribbean Studies. Washington, DC: World Bank.

Mankiw, N. Gregory, David Romer, and David N. Weil. 1992. A Contribution to the Empirics of Economic Growth. *The Quarterly Journal of Economics* 107(2):407–37.

Myrdal, Gunnar. 1957. *Economic Theory and Underdeveloped Regions*. London: Duckworth.

Naím, Moisés. 2000. Washington Consensus or Washington Confusion? *Foreign Policy* (spring):86–103.

Ocampo, José Antonio. 2004. Latin America's Growth and Equity Frustrations During Structural Reforms. *Journal of Economic Perspectives* 18(2):67–88.

Ortega, Daniel, and Francisco Rodríguez. 2006. Are Capital Shares Higher in Poor Countries? Evidence from Industrial Surveys. Reproduced, Wesleyan University.

Parente, Stephen L., and Edward C. Prescott. 2000. *Barriers to Riches*. Cambridge, MA: MIT Press.

Prebisch, Raúl. 1962. *El dessarollo economic della America Latina y algunos de sus principales problemas*. Boletin Economico de America Latina. Santiago de Chile: CEPAL.

Rodríguez, Francisco. 2006. Openness and Growth: What Have We Learned? Wesleyan Economics Working Papers 2006-011, Department of Economics, Wesleyan University.

———. 2007. Cleaning Up the Kitchen Sink: On the Consequences of the Linearity Assumption for Cross-Country Growth Empirics. Wesleyan Economics Working Papers 2006-004, Department of Economics, Wesleyan University.

Sachs, Jeffrey D. 2005. Institutions Don't Rule: Direct Effects of Geography on Per Capita Income. NBER Working Paper 9490.

Sala-i-Martin, Xavier. 1991. On Growth and States. Ph.D. Dissertation, Harvard University.

Sala-i-Martin, Xavier, Gernot Doppelhoffer, and Ronald Miller. 2004. Determinants of Long-Term Growth: A Bayesian Averaging of Classical Estimates (BACE) Approach. *American Economic Review* (September):812–35.

Stiglitz, John. 1999. The World Bank at the Millennium. *Economic Journal* 109(459):F577–97.

Stone, Robert. 1980. Optimal Rates of Convergence for Non-Parametric Estimators. *Annals of Statistics* 8:1348–60.

Temple, Jonathan. 1999. The New Growth Evidence. *Journal of Economic Literature* 37(1):112–56.

Williamson, John. 1990. What Washington Means by Policy Reform. In *Latin American Adjustment: How Much Has Happened*, ed. John Williamson. Washington, DC: Institute for International Economics.

———. 2000. What Should the World Bank Think About the Washington Consensus? *World Bank Research Observer*, August.

World Bank. 2005a. *World Development Indicators*. Electronic Database. Washington, DC: The World Bank.

———. 2005b. *Economic Growth in the 1990s: Learning from a Decade of Reform*. Washington, DC: The World Bank.

World Trade Organization (WTO). 1997. Trade Policy Review—Chile—Report by the Secretariat. Geneva: World Trade Organization.

Yatchew, Adonis. 2003. *Semiparametric Regression for the Applied Econometrician*. Cambridge: Cambridge University Press.

CHAPTER FOUR

More Market or More State for Latin America? A Reflection for the Post-Crisis

ALEJANDRO FOXLEY

INTRODUCTION

The recent global financial crisis has triggered, among other issues, an old discussion about the role of the market and the state in modern open globalized economies. It is obvious now that market failures have contributed considerably to the financial turmoil and current global recession. It is also an established fact that regulatory agencies failed in detecting imbalances and high systemic risks in the financial sector and that these failures have had a devastating effect on the real economy throughout the world. In this sense one can talk of both a market failure and a state failure.

This has opened the ground for a heated debate, with marked ideological undertones, about what the role of the state should be in the future to prevent new financial shocks of the magnitude present since 2007, and of what role free markets should play in a post-crisis scenario. This type of discussion has been going on in Latin America for decades. Every time the region suffers the consequences of an external shock, and there have been five such episodes since 1980, some blame unregulated markets. Others point to a state that has proved incapable of designing adequate policies or institutions to neutralize the negative impact of external shocks in output, employment, and social welfare.

In a striking reference to this predicament of the state in Latin America in this first decade of the twenty-first century, policymakers gathered at a meeting of the Economic Commission for Latin America and the Caribbean (ECLAC) referred to the state in Latin America as being—rather than a "welfare state"—an "ill-fare state." The remark was all the more disappointing because this erosion of state capacity occurred after a period—the first half of the 1990s—that had awakened great hopes: the structural reforms of the 1980s finally seemed to be bearing fruit, and the region at last seemed headed toward sustained economic growth.

However, the Asian crisis of the late 1990s and its damaging repercussions in Latin America ended those hopes. The pessimistic mindset that, in this region, "things don't last" took root with particular tenacity and was reinforced by heightened skepticism among the public about the efficacy of the weakening of governments that had been elected through free and fair democratic processes.

This very same process repeated itself in the 2000s. The first half of the decade showed strong growth, poverty reduction, lower inflation, and solid public finances for the region. This trend was interrupted by the global financial crisis that began in 2007. As a consequence, the deep recession and high unemployment again created a pessimistic mood through Latin America.

Thus the long-standing debate over formulas chosen to transform economies has been reopened. Some have argued that the reforms of the 1980s had a neoliberal, pro-market slant. They blamed these reforms for increasing inequalities in the region, for low investment, and consequently, for the fragility of the political systems. In this interpretation, what was needed was a stronger, more powerful state.

Others advocated the opposite view: the reforms of the 1980s had been timid and incomplete. A "second generation" of reforms was never taken up, and "third generation" reforms barely succeeded in being implemented in two or three countries in the region. A permanent fixture of these frustrated reforms was said to be a stubborn inability to tackle the modernization of the state by reducing its size and focusing its efforts on more limited tasks. According to this version, what was needed was more market and less state.

If something positive came out of the 1990s and again of most of the 2000s, it was a whole set of new approaches to transforming economies by implementing a wide range of innovative economic and social policies that had not been carried out in earlier decades. In light of the very negative consequences of the current crisis, the temptation is to discard these new approaches altogether and once again start from scratch.

My bias is the opposite. I argue that it is possible to learn from the successes and mistakes of economic policies of the last twenty years, to draw lessons and apply them cumulatively and gradually to present-day conditions. The rich experiences of the past two decades constitute a wealth of social capital residing in the actors of domestic and international development. This capital can be drawn upon to elaborate a more robust and more comprehensive road map of what must be done to achieve growth similar to that experienced by the Asian economies: self-sustaining, with fewer inequalities, and a greater capacity for innovation. At the heart of this challenge lies a critical examination of the changing role of the state and the market in Latin America's recent experience.

From the 1950s to the 2000s

The three decades from the 1950s through the 1970s can be characterized as years of "more state" in Latin America. The state was an active agent of development during this period, through industrial policy, heavy investments in infrastructure and basic industries such as steel and energy, along with increased investments in education and public health.

This phase in the development of the region succeeded in stimulating economic growth, which was plainly greater than what would be seen afterwards, in the 1980s and 1990s. However, the paradigm of import substitution and protecting national industry worked better in larger economies such as Brazil and Mexico. In the rest of the region, an initial dynamism was lost mainly due to the limited scale of smaller internal markets (Muñoz 2001).

In the 1970s, ECLAC pointed the way for a transition to a gradual opening of the economies of the region, and for their eventual integration into a common market; it also proposed boosting production through a set of stimuli from the state that would focus on small and mid-sized companies characterized by lower productivity. Through such means, ECLAC sought to reduce the structural heterogeneity and inefficiencies characteristic of Latin American economies (Torres 2007).

Subsequently, the reforms of the 1980s were introduced, driven by the debt crisis, by the need to adapt the region's economies to the globalization process, and also by a powerful pro-free market ideological offensive launched by the governments of Reagan and Thatcher and their counterparts in Latin America. By this time, the state was identified as the problem, and the market as the solution. As a consequence, state companies were privatized, markets were deregulated, and external tariffs summarily reduced (Ffrench-Davis 2005).

The debt crisis of the 1980s forced successive financial adjustments that resulted in severely weakening the ability of the state to act. Public investment was adversely affected, and resources for social protection were drastically reduced. The civil service suffered salary cuts, which in some instances transformed the civil service into a defenseless and paralyzed bureaucracy. For many civil servants, the dictum of "real socialism" became a reality: "We pretend to work, and the state pretends to pay us."

This situation was exacerbated when macroeconomic policies of automatic free market adjustment were put into effect. The most lethal combination was a sudden opening of the capital account, accompanied by fixed exchange rates. Chile, Mexico, and Argentina adopted this combination with catastrophic results: over-indebtedness of the state and the private sector, macro-devaluations, recession, high unemployment, business failures, and social crisis.[1] In the end, these economic results were accompanied by the inevitable political consequences: a commensurate weakening of political institutions, rotating governments, a crisis of the party system, and a lack of confidence in democracy where it had previously existed.

However, we need to understand the reforms of the 1980s from a perspective broader than that of the financial crises fueled by mistaken macroeconomic policies. The opening of domestic economies triggered a powerful export dynamism and compelled increased efficiency and productivity in a significant segment of the productive apparatus. The state gave up activities it was carrying out poorly and that were absorbing resources that could be earmarked instead for social priorities or modernizing the infrastructure. Dormant entrepreneurial capacity was reactivated. Accompanied by a favorable external environment, the 1990s underscored the positive results of these changes that were met with vigorous growth, unfortunately interrupted by a new external shock, the Asian crisis.[2]

To attribute a low growth rate solely to the effects of external shocks and mistaken macroeconomic policies,would be to provide only a partial and incomplete explanation. A fuller explanation must include a discussion of institutional factors. As an Inter-American Development Bank (IDB) document (2003) put it: "In the region there is as much a deficit of the State as there is of the market."

I argue that a more integrated vision is required, one in which new areas and tasks for both the market and the state are laid out in light of the successes and failures of public policy in the 1990s and 2000s, and also in view of the new circumstances posed by deepening globalization. I will attempt to articulate this integrated vision in the remainder of this chapter.

More Market?

In Latin America today, the idea predominates that we have relied too heavily on the market, and that this overreliance is the source of the dysfunctions displayed by the region's economies.

To determine whether or not there is an excessive reliance on the market, it might be useful to begin by outlining the essential, irreplaceable role played by the market, and how, when, and where it should be placed in a subsidiary role. Conversely, it would be useful to delineate the set of required roles that must ultimately be played by the state. The principal role of the market is to induce competition: that is, to encourage a more efficient economy that allocates scarce resources better, reduces costs, and evolves constantly in order to find new opportunities for production and export.

Latin American economies have advanced substantially in the direction of greater reliance on the market, deregulation, and reducing external tariffs. The unilateral opening of economies has been reinforced by a network of bilateral and multilateral free trade agreements and by ambitious agreements on subregional economic integration (Inter-American Development Bank 2002). Hemispheric Free Trade Agreements (FTAA) appeared to be the next logical step, as a way for Latin American producers to gain access to U.S. and Canadian markets. The prospect of such access would allow the region to contemplate new scales of production and investment, and to consider comparative advantages when confronted with the challenge of competing with more productive economies (Da Motta and Rios 2009).

The resistance within some North American producer groups to giving up massive state subsidies, particularly in the agricultural sector, reduced the U.S. government's room for maneuver amidst trade negotiations of an FTAA. North American proposals for trade liberalization avoided the most substantive matters (protection of agriculture and antidumping legislation) and were limited to offering modest and gradual reductions of tariffs for items on which the initial tariffs were already low and in some cases insignificant. It should be no surprise then that "FTAA lite" was met with disinterest among the major countries in the region, such as Brazil and Argentina (Foxley 2002).

Most Latin American governments have been active and constructive participants in the Doha round of Multilateral Trade Liberalization. This reflects a conviction that more market and more open markets would benefit their economies. The failure of the WTO negotiations gave new impulse to the notion of market integration within the Latin American region. A proliferation of sub-regional groups such as Mercosur, CAN,

CAFTA, and more recently UNASUR have provided the space for "more market" within the region. But progress has been slow, and the current financial crisis and recession have provided the excuse for some countries to resort, once again, to protecting their own domestic markets. In some cases, this has been accompanied by a new version of old populist, nationalist, pro-state, and anti-market rhetoric.

Latin America has not yet learned to profit from another dimension of opportunities offered by what Enrique Iglesias called "the second floor of the world economy": that is, the markets of India and China. Latin America has yet to develop a strategic orientation toward these new Asian markets. The countries that have done so in the recent past, such as Australia and New Zealand, and which are also exporters of natural resources, have expanded their growth potential in the medium term, and are less affected by the global economic downturn. Australian goods are still in high demand in China, whose economy in the midst of the crisis in 2009, is still growing at close to 7 percent.

The region also needs a greater reliance on the market through public-private partnerships in order to provide better-quality health and educational services to low and middle-income sectors heretofore excluded from quality services in these areas. The relatively low tax burden in Latin America imposes severe limitations for providing quality public services. The demand for higher quality increases with income. The dilemma is simple: either raise taxes to satisfy the demand, or open up the provision of services to the private sector, with an adequate mechanism of subsidies so as to achieve universal coverage for the lowest income sectors.[3] I will address this in more detail later.

Some Latin American countries are also expanding the role of the market by opening a system of concessions to the private sector, to carry out public works projects such as highways, ports, and airports. Chile has even initiated an experimental program of turning over to the private sector the building and running of prisons. The outcomes of this policy of granting concessions to the private sector have been mixed. A few cases have resulted in resounding failures, forcing the state to resume its role as provider. Still, it is premature to draw a definitive conclusion. What *is* clear is that private concessions make it possible to proceed with investments that the state cannot undertake, given the limited public resources available. The private sector responds rapidly and vigorously when incentives to investment are well designed (Engel, Fischer, and Galetovic 1996, 2001; Vivallos 2003).

Two sectors of the Latin American population cannot take advantage of the opportunities provided by greater market access: poor farmers, who, because of an inadequate or nonexistent transportation infrastructure cannot bring their products to the market; and small businesses that see market access for their products held back because they are unable to regularize their property rights and use them as credit guarantees, as argued by Hernando de Soto (1989, 2006).

Besides more reliance on the market, Latin America needs more competition in key markets that were deregulated or privatized and that show clear monopolistic or oligopolistic tendencies. This occurs in some countries in the fields of energy, telecommunications, and other services, where the rates charged sometimes reflect a concentrated market structure that extracts monopolistic rents from users. When one or two powerful companies confront the state periodically because their fate depends on decisions about rates, monopolistic power expresses itself by pressuring the judicial or political systems, seeking to reverse allegedly arbitrary rulings of the regulatory agency. Unnecessary recourse to the judiciary paralyzes investment. Pressure is also commonly brought to bear on the political establishment and leads to corruption. Such tactics impair the effectiveness and transparency of public decisions in a democracy. Recent experiences in Latin America poignantly illustrate what happens when transparent and reliable regulatory guidelines are not enforced equally for all. Other recent experiences show that the absence of competition among providers renders even the best regulatory guidelines ineffective (Tavares de Araujo Junior 2003; Lapuerta, Benavides, and Jorge 2003; Troya-Martínez 2006; Hilke 2006).

Latin American policymakers need to learn quickly about best practices in regulation and about legislation that has proven effective in other countries, leading to more competition in regulated sectors that provide basic services. The region also needs to promote the training of highly qualified and well-paid technical personnel from the state regulatory agencies to ensure that there is competition and predictability in the rules applying to recently privatized activities.

The experience with regulation of the financial sector in Latin America has, surprisingly, been rather positive, particularly when compared with the performance of banks and the non-bank financial sector of the developed economies during the current financial meltdown. Latin American government and legislators seem to have learned from past financial shocks. Their banks and other financial institutions did not engage, to any significant degree, in the opaque, unregulated markets of derivations, hedge funds, and credit default swaps that lie behind the collapse of financial markets in most developed economies. Their regulatory framework was significantly improved after their own experience with financial collapse in the 1980s. Thus, a note of caution must accompany the suggestion of learning from "best practices" in regulatory norms of more developed economies. It seems that domestic experience in handling financial bubbles and crises is more likely to generate adequate regulation, than importing formulas from abroad.

More State?

The "ill-fare state" of Latin America is connected principally with two notions. The first is that globalization increases economic insecurity, undermines social cohesion, and accentuates income inequality and opportunity. The second has to do with the growing precariousness of the job market. Open markets and the resulting vulnerability to external shocks supposedly make the employment situation more unstable and uncertain.

It is almost futile to engage in these arguments, for they constitute deeply held sentiments that permeate the world of politics in Latin America. Some argue that these consequences are transitory or that they might fade away with more deregulation of the economy and the promotion of new liberalizing reforms.

My focus is different. It is imperative to reconceptualize the role of the state during the next stage of Latin American development. The issue is not more state or less, but a different kind of state: a state that provides new and more effective responses to economic insecurity, insufficient job creation, and the precarious and temporary nature of many jobs. The challenge consists first of all in refocusing the role of the state so the economy can create new, better quality jobs; second, in conceiving a welfare state adapted to the new reality.

THE STATE: A CATALYST FOR DEVELOPMENT

During the phase of import substitution, the state played multiple roles in Latin American development. It was at the same time a regulatory state, an entrepreneurial state, and an agent of development that actively promoted industrialization through subsidies, tax incentives, and tariff protection.

In its first stage, this strategy was widely successful, generating strong growth in the region. It furnished a sustainable industrial base for large countries such as Brazil and Mexico, and to some extent Argentina. On the other hand, in countries with limited domestic markets, the state provided too much stimulus to an artificial, noncompetitive industry that did not withstand the battering it received from the greater interdependence that resulted from the global markets of the 1980s (Muñoz 2001).

The dilemma was particularly acute for medium- and small-sized countries, those in the Andes and Central America. The opening of their economies exposed a productive and export structure based almost entirely on natural resources. The problem is that empirical evidence indicates it is unlikely that countries can achieve sustainable development for several decades without first having diversified their productive structure, adding value and technology to their natural resources or entering into competitive production of exportable manufactured goods or services.[4]

In fact, Sachs, Larraín, and Warner suggest that the greater the concentration on natural resources, the less an economy tends to grow in the long run (1999). In addition, in such cases growth rates tend to be more volatile, with marked boom and bust cycles reflecting strong unpredictable fluctuations in the price of commodities, in the terms of trade, and in the region's capital income and expenditures (Rodrik 1999). This suggests that a traditional developmental state has a greater chance for success in the large economies of the region, such as Mexico and Brazil, than in the small ones.

This conclusion, however, has to be placed in the context of the new conditions prevailing in the global economy. Technological change has advanced at a dizzying pace, the life cycle of new products grows shorter and shorter, and the globalized markets are more volatile, as are the preferences and demands of consumers. Today, the kinds of products and services that are called for are based increasingly on knowledge and new ideas rather than on physical capital and natural resources. By definition, the generation of knowledge and ideas proceeds at different velocities, according to whether countries have or have not created the robust institutional framework that generates and utilizes knowledge from a wide variety of sources, including governmental applied research centers, private industry, customers, suppliers, a company's employees, and new potential entrepreneurs (Cooke and Morgan 2000).

Knowledge can be applied to natural resources, manufactured goods, or services. The value added by knowledge-based innovations makes it possible to diversify the composition of production (and exports) starting either from natural resources or manufactures and services.

Nevertheless, problems of development cannot be solved by an entrepreneurial state on its own. We are dealing with a complex process of collective learning in an uncertain world and in uncertain markets. Nor does the unfettered market envisioned by neoclassical theory generate, all by itself, sufficient information and knowledge to anticipate trends and compete successfully against others in global competition. It is not a matter of discovering a "silver bullet," but of forming networks that make it possible to develop a country's resources to the fullest potential through cooperation among companies, research centers, universities, public agencies, and regional and local governments (de Ferranti et al. 2002).

In short, the new demands posed by global competitiveness do not mean dismantling the state, nor increasing its size, but restructuring and fine-tuning it for a new kind of function as something like a catalyst for development. For New Zealanders, this takes the form of imagining the state as a "light rain" that produces a green pasture that invites others to sow seeds in its newly inviting environment (OECD 2003).

A superficial glance at the structures inherited for competing successfully in a knowledge society raises a red flag. Studies of leading private companies in some countries of the region reveal structures of family ownership, with a vertical and hierarchical internal organization marked by practices that are routine and repetitive. The watchword would seem to be, "doing more of the same can't hurt us." These organizations display a reluctance to dedicate resources to research and development that could result in new products, processes, and markets. Nor do they spend significant amounts on retraining personnel. They do not see learning to learn as a priority for their workers. So it is not surprising that the limited research and development undertaken in Latin America is generally carried out by public institutions and to a lesser extent by university centers that often have little connection with commercial enterprises and their drive for innovation (Benavente 2009).

Moreover, systems of industrial promotion are often fragmented and lack coordination with each other. We are dealing with superimposed layers of institutions and programs generated during different phases of development, beginning in the 1950s. In Chile, for example, there are more than one hundred government programs for promoting industry, agricultural development, small producers and farmers, and small and medium-sized businesses. The cumulative effect of these programs is barely noticeable.

They are dispersed, they duplicate efforts, and they are easy prey for a limited clientele that survives by having access time after time to the same benefits, without these benefits generating innovations in production and technology or increased productivity. Accordingly, restructuring state institutions to meet the demands of a "knowledge economy" as a basis for competing globally is an essential and urgent task.

State and the Knowledge Economy

The countries most successful at boosting their productivity and growth in the last two decades are constantly evaluating progress in reforming the state's institutions for development, adjusting designs, adopting better practices from other countries, and interacting constantly with users. These matters have a permanent place in the public agenda in Australia, New Zealand, Ireland, Finland, Korea, and other Asian countries, to mention some of the most successful experiments of the 1980s and 1990s (Yusuf 2003; Castells and Himanen 2002; Nieuwenhuysen, Lloyd, and Mead 2001; Foxley 2009).

More than two decades ago, Peter Evans, Dietrich Rueschemeyer, and Theda Skocpol published a book entitled *Bringing the State Back In* (1985). Their work stressed that despite assertions that the state had retreated, it was still taking in and distributing a third to half of the GDP in the developed capitalist countries. For the present Latin American economic situation, the title of their book remains relevant.

Let us illustrate with one example. Free trade agreements have paved the way for access to new markets, but they do not ensure that the economies that subscribe to an FTA can generate product innovation, new production methods, or permanent increases in factor productivity, all of which determine the ability to compete in these new markets. It is almost a cliché to state that technological change and globalization require advanced training for a knowledge society, and that such a society requires economic institutions and agents coordinated through networks that in some particularly successful countries combine to form a national system of innovation (de Ferranti et al. 2003).

We are not referring to arcane theoretical approaches—research done at a desk. My experience in public service studying the processes of generating ideas, mobilizing resources, and redesigning public institutions in small open market economies successful at globalization—Finland, Estonia, Ireland, Australia, New Zealand—gives us some sense of the importance of the state's "return" to promoting development. In this context, it is not a matter of protecting industries, but of helping them promote steady, permanent increases in economic productivity.

The experiences mentioned above point to certain characteristics of state activity worthy of mention. Faced with an international division of labor in constant flux, the state has to promote a process of permanent and continuous national learning with respect to changes and trends in the world markets. Quality of education, which the state must protect and guarantee, constitutes the key to survival in a constantly changing world economy. Education is the number one priority. Quality education, sustained for decades and led by the state, explains the high growth rates over the last two decades experienced by countries such as Ireland and Finland (Aho, Pitkanen, and Sahlberg 2006; Ferreira and Vanhoudt 2004; Bergin and Kearney 2004).

In the global economy, nobody survives by going it alone. Cooperation between public and private agents, and between companies, universities and regional governments, is one of the keys to new ideas, technologies, designs, and of joint access to large-scale markets. This is the essential rule of the knowledge economy: networking, sharing ideas, learning to work as a team. This principle is valid at the level of a national development strategy, on the local level, and within private industry.

The notion of "stakeholders" is pertinent here: that is, all those who share a common interest in developing new products and markets, in innovating and incorporating new technologies and lines of production, must be engaged in the network. Cooperation between stakeholders replaces the concept of the individual entrepreneur facing a static market. The purpose of strategic dialogues among stakeholders is to share a vision of the future (Foxley 2009).

With regard to key sectors and regions, it is essential to formulate questions about where those involved want to be in the future, about what others are doing, and about how to improve institutions in order to compete globally. "What kind of Finland 2020 do we want?" the top executives of that country asked themselves during a three-week collective exercise that began in China, continued in California, and culminated with a group meeting in Helsinki. Their conclusion: "We are going to work together to achieve number one status as the 2020 Welfare and Knowledge Society." In other countries, leaders are asking how the state can catalyze an effort to promote innovation in areas such as biotechnology, biomaterials, basic foods, and organic foods; and they are also asking how to detect new niches in international markets at the right time. These processes are stimulated by a "light rain" that originates in public agencies working in collaboration with research centers and private industry. Countries such as Ireland, Finland, and Australia have created instances for stakeholders' dialogue embedded in a modern and transparent state. The state facilitates the process for the relevant social actors coming together to develop a common national vision in key public policy areas.

If half the difference in per capita income is explained by an increase in total factor productivity, that is, by capacity for innovation and technical development, it is essential to ask how the state can join in this process through public institutions coordinated in a national innovation effort. The experience of countries such as Finland, Australia, and New Zealand underscores the potential value of creating national, regional, and local funds for innovation, made up initially of public resources. The money, in their experience, is allocated as grants—matched by private resources—intended for research and development to be undertaken by private industry, universities, and applied research centers. These funds are used with the criterion of rewarding partnerships between academic institutions and private enterprise, which would include networking with advanced technology research centers in other countries.

The state enters the picture again: facilitating access to capital for new entrepreneurs, attracting foreign direct investment, stimulating the creation of productive clusters, and facilitating the transfer of knowledge.

The nonexistence of a network of institutions providing capital for the different stages of a new business is an impediment to widening the base of entrepreneurial capacity in Latin American countries, in contrast with the successful innovative experiments of Korea, Israel, Finland, Ireland, New Zealand, and Australia.

The state has a central role to play in designing incentives to attract *foreign direct investment* in nontraditional categories that bring in new technological developments, new skills, and new markets. Ireland was especially successful in developing such a strategy in the 1980s through generous tax incentives that turned it into a platform for North American information technology companies operating in the European market.

The state also can contribute to stimulate the creation of *productive clusters* in local communities and regions. Regions have to identify what they can specialize in and what their strengths and weaknesses are in order to compete successfully in specific niches of the international economy. Using public funds to promote partnership at this level has also proven to be a powerful instrument for promoting innovative economies at the local level through the formation of clusters (Cooke and Morgan 2000). Another joint task for the public and private entities of each region is to design a plan—suited to the comparative advantages of the region—for improving the qualifications of its work force.

The state also has to play the role of advance guard in *internationalizing the processes of generating new knowledge and ideas* that will ultimately produce wealth for a country. Entering into partnerships with top-quality research centers in more advanced economies, participating in international capital risk funds to learn their best practices, providing educational exchanges on a large scale, especially at the graduate level, promoting the study of English and are only some of the tasks essential to successful competition in a globalized world with open economies.

THE STATE: A CATALYST FOR SOCIAL PROTECTION

Besides bringing actors together, providing the right incentives, and developing good regulations and control mechanisms, a modern state should contribute to improving the declining welfare systems of Latin America and advancing toward a welfare society in which the public and private sectors participate in the national welfare systems.

The Latin American countries with more advanced welfare states established them in the 1960s and 1970s, modeling them on the institutions developed by European countries after World War II as mechanisms of social protection. We are thinking especially of the Southern Cone countries, Costa Rica, and Colombia.

European social democracies understood social protection for workers as revolving around the workplace (Esping-Andersen et al. 2002). In the prosperous 1960s and 1970s, Europeans enjoyed job stability and strong economic growth. Unions sought to perpetuate the situation by protecting existing jobs through legal impediments for laying off workers or imposing high costs for companies that do so. In some countries it was even necessary to have union approval before a worker could be laid off. Also, negotiating salaries by sector or occupational type came into existence. The idea was for workers in high and low productivity companies to show solidarity and negotiate salaries jointly, which tended to reduce differences in income among the two groups.

The social protection system was characterized by generous retirement benefits (it is estimated that, in Italy, after basic needs are met, pensions generate a 30 percent surplus, which are then used to sustain an informal family support network[5]), unemployment insurance, and universal coverage extended to provide education and health care.

This kind of welfare state required the population to accept a high tax burden, typically more than double that prevailing in Latin American countries. The European middle classes accepted that burden because they were receiving the obvious benefits of social protection against unforeseen events, and because they had access to universal coverage for education and health care, often free and of equal quality for different socioeconomic strata. Added to all this was job stability for the head of the household.

With globalization, these favorable circumstances began to change. The first signs of change in these countries were seen in the nature of work and employment (Ferrera, Hemerijck, and Rhodes 2001). The need to adapt constantly to the changing conditions of world markets led to a high rate of job turnover. Willingly or unwillingly people left their jobs and sought new employment. Temporary and part-time work became more widespread. International financial shocks created cycles of employment and unemployment, often punctuated by long periods of searching for a new stable job. In some countries (Great Britain, Finland, Spain), a worker who has not completed high school will take an average of seven years to find a new permanent job after successive episodes of being unemployed or holding temporary short term jobs. The average for such unemployment in Germany, France, Sweden, and Belgium is between three and five years, according to OECD estimates (Esping-Andersen 2001). In the meantime, the long-term unemployed migrate between countless temporary or part-time jobs.

These profound changes in the nature of employment led to a breakdown in the traditional mechanisms of protection. The welfare state protects the "insiders": that is, workers with permanent jobs in traditional enterprises, including public sector companies and the civil service. This labor force makes up the core of the membership of union federations and confederations. These organizations defend a status quo that actually deprives those in the new mobile work force—gradually becoming a majority—of the benefits won by union members. This situation creates a crisis for the traditional welfare state and consequently weakens unions. A second issue pertains to the changing family structure and the resulting changes in the household economy. The number of married couples is decreasing and the number of single parent households is growing. A large number of female heads of households remain unprotected, as do their children. These households are especially vulnerable to the economic cycle: their economic insecurity is growing, and child poverty is being exacerbated.

The aforementioned factors, plus demographic changes and growing costs, explain the crisis of the European welfare states and the initiatives they have taken—the success of which varies from country to country—to adapt to the new conditions and characteristics of employment and of the household economy brought about by globalization. These states are forced to adopt a less onerous tax burden more compatible with stimulating employment and investment (Gilbert and Van Voorhis 2003).

Why this digression on welfare states established by European social democracies? The subject is relevant because in the period of import substitution, Latin America tried to copy the institutions that gave rise to this type of welfare state. But from the start, there was an imbalance between the welfare state that was being transplanted, and the unique labor market and character of the family in Latin America. It was wishful thinking to consider the work force of the 1960s and 1970s as homogeneous, with stable jobs and strong union organization as was the case in Europe (Ramos 2003). Nor was there a consolidated family structure with a head of household who was the breadwinner, with a stable job and income protected by his or her labor union, as was the case in Western Europe in the 1960s and 1970s when these countries designed their welfare states. In those decades in Latin America there was already a predominance of self-employed workers and individuals with temporary or sporadic jobs, combined with high unemployment among women and young people. Wage agreements, welfare programs, and social security arrangements followed the European model. They were directed toward the permanent and organized workers in the public sector, state enterprises, and a few big private companies, but they left the rest of the labor force without adequate coverage.

When we add to the above the high incidence of families headed by a female (one out of every four in Chile), it is easy to understand the gap between traditional European-type mechanisms of social protection, and the reality of jobs and households in Latin America. By way of illustration, in Chile only one out of five women in the quintile of lowest income has access to a job (often temporary or precarious) while in the top quintile the ratio is one out of two, despite notable progress in reducing poverty during the 1990s (Foxley 2003a, 2003b). The unemployment rate for women in the lowest quintile is several times higher than for those in the top quintile, which has the greatest job protection. This gap between the design of social protection networks and the reality of a heterogeneous, unprotected labor market is at the root of the malaise or "state of ill-fare" permeating Latin American societies.

Herein also lies the source of many inequalities. Take education, for example. Over several decades Latin American countries have tried to extend the coverage of their public education systems following the European model. These efforts have resulted in reforms intended to improve the quality of primary and secondary education (Puryear and Brunner 1995). However, when measured by achievement tests, the data show enormous disparities in performance according to socioeconomic strata, with stagnation in the lowest income segments (Cox 2003).

Such findings illustrate the need to refocus the welfare state in Latin America. The equalization of opportunity through the education system, which would mean equal access to good jobs for all young people regardless of socioeconomic background, will not occur as long as the following empirical data are not taken into account. A child's cognitive ability is largely determined between birth and the age of five. Children in the lowest income households live in a home environment characterized by economic insecurity and traumatic episodes—whether emotional or involving sheer survival—made worse by the economic shocks that Latin American economies suffer frequently (Rackzynski, Serrano, and Valle 2002). The first blow struck by economic crisis is often the unemployment of the head of the household. The mother really has no access to employment while her children are of preschool or school age. This, in turn, is the result of three deficiencies in Latin American social policies: overly rigid work rules that make it hard for women to obtain part-time jobs; the nonexistence of effective training programs for female heads of household, and an inadequate system of providing for children between the ages of one to five in preschool day care centers, kindergartens, and nurseries.

At the outset, the Scandinavian countries, Denmark most notably, turned their welfare states toward the creation of equal opportunity. They established a system of universal child-care coverage for the critical first five years of life, with highly qualified caregivers to stimulate their charges' social and cognitive development. Along with this, labor regulations were changed, making it possible for 75 percent of female heads of household to hold permanent part-time jobs (Ferrera, Hemerijck, and Rhodes 2001).

The above examples make it easy to understand why in the area of social protection we need more and a better state, refocused on the vulnerabilities that the lowest income sectors in Latin America face and which globalization seems to exacerbate.

In short, the state, labor unions and other actors involved in the labor markets have to face the dilemma once and for all: the institutions of the welfare system and the respective mechanisms of social participation and dialogue must be redesigned to include the "outsiders," who are the majority, and not just the "insiders," who are the workers and employees of the modern organized sector. Social cohesion must be strengthened by addressing the root cause of inequality, that is, the situation of women and children in the most vulnerable households of the low income sectors.

Private Partnership for Social Protection

In this context, in order to promote better social protection in Latin America, it is of utmost importance that a redesign of the welfare state include a re-examination of public-private partnerships and the possibility of more active participation of the private sector in providing basic social services. In many European countries, the success of state-provided universal coverage for basic services was made possible by the high tax burden prevailing in those countries, something not achievable for Latin American countries, at least not in a reasonably short period of time.

This is not, however, the only type of welfare state that prevails in developed countries. In the United States, contrary to what is usually claimed, access to basic services and social protection plans is not significantly different from that which exists in continental Europe. The difference is that in Anglo-Saxon countries a significant proportion of these services is provided by private entities and paid for out of the family budget. The tax burden is significantly less than in continental Europe, but the final cost for families is similar, as Table 4.1 shows.

The problem, a source of frustration in Latin America, is that the region designed its welfare state institutions in the European style, but with a tax base even below that of the United States measured as a percentage of GDP. As a result, universal coverage for basic services has not been achieved. These services are often underfunded, and the civil servants who manage them are poorly paid and have no incentive to improve the coverage and quality of the services they render.

The obvious question is: Why not embrace the European option in its entirety and raise the tax rate in Latin America to the levels of France, Germany, and the Scandinavian countries? There are three reasons for not doing do so. First, the institutional apparatus for collecting taxes is deficient, particularly when it comes to curbing tax evasion. In practice, the major tax burden falls on the middle sectors of workers with stable employment. These sectors, unlike their European counterparts, resist higher taxes because, in addition to being the main steady taxpayers, they do not experience—contrary to the case in northern Europe—the tangible benefits that higher taxes bring in terms of universal health care, free quality education, and protection from economic shocks such as prolonged unemployment and other catastrophic events.

Secondly, high-income groups are politically opposed to raising taxes. They exercise their influence through many channels, including powerful lobbies in national legislatures, whose representatives often depend on the financial contributions of these well-off business sectors for their re-election.

A third reason is the greater relative weakness of Latin America when it comes to competing effectively with the countries of Asia, Central Europe, and Oceania in attracting foreign capital, particularly in cutting-edge activities of greater technological sophistication. Given Latin America's political instability and unpredictability concerning the rules of the game for foreign investors, the region has had to accept smaller tax burdens than those of the developed countries, and even of stable Asian developing countries.

The way out of this vicious circle is to develop a new relationship between the state and the private sector, and to modernize the state accordingly. The state would concentrate on the essential tasks of attacking extreme poverty and reducing inequality, and providing the incentives and regulations to foster public-private cooperation. The private sector would assume the task of providing some of the basic services previously provided by the state. Deep state reform is necessary for this public-private partnership to work. The goal of the reform would be that of strengthening transparent, predictable public institutions that develop effective socio-economic policies. Such reform, however, takes time and requires a high degree of political consensus, which at the beginning of the reform process is often missing.

TABLE 4.1
Public and Private Spending on Social Protection

As Percent of GDP

	Sweden		U.S.	
	1990[a]	2001[b]	1990[a]	2001[b]
Public social spending	33.1	34.1	14.6	15.7
Tax spending	0.0	0.0	1.3	2.3
Private spending education	0.1	0.2	2.5	2.1
Private spending health	1.1	1.3	8.2	8.1
Private spending pensions	1.8	2.1	3.0	4.7
Total spending on social protection	**35.5**	**37.7**	**29.6**	**32.9**

As Percent of Household Spending

	Sweden	U.S.
	1990[a]	1990[a]
Private spending on education, health, pensions	2.7	18.8
Spending for day care	1.7	10.4
Total private spending (percent of household expenses)	4.4	29.2
Taxes	36.8	10.4
Private spending plus taxes	41.2	39.6

Note: The numbers for Sweden 1990 for spending on social protection as a percentage of GDP add up to 36.1% in the original source.
Source: [a]Esping-Andersen 1999, p. 177; [b]OECD Social Indicators 2005, Education at a Glance 2004: OECD Indicators.

Chile is one of the countries in Latin America that has made substantial progress in this direction, as is shown in Table 4.2. National social spending when we include privately financed social spending, is not significantly lower than that in some developed countries. Chile's 26% of GDP is close to the 32.9% noted for the United States in Table 4.1.

This path, however, brings with it new questions and new challenges. Basic services provided by private entities tend to cost considerably more than those provided by the state. Also, their quality is generally higher. But if access is not made equal and independent of the ability to pay,

TABLE 4.2

National Social Spending Chile, 1990, 2001, and 2005

As Percent of GDP

		1990[a]	2001[a]	2005[b]
1. Health	Public	1.9	2.7[c]	2.6[c]
	Private	2.2	3.1[c]	3.2[c]
	Total	4.1	5.8c	5.8c
2. Housing	Public	0.9	0.9	1.0
	Private	3.8	3.5	4.5[d]
	Total	4.7	4.4	5.5
3. Social Security	Public	5.6	5.4	4.8
	Private	0.4	1.4	1.8[e]
	Total	6.0	6.7	6.6
4. Education	Public	2.4	4.1	3.8
	Private	1.6	3.2	3.1
	Total	4.0	7.3	6.9
5. Subsidies	Public	0.6	0.6	0.7
	Private	0.0	0.0	0.0
	Total	0.6	0.6	0.5
6. Other social spending	Public	0.5	1.0	1.1
	Private	0.0	0.0	0.0
	Total	0.5	1.0	1.1
TOTAL	Public	11.9	14.8	14.2
	Private	7.9	11.8	11.8
	Total	19.9	26.6	26.0

Source: [a]Arellano 2005; [b]DIPRES 2005. Public Finance Statistics 1996–2005, (www.dipres.cl/publicaciones/finanzas.asp); [c]World Bank, Human Development Indicators 2005; [d]Central Bank of Chile 2007. National Accounts of Chile 2003–2006 (www.bcentral.cl/publicaciones/estadisticas/actividad-economica-gasto/aego1c.htm); [e]Superintendency of Pension Fund Administrators, (www.safp.cl/safpstats/stats).

these privately provided services could turn into a source of increasing inequality. A complete re-engineering of state subsidies to focus on those segments of the population unable to pay for services provided privately would have to be an essential component of this approach.

Incentives and competition among private sector providers of basic social services are essential to reduce the cost for users of these services. Another component would consist of regulating these privately provided benefits effectively as to quality and access, along with ensuring their design so as not to discriminate against any social sector, least of all the lowest income groups. The process we describe here consists in moving from a welfare state to a welfare society, in which broadening the system of social protection would be a task shared by the state and a broad array of organizations from the private sector and civil society. This is a fascinating field for experimentation that might be accelerated and built up by international organizations to train personnel, disseminate better practices, and make available to Latin American countries institutional blueprints that have proven effective in other parts of the world.

CONCLUSION

One conclusion to be drawn from foregoing analysis is that the debate over the paths followed by Latin American countries over the past two decades has often been misguided. The meager results of the second half of the 1990s and again those present since the current global economic crisis, have ended in mostly fruitless discussions about whether the reforms were the right ones or whether they were, in fact, counterproductive. The "ill-fare state" has rejected the "Washington Consensus," and in the most radical version, it is opposed to globalization itself. At this juncture, the ground seems well-prepared for nostalgic visions of the past or even for the reappearance of the earlier but still popular populist-nationalist discourses, with authoritarian undertones.

The root of the malaise is to be found in the new vulnerabilities arising from globalization, which are particularly relevant given Latin America's history. There are profound changes in the nature of employment in the region, toward occupations that are not permanent or are part-time or occasional. Job turnover has accelerated. Changes in family structure are making single-parent households headed by women more common. The barriers women face in access to work make such households especially vulnerable. Child poverty is growing more acute and is becoming a hindrance to the ability to learn and consequently to the academic performance of children from low-income households. This is how poverty is perpetuated from generation to generation.

Accordingly, as this chapter contends, the first reformulation of the role of the state should consist of a new type of welfare society, in which policies easing access to work for women and other vulnerable groups are a priority, in addition to a pro-child social policy that emphasizes preschool years. This refocusing must also seek to extend coverage for basic social services, education, health, and housing, until it is universal. The limits of the fiscal capacity of the state in Latin America make it necessary to reexamine the role of the private sector in providing social services complementary to those of the state. Countries such as Chile have made significant progress in that direction.

It is still too early to evaluate the results of such policies. This is a new development for Latin America, and it should be closely monitored by international organizations, which can alert us to distortions (e.g., high costs that automatically exclude the lowest income groups, oligopolistic market trends), as well as make available the experiences of best practices in more advanced countries to those that are just initiating the reform of their institution charged with the provision of basic social services.

My answer, then, to the question of whether there should be more or less state is that what we need is a radical change in the way the state and its institutions function. The task ahead is transforming the state in order to provide new answers to the underlying problems created by "the ill-fare state" in Latin America.

Another angle of the same challenge consists of the need to create permanent jobs of good quality within the context of volatile global markets and financial fluctuations. This is the most difficult task. It requires making the transition from the notion of "development from the state" or "development from the market" toward a hybrid innovative economy and a knowledge based society. Nothing more, nothing less. This requires developing the capacity, from the state, to coordinate public-private efforts and connect them with institutions generating ideas and knowledge. We need to break down barriers between air-tight compartments: public institutions and private enterprise, universities, applied research centers, productive sectors, regions and their influence on global markets through clusters, international knowledge centers and their relations with countries' exporter industries. Breaking down barriers also involves opening up the formal education system to a new environment that leads to permanent learning.

The state as the catalyst of a knowledge economy ought to have an active role beyond negotiating free trade agreements on the international level. The states of Latin America ought to move on to building strategic alliances with countries that in the last two decades have succeeded at taking advantage of globalization by stimulating innovation as a basis for diversifying their productive structures. The examples are well known. Australia, Finland, Ireland, Israel, New Zealand, and Korea are among the most prominent. At some point during the last twenty years the leaders of each of these countries either saw their main markets collapse, or faced macroeconomic crises similar to those of Latin America. They turned away from the institutions of their "ill-fare states," and reinvented the state's way of relating to a variety of agents of development, creating instances for social dialogue that increased the level of cooperation among key social actors participating in the policymaking process. This is turn helped set in motion endogenous processes that increased productivity, innovation, and international competitiveness.

Such strategies fueled the creation of better quality jobs that in the end strengthened the cohesion of their societies. As a consequence, a new culture has emerged in those economies. Key strategic actors are not working alone but are networking. Cooperation and trust are cultivated. The acquisition of knowledge is rewarded. Public policies also change. Governments learn to encourage creativity and to foster entrepreneurial capability, like a "light rain" allowing new ideas to sprout. The transition to these new forms of the welfare state and new ways for the state to function can be facilitated by working with international organizations attentive to such developments in advanced countries, as well as by profiting from the rich experience of the processes of reform in Latin America over the last two decades.

Notes

The current version of this chapter was made possible with the generous support of and facilities at the Carnegie Endowment.

1.   These crises occurred at different moments in time: Chile in 1982, Mexico in 1994, and Argentina in 2001.

2.   For further descriptions, evaluations, and measurements of the reforms see World Bank (1997), IDB (1997), ECLAC (1998, 2002), Easterly, Loayza, and Montiel (1997), Edwards (1995), Kuczynski and Williamson (2003), Ocampo (2004), and Stallings and Peres (2000).

3.   For evaluations and measurements of the role of state in Latin America see Tanzi (2008).

4.   Exceptions to this rule are Brunei and Iceland, and possibly Norway.

5.   Esping-Andersen (1999).

References

Aho, Erkki, Kari Pitkanen, and Pasi Sahlberg. 2006. Policy Development and Reform Principles of Basic and Secondary Education in Finland since 1968. Education Working Paper Series 2 (May), World Bank, Washington, DC.

Arellano, José Pablo. 2004. *Políticas sociales para el crecimiento con equidad: Chile 1990–2002.* Series Estudios Socio-Económicos, CIEPLAN, Santiago, Chile.

Benavente, J.M. 2009. El desafio dela innovacíon para la América Latina de hoy. In *A Medio Camino. Nuevos desafíos de la democracia y del desarrollo en América Latina*, ed. Fernando Henrique Cardoso and Alejandro Foxley, 313–43. Santiago, Chile: Uqbar Editores.

Bergin, Adele, and Ide Kearney. 2004. Human Capital, the Labour Market and Productivity Growth in Ireland. Working Paper 158, ESRI (Economic and Social Research Institute), Dublin.

Castells, Manuel, and Pekka Himanen. 2002. *The Information Society and the Welfare State: The Finnish Model*. Oxford and New York: Oxford University Press.

Cooke, Philip, and Kevin Morgan. 2000. *The Associational Economy: Firms, Regions and Innovation*. Oxford and New York: Oxford University Press.

Cox, Cristián. 2003. *Políticas educacionales en el cambio de siglo*. Santiago, Chile: Editorial Universitaria.

Da Motta, P., and S. Rios. 2009. "América Latina frente a los desafíos de la globalización." In *A Medio Camino. Nuevos desafíos de la democracia y el desarrollo en América Latina*, ed., Fernando Henrique Cardoso and Alejandro Foxley. Santiago: Uqbar Editores.

De Ferranti, David, Guillermo E. Perry, Indermit Gill, J. Luis Guasch, William E. Maloney, Carolina Sánchez-Páramo, and Norbert Schady. 2003. *Closing the Gap in Education and Technology*. Washington, DC: World Bank.

De Ferranti, David, Guillermo Perry, Daniel Lederman, and William Maloney. 2002. *From Natural Resources to the Knowledge Economy*. Washington, DC: World Bank.

De Soto, Hernando. 1989. *The Other Path*. New York: Basic Books.

———. 2006. The Challenge of Connecting Informal and Formal Property Systems. In *Realizing Property Rights, Swiss Human Rights Book*, Vol. 1, ed. Hernando De Soto and Francis Cheneval, 18–67. Zürich: Rüffer & Rub.

Easterly, William, Norman Loayza, and Peter Montiel. 1997. Has Latin America's Post-Reform Growth Been Disappointing? Policy Research Working Paper 1708, World Bank, Washington, DC.

ECLAC. 1998. *Políticas para mejorar la inserción en la economía mundial*, 2nd ed. Santiago, Chile: CEPAL/Fondo de Cultura Económica.

———. 2002. Globalización y desarrollo. Santiago, Chile: United Nations.

Edwards, Sebastian. 1995. *Crisis and Reform in Latin America: From Despair to Hope*. New York: World Bank/Oxford University Press.

Engel, Eduardo, Ronald Fischer, and Alexander Galetovic. 1996. *Licitación de carreteras en Chile*. Estudios Públicos 61.

———. 2001. El programa Chileno de concesiones de infraestructura: Evaluación, experiencias y perspectivas. In *La transformación económica de Chile*, 2nd ed., ed. Felipe Larraín and Rodrigo Vergara. Santiago de Chile: Centro de Estudios Públicos.

Esping-Andersen, Gøsta. 1999. *Social Foundations of Postindustrial Economies*. Oxford: Oxford University Press.

———. 2001. A Welfare State for the 21st Century. In *The Global Third Way Debate*, ed. Anthony Giddens. Oxford: Policy Press-Blackwell Publishers.

Esping-Andersen, Gøsta, Duncan Gallie, Anton Hemerijck, and John Myles. 2002. *Why We Need a New Welfare State.* Oxford: Oxford University Press.

Evans, Peter, Dietrich Rueschemeyer, and Theda Skocpol, eds. 1985. *Bringing the State Back In.* Cambridge: Cambridge University Press.

Ferreira, M. Luisa, and Patrick Vanhoudt. 2004. Catching the Celtic Tiger By Its Tail. *European Journal of Education* 39(2).

Ferrera, Maurizio, Anton Hemerijck, and Martin Rhodes. 2001. The Future of Social Europe: Recasting Work and Welfare in the New Economy. In *The Global Third Way Debate*, ed. Anthony Giddens. Oxford, UK: Blackwell Publishers.

Ffrench-Davis, Ricardo. 2005. *Reformas para América Latina después del fundamentalismo neoliberal.* Buenos Aires: Siglo XXI.

Foxley, Alejandro. 2002. La economía política del libre comercio en las Américas: Mercosur y ALCA. Paper prepared for the Conferencia del Diálogo Interamericano, Washington, DC.

————. 2003a. Development Lessons of the 90s: Chile. Paper prepared for the Practitioners of Development series, World Bank, Washington, DC.

————. 2003b. Successes and Failures in Poverty Eradication: Chile. Paper prepared for the World Bank, Washington, DC.

————, ed. 2009. *Caminos al Desarrollo: Lecciones de países afines exitosos*, Santiago, Chile: Inter-American Development Bank and Ministry of Foreign Affairs of Chile.

Giddens, Anthony, ed. 2001. *The Global Third Way Debate.* Oxford, UK: Policy Press-Blackwell Publishers.

Gilbert, Neil, and Rebecca Van Voorhis, eds. 2003. *Changing Patterns of Social Protection.* London: Transaction Publishers.

Hilke, John. 2006. Improving Relationships Between Competition Policy and Sectoral Regulation. Paper prepared for the Fourth Meeting of the Latin American Competition Forum, San Salvador.

Inter-American Development Bank (IDB). 1997. *América Latina tras una década de reformas: Progreso económico y social; Informe 1997.* Washington, DC: IDB.

————. 2002. *Beyond Borders: The New Regionalism in Latin America.* Washington, DC: IDB.

————. 2003. *Modernizing the State.* Washington, DC: IDB.

Kuczynski, Pedro-Pablo, and John Williamson, eds. 2003. *After the Washington Consensus: Restarting Growth and Reform in Latin America.* Washington, DC: Institute for International Economics.

Lapuerta, Carlos, Juan Benavides, and Sonia Jorge. 2003. Regulation and Competition in Mobile Telephony in Latin America. Paper prepared for the First Meeting of the Latin American Competition Forum, Paris.

Muñoz, Oscar. 2001. *Estrategias de desarrollo en economías emergentes: Lecciones de la experiencia latinoamericana.* Santiago, Chile: Serie Libros FLACSO.

Nieuwenhuysen, John, Peter Lloyd, and Margaret Mead, eds. 2001. *Reshaping Australia's Economy.* Cambridge: Cambridge University Press.

Ocampo, José Antonio. 2004. Latin America's Growth and Equity Frustrations During Structural Reforms. *Journal of Economic Perspectives* 12(2).

OECD. 2003. *New Zealand: An Economic Survey.* Paris: OECD.

Puryear, Jeffrey, and José Joaquín Brunner. 1995. *Education, Equity, and Economic Competition in the Americas.* Washington, DC: INTERAMER Collection, OAS.

Rackzynski, Dagmar, Claudia Serrano, and Manuela Valle. 2002. Eventos de quiebre de ingreso y mecanismos de protección social. Draft of a project for the World Bank.

Ramos, Joseph, ed. 2003. *Políticas de empleo e institucionalidad laboral para el siglo XXI.* Santiago, Chile: Editorial Universitaria.

Rodrik, Dani. 1999. Why Is There So Much Economic Insecurity in Latin America? Paper presented at the Kennedy School, Harvard University.

Sachs, Jeffrey, Felipe Larraín, and Andrew Warner. 1999. A Structural Analysis of Chile's Long Term Growth. Paper prepared for the government of Chile.

Stallings, Barbara, and Wilson Peres. 2000. *Crecimiento, empleo y equidad: El impacto de las reformas económicas en América Latina y el Caribe.* Santiago, Chile: Fondo de Cultura Económica/CEPAL.

Tanzi, Vito. 2008. The Role of the State and Public Finance in the Next Generation. Paper presented at the 20 Seminario Regional de Politica Fiscal, ECLAC, Santiago, Chile.

Tavares de Araujo Junior, José. 2003. Challenges in the Introduction of Competition in Latin America. Paper prepared for the First Meeting of the Latin American Competition Forum, Paris.

Torres, Miguel. 2007. *Evolución del pensamiento cepalino: Sesenta años de economía política. III Curso Internacional políticas macroeconómicas y finanzas públicas,* Santiago de Chile, ECLAC.

Troya-Martínez, Marta. 2006. La política de competencia en el sector financiero de América Latina. Paper prepared for the Fourth Meeting of the Latin American Competition Forum, San Salvador.

Vivallos, Leonel. 2003. *La experiencia de Chile en el otorgamiento de concesiones de obras viales: Lecciones y desafíos.* www.eclac.org/Transporte/noticias/noticias/8/13708/ Proyectos%20VIALES%20CDGP2a.ppt -.

World Bank. 1997. *The Long March: A Reform Agenda for Latin America and the Caribbean in the Next Decade.* Washington, DC: World Bank.

Yusuf, Shahid. 2003. *Innovative East Asia.* Oxford and New York: Oxford University Press-World Bank Publication.

CHAPTER FIVE

Successful Social Policy Regimes? Political Economy, Politics, and Social Policy in Argentina, Chile, Uruguay, and Costa Rica

EVELYNE HUBER AND JOHN D. STEPHENS

IMPORTANCE AND CONTEXT OF SOCIAL POLICY REGIMES

If we accept the conceptualization of successful democratic governance developed by Mainwaring and Scully in their introductory chapter as "governments that succeed in maintaining a reasonably high quality of democratic practice, help their countries advance economically, provide citizen security, and help address the serious social problems...that affect...Latin American countries," it becomes obvious that a successful social policy regime is an essential component of successful democratic governance. Normatively, the case that poverty and inequality are incompatible with a full democracy of citizenship has been made compellingly by Guillermo O'Donnell and others in the PNUD (2004) report on the State of Democracy in Latin America. From an empirical point of view, we can state that a good part of declining popular support for democracy has to do with the failure of democratic regimes successfully to address questions of people's welfare, from outright poverty to poor quality education and health services.

The basic questions we address in this chapter are whether we can identify successful social policy regimes in Latin America, where and why they are successful or not, and how they could be made more successful. The question of the reasons for success or lack thereof forces us to analyze changes in the economic and social context, as well as political power distributions and processes that shape social policy regimes. We begin by establishing criteria to differentiate more successful social policy regimes from less successful social policy regimes. We then use these criteria to identify the comparatively most successful social policy regimes in Latin America as of the 1990s, which turn out to be the social policy regimes of Argentina, Chile, Costa Rica, and Uruguay, and differentiate them from some of the others.

It is no accident that Costa Rica, Chile, and Uruguay also rank by far the highest on the democracy, rule of law, and corruption measures in Table 1.2 of Chapter 1, with Argentina lagging behind Panama. As we shall demonstrate below, long periods of democracy make it possible for parties representing the interests of the underprivileged to consolidate and influence policy. We examine why and how these regimes were comparatively successful and argue that one needs to understand their functioning and effects in relationship to the economic and social structures in which they are embedded, as well as in the light of policy legacies from earlier periods. We proceed to tracing the contours of the social policy regimes in our four cases in their economic and social context as of the 1970s and then to an examination of the impact of the economic crisis and structural adjustment on the social policy regimes. We explain how the political economies and political institutions shaped the transformations and effectiveness of these regimes in response to these pressures and a changing international context. We conclude that all of these regimes continue to be under pressure and have difficulty protecting previous achievements. We end with some recommendations for future social policy directions.

IDENTIFYING MORE OR LESS SUCCESSFUL
SOCIAL POLICY REGIMES

We conceptualize a social policy regime as the institutional configuration of social policy schemes, that is, the types and structure of programs that provide cash transfers or free or subsidized goods and services to the population. The important structural features are the coverage of programs (the percentage of the relevant population covered), the rules for entitlement to benefits, the magnitude of the benefits, and the mode of financing of the schemes. A welfare state worthy of the name is a social policy regime with a wide variety of programs, universal coverage (or close to it), universalistic rules, benefits of a magnitude to keep people out of poverty, and a secure financial base in the country's tax system.

In order to establish criteria for differentiating more from less successful social policy regimes, it makes sense to begin with the desired outcomes. Successful social policy regimes should result in comparatively low levels of poverty and inequality and high levels of human capital, or at least in significant and sustained movement toward lowering levels of poverty and inequality and improving the human capital base. In addition, one would want to stipulate that indeed the social policy regime make a major contribution to such an outcome by making a significant welfare state or social policy effort, expressed in social spending as a percentage of GDP, and by allocating spending in a progressive way. *Progressive spending* is defined as spending that benefits lower income groups more than higher income groups in relationship to their market income. Progressive spending is designed to prevent or reduce poverty and to offer access to good quality basic services to all members of society.

According to these criteria, there are no fully successful social policy regimes in Latin America. All countries have rather large groups that live in poverty, with Uruguay being the only country in the 1990s where less than 10% of households were below the poverty level defined either by a basket of basic necessities (ECLAC) or by the $2 per day in purchasing power parity (World Bank) (see Table 5.1). The economic crisis of the early 2000s in Argentina and Uruguay saw poverty rates there shoot up to 26% in Argentina and 19% in Uruguay in 2005. In that year, Uruguay and Chile had the lowest poverty rates in Latin America with 19%, thus leaving close to a fifth of their populations in poverty. Moreover, almost all countries have rather large groups with access to poor quality education and health care only. However, different countries have different programs that are particularly successful, or were particularly successful at some point. Uruguay had a successful regime as of the 1970s, but it has come under increasing pressure, both in pensions and health care; the same can be said about Argentina in the 1960s, but the system there has been damaged to an even greater extent than in Uruguay. Costa Rica has a successful health care system, but it is limited in pension coverage and other anti-poverty policies. In general, all regimes are weak in anti-poverty policy schemes for the working age population.

As we've noted, any social policy regime needs to be understood within the economic and social structure of the country in question. The same kinds of programs have different effects in different economic

TABLE 5.1
Poverty, Inequality, and Education

	Percent of Households on $2 PPP*		Percent of Households below ECLAC Poverty Line			Gini			Average Years of Education		
	1981–1990	1991–2001	1970–1980	1981–1990	1991–2001	1970–1980	1981–1990	1991–2001	1970–1980	1981–1990	1991–2001
Argentina	1.4	11.4	8.5	21.6	18.7	40.2	46.5	46.7	6.2	7.2	8.3
Chile	22.9	14.6	17.0	36.0	21.2	50.1	53.1	54.5	5.6	6.2	7.3
Costa Rica	22.1	12.3	24.0	23.7	21.0	48.7	45.9	45.1	4.3	5.4	5.9
Uruguay	3.2	4.3	14.5	13.2	5.6	47.4	43.4	43.2	5.4	6.6	7.1
Average	12.4	10.7	16.0	23.6	16.6	46.6	47.2	47.4	5.4	6.4	7.2
Brazil	33.2	26.5	44.0	40.5	33.0	61.1	56.4	57.1	2.9	3.6	4.4
Mexico	32.3	28.4	33.0	36.2	37.2	52.2	51.0	53.8	3.4	5.1	6.6
Average	32.8	27.5	38.5	38.4	35.1	56.7	53.7	55.5	3.2	4.4	5.5
Bahamas						55.2	44.4	42.4			
Barbados						50.0			8.0	7.5	
Guyana		19.1						53.5	4.3	5.1	
Jamaica	21.5	23.1				60.7	52.3	54.5	3.4	4.2	

Trinidad and Tobago	15.3	20.0		48.8	42.6	46.4	40.2	5.5	6.5
Average	18.4	20.7			53.7	46.4	47.7	5.3	5.8
Bolivia	37.7	36.7		55.5	53.0		59.8	3.8	5.4
Colombia	13.4	19.1	42.0	39.4	47.3		54.6	3.8	4.8
Ecuador	3.1	32.5		62.8	60.0		55.9	4.2	6.4
Paraguay	26.3	32.6			49.5		56.2	4.2	5.7
Peru	10.1	32.6	48.0	52.0	42.7		51.3	4.5	7.1
Venezuela	21.3	28.5	25.0	27.7	40.3		47.5	3.9	5.5
Average	18.7	30.3	38.3	47.5	48.8	50.4	54.2	4.1	5.2
Dominican Republic	23.1	10.7			29.0		49.6	3.3	5.0
El Salvador	43.0	51.1			45.7		53.2	2.7	4.3
Guatemala	66.0	33.5	65.0	65.5	54.0		56.9	2.0	3.0
Honduras	61.6	48.3	65.0	72.3	73.5		55.2	2.2	4.0
Nicaragua		78.9			65.3		55.1	2.5	4.2
Panama	23.8	18.1	24.5	36.0	29.3		57.0	5.2	7.8
Average	43.5	40.1	51.5	57.9	49.5	54.2	54.5	3.0	4.7

*See Appendix for variable definition and data sources.

and social contexts. The most obvious and important example for Latin America is the differential effectiveness of occupationally based social policy schemes in countries with small versus large informal sectors. Where most of the working age population is economically active and employed in the formal sector, an occupationally based pension scheme or health insurance scheme that also covers dependents can be highly effective in providing very wide coverage. Where most of the working age population is either unemployed or self-employed or employed in the informal sector, an occupationally based scheme can be very exclusionary and cover only a privileged minority.

Similarly, a larger formal sector provides a better base to construct an effective system of taxation, which is crucial for the ability to fund social policy schemes in a sustainable way. Ultimately, what one would want to understand is models of capitalism, or varieties of capitalism as they have been conceptualized in advanced industrial countries, with growth and distribution components, and physical and human capital components. Here we are making a first step toward this larger goal by identifying social policy regimes that have been successful in terms of the distribution and human capital components, and by locating them in the economic and social contexts of the respective countries.

Our procedure is empirical and inductive. We work backward from data on poverty, inequality, and human development, and then we look at the social policy regimes in the countries with the best outcomes, and at their economic and social context. We take the 1990s and the first half decade of the 2000s as the end point and the 1970s as the starting point, analyzing the transformation of the social policy schemes of these countries since the 1970s. We chose the 1970s as the starting point because this was the last decade of ISI pursuit before the debt crisis of the 1980s forced an abandonment of that model. We analyze the economic and political determinants of these transformations, as well as the effect of the transformations on the present and probable future welfare of the population.

We are not attempting to elaborate a typology of all welfare states or social policy regimes in Latin America here. Filgueira's (2005) typology is a reasonable attempt for the period up to the 1970s. He distinguishes three types: stratified universalism (Argentina, Chile, Uruguay, and Costa Rica as a special case), dual regimes (Brazil and Mexico, with Peru as a borderline case), and exclusionary regimes (Guatemala, Honduras, El Salvador, Nicaragua, and Bolivia). He argues that the regimes with stratified universalism covered virtually the entire population with a social security scheme and basic health services, and they also had universal access to primary education and broad access to some secondary education. The stratified nature of the regimes resulted from differential cash benefits and quality of services. The dual regimes resembled the stratified universalistic ones in the near universal access to basic health care and primary education, but their social security systems were much more restricted in coverage as well as stratified, covering just about half the population. The exclusionary regimes offered social security protection to less than a quarter of their population only, and access to health care was very restricted as well. Primary education had formally relatively wide coverage, but its quality in rural and in urban poor areas was very low.

We agree with Filgueira that coverage through social security, health, and education policies, along with the extent of spending on these policies, are relevant characteristics for a welfare state typology. We would add the differential emphasis of the social policy regime on social security transfers (essentially pensions) versus on health and education, and the allocation of expenditures within these categories on basic transfers and services versus on income-related transfers and higher level services. On this basis, we would roughly distinguish the following clusters or types:

1. Chile, Argentina, Uruguay, and Costa Rica
2. Brazil and Mexico
3. the Andean countries (including Colombia and Venezuela, excluding Chile)
4. Central America (without Costa Rica) and the Dominican Republic
5. the English-speaking Caribbean

The first four clusters show roughly declining degrees of coverage and effort; the fifth is different in its stronger emphasis on health and education relative to social security spending. This is also what makes Costa Rica different from the other three members of the top category.

An examination of average figures for the period 1991 to 2001 shows the following pattern (see Table 5.1): The lowest average poverty rates according to the ECLAC basic needs basket poverty line were to be found in Uruguay with 5.6% of households, followed by Argentina with 18.7%, and Costa Rica and Chile with 21% each. In contrast, Brazil had 33% of households below the poverty line, and the next lowest were Panama and the Dominican Republic with 29% each. The World Bank $2 per day poverty line gives roughly the same ordering, except that Costa Rica is doing better than Chile, with Uruguay at 4%, Argentina at 11%, Costa Rica at 12%, and Chile at 15%. The next lowest countries are the Dominican Republic with 11% (though the data here are hard to believe), Panama with 18%, Colombia and Guyana with 19%, Trinidad and Tobago with 20%, Jamaica with 23%, and Brazil with 26%. By 2003–2005, poverty in Argentina and Uruguay had increased considerably (to 26% and 19% respectively), but these two countries along with Chile and Costa Rica (with 19% and 21% respectively) still retained the lowest poverty rates (ECLAC 2006, 8).

Outside the two former English colonies, Bahamas and Trinidad, the country with the lowest inequality in the 1990s was Uruguay with a Gini index of 43, followed by Costa Rica (45) and Argentina (47). By contrast, Chile is among the more inegalitarian countries in Latin America with a Gini of 55. The trajectory of these four countries is also rather different: Uruguay and Costa Rica experienced modest reductions in inequality from the 1970s to the 1980s, while Argentina and Chile witnessed substantial increases in inequality. In both cases these increases in inequality continued into the democratic period. In the case of Chile, this is remarkable given the decline of poverty on both poverty indicators in Table 5.1. Both poverty indicators are absolute measures, so this combination of growing inequality and declining poverty is possible.[1] What made this possibility materialize in the Chilean case was the combination of rapid growth and government policy aimed at poverty reduction since the return of democracy. However, as we point out below, statistical analysis shows that Chile is very much the exception to the rule in this regard. Outside of our four focal countries, inequality in Latin America and the Caribbean changed little in the last two decades of the twentieth century. It stayed at its historically and comparatively (to other regions of the world) high level.

If we look at average years of education among the adult population as an indicator of the quality of human capital in the 1990s, we see Argentina in a clearly leading position, with 8.3 years, followed by Panama with 7.8 years, and Chile and Uruguay with 7.3 and 7.1 years, respectively. Costa Rica's 5.9 years place it behind Mexico with 6.6, and even Peru and Ecuador with 7.1 and 6.4 years, respectively. However, the last two figures strain credulity, and even if we take the figures at face value, the effort indicators in terms of education spending suggest a significantly higher quality of education in Costa Rica than in the three other countries. The figures for adult literacy would support this assessment, with Argentina, Chile, Costa Rica, and Uruguay all having literacy rates of 96% or above, and Panama, Mexico, and Peru with rates of 92%, 91%, and 90%, respectively (World Bank 2008).

Our outcome indicators have parallels in effort indicators (see Table 5.2). Costa Rica was consistently (over all three time periods) the highest spender in health and education, rivaled only by Jamaica, with 5.2%

TABLE 5.2
Government Social Spending as a Percentage of GDP

	Education			Health			Social Security and Welfare			Total		
	1970–1980	1981–1990	1991–2001	1970–1980	1981–1990	1991–2001	1970–1980	1981–1990	1991–2001	1970–1980	1981–1990	1991–2001
Argentina	1.5	3.4	4.1	0.6	3.0	4.5	4.7	4.7	7.6	6.8	11.1	16.2
Chile	4.4	3.7	3.0	2.4	2.0	2.3	8.5	10.6	6.9	15.3	16.3	12.2
Costa Rica	5.4	4.6	4.3	2.3	5.9	5.2	3.8	3.2	4.1	11.5	13.7	13.6
Uruguay	2.6	2.9	2.7	1.1	2.6	3.1	10.8	12.8	17.8	14.5	18.3	23.6
Average	3.5	3.7	3.5	1.6	3.4	3.8	7.0	7.8	9.1	12.0	14.9	16.4
Brazil	1.1	2.5	3.8	1.6	2.6	3.2	6.4	7.0	10.2	9.1	12.1	17.2
Colombia	2.0	3.0	3.8	2.9	1.2	3.0		2.4	1.4	4.9	6.6	8.2
Mexico	2.7	2.9	3.8	0.7	3.0	3.6	3.3	2.4	3.2	6.7	8.3	10.6
Venezuela	3.9	4.2	3.6	1.5	1.6	1.3	1.4	1.8	2.4	6.8	7.6	7.3
Average	2.4	3.2	3.8	1.7	2.1	2.8	3.7	3.4	4.3	6.9	8.7	10.8
Jamaica	5.6	3.4	5.3	2.4	7.1	2.3	1.2		0.5	9.2	10.5	8.1

of GDP spent on health and 4.3% on education in the 1990s. Argentina was a close second in this decade in health and education spending, with 4.5% and 4.1%, respectively. Both Chile and Uruguay clearly lagged behind Argentina and Costa Rica, and by the 1990s even behind Brazil, Colombia, Mexico, and Venezuela in education spending. In health spending in the 1990s Uruguay also lagged behind Brazil and Mexico, and among our comparison group only Venezuela spent a lower percentage of GDP on health than Chile. However, in the case of Uruguay we have to take into account that a large share of health care is financed by mutual insurance, to which employers and employees contribute on a mandatory basis but which is not showing up in these public spending figures because it is counted as private spending.

In social security and welfare spending, in contrast, Uruguay was way out in front, with 17.8% of GDP in the 1990s, followed by Brazil with 10.2%, Argentina with 7.6%, Chile with 6.9%, and—at a considerable distance—Costa Rica with 4.1%. It is worth noting here how much Brazil spent on social security and welfare, without apparently commensurate effects on poverty. If we look at total social spending over the three decades, Uruguay, Chile, and Costa Rica were clearly ahead of any of the other countries in the 1970s and 1980s; in the 1990s Brazil greatly increased spending and joined this top group, as did Argentina.[2] In the 1990s, Uruguay was the leader in total social spending, with 23.6% of GDP (mainly due to its heavy outlays on social security), followed by Argentina, Costa Rica, and then Chile, the lowest spender in the top group with 12.2%.

According to our criteria, then, it is correct to identify Argentina, Chile, Costa Rica, and Uruguay as comparatively successful cases. These cases are consistently in the top group in both outcome and effort indicators. Some other cases are close to these four on some indicators but not on others. A close competitor on poverty and educational indicators is Panama, but that country is a very special case because of the Canal Zone; that is, we cannot regard it as an entirely home-grown model. Venezuela in the 1990s still showed the heritage of better social policy up to the 1980s (e.g., in adult literacy and average years of education), but the profound crisis increased poverty in the 1990s and possibly is eroding previous achievements. The English-speaking Caribbean forms a special group. These countries rank high on education and health spending, but not as uniformly high on education outcome indicators. Moreover, they rank relatively low on social security and welfare spending and have intermediate levels of poverty. Thus, we will focus the analysis here on the four cases with the relatively best outcomes and strongest efforts.

If we compare Argentina, Chile, Costa Rica, and Uruguay, we can see that the rank order in welfare state effort among those four is not

TABLE 5.3
GDP and Growth

	GDP Per Capita			Growth of GDP Per Capita		
	1970–1980	1981–1990	1991–2001	1970–1980	1981–1990	1991–2001
Argentina	9876	8773	10372	1.5	−3.6	4.5
Chile	4846	5320	8530	1.5	1.5	5.0
Costa Rica	4907	4756	5329	2.6	−0.8	1.8
Uruguay	6654	7027	9058	2.8	−0.8	2.9
Average	6571	6469	8322	2.1	−0.9	3.6
Brazil	5111	6194	6663	5.9	−0.2	1.5
Colombia	3739	4502	5349	3.2	1.4	0.9
Mexico	6449	7495	7673	3.3	−0.4	1.9
Venezuela	8800	7112	6996	−2.7	−1.3	−0.7
Average	6025	6326	6670	2.4	−0.1	0.9
Jamaica	3917	3552	3788	−0.9	1.8	−1.0

associated with the rank order in GDP per capita, where in the 1990s Argentina had more than a $1,000 lead over Uruguay; Uruguay in turn was followed by Chile with a $500 lag, and finally Costa Rica was almost at half the level of Argentina (see Table 5.3). Thus, within this group of leaders, compared to their relative level of economic strength, Costa Rica was making a disproportionate effort and Chile was a laggard. If we look at the 1970s and 1980s, Argentina stands out as a real laggard, given the even greater lead in GDP per capita in these earlier decades.

REASONS FOR THE SUCCESS OF THESE POLICY REGIMES: POLITICAL ECONOMY AND REGIME STRUCTURE

Economic Structure

If we inquire into the reasons why the social policy regimes in Argentina, Chile, Costa Rica, and Uruguay were the most successful ones in Latin America as of the early 1970s, we have to understand them in the context of these countries' economies. One key reason for the low levels of poverty in Argentina was that it was the most industrialized of the Latin American countries, with 46% of GDP value added in industry, with the lowest level of urban unemployment at 3%, and the smallest informal sector with 24% (see Tables 5.4 and 5.5).

This type of labor market meant that the great majority of adult males were employed in formal sector jobs, which paid a decent wage and also made occupationally based social security schemes and health care schemes with coverage for dependents highly effective.

Uruguay had still a stronger agricultural sector, with 17% of GDP value added, compared to 31% in industry, but also a comparatively small informal sector, with 25%, and low urban unemployment at 7%. Again, this provided for comparatively high formal sector employment and thus a favorable context for the traditional occupationally based social security approach pursued in the Continental European countries and diffused internationally by the International Labour Organization (ILO).

Chile's value added in industry was 40% of GDP, with only 8% in agriculture, but average urban unemployment in the 1970s was at 12% already and the informal sector comprised 36% of the economically active population. The size of the informal sector in this period was comparable to that of Brazil and Colombia and clearly hampered the effectiveness of cash transfer and health care schemes tied to employment.

Costa Rica was the most agricultural of the four countries, with 23% of GDP value added in agriculture and only 30% in industry (close to Uruguay); the country had comparatively low urban unemployment and an informal sector of intermediate size, between Argentina/Uruguay and Chile, with 30%, which was still comparatively low in the Latin American context.

STRUCTURE OF SOCIAL POLICY REGIMES

The social security systems of Argentina, Chile, and Uruguay had historically been highly fragmented, with different schemes providing different benefits for different categories of workers, but in Uruguay in the 1960s a process of unification brought close to 90 percent of the insured into the same fund under the Banco de Previsión Social (BPS). The Costa Rican system was set up from the beginning as a more unified system, with only a few privileged schemes. All of these countries had a social assistance pension for the elderly without any other sources of income; typically it was means tested, for people over seventy years of age, and provided low benefits. Still, these pensions could make an important

TABLE 5.4
Industry, Agriculture, and Foreign Investment

	Value Added in Industry			Value Added in Agriculture			Industrial Employment			Net FDI Inflows		
	1970–1980	1981–1990	1991–2001	1970–1980	1981–1990	1991–2001	1970–1980	1981–1990	1991–2001	1970–1980	1981–1990	1991–2001
Argentina	45.5	39.4	28.9	8.9	8.3	5.6			28.1	0.3	0.7	2.7
Chile	39.7	39.0	35.7	7.6	7.7	9.0	23.7	22.1	26.4	-0.1	2.2	5.6
Costa Rica	29.9	31.3	30.3	22.6	22.8	12.3	24.0	23.0	24.3	2.6	2.0	3.1
Uruguay	31.4	34.0	29.2	16.7	12.3	7.4		32.8	28.1	0.9	0.2	0.8
Average	36.6	35.9	31.0	14.0	12.8	8.6	23.9	26.0	26.7	0.9	1.3	3.1
Brazil	39.7	44.0	33.7	12.5	10.2	8.2		23.5	20.1	1.1	0.6	2.3
Colombia	30.3	35.2	31.6	7.6	7.7	9.0	34.0	29.9	29.0	0.4	1.4	2.3
Mexico	32.3	33.5	27.9	11.4	8.9	5.6	20.6	27.2	23.5	0.8	1.1	2.5
Venezuela	44.4	42.9	43.5	5.1	5.8	5.1	27.7	26.4	24.6	-0.3	0.2	2.9
Average	36.7	38.9	34.2	9.2	8.2	7.0	27.4	26.8	24.3	0.5	0.8	2.5
Jamaica	38.5	37.1	33.8	7.6	7.2	7.5	15.2	22.6	19.2	3.1	0.4	4.1

TABLE 5.5
Unemployment and Informal Sector Employment

	Unemployment				Urban Unemployment				Informal Sector Employment		
	1970–1980	1998–1990	1991–2001		1970–1980	1981–1990	1991–2001		1970–1980	1981–1990	1991–2001
Argentina	2.3	5.3	12.3		2.6	5.8	13.1		24.3	34.5	60.0
Chile	10.4	10.6	6.6		11.7	14.4	7.7		36.1	39.4	47.0
Costa Rica	5.9	6.5	5.3		6.0	6.9	5.4		30.0	33.1	44.2
Uruguay		9.0	9.7		7.4	10.6	10.8		25.4	39.1	42.9
Average	6.2	7.9	8.5		6.9	9.4	9.3		29.0	36.5	48.5
Brazil	2.8	3.3	7.0		6.3	5.2	5.9		36.2	35.3	52.1
Colombia	9.1	10.9	12.3		10.0	11.3	12.8		36.0	39.8	55.6
Mexico		2.7	3.5		4.5	4.2	3.5		33.7	34.0	52.7
Venezuela	5.9	9.7	10.2		6.0	9.7	10.9		34.0	30.7	43.9
Average	5.9	6.7	8.3		6.7	7.6	8.3		35.0	35.0	51.1
Jamaica	27.3	22.7	15.9			15.3	15.7				

contribution to poverty reduction among the aged by contributing to the extended households most of them were living in. The regular pensions themselves, of course, were important in preventing retired people from falling into poverty. This was particularly important in periods of high inflation, when the real value of savings was being rapidly eroded. Benefit adjustment mechanisms were part of all the pension systems, albeit generally a controversial part and subject to much political manipulation.[3]

The health care systems in Argentina and Uruguay were organized along similar lines, based on a combination of mutual insurance schemes, historically grown out of working class immigrant communities and later linked to the place of employment through union contracts, a public health service, and private provision. In both cases, coverage was extensive due to the favorable employment structure, and indigents could receive health care through the Ministry of Health. Access to these public health services was problematic in rural areas, but the comparatively high degree of urbanization mitigated these problems. Again in both cases, coordination of financing and service provision between the public and the private sectors (including the mutual insurance schemes) would become highly problematic in the 1980s and beyond.

The Chilean health system was also divided between public and private sectors, and in addition the public health sector was divided between the Servicio Nacional de Salud (SNS) in charge of providing health care to blue collar workers, some white collar workers insured through social security, and the indigent, and a separate entity in charge of financing private service provision for civil servants and sectors of white collar workers insured through social security. The result of this division was significant inequality in the accessibility and quality of services, as the SNS was seriously underfunded. To counteract some of the consequences of these deficiencies, such as high infant mortality, the Frei and Allende governments targeted resources to pregnant women and children and to medical centers in poor and peripheral areas, with tangible results in the form of improvement in corresponding health statistics (Borzutzky 2002; McGuire, forthcoming).

In Costa Rica, health insurance was also provided through the social security institute, the Caja Costarricense de Seguro Social (CCSS). It had been set up in 1941 but reached only about a quarter of the economically active population in 1960. The constitutional amendment of 1961 mandating universalization of coverage within a decade propelled an expansion of coverage to 43% of the population by 1971 (Rosenberg 1979, 24). In 1973, all public hospitals were transferred to the CCSS and an integrated national health service was established—such that by 1980 only 14% of consultations were done on a private basis (Casas and Vargas 1980, 268). Standardized and comprehensive coverage for services greatly improved health statistics for Costa Rica.

By the early 1970s, Argentina, Chile, and Uruguay had reached comparatively high coverage in their social security systems, close to 70% of the economically active population in Argentina, about 75% in Chile, and over 90% in Uruguay; whereas Costa Rica lagged far behind, with just below 40% (Mesa-Lago 1994, 22).[4] The first three countries had gradually expanded pension coverage from the security forces and higher civil servants to ever larger groups, including blue collar workers. Costa Rica's push for expansion began in earnest in the 1960s only. Social security schemes were typically based on employment and financed by a combination of employer and employee contributions, calculated as a percentage of earnings, sometimes supplemented by the state. They covered sickness/maternity (health care and often some cash subsidy as well), pensions, employment injury, and family allowances. The weight of the different components varied by country. In the late 1960s and early 1970s, the great majority of the funds went to pensions in Uruguay (over 70%) and Argentina (close to 60%), whereas in Chile it was less than 40%, with over 40% going to family allowances. In Costa Rica, the bulk of the spending went to sickness/maternity, with close to 80%, which in part reflects the fact that the pension system had not matured yet. None of these countries had any significant unemployment insurance; if there was one, only a very small percentage of the workforce was covered (Mesa-Lago 1994, 53).

Argentina and Uruguay, then, were most successful economically and in terms of poverty and inequality, though on a somewhat different basis, with a stronger weight of agriculture in Uruguay. The key to relatively low poverty and inequality and to close to universal coverage through pension and health care schemes in both was the comparatively small informal sector and low or moderate urban unemployment. This kept wages above the poverty level and made the traditional social security system that they had established relatively effective. Both had comparatively low public expenditures on health, but the mutual insurance schemes—a large part of whose expenditures are considered private sector expenditures and thus do not appear in the data for public spending—provided wide coverage; in Argentina they were administered by the trade unions. Uruguay was already the highest spender on social security and welfare, as its pension system was relatively generous and had virtually fully matured.

Costa Rica was the most agricultural of the four countries and had a comparatively high poverty rate. However, the country already was the highest public spender on education and tied with Chile for public

health expenditures. Social security and welfare spending was comparatively low, as efforts were just being undertaken to expand coverage.
The figures for Chile in the 1970s already reflect the first wave of economic restructuring under Pinochet, resulting in relatively high urban
unemployment and a large informal sector. However, the legacy of the
pre-Pinochet policies in health, education, and social security are still
visible in the comparatively high expenditures in those categories. The
big restructuring of social policy in Chile occurred in the 1980s.

Effectiveness of Social Policy

One might hypothesize that Argentina, Uruguay, Chile, and Costa Rica
were simply the most affluent societies and therefore had the lowest poverty rates and highest educational levels. Given that the most commonly
used poverty measures (the ECLAC measure and the World Bank $2 per
day measure) are measures of absolute poverty, we would certainly expect a strong relationship between affluence of the society and satisfaction of basic human needs. Thus, we need to look for systematic patterns
of deviation of the actual level of poverty from the level we would predict
on the basis of the society's GDP per capita. We have data on poverty
levels for the 1970s for twelve countries only, so we cannot perform
multivariate regression. The scatter plot of a bivariate regression suggests
that there is more to low poverty levels than just GDP per capita. This
argument works reasonably well for Argentina, which is right on the
regression line, but Costa Rica, Chile, and Uruguay are clearly below the
regression line, indicating that they have lower poverty rates than one
would predict on the basis of their GDP per capita (see Figure 5.1).

We find a similar pattern in the scatter plot for average years of education and GDP per capita. Again, Argentina conforms to expectations,
sitting right on the regression line, as does Costa Rica in this case (see
Figure 5.2). However, Uruguay and Chile have higher educational levels
than predicted. If we look at the relationship between average years of
education and poverty levels, which can be viewed both as indicators of
policy regimes success and as cause (educational level) and effect (poverty level), we see a very close relationship. The zero order correlation is
−.89, which means that education explains close to 80% of the variation
in poverty. Indeed, Argentina, Chile, and Uruguay are very close to the
regression line, whereas Costa Rica has lower poverty than predicted by
the educational levels of the population (see Figure 5.3).

Income inequality stands in a similar relationship to poverty as educational levels. Poverty and inequality are both shaped by the policy
regime, but inequality is also a very strong predictor of poverty. The

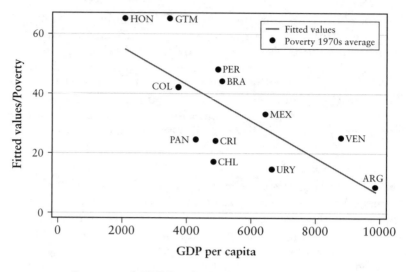

FIGURE 5.1 Poverty and GDP Per Capita, 1970s Averages
R = −.72

Source: Author calculations on basis of Huber, Stephens, Mustillo, and Pribble dataset.
See Appendix.

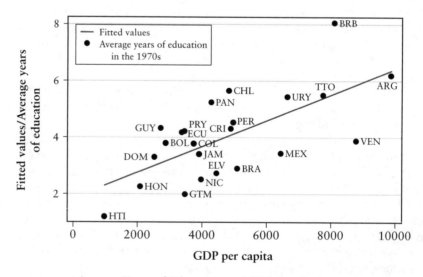

FIGURE 5.2 Average Years of Education and GDP Per Capita, 1970s Averages
R = .67

Source: Author calculations on basis of Huber, Stephens, Mustillo, and Pribble dataset.
See Appendix.

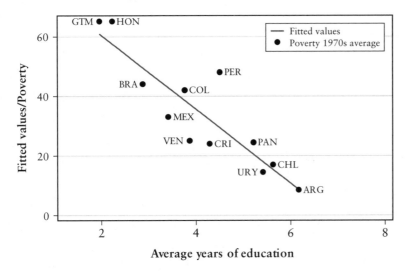

FIGURE 5.3 Poverty and Average Years of Education, 1970s Averages
R = −.89
Source: Author calculations on basis of Huber, Stephens, Mustillo, and Pribble dataset.
See Appendix.

zero order correlation is .84, indicating that inequality explains about two thirds of the variation in poverty.[5] Costa Rica is very close to the regression line here, Argentina is slightly above, and Uruguay and Chile below, indicating that the latter two countries have lower poverty than expected on the basis of their inequality (see Figure 5.4).

The zero order correlation between poverty and total social spending (social security and welfare, health, and education combined) is −.68, clearly lower than for inequality and education but not inconsequential. The scatter plot of total social spending and poverty confirms that our four countries were the leading spenders in the 1970s, along with Panama and followed by Brazil. However, Brazil is far above the regression line, indicating that its social security and welfare spending is not very effective as an anti-poverty weapon (see Figure 5.5). Uruguay and Costa Rica are right on the regression line, Chile slightly above, and Argentina well below, suggesting that Uruguay and Costa Rica were getting average levels of poverty given their social spending, whereas Argentina had lower levels of poverty than one might expect on the basis of its social spending.[6]

One of the main mechanisms through which we would expect development to affect poverty levels is the size of the informal sector. Jobs in

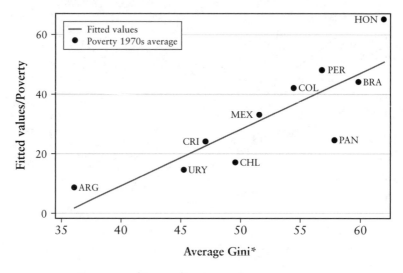

FIGURE 5.4 Poverty and Inequality, 1970s Averages
R = .84

Note: Urg is urban, Hon is 1968.

Source: Author calculations on basis of Huber, Stephens, Mustillo, and Pribble dataset. See Appendix.

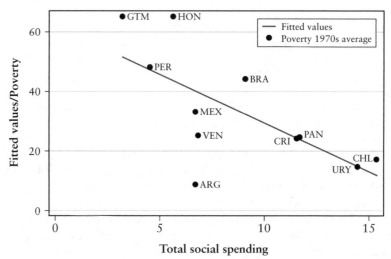

FIGURE 5.5 Poverty and Spending on Health, Education, Social Security, and Welfare, 1970s Averages
R = −.68

Source: Author calculations on basis of Huber, Stephens, Mustillo, and Pribble dataset. See Appendix.

the informal sector are on average less productive and lower paid than jobs in the formal sector. Indeed, introducing the size of the informal sector increases our capacity to explain variations in poverty levels. GDP per capita alone explains 47% of the variation in poverty in a simple regression, and when we add size of the informal sector to GDP per capita, we increase the variation explained to 55%.

However, if we add measures of social spending to GDP per capita, the increase in variation explained is greater. GDP per capita and spending on education together explain 59% of the variation in poverty. Spending on health and spending on social security and welfare have even stronger explanatory power; GDP per capita and spending on health together explain 68% of the variation, the same as GDP per capita and spending on social security and welfare. Finally, if we measure total social spending and enter it with GDP per capita, we can explain 92% of the variation in poverty. This is a very strong increase in explanatory power that suggests a substantial impact of social expenditures on poverty levels.

If we turn to our cases, we see that Uruguay and Chile were by far the largest spenders on social security and welfare in this period, and Chile and Costa Rica spent the highest percentage of their GDP on health and education. The low figures for health spending in Argentina and Uruguay vastly underestimate the real spending on health care. As noted, the reason for these low figures is the provision of health care through mutual insurance schemes, the *obras sociales* run by the unions in Argentina, and the *mutuales* in Uruguay, whose expenditures do not count as public spending. In both cases, these were alternatives to state-run social security health care schemes, in so far as the compulsory payroll contributions from employees and employers went to these alternative schemes. Given the high levels of formal sector employment, they provided wide coverage of the population.

Health and education spending affect poverty levels indirectly, through better human capital. Social security and welfare spending affect them very directly, through cash transfers. Both Uruguay and Chile had well-established pension systems and family allowances by the early 1970s. The systems were highly fragmented and unequal, but they undoubtedly made an important contribution to keeping poverty levels low, through family allowances among the working age population and pensions among the elderly. In Uruguay in 1969 to 1970, social security expenditures amounted to 14% of GDP, 66% of which went to pensions and 21% to family allowances, amounting to 9.3% of GDP for pensions and 2.8% of GDP for family allowances (Mesa-Lago 1989, 224–25). Family allowances were actually remarkably egalitarian, consisting of a flat amount for all those contributing to social security, except for the armed forces and civil servants. Uruguay also had non-contributory social assistance pensions for those not entitled to a regular pension. Even though the amount of these benefits was low, they made important contributions to the income of extended households with children and elderly members and thus to keeping those households out of poverty.

In Chile, total social security expenditures in 1971 amounted to 17% of GDP, and in 1970 family allowances accounted for 31% of all social security expenditures, so roughly for somewhat over 5% of GDP (Mesa-Lago 1989, 131–33). In contrast to Uruguay, there was more diversity in the level of benefits, for family allowances as well as pensions, because there were more programs for different groups. Argentina also had family allowances, and they were standardized among different systems in 1969, though civil servants and the armed forces kept their own, like in Uruguay. However, the total expenditures on social security were significantly lower than in Chile and Uruguay, with 4.2% of GDP in 1970, which suggests that family allowances did not have the same magnitude of impact on family incomes as in these other two countries. Costa Rica did not have any family allowances, and the social security system just began to expand greatly in the 1960s. An important social assistance program for indigents did not start until 1974. Thus, cash transfers did not make a big contribution to low poverty levels in Costa Rica in that time period. We would hypothesize that two of the main reasons for the low poverty were the comparatively low degree of inequality and the comparatively strong human capital base.

Though minimum wage legislation is considered part of labor market policy rather than social policy, it actually is very closely connected to social policy in those countries that use the minimum wage to index social assistance and insurance benefits. Also, it is important to consider the impact of the minimum wage if we attempt to explain differences in poverty levels. Chile, Costa Rica, and Uruguay all had minimum wages in this period; Argentina before 1973 only for the rural sector. In Costa Rica and Uruguay, tripartite bodies were in charge of setting the minimum wage; in Chile, it was the President. Data to calculate the ratio of the minimum to the mean wage are available for Argentina starting in 1996 only, in Chile and Costa Rica in 1976, and in Uruguay in 1990. In Chile in 1976, the ratio was 31% and in Costa Rica 57%, indicating that the minimum wage was clearly worth more compared to average earnings in Costa Rica. In most of the years for which data are available, this ratio is higher in Costa Rica than in the other three countries. Thus, we can add the minimum wage as an additional reason for the comparatively low level of poverty in the 1970s in Costa Rica.

Political Determinants

When we look for political explanations of these policy patterns and outcomes, democracy looms large. As of 1971—that is, in the period between 1945 and 1970—three of our four countries had by far the longest records of democratic rule; Chile and Uruguay were the leaders with 26 years, followed by Costa Rica with 25 years. Argentina with 12 lagged behind Brazil (19), Colombia (16), Peru (15), and Venezuela (14). If we look at full democracy only, without restrictions on the franchise of adult males, military intervention behind the scenes, prohibition of certain parties, lack of a secret ballot, large-scale election fraud, etc., two countries are far and above all others: Uruguay with 26 years and Costa Rica with 16; Argentina only had 6 such years—if we classify the first years of Perón as fully democratic, which is not uncontroversial. If we reject this classification, then Argentina had no fully democratic years, just like Chile, where illiterates were disenfranchised until 1970.[7] No other Latin American country had ten or more years of full democracy in this period.

One of the essential effects of democracy is that it affords the opportunity for groups representing the underprivileged to organize and attempt to influence policy. The main instrument to influence policy in favor of low-income groups and the poor is the political party, more specifically political parties of the center-left or left. To measure the influence of parties on policy, we added up the proportion of seats held by parties with distinctive political orientations during all the years from 1945 to 1970 that were democratic (full and restricted democracies). So, if a country was democratic for the entire period and center-left and left parties had been in full control of the legislature for the entire time, our measure of left legislative strength would indicate 26. A score of 13 could hypothetically indicate that roughly half of the years were democratic and center-left and left parties controlled all seats in the legislature during that period; or it could indicate that all of the years were democratic and center-left and left parties controlled half the seats.

Left-of-center legislative strength in the period leading up to the 1970s was dominant only in Uruguay, with a score of 14. Costa Rica came closest with 11, followed by Chile with 9. The only other countries with scores above 5 were Venezuela with 10 and Bolivia with 7. Thus, despite the restrictions on the franchise, democracy offered the opportunity for the organizing capacity of Chilean parties to the left of center to grow and consolidate a support base. So, essentially we can identify two paths to comparatively high social expenditures, high average educational achievement, and low poverty as of the 1970s; democracy and left of center party strength (Uruguay, Costa Rica, and Chile), or populism on the borderline between restricted democracy and authoritarianism (Argentina). As we saw, the latter path by the 1970s did not entail the same commitment to social expenditure as the former; rather, the low levels of poverty in Argentina were explained to a larger extent than in the other three countries by high GDP per capita, low inequality, low urban unemployment, and low informal sector employment, all linked to the strength of the ISI thrust.

The PLN in Costa Rica dominated the legislature in 1961 when the constitutional amendment for universalization of social security was passed (Rosenberg 1979). The Colorados inspired by reformist President Batlle (1903–1907 and 1911–1916) dominated in Uruguay in the 1910s, when the social security system was first established (Filgueira 1995), and in the period 1948–1954 when it was expanded and reorganized (Papadopoulos 1992). In Chile, the origins of the social security system for blue collar workers are in the period of turmoil in 1925, when military intervention terminated the stalemate between reformist President Alessandri and the conservative congress, but significant efforts to expand coverage came in the 1960s and early 1970s in the competition between the Christian democrats and the left and under pressure from unions (Borzutzky 2002, 48, 97–120, 139–45). Argentina illustrates an alternative to democracy, the path to a social security system with wide coverage via populist authoritarianism and semi-democracy, because the social security system for the bulk of the population was established by Perón, as part of his popular mobilization and support building strategy, beginning in 1944 as Minister of Labor under the military government and extending through his democratic and then authoritarian periods as president. Subsequently the Peronist movement, particularly the unions, became the key defenders of the system.

Our quantitative analyses of pooled time series data for eighteen Latin American and Caribbean countries show that these observations about the relationship between democracy and parties and social policy, poverty, and inequality are generalizable. The cumulative records of democracy and left party strength are negatively related to inequality and poverty (Pribble, Huber, and Stephens 2009), and the cumulative record of democracy is positively related to spending on social security and welfare and on health and education (Huber, Mustillo, and Stephens 2008). Social security and welfare spending is positively related to inequality, but when it takes place in a democratic context (measured with an interaction term) it is negatively related to inequality (Huber et al. 2006). This makes sense because typically more than 80 percent of social security and welfare spending goes to social security, and contributory pensions constitute the lion's share of social security spending. They accrue only to formal sector workers with significant histories of contributions, and even among formal sector workers they are unequally distributed to the especially generous schemes covering privileged groups such as judges, the military, and university professors. Democracies, though, are more likely to shift the composition of spending toward lower income groups than nondemocracies.

ECONOMIC CRISIS AND STRUCTURAL REFORM

The mature social security systems of Argentina, Chile, and Uruguay all began to experience fiscal problems in the 1970s. The active/passive ratio deteriorated because of the aging of the population, reserves had not been invested properly, inflation eroded benefits and economic stagnation meant stagnation of contributions, and the privileged schemes imposed ever greater financing burdens on the state budget. Various governments made efforts to unify and simplify the systems and shore up their fiscal base, but these efforts were politically difficult and insufficient to turn them into solid safety nets. The combination of economic crisis in the 1980s and economic liberalization, then, which caused a shrinking of the industrial and public sectors and thus of formal sector employment and of real wages, aggravated the fiscal crisis of the systems by reducing the number of contributors and the value of contributions, and it reduced their effective coverage. These problems also affected the pension part of the social security system in Costa Rica and the health systems of all four countries, and they prompted responses in the form of social policy reforms of different scope and character.

The problems went much deeper, though, than the fiscal crises of the social security systems. These traditional employment-based systems became increasingly inappropriate for the new structure of labor markets and family patterns. The decline of formal sector employment caused increasing poverty and decreasing social security coverage. Increasing divorce rates and births out of wedlock aggravated the problem of lack of social security coverage through the mechanism of coverage for dependents of the family breadwinner. At the same time, under the impact of the debt crisis, all governments were forced to implement stringent austerity measures, which prevented even those governments wanting to combat poverty from establishing new programs on a sufficiently large scale to be effective. Rather, the responses promoted by the International Financial Institutions (IFIs) were emergency social programs presumably targeted at the poorest sectors. Only in the 1990s did the IFIs and many Latin American governments begin to think more comprehensively about anti-poverty policies and universalistic health care policies. With the shift to the left after the turn of the century such efforts were intensified.

Argentina experienced a severe bout of fiscal crisis in the mid-1970s. After the military coup in 1976, the government imposed a major increase in financial liberalization and significant trade liberalization as well, in the context of an austerity program. The result was a decline in industrial and public sector employment, which reduced effective coverage of the welfare state. The next episode of fiscal crisis and economic decline in 1981 led right into the generalized debt crisis with high inflation, which continued until 1991. The Alfonsín government undertook several unsuccessful heterodox stabilization efforts. The country suffered the deepest economic decline of our four cases (see Table 5.3), with predictably dire consequences for the coverage and financial base of social security schemes and social services. In the 1990s, the Menem government imposed a radical program of liberalization and introduced the convertibility regime, which brought inflation under control and restored confidence in the emerging Argentine market, and thus stimulated capital inflows. Growth resumed, only to end up in a renewed profound crisis in 2001. What was different from earlier periods, though, was that the economic growth in the 1990s was accompanied by high unemployment, growth of the informal sector, and instability of employment (see Tables 5.3 and 5.5). In 1991, reforms of the labor market were implemented to make it more flexible, and the number of full-time, stable jobs decreased.

Chile's experience with economic reform and structural adjustment was very different from that of our other three cases, essentially taking place under the dictatorship of General Pinochet. After a radical economic stabilization program and a deep recession in 1975, the economic team led by economists trained at the University of Chicago embarked on a systematic and sustained program of trade and financial liberalization, privatization, labor market reform, and finally social policy reform. Capital poured into Chile and fueled economic growth until the financial bubble burst in 1981 and ushered in another major economic crisis. From the mid-1980s on, the economy embarked on a steady growth process with comparatively high growth rates, turning Chile into the poster child for advocates of neoliberalism. Ironically, these advocates conveniently overlooked the more statist elements in Chile's post-1983 approach, such as controls on short-term capital flows and export promotion measures. Similar to Argentina, economic growth was accompanied by increasing insecurity and informality of employment, increasing inequality, and—until the democratic government significantly increased social expenditures—also deterioration of social services and high levels of poverty.

Uruguay entered a period of slow economic growth and frequent balance of payments problems in the 1950s already. Between 1973 and 1985 the military government imposed an austerity program and undertook significant economic liberalization, particularly in trade and financial markets and domestic consumer prices, and it also increased the value added tax (VAT) and reduced social security taxes. The debt crisis led to a harsh IMF program and a very steep economic decline, which ended in 1985. Between 1973 and 1985 the military repressed the left and organized labor, and real wages had declined by 49 percent (Cassoni, Labadie, and Allen 1995). However, compared to Chile, labor was less debilitated, and after the transition to democracy the traditional wage-councils were reinstituted and resumed their function of wage-setting until they were disbanded in 1992.

In the 1990s, Uruguay grew more slowly than Argentina and Chile and remained below Argentina in level of GDP per capita, maintaining much lower poverty levels and lower inequality. In part, this is certainly a result of the slower and less extensive process of liberalization from 1985 on. As of 1985, Uruguay's liberalization index stood at .37, second only to Chile's (see Table 5.6), but by 1998 it had climbed to .46 only, an

TABLE 5.6
Index of Economic Liberalization

	General Structural Reform Index			
	1985	1990	1995	1998
Argentina	.34	.47	.60	.60
Chile	.49	.57	.58	.58
Costa Rica	.31	.42	.54	.56
Uruguay	.37	.37	.45	.46
Average	.38	.46	.54	.55
Brazil	.26	.43	.52	.58
Colombia	.29	.41	.54	.56
Mexico	.29	.42	.53	.51
Venezuela	.28	.34	.48	.51
Average	.28	.40	.52	.54
Jamaica	.40	.50	.55	.65

increase of .09, compared to a level of .60 in Argentina (an increase of
.26 there between 1985 and 1995). Comparative evidence suggests that
countries that underwent drastic reforms performed more poorly in a
variety of areas, including poverty, than countries that liberalized more
moderately (Huber and Solt 2004). In line with the more moderate approach to liberalization, Uruguay also managed to keep the size of the
informal sector slightly below those of Chile and Costa Rica, and well
below that of Argentina. Within the formal sector, labor rights were
better protected than in Chile. Finally, Uruguay sustained by far the
highest spending effort on social security and welfare in the 1990s. The
Argentine economic meltdown also affected Uruguay highly negatively,
and poverty in urban areas rose to a high of 15 percent of the population
(9 percent of households) by 2002, still well below the levels of the other
countries.

Unlike the other three countries, Costa Rica made no significant efforts at structural adjustment through economic liberalization before the
debt crisis. The country experienced an early onset of the debt crisis and
the government put a moratorium on external debt payments in 1981
already. In 1982, the new PLN government under Monge imposed an
austerity program supported by USAID and later in the year concluded
a stabilization agreement with the IMF. USAID played a critical role
and provided massive amounts of aid throughout the 1980s because of
Costa Rica's strategic location in the Central American conflict. In the
1980s, Costa Rica negotiated five IMF agreements and two major structural adjustment loans from the World Bank, as well as many separate
agreements with USAID. In the 1990s, then, USAID support diminished
greatly, and Costa Rica remained heavily dependent on the World Bank
and thus had to meet liberalization requirements. The liberalization
index increased from a low of .31 in 1985 to .42 in 1990 and .56 in 1998,
the latter level close to that of Chile. Accordingly, Costa Rica also experienced a substantial increase in the size of the informal sector, which
made it roughly similar to that of Chile on average in the 1990s. Finally,
Costa Rica had the lowest average growth rates of our four countries in
the 1990s.

Despite this problematic economic performance, Costa Rica continued to do comparatively well in levels of poverty and inequality. In the
1990s, Costa Rica had an average poverty level similar to that of Chile,
despite a much lower GDP per capita. Looking at the trajectory, Chile
had 39% of the population below the ECLAC poverty line in 1990 and
reduced that level to 21% in 2000, whereas Costa Rica began at 26%
in 1990 and reduced it to 20% by 1999 (CEPAL 2004, 324). Costa Rica
also managed to protect a much lower degree of inequality than that of

Chile, keeping its Gini close to that of Uruguay. All through the 1980s and 1990s Costa Rica continued with a tripartite wage setting arrangement and with a consistent policy to favor lower income earners through minimum wages in different sectors and absolute raises that benefited lower income workers most (Villasuso 2000, 21). Costa Rica also continued with a stronger welfare state effort than Chile in the 1990s, devoting a higher average percentage of GDP to total social spending.

REFORMS OF THE SOCIAL POLICY SCHEMES

All four countries, like the rest of the countries in Latin America and the Caribbean, undertook significant reforms of their social policy regimes in the 1980s and 1990s. Chile's reforms under the dictatorship were most radical and conformed most closely to the neoliberal prescriptions of reducing the role of the state and expanding the role of private provision of pensions and services in health and education. The democratic governments in the 1990s increased expenditures, but a serious rethinking of the balance between state and private provision of social policy did not take place until the turn of the century. Costa Rica stands at the other end of the spectrum, resisting pressures from external agents for neoliberal social policy reforms and instead concentrating on strengthening public schemes, and Uruguay and Argentina occupy an intermediate position in terms of private sector participation in pensions and health care, with Uruguay having protected the value of pension benefits to a much greater extent. Upon taking power in 2005, the Frente Amplio government began to pursue social policy reform with urgency and a clear universalistic and redistributive bent.

The Chilean pension reform and its effects have been well analyzed (Borzutsky 1998; Mesa-Lago and Arenas de Mesa 1998; Kay 1999), so a brief summary will suffice. A new statutory fully funded pension system with private individual accounts was established in 1981 to replace the old pay-as-you-go public system, and employer contributions were abolished for both systems. These new accounts are administered by private financial firms, the Administradores de Fondos de Pensiones (AFPs), and their yield depends on the returns on the investments made by these firms minus the fees and commissions charged. The old public system was closed for new entrants, and employees who had already made contributions to the old system had a choice whether to remain there or switch to the new private system. A large proportion of existing contributors were enticed to switch by heavy advertising, lower contribution rates, and the promise of recognition bonds for past contributions.

The privatization put a significant burden on the budget because the state needed to pay the benefits of existing pensioners without receiving the contributions of most active workers. Essentially, the whole reform constituted a massive transfer of funds from the public to the private sector. Despite the initially high returns on the investments in the pension funds, which were broadcast by the neoliberal reformers, the results in the longer run have failed to meet promises of reformers in virtually every respect: Effective coverage, that is, the proportion of the workforce making contributions to the pension system, did not increase; administrative costs are very high, mainly because of marketing expenses; the system of commissions and fees weighs particularly heavily on lower income earners and significantly lowers the real rate of return compared to the one claimed by the AFPs (Mesa-Lago and Arenas de Mesa 1998, 69); and there is no evidence that the new system caused an increase in the national savings rate (Uthoff 1995). Given the instability in the labor market, the low wages, and the size of the informal sector, a large percentage of the workforce will not have contributed for the required twenty years and thus be dependent on social assistance pensions, and another large percentage will not have accumulated enough in their accounts to get beyond a subsidized minimum pension. In other words, the state will have to subsidize the pensions of low income earners without having the benefit of the contributions from middle and high income earners.[8] All these problems prompted a re-reform of the pension system under President Bachelet in 2007, with emphasis on non-contributory and subsidized minimum pensions.

In both Argentina and Uruguay, pension privatization was put on the reform agenda and the Chilean model was propagated by the IFIs, but in both countries domestic resistance to full privatization was strong, and both ended up with mixed systems, retaining a strong public basic tier. In Argentina, the reformed system began operating in 1994 and gave employees a choice between putting their own contributions into the public pay-as-you-go system where all the employer contributions go, or into the new private system of individual accounts invested through AFPs. The public system provides a basic flat rate benefit to all retirees with thirty years of contributions, and supplementary benefits in the public system depend on the length of time during which the employee made contributions and previous earnings, and in the private system on the amount of contributions and the returns on the investment minus fees and commissions. The basic pension benefit is calculated on the basis of average compulsory pension contributions, which provides some adjustments to inflation. In 2007, new legislation was passed that makes it possible for individuals to return from the private to the public system.

Since 1996, Uruguay has had a mixed system also, with a public basic tier and a private supplementary tier. All employer contributions go to the basic public tier, as do employee contributions up to a specified income limit (originally the equivalent of $800 per month). Unlike in Argentina, however, there is no choice for employees but rather contributions to the supplementary private system are mandatory for all new entrants to the labor force and all those who were under forty at the time of the reform and have earnings above this income limit. All pensioners receive a pension from the public system calculated on the basis of earnings of the best twenty years, and higher income earners receive an additional benefit from their private individual accounts. Due to a constitutional amendment called for by a referendum in 1989, the real value of public pensions is tied to remunerations of public sector employees.

The Costa Rican pension system was the last one of the four to be reformed. After extensive public consultation and debate, the Ley de Protección del Trabajador (LPT) was passed in 2000 and established a mixed system that began operation in 2001. Half of the employee contributions and most of the employer contributions, as well as a small state subsidy, go to the public basic tier, the remainder to a second tier with individual capitalized accounts invested in public or private pension funds. The default option is the public fund administered by the Banco Popular, which had the large majority of all accounts as of 2002. The non-contributory income-tested pensions were reformed in 2003 and benefits set at no less then half of the minimum pension in the contributory system.

If we compare the four pension systems, we can identify two features that make Chile unique. Chile is the only one of the four countries where employers do not contribute anything to pensions and also the only one where coverage for the self-employed is voluntary by law. In Costa Rica, coverage for the self-employed was made mandatory by the LPT, though virtually no progress had been made on implementation by 2003. Similarly, in Uruguay and Argentina, de facto coverage of the self-employed as measured by active contributors is very low. The more important difference is the presence or absence of employer contributions; in Argentina employer contributions are set at 16% of wages, in Uruguay at 12.5%, and in Costa Rica at 6.5%. Thus, compared to Argentina and Uruguay, Chile is foregoing a major source of financial support for the pension system.

The great majority of those covered in all four countries now belong to one and the same pension scheme. Nevertheless, special schemes with better benefits than those offered by the general system persist, most prominently for the military in Argentina, Chile, and Uruguay. In

Argentina, provinces and municipalities have their own pension schemes as well; in Costa Rica the teachers and judicial employees, and in Uruguay workers in the financial sector, university professionals, public notaries, and the police do.

In the health sector, Pinochet in Chile again imposed the most radical reform, greatly strengthening the role of the private sector in the provision and financing of health care. All those covered by mandatory health insurance have a choice whether to direct their contributions to the public system through the Fondo Nacional de Salud (FONASA) or one of many private, for-profit health care organizations (Instituciones de salud previsional, ISAPREs).

The democratic governments inherited a public health system with clinics and hospitals whose maintenance and expansion to keep pace with population growth had been neglected under the military and whose personnel was underpaid. The government of Ricardo Lagos undertook a major reform by introducing the plan AUGE (Acceso Universal con Garantías Explícitas). This plan was to offer protection to all Chileans for fifty-six major illnesses, with equal quality of care and financial protection, regardless of income. In order to make this possible, it specifies maximum waiting times, prices to be charged for treatment by all providers, and the right to access to private clinics or hospitals if public ones are not available. The legislation was to create a compensation fund that would redistribute the costs between members of the public and private systems, financed by part of the mandatory contributions, and state funding was to cover indigents. After two years of intense negotiations during which Lagos had to withdraw the compensation fund and reduce the number of illnesses covered initially to 25, the legislation was passed and the program began operating in July of 2005. Treatment is free for FONASA members in the lower income categories and for the uninsured poor and requires a 20 percent copay from higher income members. The number of illnesses covered is to increase to 56 by 2007. New financing is coming from a 0.5% increase in the value added tax; other tax increases were rejected by parliament. Essentially, the right opposed the provisions that would have increased equity and solidarity and infringed on the interests of the private sector, and they managed to get support from some members of the governing coalition from the Christian Democratic Party and thus to force modifications of the legislation (Dávila 2005; Pribble 2008).

In Argentina and Uruguay, the changes in the labor market reduced the percentage of the labor force covered by mutual health insurance schemes, which—together with low funding for public institutions—stimulated growth of private insurance and provision on the one hand

and greater reliance on the increasingly financially stressed public system on the other hand. In Argentina, all efforts to unify the system failed because of resistance from the unions and the Peronists. The responsibility for the financing of public hospitals was transferred to the provinces (beginning in the 1970s already), and self-management and self-financing of public hospitals was favored, with predictable consequences for the quality of care given to the uninsured poor. In Uruguay, as in Argentina, health sector reform has also been stymied by the involvement of too many powerful stakeholders, despite insistent encouragement on the part of the IFIs. The public sector and the *mutuales* work in partnership, with the *mutuales* using public sector facilities under contracts, but overall coordination is deficient, which leads to inefficient use of resources and uneven quality of services. Moreover, as in the other cases, investment in public sector facilities has been lower than needed to provide high quality services across the board.

Costa Rica's unified public health system also began experiencing the problems of long lines and long waits for major treatments in the 1980s, with the result that higher income earners began to leave the system for the private sector and the private share of health expenditures rose from 26% in 1991 to 32% in 2000 (Martínez and Mesa-Lago 2003). The government did implement a reform that improved the access of poorer sectors to health care via the primary care centers, but it did not strengthen the public sector as a whole relative to the private sector.

EFFECTIVENESS OF THESE SOCIAL POLICY REGIMES IN THE NEW MILLENNIUM

As demonstrated at the outset, the social policy regimes of Argentina, Chile, Costa Rica, and Uruguay remain the comparatively most successful ones in Latin America, despite growing challenges. In Argentina and Chile, poverty increased greatly in the 1980s and declined again in the 1990s. In Costa Rica, poverty increased moderately in the 1980s and decreased in the 1990s, and in Uruguay it remained roughly at the same level in the 1980s as in the 1970s and then declined in the 1990s. In both Argentina and Uruguay, poverty shot up very sharply as a result of the economic crisis in the early 2000s.

If we compare the data on the determinants of poverty in Latin American countries for the 1990s with those for the 1970s, what stands out is the stronger relationship to economic indicators and the somewhat weaker relationship to spending indicators. Again, we have a limited number of observations and thus are looking at simple measures. The variation explained in a simple regression of poverty on GDP per capita is 63%, compared to 47% in the 1970s.[9] Adding the size of the informal sector to GDP per capita increased the variation explained in the 1970s to 55% and in the 1990s to 69%; adding the Gini increased it to 63% in the 1970s and 71% in the 1990s. In contrast, adding spending on education to GDP per capita increased the variation explained in the 1970s by 12% (to 59%) but lowered it by 3% (to 60%) in the 1990s; adding spending on social security and welfare increased it by 21% (to 68%) in the 1970s but by 3% only (to 69%) in the 1990s. The broad picture, then, is that the level of affluence of the society, the degree of inequality, and the size of the informal sector became stronger determinants of poverty relative to social expenditures than they had been two decades earlier.

However, this is a broad picture looking at averages for twelve to eighteen Latin American countries. If we look at scatter plots of averages for the 1990s, we see that there remains unexplained variation. In particular, Costa Rica and Uruguay remain considerably below the regression line of poverty on GDP per capita, whereas Chile sits exactly on that line and Argentina above it (see Figure 5.6). If we look at the scatter plots for poverty and the Gini, and for poverty and the size of the informal sector, all four of our countries are below the regression line.

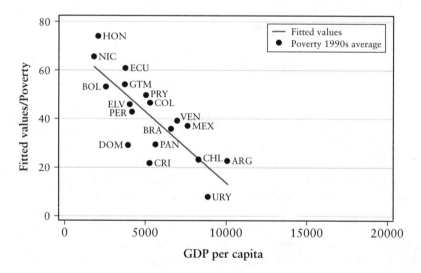

FIGURE 5.6 Poverty and GDP Per Capita, 1990s Averages
R = −.81

Author calculations on basis of Huber, Stephens, Mustillo, and Pribble dataset. See Appendix.

This suggests that their policy regimes manage to keep poverty lower than would be expected on the basis of these economic indicators. Magnitude of expenditures has something to do with it, but the fact that they are below the regression line of poverty on total social expenditures also suggests that they allocate their expenditures and implement their policies more effectively than other countries, in particular than Brazil, the second highest spender.

These four countries have begun to address the crucial challenge posed by economic informalization and the decline of the traditional male breadwinner family by strengthening social assistance programs and non-employment-based access to health care. Actual outlays on social assistance are still a small proportion of social expenditures, but these programs are receiving more political attention. In Argentina in 2003, social assistance accounted for 7.1% of total social spending and 1.4% of GDP, compared to social insurance with 43.2% of social expenditures and 8.3% of GDP. The corresponding figures for Chile in the same year were 4.4% and 0.7% for social assistance and 43.1% and 6.9% for social insurance (Lindert, Skoufias, and Shapiro 2005). In other words, Chile still spent ten times more on social insurance than on social assistance.

The reformed pension systems demonstrate the challenges faced by social insurance schemes and the need for greater emphasis on social assistance. Coverage of the pension systems is problematic in all four countries. Even where the self-employed are covered on a mandatory basis, few of them affiliate and even fewer contribute on a regular basis. Because of the precarious labor market conditions, even among employees only a fraction contributes regularly. In Argentina in 1998, way before the economic crisis, only 52% of affiliates contributed, in Uruguay 67%, and in Chile 54% (Cruz-Saco and Mesa-Lago 1998). By 2004, a study done by the Chilean Supervisory Agency of Pension Fund Administrators (cited in Riesco 2005) showed less than half of affiliates making contributions regularly enough to accumulate the twenty years required for a minimum pension. We have not been able to find comparable figures for Costa Rica, but figures for coverage for 2001 show that 65% of employees and 24% of self-employed were covered by the pension system, for a total of 53% of the economically active population. We can assume that the ratio of contributors to affiliated is somewhat higher in Costa Rica than in the other three countries because contributions are lower and for the self-employed they are differentiated by educational/skill level, but even with a higher ratio this still implies that in Costa Rica too the majority of elderly will depend on social assistance pensions.

All four systems have minimum pensions and income-tested social assistance pensions. As just noted, given the comparatively low ratio of active contributors to legally covered employees, and the requirements of twenty or thirty years of contributions to qualify for a minimum pension, a large proportion of employees is and will be dependent on those social assistance pensions. However, the level of these social assistance pensions is very low and not all elderly who would qualify actually receive them. In Chile, the value of a social assistance pension in 2001 was the equivalent of US $50 per month, in Costa Rica in 2000 it was $33.50, in Argentina after the devaluation of January 2002 it was $50, and in Uruguay in 2000 it was $120 (OIT 2002, 20).[10] In Uruguay, the social assistance pension is comparatively generously set at 45% of the average (not the minimum) pension in the general system. The urban poverty line per person in Chile in 2000 was $77 (indigence $39), in Costa Rica it was $75 in 1999 (indigence $38), in Argentina in 2002 it was $55 (indigence $28), and in Uruguay in 1999 it was $113 (indigence $56) (CEPAL 2004, 326–27). Thus, social assistance pensions clearly left individuals in poverty everywhere except for Uruguay, and in Costa Rica even in extreme poverty, whereas the minimum pension raised them above the poverty line. However, even this assessment is too rosy, since estimates were that in 2003 in Costa Rica only about 45% of the target population received the benefits (between 10,000 and 12,000 people), and some 11,000 people were on the waiting list (Martínez and Mesa-Lago 2003). Similarly, in Chile there was a quota for the maximum possible number of recipients. The OIT Report (OIT 2002, 22, 143) acknowledges the existence of an annual quota and a waiting list in Chile, but also gives figures based on household surveys that show more than 100 percent of the target population (impoverished people over 65) receiving such pensions by 2000.

According to OIT figures (2002, 17) noncontributory and social assistance pensions covered 0.9% of the total population (NOT the target population) in Argentina, 1.8% in Costa Rica, 2.0% in Uruguay, and 2.3% in Chile in 2000–01. Given the differential levels of poverty and thus the size of the target population, this suggests that Uruguay offers much better coverage than the other countries. These figures also show that non-contributory and social assistance pensions go only in part to the elderly, the other parts going to invalids, or survivors, or some other recipients. This is particularly true for Argentina and Uruguay, with 11% and 29% of these pensions going to the elderly only, whereas 46% in Chile and 61% in Costa Rica went to the elderly. The figures for Chile and Costa Rica sound plausible; that is, it is reasonable to assume that about half of noncontributory pensions could go to non-elderly, but the figures for Uruguay and Argentina suggest that these programs might not have strict eligibility rules and thus open room for discretion. Indeed, in Uruguay, traditionally noncontributory pensions were handed out through politicians, and the local party groups played an important mediating role (Rama 1972; Luna 2006). Nevertheless, the available figures suggest that in all four countries noncontributory and social assistance pensions were very effective in reducing indigence and poverty among households with recipients of such pensions (OIT 2002, 26). The reason why this is so, despite the fact that the benefits are so low as to leave individuals below the poverty line, is that they make contributions to the household budget that otherwise would have to cover the recipient as a dependent without income.

Unemployment insurance is another potentially effective antipoverty tool. However, unemployment insurance covers only a small percentage of the population, not even all formal sector workers. In Uruguay, under the oldest program with the best potential reach because of the smallest informal sector, only about 15 percent of the unemployed received benefits in the 1990s on average (OIT 2004, 69). Argentina in the 1990s and Chile in the early 2000s introduced unemployment insurance and active labor market programs, but their effects have remained very limited so far. The rules for eligibility in Argentina were so stringent that by 1995 only some 6 percent of the unemployed received benefits (Lo Vuolo 1997, 41).

In Argentina in the late 1990s, various emergency employment programs were introduced to provide some support to the large numbers of unemployed, and during the height of the economic crisis in 2001 and 2002 this program was supposed to be made universal, but coverage and the value of the benefits were too low to stem a massive increase in poverty. Whereas the average poverty rate in urban areas for the 1990s was 19 percent of households, the rate shot up to 32 percent in 2002 (CEPAL 2004, 324). The crisis also aggravated inequality in Argentina, driving the Gini index for the Greater Buenos Aires area from 50 in 1990 (already high by historical standards) to 59 in 2002, second only to Brazil in that year (CEPAL 2004, 12). The longest running emergency employment program is in its latest incarnation called *Jefes y Jefas de Hogar Desocupados*. The program is means-tested and grew from 26,000 beneficiaries in 1993 to 1.4 million beneficiaries in 2002, offering the equivalent of US $50 per month in 2002 (Giraudy 2007). It received co-financing from the World Bank. Funds were allocated from the central government to provincial governments, and those allocations favored provinces with Peronist or conservative governors (i.e., non-Radical, non-Alianza governors) and small peripheral provinces with overrepresentation in the

Senate, i.e., they were clearly responding to political purposes in addition to the poverty alleviation purpose (Giraudy 2007).

Chile has a relatively large number of programs directed at the poor, in the form of both subsidies and goods and services. The value of cash transfers is low, though. All of these programs have strict eligibility rules, and throughout the 1990s there was little coordination between them. Chile Solidario was launched in 2002 with the purpose of targeting the 225,000 poorest families in the country and assigning them to a social worker who would coordinate for them access to all the transfers and services they are entitled to under the condition that they comply with certain requirements. These requirements are designed to keep the most vulnerable members of the households, primarily children, healthy and in school (Serrano and Raczynski 2004). It is worth noting here that Chile made major progress in the provision of basic health services, managing to reduce infant mortality from 17 to 9 per 1000 from 1990 to 2004 (McGuire, forthcoming). Chile Solidario is an example of the contingent transfer programs that sprang up as pilot programs in several Latin American countries. In general, early evaluations of these programs have been favorable, and in a few countries their reach has grown to make a major contribution to poverty reduction, particularly in Brazil.

In Costa Rica, the annual reports on *The State of the Nation in Sustainable Human Development*, issued by the Proyecto Estado de la Nación since its foundation in 1994, and with the collaboration of the Contraloría General de la República and other state agencies, evaluate efforts to overcome poverty and social exclusion. The report with data for 2002 shows that 39% of all pensions paid in that year were noncontributory. According to the OIT report (OIT 2002, 17), over 60% of these pensions go to the elderly. A systematic examination of the incidence of social expenditures shows that children less than six years old and young people aged fifteen to seventeen years old receive the smallest share of total social expenditures, counting health and education expenditures, as well as cash transfers and other programs. Costa Rica, like Chile, maintains a register of poor families, categorized into four priority groups to receive support. The main programs to combat poverty and their effective coverage in the lowest income quintile in 2003 were school feeding programs (68% coverage), social assistance (54%), and housing support (43%) (Estado de la Nación 2004, 110). As this report makes clear, funding for these programs is pro-cyclical because it comes from a proportion of the sales tax, and the programs do not regularly receive the 20% of the sales tax that they should according to the law.

In Uruguay before the crisis of 2002, the social policy regime functioned relatively well in keeping poverty low because of comparatively high formal sector employment that made social security coverage effective, supplemented by the over 70% of non-contributory pensions going to the non-elderly. The aged continue to do relatively well in levels of poverty, but not children. Some 90% of people over 65 receive some kind of pension (OIT 2004, 66), contributory or not, whereas there is very little support for working age parents who are poor and their children. Accordingly, poverty is concentrated among children (40). The program of family allowances was reformed in 1995 and 2004, to improve its real value, target it to low income earners, and detach it from social security contributions and thus from formal sector employment. In 1995, the value of family allowances for private sector employees, the unemployed, pensioners, and small producers, was set at 16% of the national minimum wage for those with household income of less than six times the national minimum wage. Whereas the monetary value is low, it amounted to between 17% and 25% of the value of the basic nutrition basket for the poverty line in Montevideo between 2000 and 2004, and for 20% to 30% of that value in the Interior (Vigorito 2007). Still, coverage remained restricted; only about 30% of families with children in the lowest income quintile received the allowances in 2003. Coverage expanded as a result of the 2004 reforms and has made a difference in lowering extreme poverty (Vigorito 2007). Since total social expenditures are the highest in Latin America already, and the pension system weighs heavily and had a deficit of 4.5% of GDP in 2000 (before the crisis), the challenge for Uruguay is to redirect more resources from the elderly to working age unemployed or underemployed poor adults and their children. This, of course, is very difficult to do politically.

Since the 1990s, the experience with the minimum wage differed greatly across our four countries. At one extreme in Uruguay, where it was the marker for social security benefits, it lost all function as a labor market income policy tool, and at the other extreme in Chile it became an important factor lifting people out of poverty.

In Uruguay the value of the minimum wage deteriorated consistently and strongly from 1985 on; in Argentina it remained roughly constant from 1994 to 2001 and then deteriorated dramatically, whereas it increased consistently and substantially in Chile from 1990 on (Marinakis 2006, 4; BADEINSO/ECLAC) and remained relatively stable with a slight upward trajectory in Costa Rica (Estado de la Nación 2004, 410). If we look at its value as a proportion of median wages, we see that in Uruguay it was much lower in 1997 and 2002 than in Argentina and Chile; the ratio of median wage for all wage and salary earners to the minimum wage in 2002 was roughly 6:1 in Uruguay, 3.5:1 in Argentina, and 2.8:1 in Chile (Marinakis 2006, 6), and in Costa Rica it was 2.2:1 (Estado de la Nación 2004, 409–10). If we just look at wage and salary earners in small enterprises (up to five workers), i.e., the low paid sector, this ratio was roughly 3.5:1 in Uruguay, 2.5:1 in Argentina, and 1.3:1 in Chile (Marinakis 2006, 6). In Costa Rica for the private sector only (where the average wage is lower than in the public sector) it was 1.6:1 (Estado de la Nación 2004, 409–10). As a consequence, the minimum wage in 2002 was clearly below the poverty line for one person in Uruguay, just about at the poverty line in Argentina, and almost twice the poverty line in Chile (indicating that it would keep a worker and a spouse just out of poverty), and in Costa Rica it was three times the poverty line for households in urban areas. If we look at the proportion of all wage and salary earners receiving less than one minimum wage, we see only 3% in Uruguay, but 10% in Argentina and 13% in Chile; the proportion of all wage and salary earners receiving between 1 and 1.5 minimum wages (where we can assume that the value of the minimum wage is indeed important) is only 6% in Uruguay and 7% in Argentina, but 26% in Chile (Marinakis 2006, 5). In other words, about one quarter of wage and salary earners in Chile in 2002–2003 earned an income arguably influenced by the minimum wage legislation that was sufficient to keep themselves and a spouse out of poverty. The nominal value of the minimum wage in Chile increased by 640% from 1990 to 2003, while the consumer price index increased by 280% in the same period.

If we look at the whole picture since the 1990s—the greater importance of economic indicators in explaining poverty, the use of minimum wage legislation, and the development of social expenditures and their allocation, we can say that Chile's success in reducing poverty to the extent that it has was more due to economic growth and the use of minimum wage legislation than generous social policy, whereas Uruguay has been at the opposite end, relying more on social policy to compensate for lower economic growth and the abandonment of the minimum wage as a meaningful policy tool. In Argentina, the real minimum wage remained flat in the 1990s, declined during the crisis, and did not surpass the level of the mid-1990s again until 2005, so it was not a critical tool in fighting poverty. More important were the emergency employment programs that were introduced during the crisis and persisted afterward. In Costa Rica, the average wage in agriculture and in domestic service was below the minimum wage in 2000–2003 (Estado de la Nación 2004, 410), indicating that a significant proportion of wage earners fell below the minimum wage, as in Chile. Thus, the minimum wage appears to work as in Chile, being relatively high and an effective anti-poverty instrument for a good proportion of wage earners.

THE POLITICS OF SOCIAL POLICY

As previously discussed, the record of democracy and strength of political cal parties with commitments to redistribution, or alternatively incumbency of a populist leader with a labor base, are key factors to explain the original formation of the social policy regimes. To understand reforms of the social policy regimes since the 1980s we have to take into account again power constellations in the sense of the distribution of power between parties and interest groups on the left versus the right, or forces that defend the interests of the underprivileged versus those that defend the interests of the economically dominant groups, as well as the degree of power concentration through political institutions. In addition, we have to consider two important factors that are specific to the reform process and to the time period in which it occurred: policy legacies and external pressures.

The most straightforward explanation can be offered for policy reform under Pinochet: A radical right-wing dictatorship with extreme power concentration bulldozed over any possible opposition as well as policy legacies and instituted reforms before the IFIs were pushing for them, but then received lots of support for these policies. This same dictatorship also restructured economy and society in a way to emasculate labor and the economic capacity of the state, which left the democratic governments in a very weak position to change the social policy regime. The weakness of their position was reinforced by the institutional legacies of the dictatorship that favor the right, specifically the electoral system and the appointed senators. Finally, the composition of the Concertación itself, that is, the presence of some leading members with economically quite conservative views, made bold reform initiatives in social policy difficult. Under the two Christian Democratic presidents, priority was given to increasing social spending, but resistance to increased taxation from the business community and the right set limits to that strategy. As the figures show, Chile in the 1990s remained a laggard among our four cases in terms of its percentage of GDP devoted to social expenditures. When Lagos, the Socialist president, launched his major reform initiative in health care, he ran up against obstacles in the form of policy legacies and unfavorable power distributions. The private sector in health care had been given a key role under Pinochet and strenuously opposed the redistributive elements of the reform, as did the political right (Pribble 2008). Some Christian democrats sided with the right in opposition to the compensation fund, which forced its elimination from the legislation (Dávila 2005). Similarly, the right successfully opposed most of the tax increases proposed to fund the new system.

196 Variance in Success: Economics, Social Policy, and the State

In the other three cases, the reforms were carried out—or failed to be carried out—under democratic governments. Power concentration was arguably strongest in Argentina under Menem, as he had a majority or close to it in both houses of parliament and was also willing to use strong-arm tactics to push his initiatives through (Madrid 2003). In terms of opposition from society, he had to make concessions to the unions (and their allies in parliament), which obstructed the imposition of the Chilean model of pension reform and paralyzed health sector reform. Policy legacies were crucial in the health sector reforms; the reason why the unions so strenuously opposed reforms of the *obras sociales* was that they played an important administrative role. Pressures from civil society were very important for the great increase in expenditures for the *Jefes y Jefas* emergency employment program and for their allocation. Regression analyses show that the number of road blocks organized by the *piqueteros* was a significant determinant of the number of positions in the emergency employment programs given out (Giraudy 2007). Finally, external pressures were important but not decisive; the pension reform deviated from the Chilean model that was pushed by the IFIs, and health sector reform stalled. Just how important external pressures were is difficult to assess, because they have worked in the subtle ways of persuasion through policy networks (Teichman 2001), as well as through the tangible incentives of financing of reform initiatives.

In Uruguay, the ideological differences between the two traditional parties had largely disappeared by the mid-1980s, and a new divide between them and the left over the economic model and redistribution emerged (Luna 2006). Presidents from both of the traditional parties put reform proposals inspired by the IFIs on the agenda, but these proposals were unpopular and thus the traditional party in opposition and even factions of the president's own party failed to support them, along with the left opposition, of course. Moreover, power dispersion was the highest of our four cases despite the small size and unitary system of the country. It was high because of the existence of the referendum and the fractionalized structure of the parties. The threat and reality of the referendum hampered pension reform for a long time, and in the end the referendum protected the value of public pensions, but it failed to integrate the few remaining privileged schemes into the general one. The competition between fractions within the parties made it very difficult for presidents to forge majority coalitions in support of any specific reforms. It was only after the two traditional parties had formed a coalition to prevent a victory of the left that a pension reform could be passed (Hernández 2003). Resistance from civil society against pension privatization was strong, as leaders with union experience mobilized a strong pensioners' movement. Accordingly, the reform protected a strong public tier and introduced private individual accounts for relatively high incomes only. In health sector reform, policy legacies were problematic as in Argentina, as the *mutuales* strongly resisted a reduction of their role and stronger supervision and coordination by the Ministry of Health. Finally, here too strong pro-reform pressures and financial incentives from the IFIs sustained reform efforts but were not able to push them through against strong societal resistance and in a context of fragmentation of political power.

In Costa Rica, the political power distribution and policy legacies were the most favorable toward preserving a universalistic and solidaristic social policy regime. Though presidents from both traditional parties had to accept economic austerity and structural adjustment policies, resistance against neoliberal reforms of social policy from both the PLN and social sectors was strong and made it politically too costly for PUSC presidents also to push such reform models. An intermediate degree of dispersion of political power contributed to making reforms slow. The 1994–1998 PLN government did not have a majority in parliament and party discipline in controversial questions is difficult for any president because the no-reelection rule makes deputies look to the next probable presidential candidate of their party, who may have an interest in distancing himself (herself?—not quite yet!) from unpopular policy initiatives of the incumbent (Carey 1996; Lehoucq 2005). Finally, the introduction of the Constitutional Chamber made the judicial system an important player in—among other areas—social policy.[11]

Costa Rica does have a tradition of tripartite or multipartite consultation in important questions, and this tradition was followed in the social policy reforms as well. In 1998, a national forum was established to make recommendations that then profoundly shaped the LPT adopted in 2000 and thus the pension reform (Martínez and Mesa-Lago 2003). In the health sector, the policy legacies pushed in a universalistic direction in so far as the private sector was not nearly as large and as powerful as in the other three countries. Indeed, the World Bank had paid for Chilean consultants on health sector reform who suggested the establishment of ISAPREs, a suggestion roundly rejected by the Costa Ricans, whose main goal was to improve primary care for everybody. On a speculative note, one might add that IFI pressures for social sector reforms were not as intense on Costa Rica as on the other countries because Costa Rica spends a comparatively low amount on pensions, which are regarded as nonproductive spending by the IFIs, and more on health and education, which are regarded as contributing to human capital formation and thus economic growth.

CHALLENGES IN 2005 AND BEYOND

None of these countries have an optimal social policy regime, which makes it essential for them to undertake steps for improvement. Argentina suffered the greatest deterioration; Chile managed the greatest reduction in poverty but still faces huge inequalities in access to health and education; Uruguay and Costa Rica managed to stem off a major deterioration in outcomes so far but continue to face major fiscal pressures that affect their social policy regimes negatively.

Argentina saw an enormous increase in unemployment and poverty as a result of the economic crisis, with poverty rising from 21% of the population in 1990 to 45% in 2002 and then falling back to 21% in 2006 (ECLAC 2007, 11). The financial crisis destroyed a large share of the value of private pension funds, which will make problems of poverty among the elderly persist for years to come, unless the state improves its social assistance pensions. In 2007, the government passed a reform that makes it possible for people to return from the private to the public pension system and makes the public the default system. Yet, this reform was not accompanied by plans for how to meet financial obligations in the long run. The health system has remained inefficient and increasingly incapable of providing universal coverage. On the positive side, provision of primary health care for the poor by provincial governments has improved (McGuire, forthcoming).

Uruguay was heavily affected by the Argentine crisis and suffered a full-blown financial crisis also. Accordingly, the country also saw an increase in unemployment and poverty. Poverty had been reduced from 18% of the urban population in 1990 to 9% in 1999, but rose again to 15% in 2002 and 18.5% in 2006 (ECLAC 2007, 11). The health system is facing problems in financing and public-private sector coordination. The fiscal crisis also damaged the value of the private pension funds, to the extent that they had been invested in government bonds. The referendum locked in pension adjustments that absorb a large share of resources. The privileged schemes still exist. As noted, poverty is concentrated among families with children, so resources have to be redirected. The FA government is committed to change and has taken bold initiatives with the Plan Equidad (increase in the value of the universalistic family allowances for low incomes and lowering of the minimum age for the social assistance pensions to 65), as well as health sector reforms (Pribble 2008). However, the government has encountered considerable external opposition, as well as having to deal with internal tensions because of a very heterogeneous social base, ranging from the poor to recipients of comparatively generous benefits (Luna 2007).

In Costa Rica, poverty was actually reduced from 26% of the population in 1990 to 20% in 2002, rising to 21% in 2005 but falling back to 19% in 2006 (ECLAC 2007, 11). The adaptation of the health system can be regarded as successful in so far as the basic principles of equality of access have been preserved and the EBAIS primary health care program has been effective in delivering basic health services to virtually the entire population (McGuire, forthcoming). However, the problems of waiting times for more complicated treatments persist, as does the problem of exit of higher income earners. Implementation of the mandatory inclusion of the self-employed into the health insurance and pension systems is way behind schedule. Both of the established parties have been losing support, and it is not yet clear whether the Partido de Acción Ciudadana (PAC), a left splinter from the PLN, could replace them, as the FA has done in Uruguay (Lehoucq 2007). There is spreading alienation from politics and increased electoral volatility (Seligson 2002; Straface 2007; Seligson and Martínez Franzoni in this volume).

In Chile, poverty was reduced from 39% of the population in 1990 to 19% in 2003 and 14% in 2006 (ECLAC 2007, 11), and the economy is the strongest of our four cases. This should provide an excellent basis for further advances, but rapid progress in combating poverty and improving health and education for all is hampered by the distribution of power. There are potentially very effective programs in place for the poorest families, such as Chile Solidario and a number of progressive transfers. However, the proportion of total social expenditures (4.4%) and even more so of total GDP (0.7%) spent on these transfers remains highly limited (Lindert, Skoufias, and Shapiro 2005). The minimum wage has served as an important instrument so far, but there are limits to its further use because it does not reach into the informal sector. Business and the right strenuously resist tax increases, and the right has been overrepresented in the Senate and through the electoral system, which made it very difficult for the Concertación to get its policies passed. The constitutional reforms passed in 2005 reduced the problem in the Senate, but the distorting effect of the electoral system remains. Moreover, there are increasing tensions within the Concertación, to the extent that some members in the Senate defied the leadership in late 2007.

In identifying promising paths of action, then, we need to address both the design of social policy regimes and the politics of social policy. As far as designs are concerned, the crucial elements to combat poverty in this generation and the coming ones—in addition to the enforcement of above poverty minimum wages—are transfers, both to the elderly and the working-age population for their children. In the longer run, essential tools to prevent poverty are equal access to high quality health care and education. With regard to the health care systems, we know from comparative research that the systems with the greatest reliance on private delivery and financing of health care among advanced industrial societies (the United States and Switzerland) have the most expensive and inegalitarian health care systems, whereas the countries with the greatest reliance on public provision and financing (the Nordic countries and Britain) have much more inclusive systems and spend a lower percentage of GDP on them. The lessons for our Latin American countries are that the public components need to be strengthened and the regulatory role of the Ministry of Health expanded, in order to improve access to equal quality health care for all sectors of the population. This is precisely what the FA in Uruguay is attempting to do. The path advocated by Foxley (Chapter 4), in contrast, toward greater reliance on private provision of services with preservation of low taxes (and by implication also low transfers) would lead toward the American "model," which offers very little redistribution (Bradley et al. 2003), the least poverty reduction (Moller et al. 2003), and the most expensive and most inegalitarian health care system of any advanced industrial society.

It is important to emphasize transfers to the current generation of parents, that is, people of working age, precisely because such transfers have been condemned by the IFIs as unproductive expenditures at best and tools for political manipulation at worst. Of course, there are plenty of examples to support the latter view. However, investment in health and education alone, without intervention in poor households, simply will not break the cycle of intergenerational poverty. As long as basic needs for food and shelter are unmet, children will be integrated into family survival strategies and will not attend school on a regular enough basis to acquire the skills necessary to escape poverty in adult life. Data from the OECD and Statistics Canada (OECD/HRDC 2000) indicate that poverty and inequality remain important determinants of literacy skill distributions and literacy skill levels in society even in advanced industrial countries. The correlations for thirteen advanced industrial countries in the late 1990s between the literacy skills of the bottom five percentile and poverty (-.68) and inequality (-.85) are actually much higher than the correlation with public education spending (.54) (calculations by the authors).

At present, our four countries with the most successful social policy regimes in Latin America have made major efforts in expanding the coverage and raising the value of minimum pensions and non-contributory pensions (with the exception of Argentina), and in investing in health and education. However, the total amount of funds spent on transfers to the working age poor and their children has remained highly limited and has kept these programs from becoming truly effective instruments of poverty reduction. There are very promising experiences with programs of conditional transfers to the working age poor, conditional on educational participation of children and their use of health service, and in some cases also on participation in public service projects (de Ferranti et al. 2004, 272–80). The challenge is to let these programs grow to reach universal coverage of poor households. The FA in Uruguay is the only government in Latin America to have taken this step with the passage of legislation in December 2007.

At present, the dominant approach to targeting of poor households is expensive, as it entails repeated visits of social workers to take inventory of the possessions of the household as well as its income sources. This system is also intrusive and stigmatizing and sets the poor in competition with each other for favorable classification. A much more useful approach in the longer run would be to invest in improving the income tax system. This then would make it possible, for instance, to offer universal flat rate basic child allowances to parents whose children remain in school, and to reclaim them from the nonpoor through the income tax system. Or, it could make possible the introduction of a negative income tax for low income earners, an approach that has proven very effective in Canada (Myles 2002, 350–55). Tax reform efforts have been reasonably high on the agenda, but their thrust has gone in a different direction—toward greater reliance on indirect taxes and a lowering of marginal tax rates on income taxes (Tanzi 2000).

Where all of our countries are weak is in enforcing income tax collection and curbing tax evasion and avoidance. Latin America as a whole severely underperformed in tax collection in the early 2000s, if we control for per capita income levels. Median undercollection was 4% of GDP, with Argentina by far the worst performer with 12.3%, Chile (3.6%) and Costa Rica (3.3%) slightly below the mean, and Uruguay one of only three countries exceeding expectations, by 1.8%. Latin American countries undercollect particularly in personal income taxes, with a mean undercollection of 2.9% of GDP. Argentina undercollected by 4.4%, Chile by 4%, Costa Rica by 3%, and Uruguay by 3.4% (Perry et al. 2006, 95–96).

The strong correlations we show above between decade averages of GDP per capita and poverty for the 1970s and the 1990s might be interpreted as indicating that growth will solve the problem of poverty. However, these correlations are driven by cross-country differences and not change through time. In pooled time series analyses of this measure of poverty, we found that GDP per capita had only a modest and not robust effect (Pribble, Huber, and Stephens 2009). The reason for this difference is that growth in GDP per capita over time within countries was accompanied by increasing informalization, and variations in size of the informal sector were strongly and robustly related to poverty. These statistical findings are corroborated by our case studies. The clearest case experience is Argentina, where growth in the 1990s was indeed accompanied by rising unemployment and poverty. Of course, the economic crisis greatly aggravated these problems. So, economic decline—particularly precipitous decline—is to be avoided, but growth alone is not the solution. Social policies need to compensate for increasing informalization.

One of the keys for a government committed to poverty reduction is maintenance of macroeconomic stability. Financial crises wreak havoc with employment and real wages, tax revenues, and social expenditures. This is even true for advanced industrial democracies. The financial crisis in the Nordic countries in the early 1990s forced major (if to some extent temporary) cuts in welfare state entitlements. The effect of the crisis on popular living standards was largely cushioned through a strong social safety net, primarily unemployment compensation and active labor market policies to reintegrate people into the labor market, but financing for social services and generosity of transfers were cut (Huber and Stephens 2001). In Latin America, the blow from such crises is much harsher, because the social safety net is much weaker to begin with and the cuts tend to be more drastic. In particular, as we saw, unemployment insurance is rudimentary and active labor market policies are all but nonexistent.

The fundamental problem is that control of macroeconomic stability is only partly in the hands of Latin American governments. Fiscally responsible tax and expenditure policies are a necessary but not sufficient condition to ensure such stability. Controls over capital flows in and out of the country are an essential complement, but they run counter to neoliberal orthodoxy. Thus, in order to construct effective social safety nets, we need to rethink not only the traditional approaches to social policy regimes, but also the relationship between social policy regimes and economic policies more generally.

For too long, the debate about economic and social policy in Latin America has been dominated by economists. Social scientists from other fields need to reclaim the debate about policy, starting from questions about a desirable society and about ways to move in that direction both in terms of specific policies and in terms of political strategies. This requires us all to think broadly and include issues of public opinion formation in democracies, of the influence of media and the shaping of media contents by economically dominant groups, and possible counterweights from public media and the educational function of political parties in the area of public opinion formation. Social policy itself can have a powerful feedback effect on public opinion. Contrary to Meltzer and Richard (1975), support for redistribution in OECD countries is higher in countries with more equal income distributions (Mehrtens 2004). In the Latin American context, it is telling that Uruguay and Costa Rica, the two countries with the least unequal income distributions in Latin America, also have the highest levels of support for the political instruments of redistribution, democracy and political parties (PNUD 2004).

APPENDIX: DEFINITION AND DATA SOURCES

All the data used in this paper are contained in Evelyne Huber, John D. Stephens, Tom Mustillo, and Jenny Pribble. 2008. "Social Policy in Latin America and the Caribbean Dataset, 1960–2006." Department of Political Science, University of North Carolina. This dataset is available at www.unc.edu/~jdsteph/common/data-common.html. The variable definitions and original data sources are listed below.

> *Percent of households on $2 PPP:* World Bank poverty line, poverty is defined as households that live on 2 purchasing power parity dollars per day or less. Variable downloaded from the Cepal online database on April 5, 2005.
>
> *Percent of households in poverty:* ECLAC country-specific poverty lines and indigent poverty lines. The value of the poverty line(s) can be found in ECLAC's "Statistical Yearbook of Latin America and the Caribbean."
>
> *Gini:* United Nations University World Income Inequality Database Volume 2.0a (June 2005), which is available at: www.wider.unu.edu/wiid/wiid-introduction-2005-1.htm.
>
> *Average years of education:* Robert Barro and Jong-Wha Lee. 2000. "International Data on Educational Attainment: Updates and Implications." Harvard Center for International Development Working Paper 42, appendix table A1.
>
> The social spending variables are compiled using values from four spending series included in this Huber et al. (2007) dataset: (1) the IMF series, (2) the first Cepal series, (3) the second Cepal series, and (4) the Cominetti (2006) series. See Huber, Mustillo, and Stephens (2008) for an explanation of how the data were selected.

GDP per capita: Real GDP per capita in constant dollars using the Chain index based on

PPPs (Purchasing Power Parities) in 1996 international prices. Mark 6.1 of the Penn World Tables, Alan Heston, Robert Summers and Bettina Aten, Penn World Table Version 6.0, Center for International Comparisons at the University of Pennsylvania (CICUP), December 2001.

Growth in GDP per capita: Calculated from GDP per capita.

Value added in industry and agriculture: Value added is the net output of a sector after adding up all outputs and subtracting intermediate inputs. World Bank, *World Development Indicators*.

Industrial employment: Employment in industry as a percent of total employment. International Labour Organization, Key Indicators of the Labour Market database.

Net FDI inflows: Foreign direct investment, net inflows, as a percent of gross capital formation. World Bank, *World Development Indicators*.

Unemployment: Unemployment as a percent of total labor force. World Bank, *World Development Indicators*.

Urban Unemployment: Urban unemployment as a percent of total labor force. Cepal.

Informal sector employment: Percentage of workers classified as informal or non-agricultural labor force. International Labour Organization.

General Structural Reform Index: Values are bound between 0–1. (Eduardo Lora. 2001. Structural Reforms in Latin America: What Has Been Reformed and How to Measure It. Inter-American Development Bank Working Paper 348, Appendix 2, p. 30.)

Notes

We would like to thank Scott Mainwaring, Tim Scully, and Jim McGuire for comments on an earlier draft of this chapter.

1. Theoretically, it is possible even for a relative measure of poverty to decrease while inequality as measured by the Gini index is increasing. If the key factor driving inequality is the concentration in the top decile (as it is in Latin America; see Morley 2001), then poverty defined as a percentage of the median income can decline while concentration at the top increases. In Chile, growth arguably reduced absolute poverty, while government policy reduced both absolute and relative poverty by transferring resources to the poor.

2. It is important here to emphasize the importance of consistency in social policy effort. Nicaragua in the 1980s and 1990s was comparable to the top group in health and education spending, and in the 1990s in social security and welfare spending also, but the country had so much ground to make up that it remained highest in poverty, along with Honduras, and very high on inequality, as well as very low on literacy and life expectancy

3. For instance, Papadopoulos (1992, 63) notes that in the period 1962–1972 in Uruguay, election years regularly saw a significant increase in the value of pensions, and in between elections the value deteriorated.

4. These figures have to be taken with some caution. In general, Mesa-Lago's figures are on the high side, because he looks at legal coverage, whereas other scholars look at actual contributors to social security schemes. Isuani (1985, 95) gives coverage for Argentina in 1970 as 68% and Chile as 69%, and Papadopoulos for Uruguay as somewhat over 80% (1992, 55ff); still, the figures give a reasonable picture of the relative position of these countries.

5. For this period, we only have data on poverty and inequality for ten countries.

6. One needs to keep in mind, though, that the Argentine figures for spending on health do not include the *obras sociales*.

7. In Chile, the main restrictions were a ban of the Communist Party, lack of a secret ballot, and other infringements on free and fair elections in the rural areas until the late 1950s and exclusion of illiterates until 1970. In Argentina, the restrictions consisted of harassment of the opposition under Perón, and proscription of the Peronist party and military intervention behind the scenes after his overthrow, and in Costa Rica, mainly of irregularities in elections before the mid-1950s.

8. As we note elsewhere, one can get the benefits of a funded scheme (increased saving rates and insulation from demographic change) without many of the flaws of the Chilean systems such as high administrative costs, cohort risk, and individual account risk (Huber and Stephens 2000). However, any system, funded or PAYGO, which ties benefits to a contribution record, will leave many aged people in poverty in the Latin American context due to the large size of the informal sector.

9. We had more countries for which data were available for the 1990s than for the 1970s. Since these were mostly smaller and poorer countries, we ran our regressions with all the observations available as well as with those countries only for which we also had data in the 1970s. The pattern of results was essentially the same. The data presented here cover all the available observations for the 1990s.

10. In Costa Rica, in January of 2003 it was US $36.50, but according to the law it should have been $48.50, since the minimum pension was set at $97 and the law stipulates a value of half the minimum pension (Martínez and Mesa-Lago 2003).

11. For instance, the Constitutional Chamber ruled that the lack of cash benefits in case of sickness for the self-employed was discriminatory and thus forced the CCSS to introduce this benefit.

References

BADEINSO/ECLAC. Available at www.eclac.cl/badeinso/SistemasDisponibles. asp.

Borzutsky, Silvia. 1998. Chile: The Politics of Privatization. In *Do Options Exist: The Reform of Pension and Health Care Systems in Latin America*, ed. María Amparo Cruz-Saco and Carmelo Mesa-Lago. Pittsburgh, PA: Pittsburgh University Press.

———. 2002. *Vital Connections: Politics, Social Security, and Inequality in Chile.* Notre Dame, IN: University of Notre Dame Press.

Bradley, David, Evelyne Huber, Stephanie Moller, Francois Nielsen, and John D. Stephens. 2003. Distribution and Redistribution in Postindustrial Democracies. *World Politics* 55 (January):193–228.

Carey, John M. 1996. *Term Limits and Legislative Representation.* New York: Cambridge University Press.

Casas, Antonio, and Herman Vargas. 1980. The Health System of Costa Rica: Toward a National Health Service. *Journal of Public Health Policy* (September): 258–79.

Cassoni, Adriana, Gastón J. Labadie, and Steve Allen. 1995. Uruguay. In *Reforming the Labor Market in a Liberalized Economy*, ed. Gustavo Márquez. Washington, DC: Inter-American Development Bank.

CEPAL (Economic Commission for Latin America and the Caribbean). 2004. *Economic Panorama of Latin America 2004.* United Nations.

Cominetti, Rossella. 1996. *Social Expenditure in Latin America—An Update.* Santiago, Chile: CEPAL.

Cruz-Saco, María Amparo, and Carmelo Mesa-Lago. 1998. Conclusion: Conditioning Factors, Cross-Country Comparisons, and Recommendations. In *Do Options Exist? The Reform of Pension and Health Care Systems in Latin America*, ed. María Amparo Cruz-Saco and Carmelo Mesa-Lago. Pittsburgh, PA: University of Pittsburgh Press.

Dávila, Mireya. 2005. Health Reform in Contemporary Chile: Does Politics Matter? Master's thesis, Department of Political Science, University of North Carolina, Chapel Hill.

De Ferranti, David, Guillermo E. Perry, Francisco H.G. Ferreira, and Michael Walton. 2004. *Inequality in Latin America: Breaking with History?* Washington, DC: The World Bank.

ECLAC. 2006. *Social Panorama of Latin America 2006.* Santiago, Chile: United Nations Economic Commission on Latin America and the Caribbean.

———. 2007. *Social Panorama of Latin America 2007.* Santiago, Chile: United Nations Economic Commission on Latin America and the Caribbean.

Estado de la Nación. 2004. *Estado de la nación en desarrollo humano sostenible.* San José, Costa Rica: Proyecto Estado de la Nación.

Filgueira, Fernando. 1995. A Century of Social Welfare in Uruguay: Growth to the Limit of the Batllista Social State. Working Paper 5, Democracy and Social Policy Series, Kellogg Institute, University of Notre Dame.

————. 2005. The Structural and Political Keys of the Reluctant Latin American Social State and its Interplay with Democracy. Paper prepared for the United Nations Research Institute for Social Development. Geneva: UNRISD.

Giraudy, Agustina. 2007. The Distributive Politics of Emergency Employment Programs in Argentina (1993–2002). *Latin American Research Review* 42(2):33–55.

Hernández, Diego. 2003. Pension Reform in Uruguay. Master's thesis, Department of Political Science, University of North Carolina, Chapel Hill.

Huber, Evelyne, Thomas Mustillo, and John D. Stephens. 2008. Politics and Social Spending in Latin America. *Journal of Politics* 70(2):420–36.

Huber, Evelyne, Francois Nielsen, Jenny Pribble, and John D. Stephens. 2006. Politics and Inequality in Latin America and the Caribbean. *American Sociological Review* 71(6):943–63.

Huber, Evelyne, and Fred Solt. 2004. Successes and Failures of Neoliberalism. *Latin American Research Review* 39(3).

Huber, Evelyne, and John D. Stephens. 2000. The Political Economy of Pension Reform: Latin America in Comparative Perspective. Occasional Paper 7 for Geneva 2000, Geneva: United Nations Research Institute for Social Development.

————. 2001. *Development and Crisis of the Welfare State: Parties and Policies in Global Markets.* Chicago: University of Chicago Press.

Isuani, Ernesto Aldo. 1985. Social Security and Public Assistance. In *The Crisis of Social Security and Health Care: Latin American Experiences and Lessons,* ed. Carmelo Mesa-Lago. Latin American Monograph and Document Series 9, Center for Latin American Studies, University of Pittsburgh.

Kay, Stephen James. 1999. Unexpected Privatizations: Politics and Social Security Reform in the Southern Cone. *Comparative Politics* (April):357–75.

Lehoucq, Fabrice. 2005. Trouble in the Tropics: Two-Party System Collapse and Institutional Shortcomings in Costa Rica. *Journal of Democracy* (July).

————. 2007. Proceso de políticas, partidos e instituciones en la Costa Rica democrática. In *Democracia estable alcanza? Análisis de la gobernabilidad en Costa Rica,* ed. Miguel Gutiérrez Saxe and Fernando Straface. Washington, DC: Inter-American Development Bank.

Lindert, Kathy, Emmanuel Skoufias, and Joseph Shapiro. 2005. Redistributing Income to the Poor and the Rich: Public Transfers in Latin America and the Caribbean. Discussion Paper, LACEA. Washington, DC: The World Bank.

Lo Vuolo, Rubén M. 1997. La retracción del estado de bienestar en la Argentina. Buenos Aires: Centro Interdisciplinario para el Estudio de Políticas Públicas.

Luna, Juan. 2006. Programmatic and Non-Programmatic Party-Voter Linkages in Two Institutionalized Party Systems: Chile and Uruguay in Comparative Perspective. Ph.D. dissertation, Department of Political Science, University of North Carolina, Chapel Hill.

————. 2007. The Frente Amplio and the Crafting of a Social Democratic Alternative in Uruguay. *Latin American Politics and Society* 49(4):1–30.

Madrid, Raúl L. 2003. *Retiring the State: The Politics of Pension Privatization in Latin America and Beyond.* Stanford, CA: Stanford University Press.

Marinakis, Andrés. 2006. Desempolvando el salario mínimo: Reflexiones a partir de la experiencia en el Cono Sur." In *Para qué sirve el salario mínimo? Elementos para su determinación en los países del Cono Sur,* ed. Andrés Marinakis and Juan Jacobo Velasco. Santiago, Chile: Oficina Internacional del Trabajo.

Martínez Franzoni, Juliana, and Carmelo Mesa-Lago. 2003. La reforma de la seguridad social en Costa Rica en pensiones y salud: Avances, problemas pendients y recomendaciones. San José, Costa Rica: Fundación Friedrich Ebert.

McGuire, James. Forthcoming. *Politics, Policy, and Mortality Decline in East Asia and Latin America.* New York: Cambridge University Press.

Mehrtens, John. 2004. Three Worlds of Public Opinion? Values, Variation, and the Effect of Social Policy. *International Journal of Public Opinion Research* 16.

Meltzer, Allan H., and Scott F. Richard. 1975. A Rational Theory of the Size of Government. *Journal of Political Economy* 89(October):914–27.

Mesa-Lago, Carmelo. 1989. *Ascent to Bankruptcy: Financing Social Security in Latin America.* Pittsburgh, PA: Pittsburgh University Press.

———. 1994. *Changing Social Security in Latin America: Toward Alleviating the Social Costs of Economic Reform.* Boulder, CO: Lynne Rienner Publishers.

Mesa-Lago, Carmelo, and Alberto Arenas de Mesa. 1998. The Chilean Pension System: Evaluation, Lessons, and Challenges. In *Do Options Exist: The Reform of Pension and Health Care Systems in Latin America,* ed. María Amparo Cruz-Saco and Carmelo Mesa-Lago. Pittsburgh, PA: Pittsburgh University Press.

Moller, Stephanie, David Bradley, Evelyne Huber, Francois Nielsen, and John D. Stephens. 2003. Determinants of Relative Poverty in Advanced Capitalist Democracies. *American Sociological Review* 68(1):22–51.

Morley, Samuel A. 1995. *Poverty and Inequality in Latin America: The Impact of Adjustment and Recovery in the 1980s.* Baltimore, MD: Johns Hopkins University Press.

———.2001. *The Income Distribution Problem in Latin America and the Caribbean.* Santiago, Chile: United Nations Press.

Myles, John. 2002. How to Design a Liberal Welfare State: A Comparison of Canada and the United States. In *Models of Capitalism: Lessons for Latin America,* ed. Evelyne Huber, 339–66. University Park, PA: Pennsylvania State University Press.

OECD/HRDC. 2000. *Literacy in the Information Age: Final Report of the International Adult Literacy Survey.* Paris: Organization for Economic Co-operation and Development; Statistics Canada.

OIT. 2002. *Pensiones no contributivas y asistenciales.* Santiago, Chile: Oficina Internacional del Trabajo.

———. 2004. *El futuro de la previsión social en Argentina y el mundo: Evaluación y desafíos.* Santiago, Chile: Oficina Internacional del Trabajo.

Papadópoulos, Jorge. 1992. *Seguridad social y política en el Uruguay.* Montevideo: Centro de Informaciones y Estudios del Uruguay.

Perry, Guillermo E., Omar S. Arias, J. Humberto López, William F. Maloney, and Louis Servén. 2006. *Poverty Reduction and Growth: Virtuous and Vicious Circles.* Washington, DC: The World Bank.

PNUD. 2004. Programa de las Naciones Unidas para el Desarrollo. *La Democracia en América Latina.* Buenos Aires.

Pribble, Jennifer E. 2008. Protecting the Poor: Welfare Politics in Latin America's Free Market Era. Ph.D. dissertation, Department of Political Science, University of North Carolina, Chapel Hill.

Pribble, Jennifer, Evelyne Huber, and John D. Stephens. 2009. Politics, Policies, and Poverty in Latin America. *Comparative Politics.* 41(4), July.

Rama, German. 1972. *Club Político.* Montevideo: Arca Editorial.

Riesco, Manuel. 2005. 25 Years Reveal Myths of Privatized Federal Pensions in Chile: Lessons for Proposed U.S. Social Security Reform. *Americas Program Commentary.* Americas Program, Center for International Policy (March 10). Available at www.americaspolicy.org.

Rosenberg, Mark B. 1979. Social Security Policy-Making in Costa Rica: A Research Report. *Latin American Research Review* 15(1):116–33.

Seligson, Mitchell A. 2002. Trouble in Paradise? The Erosion of System Support in Costa Rica, 1978–1999. *Latin American Research Review* 37(1):160–85.

Serrano, Claudia, and Dagmar Raczynski. 2004. Programas sociales innovadores de superación de la pobreza en Brasil y Chile. In *Equidad y protección social,* ed. Clarisa Hardy. Santiago, Chile: LOM Ediciones, Fundación Chile 21.

Straface, Fernando. 2007. Gobernabilidad democrática en Costa Rica: "Hipergradualismo," cansancio reformista o desacuerdo sobre el modelo deseado? In *Democracia estable alcanza? Análisis de la gobernabilidad en Costa Rica,* ed. Miguel Gutiérrez Saxe and Fernando Straface. Washington, DC: Inter-American Development Bank.

Tanzi, Vito. 2000. Taxation in Latin America in the Last Decade. Paper prepared for the Conference on Fiscal and Financial Reforms in Latin America, Stanford University, November 9–10.

Teichman, Judith. 2001. *The Politics of Freeing Markets in Latin America: Chile, Argentina, and Mexico.* Chapel Hill, NC: University of North Carolina Press.

Uthoff, Andras. 1995. *Reformas a los sistemas de pensiones en América Latina y el Caribe.* Santiago, Chile: CEPAL.

Vigorito, Andrea. 2007. El impacto de las asignaciones familiares sobre la pobreza y la distribución del ingreso en los años recientes. Unpublished paper. Montevideo, Uruguay: Instituto de Economía, Universidad de la República.

Villasuso, Juan Manuel. 2000. Reformas estructurales y política económica en Costa Rica. San Jose, Costa Rica: Instituto de Investigaciones Economicas de la Universidad de Costa Rica, Serie Reformas Economicas 64.

World Bank, 2008. CD-Rom. *World Development Indicators 2007.*

CHAPTER SIX

Institutional Design and Judicial Effectiveness: Lessons from the Prosecution of Rights Violations for Democratic Governance and the Rule of Law

DANIEL M. BRINKS

This chapter addresses an especially important challenge for democratic governance in Latin America. In it, I first briefly describe some facets of the violent response to crime on the part of the police—the all-too-quick decision to shoot and kill crime suspects and others who run afoul of the police—and then analyze in more detail (the failures of) the judicial response to this violence. I argue that the failure to enforce criminal laws against violent police can be traced back to two principal dynamics, operating to different degrees in different environments: first, the willingness of some judges and prosecutors to take an overly lenient stance in these cases when there is important political pressure to look the other way, what I will call a normative failure; and second, the inability of even willing judges and prosecutors to penetrate the wall of silence put up by the police in these cases, what I will call an informational failure. I conclude with a review of the lessons we can extract from these findings, for governments that wish to combat police violence or establish a more effective rule of law more generally.

As Mainwaring et al. make abundantly clear in the Introduction to this book and in Chapter 1, the impunity of police officers who kill is a crucial challenge for *democratic* governance for at least three reasons. In the first place, these violations strike at the very core of what it means to be a true democracy. If police violence is so pervasive, and impunity so common, that citizens still walk the streets in fear of the state's repressive apparatus; if important parts of the state are still *de legibus solutus* as a matter of fact, if not as a matter of law; then we might begin to question just how democratic these regimes are, at least for the most vulnerable populations (O'Donnell 2001, 2004). The effective, not just the nominal, protection of basic human and civil rights is part of what it means to be a democracy.

Secondly, police violence attains epidemic proportions in many Latin American cities. Crime has become one of the major problems Latin American governments are facing, and Latin American publics are making ever more pressing demands for an effective response to crime (Hojman 2004; Mainwaring 2006). Increasing levels of police violence are partly explained by these demands, but police abuses in turn contribute to the rising sensation of lawlessness and violence (Stanley 2005). When the police (in São Paulo, in 1992, for example), kill more than 1,400 people in a single year, representing 27% of all homicides; when per capita rates of police homicides in Salvador da Bahia are four times higher than the overall homicide rate in most European advanced industrial democracies; when the rate at which Buenos Aires police kill civilians grows every year, we might soon begin to question whether these governments are at all in control of their own police forces—and if they are, whether they merit the democratic label. Controlling the various parts of the state is, of course, a governance challenge for any regime, but especially so for democratic ones, which implicitly promise an accountable state, respectful of legal limits and citizen rights.

Finally, once the initial excitement of the restoration of democracy had passed, it became increasingly clear that one of the areas in which Latin American democracies were falling short was in establishing an effective rule of law and effective judiciaries (Shifter 1997, 116; Diamond 1999). Billions of dollars have been poured into justice reform efforts, with decidedly mixed results (Stotzky 1993; Hammergren 1999; Méndez, O'Donnell, and Pinheiro 1999; Prillaman 2000; Ungar 2001; Mainwaring and Welna 2003). The inability to convict police officers who murder unarmed civilians is yet another indication that the courts are failing in some of their core purposes.

There is at least one additional reason why it is appropriate to address this issue in a volume dedicated to governance. In many ways, establishing the rule of law is a governance issue no different than many others. The democratic rule of law has both a substantive component, requiring the selection of certain rules such as due process and an independent arbiter, and a more procedural component, requiring the universal application of those rules (Raz 1979). Similarly, successful governance requires first choosing the right policy, and then effectively implementing that policy. Governance and the rule of law, therefore, share two dimensions: successful policy selection—for the rule of law, the choice of adequate, democratic, substantive or procedural rules—and effective implementation—for the rule of law, legal enforcement. In this paper I address almost exclusively the latter, in the context of the prosecution of police officers for arbitrary killings.

A focus on implementation when examining the failures of the rule of law in Latin America is more than justified. The lack of a fully democratic rule of law in the region is partly related, to be sure, to the selection of rules. There are outmoded procedural codes; laws governing freedom of expression, defamation, or states of emergency that are "bad" from a democratic perspective; ill-advised rules concerning foreign investment and the regulation of financial markets; undefined and unprotected basic rights, and many other instances of poorly chosen or designed laws. But many of these substantive deficiencies are being or have been corrected. New procedural codes have been put in place in almost all the countries of the region, and new constitutions or constitutional amendments addressing the worst substantive defects have been enacted in many countries. Indigenous rights are being included in ever more constitutions (Yashar 1999; Van Cott 2000). Gender equality is finding its way into formal laws, and now "the majority of Latin American and Caribbean countries have passed legislation that addresses intra-family or domestic violence, or violence against women" (ISIS International 2006, 1). Legal reform has swept the continent and continues to produce improvements—at least in the text of the law.

Despite all this normative innovation, however, many of the old problems remain. Substantive rights guaranteed in constitutions too often remain a dead letter, procedural codes are ignored in practice; in brief, formal laws still fail to structure reality in many ways. Now that a democratic formal legality is the norm in the region, the most basic difficulty for a government pursuing the rule of law is not so much choosing the right laws but making the chosen laws "stick." In this chapter, therefore, I propose some answers to this basic difficulty, by examining why different judicial systems succeed or fail to enforce existing laws against arbitrary killing by the police. I use the criminal prosecution of police officers who kill as a window to evaluate the success of the state in establishing the rule of law in five different legal environments—the federal and provincial courts of the City of Buenos Aires and its metropolitan area, the state courts of São Paulo and Salvador da Bahia in Brazil, the state courts of the Córdoba metropolitan area in North-Central Argentina, and the national courts of Uruguay.

A brief word is in order about the countries and cities chosen for this study. Argentina has a long history of transitions back and forth to democracy, but it returned to democracy in 1983 with the election of Raúl Alfonsín and has since had a series of peaceful alternations in power. The democratic regime itself seems stable, surviving serious economic crises and perceived mismanagement that forced two presidents, Alfonsín and de la Rúa, to step down early. Argentina is a federal country. Buenos Aires, the capital city, has autonomous legal status, its own judiciary, and one third of the country's population in its metropolitan area. Events that take place in the Buenos Aires metropolitan area but outside city limits fall under the jurisdiction of the provincial courts of the province of Buenos Aires. Córdoba, the second city examined here, is the second largest city in Argentina, with a strong industrial base. It is known as "la docta," a reference to the numerous and distinguished lawyers it has produced and its prominent place in Argentine legal history. Argentina in general and Buenos Aires in particular have a reputation for weak courts (Verbitsky 1993; Larkins 1998; Miller 2000) and a violent police (Dutil and Ragendorfer 1997), while the reputation of the courts in Córdoba is better (FORES and Colegio de Abogados de Buenos Aires 1999).

Brazil is the largest and most populous country in South America. It has the largest economy in the region, and has experienced slow but, at least recently, steady economic growth since its own transition back to democracy, in 1985. It too has a strong and stable democratic government. In contrast to Argentina and Uruguay, however, it is characterized by a much more fragmented party system. Like Argentina, Brazil is a federal country with separate state judiciaries. São Paulo is its largest and wealthiest city, while Salvador is the third largest city in the country. Again like Argentina's, Brazil's legal system is often the target of domestic and foreign critics (Faria 1988, 1994, 1996; Prillaman 2000). The police in Brazil generally and in São Paulo in particular, meanwhile, are also viewed as violent and barely under control (Barcellos 1992; Cano 1999; Amnesty International 2005). Salvador, in turn, is the capital of Bahia, which, as Ames notes, "For many years,...has been the strongest bailiwick of the Brazilian Right" (2001, 129).

Uruguay has also established a stable democracy since the end of the 1973–1985 military dictatorship. For most of its history, it was dominated by two large parties, until the recent rise of a coalition of leftist parties, who now hold the presidency. In contrast to the other two countries in the study, Uruguay is a unitary country with a national legal system and has acquired a deserved reputation for respect for civil rights and the rule of law. O'Donnell, for example, highlights Uruguay as a positive case for an effective and egalitarian legal system (1999b, 311). Uruguay and Córdoba, therefore, anchor one end of the continuum between well regarded legal systems, with a reputation for less violence and more legality, and less successful legal systems, with more violent police forces. Buenos Aires, São Paulo, and Salvador, in roughly that order, lie closer to the other end of the continuum.

The frequency with which the police kill in the most violent of these cities is truly shocking. Over the course of the 1990s, in democracy, the police in the state of São Paulo, Brazil, killed more than 7,500 people, for an average annual rate of about two per hundred thousand of population. That is two and half times as many people as Pinochet's regime murdered in all of Chile, over its entire seventeen year course. In some years, the São Paulo police killed, on average, one person every six hours. Nor are São Paulo's police the most violent. In Salvador da Bahia, in Northeastern Brazil, the per capita rate of police killings for a three year period in the mid-1990s was three times higher than São Paulo's. Many other places show equally dismal results. In the second half of the decade, the police in Buenos Aires killed, on a population-adjusted basis, just as often as the police in São Paulo, ending the decade with an annual average of about 1.5/100,000. There is information to suggest that in Venezuela, which is not a part of this study, the police killed twice as often as in Salvador.[1] For comparison, consider that police killings in Los Angeles, the U.S. city with the most violent police force, occur at a rate of about 0.5/100,000, less than one tenth the rate in Salvador, while in New York the rate is about 0.34 (Chevigny 1995).

The phenomenon, however, is not universal; in the Argentine province of Córdoba and in Uruguay, for example, rates of killing are very much lower. Uruguay has the lowest rates, reporting an average of two or three deaths per year at the hands of the police, and Córdoba follows with about 30 killings per year. Adjusted for population levels, Uruguay's rate is about 0.1 per hundred thousand, and Córdoba's about 0.3, compared to more than 6 per hundred thousand for Salvador. Despite these occasional variations, in many countries police violence is an everyday occurrence, and the phenomenon seems to be growing.

Unfortunately, the courts have not always responded well to the problem. While Uruguay and Córdoba succeed with some regularity, Buenos Aires, São Paulo, and Salvador da Bahia largely fail to enforce laws against police violence. As seen in Figure 6.1, the conviction rate following a police killing is about 50% in Uruguay, about 45% in Córdoba, 20% in Buenos Aires, and 5% or less in São Paulo and Salvador. The dif-

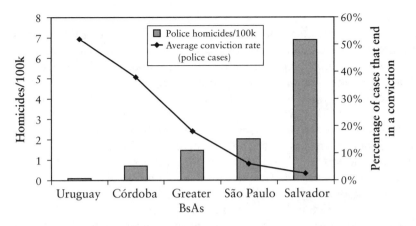

FIGURE 6.1 Average Per Capita Police Killings and Conviction Rates in Police Cases in Uruguay, Brazil, and Argentina for the 1990s

ference in conviction rates cannot reasonably be attributed to a greater propensity on the part of Uruguay's and Córdoba's police forces to kill in violation of the law. As Figure 6.1 also shows, these two are by far the least violent of all five police forces. In fact, there is an almost perfect inverse relationship between conviction rates and the level of police violence in each of these places.[2]

The focus on the enforcement problem conforms to narrow or formal notions of the rule of law—similar to what Barros (2003), for example, calls rule *by* law, or Holmes (2003) calls rule *through* law. The paper focuses not on substantive virtues or defects in the law, but on the political, social and institutional roots of the law's failure to structure social interactions; and, more specifically, on the role of the criminal justice system in channeling the structuring force of law, in the area of police violence. This is not, in principle, a different problem than what is involved in the implementation aspect of governance more generally. Policies are expressed in laws more often than not, and the decision to protect civil rights is a policy decision like many others.

In a functioning democratic system, the legally empowered law-giver (a Constitutional assembly, legislature, or regulatory agency, among others) establishes a rule defining a range of permissible rules of decision.[3] The rule of law requires that subordinate actors, defined as those to whom the primary rule is made applicable plus all enforcement instances, use a more or less faithful reproduction of that rule in making their own decisions. The first governance problem in creating the rule of law is generating this top-down normative homogeneity: ensuring that the rules of decision used by subordinate actors in practice do not exceed the permissible range established in the superior law. A failure here is what I have labeled a normative failure. In the area of police misconduct, the rules are primarily applicable to the police, and the enforcement actors are, among others, prosecutors and judges.

I take the view, perhaps most forcefully and most recently expressed by Maravall and Przeworski (2003), that inducing compliance with norms—including the law—is primarily a matter of ensuring that individual actors' incentives favor compliance. In addition to positive incentives for those who excel at norm compliance, this prominently includes, of course, the presence of effective enforcement mechanisms that impose costs for noncompliance. While there may well be a "normative component" to rules which induces compliance for the sake of the rule (something these authors deny), the best way to ensure a general tendency toward compliance is to structure incentives so that they tend in that direction. We have known this at least since Madison said, "If men were angels, no government would be necessary. If angels were to govern men, neither internal nor external controls on government would be necessary" (Federalist No. 51, Hamilton, Madison, and Jay 1961).

If knowledge of the rule were sufficient to induce compliance, then solving the problem would require no more than enacting the right rules and adequately informing all the various actors of their content. But the problem is not so much that the police, as the subjects of the rules against arbitrary police violence, do not know the rules. It is that far too many of them consider human rights to be *bobagem* or foolishness, as a judge who teaches human rights classes to police officers once told me.[4] Rules that purport to limit police discretion in the use and abuse of lethal force, rules that purport to give socially marginal, possibly criminal, actors some leverage over the police, run sharply against the incentives and normative expectations of police officers in places like São Paulo, Salvador, or Buenos Aires. In consequence, the rule the police often in fact apply ("human rights is *bobagem*, we can shoot to kill any time we decide to do so") falls outside the permissible range of rules, as defined in the law. Oversight instances, such as prosecutors and judges, are supposed to evaluate and punish this deviation, applying the correct rule of decision.

Even this narrow notion of the rule of law requires a second element, however: the application of the right rule of decision to the right information. At least some of the failures of the legal system can be attributed to what we might call an informational failure. The oversight decision can fail to make a rule effective because it is based on a biased version of the rule, or because it is based on biased information about the object of the rule. That information, in contrast to normative direction, typically flows from the bottom up, rather than from the top down. And in the legal system, more often than not, the information used by prosecutors and judges is generated by the police. When the police are applying the wrong rule, this flow of information is compromised. The police know what the true facts are, but their more lenient normative assessment of them causes them to classify those facts as not a violation of (their) rule and therefore not punishable. To ensure that the official outcome matches their own preferred outcome, they can attempt to pass on to prosecutors a sanitized version of the facts that produces an acquittal even under the prosecutor's stricter version of the rule.

Certainly the police know this. In all the places I have examined, the police, usually with the more or less active participation of senior officers, resist enforcement of these rules in exactly this way. I will discuss some of the details of this resistance below. For now, suffice it to say that the police corrupt or hide evidence of abuses, plant weapons near victims' bodies, produce misleading forensic reports, intimidate and even kill witnesses. Even in Uruguay, where the conviction rate is the highest of any place I examine, the police in one case planted a gun on the victim, after using it to shoot holes in their own clothing and in the police car, and in general resist cooperation with prosecutors and investigative judges by impeding an honest investigation. In short, the police not only violate the rules, they predictably resist efforts to enforce compliance by stifling the production of information about their illegal conduct.

Solving this informational problem in the area of police violence poses some special difficulties. In the criminal justice area, the police force, or some subdivision of it, is the agency typically assigned the task of producing information for the use of prosecutors and judges.[5] For enforcement of criminal laws, policy makers generally rely on the resources and incentives endogenous to the legal system to produce the requisite enforcement behavior: the police will investigate because that is what they are paid to do, prosecutors will prosecute (and defense attorneys will defend) because their jobs depend on it. But in these cases, these endogenous incentives and resources fail to work. When the police reliably fail to produce adequate information, prosecutors are forced either to carry out an investigation for which they have few resources and organizational capacity, or to rely more heavily on the efforts of interested parties. The ordinary incentives and capabilities are insufficient.

In effect, the failure of the police to carry out their assigned task forces the criminal justice system to work a little more like the ordinary civil justice system in the common law world, which relies on interested parties on both sides to produce most of the relevant information. When the police resist enforcement, then, the adjudicatory process begins to look a lot like an adversarial process, pitting the defendant (possibly with the endorsement of the police corporation) against representatives of the victim (possibly with the endorsement of the prosecutor's office).

In summary, the courts may be acquitting murderous police officers because judges and prosecutors have no intention of enforcing rights (a normative failure) *or* because they are trying to enforce them but cannot get the information they need to do so effectively (an informational failure). The outcome in each case—a low conviction rate—looks the same, but the underlying source of that failure is different, and the governance solution will have to be different. The challenge for a government wishing to effectively prosecute police misconduct, therefore, is to design oversight institutions in such a way that prosecutors and judges have (a) the incentives to apply the correct rule of decision themselves, thus undertaking these prosecutions with sufficient interest to overcome the resistance of the police, and (b) the capacity to obtain the information required to monitor the relevant conduct.

The matter of incentives is, conceptually at least, straightforward. The literature on judicial decision making suggests that judges are responsive to their political environment. This may be because their appointment is controlled by dominant political actors (Dahl 1957; Segal and Spaeth 2002), or because judges act strategically in order to please political actors that have some power over them (Epstein and Knight 1998; Helmke 2002). Or it may simply be that judges are, like any other members of society, a product of their environment. And if judges, who are typically expected to be independent, respond to political pressure, then prosecutors, who in most cases are expected to respond to political direction, should be no different. In either case, if this view of legal actors as embedded in their political context is correct, we should see conviction rates track political pressures: all else equal, there will be higher conviction rates when there is external pressure to convict, and lower conviction rates when there is broad support for violent police tactics.

As we will see in the discussion of particular systems, below, there is one additional wrinkle to consider on this issue. Different institutional arrangements channel popular and political pressures in different ways. Some judicial and prosecutorial institutions are designed to be more responsive to political direction, while others are specifically designed to be more independent. Thus we should see these exogenous pressures matter more when judicial and prosecutorial institutions more efficiently translate outside pressure into career and similar personal incentives for individual legal actors, and matter less when these institutions are designed to be more insulated from outside pressures.

Giving prosecutors, or in their defect, the representatives of the victim, sufficient capacity to overcome police resistance is a more difficult problem. When there is strong pressure to acquit—say, because a city is in the midst of a perceived epidemic of violent crime, and police violence is presented as the only possible solution—almost no amount of information will suffice. When there is little pressure on prosecutors or judges in either direction, the entire burden will fall squarely on victims' representatives, and convictions will respond to their personal capabilities. When there is more pressure to convict, the state, in the form of judges and prosecutors, will take a stronger hand in the process, but will still rely on interactions with representatives of the victim or members of the victim's immediate surroundings to generate much of the requisite information. As a result, even if prosecutors and judges are motivated to prosecute, a prosecution may still be stymied if the police have the ability to impose silence on witnesses and family members. This leads to the second prediction: when judges and prosecutors are neutral, the likelihood of a conviction will closely respond to the socioeconomic status of the victim. The victim's socioeconomic status will be less relevant when there is stronger political pressure either for or against these prosecutions.

In the next section, I show how these predictions match up to the data. As anticipated, the dependent variable, the main indicator of success, is the conviction rate of police officers who have been accused of killing someone. The point, of course, is not that the conviction rate should be 100% everywhere. On this measure, Stalin's judiciary was almost certainly among the most effective in history. The flip side of a successful prosecution is the success of the institution in protecting the rights of those who are accused on the basis of insufficient or inaccurate evidence. But the rate of appropriate convictions should be higher where the investigative, prosecutorial, and judicial functions are most effective, so long as the system is not simply rubber-stamping political decisions by convicting everyone who is accused. And comparisons across social groups and across legal systems should be valid so long as there are no significant, systematic variations in the underlying proportion of meritorious to meritless cases.

To obtain conviction rates, examine the characteristics of victims, and uncover possible reasons for the failure of courts to convict, I put together lists of victims of police homicides in each of the five cities.[6] I used these lists as the starting point to uncover the course of subsequent prosecutions or investigations. The result is a database of more than 500 cases in which the police killed someone, with more or less complete information on the characteristics of the victim, the process the case underwent, the outcome of the case, and other variables.

By analyzing these cases, we can infer the extent to which, in a particular city, normative or informational failures are behind the failure to convict. As explained in a little more detail below, I take the effect of the socioeconomic status of the victim and the impact of a private attorney as evidence that there was an informational failure—poorer victims have greater difficulty producing high quality information for legal consumption, and the intervention of a private attorney can improve the quality of the prosecution. Conversely, I take the impact of demonstrations as evidence of normative failures—demonstrations do not add any legally relevant information, but they do generate pressure to convict.[7] Within-city comparisons show that both the victims' resources and the political construction of a case affect the performance of judges and prosecutors. As predicted, they show that socioeconomic variables matter most where political pressures are neutral (Córdoba) or neutralized by insulated judicial institutions (São Paulo). Table 6.1 shows the impact of the victim's socioeconomic status on prosecutorial success in each location. This result is confirmed in individual level analyses showing that the intervention of a private attorney to assist the prosecution is crucial in all the systems but Uruguay (Table 6.2). Politics also matters. Pointed political pressure in individual cases, such as demonstrations, strongly affects the probability of a conviction in most cities (Table 6.2). The importance of resources and politics is further confirmed in the cross-national comparisons detailed further here, where I show how broad political variables predict higher or lower overall conviction rates.

The effect of the victims' socioeconomic condition varies considerably across different systems, as does the impact of more political variables. In Córdoba, although the average conviction rate is high, we see a very high impact of socioeconomic inequality on legal outcomes: raising the victim's status from lower to middle class more than doubles the conviction rate from 33 to 79% (see Table 6.1). Similarly, in São Paulo the most marginal victims secure a much lower conviction rate than those who are slightly better off, who see a conviction rate more than two and a half times higher. In Buenos Aires, class matters but to a lesser degree. In Uruguay, in contrast, the socioeconomic status of the victim is not significantly related to the outcome of the prosecution—there is a higher conviction rate among cases involving non-middle class victims, but the relationship is not significant.

Socioeconomic status also seems almost irrelevant in Salvador, where convictions fail no matter what the condition of the victim. In Salvador, I was unable to review the records in a systematic sample of cases so as to draw statistical conclusions, but I gathered information on about 40 cases by interviewing advocates, judges, and prosecutors, and review-

TABLE 6.1

Conviction Rates by Socioeconomic Condition in Police Action Cases
in Uruguay, Buenos Aires, Córdoba, and São Paulo

	Lower and lower working class	All others	Significance (1-tailed Z-test for difference between two proportions)
Uruguay	47.37% (*n* = 19)	25% (*n* = 4)	*p* = .206
Buenos Aires	25% (*n* = 100)	44.44% (*n* = 27)	*p* = .024
Córdoba	32.56% (*n* = 43)	78.95% (*n* = 19)	*p* = .000
São Paulo*	Lowest	Low/Low Working Class	
	6.02% (*n* = 133)	16.67% (*n* = 24)	*p* = .035

Note: Since in São Paulo there are virtually no middle class victims, I created a new
category including only unemployed shantytown dwellers who had not completed their
primary education. I compare the outcomes in their cases against cases involving all
other low and lower working class victims.

Two clarifications regarding these tables are necessary. First, Salvador is not included in
Table 6.1 or Table 6.2 because the sample there was not a systematic one, so the results
would be misleading. The conclusions for Salvador are based on a qualitative analysis of
cases that generated a great deal of attention on the part of the media and civil society.
Secondly, cases with missing data are excluded from this analysis, and are less likely
to end in a conviction, producing a higher average conviction rate than in the entire
sample. Because there is less information on cases dismissed early on, these results are
likely to *under*state the impact of class on judicial effectiveness.

ing the principal newspaper, *A Tarde*. In addition, I obtained secondary, summary information on about 80 cases followed by CEDECA, a
children's advocacy organization. All these are high profile cases that
generated a great deal of interest, and do not include the hundreds of
routine cases that go unnoticed by the daily newspaper. Even this limited
and unrepresentative information, however, suggests a generalized tolerance for police violence on the part of judges, police investigators, and
many prosecutors, regardless, almost, of the status of the victim or the
visibility of the case. Cases involving nurses and former police officers,

cases involving journalists and politicians, all end without any action by the courts.

Perhaps the most visible manifestation of this can be found in a series of notorious cases in which the police executed persons after they were arrested, or on the flimsiest of pretenses, and no conviction ensued. In one particularly egregious case, the police were photographed placing a bank robber in the back of a police wagon with his hands cuffed behind his back—alive, but wounded in the leg. The bank robber arrived at the hospital with two new gunshots to the chest. No one was convicted. CEDECA reports similar evidence for a number of killings of street children. In Salvador it is clear that the problem is not, as a general rule, a lack of information—though that too surfaces, whenever it appears that someone might actually be prosecuted for a murder—but rather a normative shift that allows the police to kill with impunity.

In summary, then, the socioeconomic resources of the victim matter most in Córdoba and São Paulo, though the conviction rate is considerably higher in the former. From this we can infer (a) that the failure to convict in those two systems is closely tied to informational failures, but (b) that informational failures are far more common in São Paulo than in Cordoba. The failures in Buenos Aires, on the other hand, should be a combination of informational and normative failures, while the consistent failure to convict in Salvador can be attributed largely to an overly lenient rule of decision. Since the impact of socioeconomic status is not significant in Uruguay, we can also assume state-based legal actors are generating the requisite information themselves, and doing so often enough to produce a high conviction rate. There is no evidence here of systematic informational failures.

There is additional evidence for these conclusions. In Table 6.2, I show both the impact of legal resources that improve the quality of the prosecution's case, in the form of a privately retained attorney, and the impact of direct political pressures in particular cases. In four of the five systems (except Uruguay), those who have an interest in the case may obtain official recognition as a party to the criminal prosecution. These interested parties are then authorized to present testimony and other evidence, participating as private prosecutors in the case. If the presence of a private prosecutor has a strong positive effect on the outcome, then it is likely that the difference lies in the quality of the information the judge is using to reach a decision.[8] If, on the other hand, public demonstrations strongly affect the outcome, this is likely an indication that judges and prosecutors are shifting their rule of decision in response to political pressure.

Table 6.2 demonstrates the importance of both private resources and political incentives in Buenos Aires. Without the intervention of a

TABLE 6.2
Impact of Private Prosecutor and Popular Demonstrations on Conviction Rates in Uruguay, Buenos Aires, Córdoba, and São Paulo

	No Private Prosecutor		Private Prosecutor		Average (total *n*)
	No demonstrations	Popular demonstrations	No demonstrations	Popular demonstrations	
Buenos Aires	6.67% (*n* = 45)	—	13.64% (*n* = 44)	41.43% (*n* = 70)	23.9% (*n* = 159)
Córdoba	13.33% (*n* = 30)	0% (*n* = 2)	20% (*n* = 10)	80% (*n* = 30)	41.66% (*n* = 72)
São Paulo	1.68% (*n* = 179)	—	35.14% (*n* = 37)	—	7.41% (*n* = 216)
Uruguay	50% (*n* = 22)	37.5% (*n* = 8)	n/a	n/a	46.67% (*n* = 30)

All differences, except for Uruguay's, statistically significant (p < .01).

private attorney and without the help of popular demonstrations, victims can expect a conviction rate that is no higher than São Paulo's average conviction rate. Adding a private attorney to supplement the prosecutor doubles the likelihood of a conviction, but it remains at a relatively low 14%. It is only with the addition of political pressure that we observe a conviction rate close to 50%. Clearly, judges must feel political pressure before they will be motivated to convict, and they are strongly responsive to this pressure. Similarly, in Córdoba, popular demonstrations plus private resources push the conviction rate all the way to 80%.

In São Paulo, there are no demonstrations in the cases in the sample apparently because, as we will see below, advocates correctly understand that the best way to motivate the well-insulated judges in this city is not by applying political pressure but by improving the legal case. But the addition of a private prosecutor, and the consequent improvement in the quality of the information presented to the judge, produces an improvement in the conviction rate from less than 2 to 35%. In all three locations, the state's prosecutors seem to be failing miserably in their task.

To summarize the individual case-level results for all these locations, then, Uruguay and Córdoba manage to convict a significantly higher number of police officers than Buenos Aires, São Paulo, and Salvador. But Uruguay does so without regard to the victim's social class or political interventions, while Córdoba sharply favors victims whose families have the resources to assist the prosecution, especially when they also garner political support. The conviction rate in Córdoba would be higher still if it were not for repeated informational failures in cases affecting underprivileged victims, and if prosecutors (and judges) could be persuaded to take these cases seriously even in the absence of demonstrations.

In Buenos Aires, the evidence suggests that *both* normative and informational failures are at work. Judges respond more readily in cases that attract considerable public attention, and they are better able to succeed when a private attorney assists in the presentation of the case. The crosscutting effect of political variables and CORREPI's strong investment of resources in cases affecting the poor renders the personal resources of the victims a less clear predictor of legal outcomes, as we saw in Table 6.1, though they remain significant. In São Paulo, the dismal conviction rate appears to be linked to widespread informational failures. A strong personal investment, usually with the help of an NGO, produces a dramatic improvement: the likelihood of a conviction exceeds 35% when the case is prepared by a private lawyer compared to less than 2% in cases spearheaded by the public prosecutor. Finally, Salvador stands alone as an instance of a system that almost uniformly applies a rule that departs from the formal laws—actors at all levels of the legal system simply apply a rule of impunity for police officers.

If the goal is to produce not only a high conviction rate, but also one that does not rely on and respond to such extra-legal considerations as the resources of the victim or the public attention the case generates, we must examine what system-level features are behind these individual-level results. What explains these varying degrees of success (or utter failure) in solving the two governance problems identified earlier? What about the institutional, political, or economic context accounts for the similar informational failures in São Paulo and Córdoba, despite quite different overall success rates? Why do Buenos Aires and Salvador show considerable infiltration of extra-legal norms into decision-making, and consequent normative failures? How did Uruguay apparently solve both informational and normative problems without relying on mass demonstrations or personal investments?

The key to solving the normative problem is, as noted earlier, a matter of structuring incentives so the key actors apply the right rule. Where the political context is favorable to these prosecutions—that is, where there is considerable political support for curbs on police violence—we might expect politically embedded prosecutors and judges to take these cases seriously, investing the resources at their disposal in an effort to secure convictions. On the other hand, where the political context is unfavorable to victims' rights, it is hard to imagine an institutional solution that would produce the requisite incentives (and harder yet to imagine the political process that might produce such a solution). Under these conditions, if courts and prosecutors are wide open to political pressures, we should expect a very lenient rule for police officers who take the law into their own hands. Designing these institutions so that judges and prosecutors are more insulated from political or popular pressure might neutralize the vagaries of public opinion, but in and of itself it does very little to create incentives for prosecutors to expend scarce resources on this class of cases in particular.

It is largely beyond the scope of this paper to address the origins of the political conditions that favor or disfavor the prosecution of police homicides. Some factors, however, readily stand out. The perception that there is an epidemic of violent crime (a perception more or less equally present in São Paulo, Salvador, and Buenos Aires, despite considerable differences in actual crime rates) obviously disfavors the victims of police violence. So does the consistent public representation of the victims by police (and, in Buenos Aires and Salvador by politicians in general) as violent criminals, despite considerable evidence that the victims are only rarely criminals, and almost never violent (Brinks 2008; Ouvidoria da

Polícia 1999).[9] Surely the fact that most of the victims are poor and marginalized urban males in sharply unequal societies does not help their cause, as it is hard to believe the same apathy would accompany the systematic execution of, say, white middle class cocaine users. In any event, the point is that adverse political conditions fail to generate incentives for state actors to undertake a vigorous investigation and prosecution of these violations.

The key to solving the informational problem, on the other hand, is empowering victims and prosecutors to overcome police resistance to these prosecutions. Victims' advocates and (often but not always) prosecutors seek a conviction, while the defendant and (often but not always) the police more generally, seek an acquittal in these cases. When the contestants are radically unequal, it is no surprise that one class of disputants is favored in the outcomes, even (or especially) if the arbiter is neutral. In the case of police violence, the police have some clear advantages: the police are in charge of the official investigation, and are given the resources, tools and experts to produce evidence. Moreover, the police have access to the process of compiling and organizing that evidence, and have frequent interactions with other actors in the legal system (see the discussion in Galanter 1974, for an analysis of the advantages repeat players have in the legal arena). And if their strong position within the legal system were not enough, the police have access to coercive resources that they can use to intimidate and silence complainants and witnesses.

This is especially true when the victims are drawn, as they often are, from among the most vulnerable sectors of society. The victims are typically poor young males, often with a criminal record and no fixed employment. The families they leave behind are no better off, usually having little experience interacting with the legal system, and the witnesses will be drawn from the same environment. As a result, the more the violence is focused on a marginal population, the more often oversight institutions will fail to secure the necessary information, and the lower the conviction rate overall. To solve the informational problem the government must address this imbalance of power in one way or another—strengthening and protecting those who claim on behalf of the victims, motivating prosecutors to be more proactive. The challenge for *democratic* governance is to enhance citizen capacity to engage with the legal system, so the law is more evenly applied regardless of social status. And where inequalities persist, the challenge is to place state resources well within reach of those who would otherwise remain on the margins of the democratic legal order.

In this and following paragraphs, I turn to the next set of questions. How likely is it that these deficiencies will actually be addressed, and what are the macro factors that produce the variation in informational and normative success described in the preceding section? As we have seen, the political context in São Paulo is not especially propitious for the aggressive prosecution of violent police officers. On the one hand, its elected leaders have not been hostile to civil rights, and some have instituted important innovations in an attempt to control police violence. On the other, a long-standing problem with violent crime leads to a deep-seated popular acceptance of, even demand for, aggressive police action in response to crime. Holston and Caldeira attribute "massive support for illegal and/or authoritarian measures of control" to the population as a whole (1998, 267). They argue that "shooting to kill not only has broad popular support but it is also 'accepted' by the 'tough talk' of official policy" (271). Even Caetano Veloso, in his song "Haiti," describes São Paulo's "smiling silence when faced with the massacre of 111 defenseless inmates"[10] of that city's immense (and now demolished) house of detention.

Certainly, there is a consensus among operators and observers of the justice system that the population continues to accept the use of lethal force as an instrument to fight crime. I repeatedly heard public opinion described this way from people such as Luiz Eduardo Greenhalgh, a Workers' Party (PT) national senator from São Paulo; Hélio Bicudo, a former national congressman, vice-mayor of São Paulo, the primary sponsor of the law subjecting the military police to civilian justice, and a member of the Inter-American Human Rights Commission; Benedito Mariano, first director of the *Ouvidoria da Polícia*; Mário Papaterra, São Paulo's Adjunct Secretary of State for Public Security, a former prosecutor who was, when I spoke to him, the civilian in charge of the civil and military police forces for the state ministry of security; Antônio Carlos da Ponte, a prosecutor in the jury division (which has jurisdiction over homicide cases). Norberto Jóia, another prosecutor in the jury division, said roughly the same thing, although he framed it as a slightly less absolute rule, arguing that if the victim has a violent criminal past the police get the benefit of the doubt, while otherwise there is stricter scrutiny.[11] No one disagreed with this assessment.

In spite of this apparent popular support for police killings, however, the earlier analysis showed that São Paulo manages to maintain judicial and prosecutorial support for the rule, at least at a higher level than Buenos Aires or Salvador. This is possible because a relatively "closed" institutional design—with strong and effective tenure protections and an entry and promotions structure that is meritocratic and internally regulated—divorces both the judiciary and prosecutors from everyday politics. This leaves judges free to rule in accordance with the law in these cases, and prosecutors free to act as they see fit, though it does not prompt any particular zeal in the prosecution of these cases. This same feature explains the lack of popular demonstrations in these cases. Advocates like the *Centro Santo Dias* invest resources in lobbying legislators to improve the legal framework, in generating forensic and other evidence for particular cases, and in legal argumentation. They waste little time and effort in lobbying sitting judges in individual cases. In other words, they seek to improve the legal features of their case, trusting judges to use the right rule of decision, rather than organizing demonstrations in an attempt to force judges to apply the law.

São Paulo, in short, seems to have solved the normative problem, despite a lack of popular support for these cases. Judges and prosecutors' incentives are structured in such a way that they are insulated from pressures to acquit, and more concerned with enforcing the letter of the law. These incentives are not sufficient, however, to move them away from strict neutrality in these cases.

Partly for this reason, and partly because of the socioeconomic context, São Paulo has not solved the informational problem. The official investigative agent in these cases is the Military Police, and the vast majority of victims are killed by members of this same entity. The Military Police, by virtue of its dominant position in the official investigation and its overwhelming superiority of force in interactions with the victim population, imposes a virtual wall of silence in these cases. Prosecutors, although insulated from direct pressures to turn a blind eye, have no real incentive to invest extraordinary resources in these cases. And even in those cases in which prosecutors are inclined to take the unusual step of conducting their own investigation, they are hampered by the lack of significant independent investigative resources.

The other potential source of information for the system—the victims and their relatives—cannot effectively meet the challenge because the victims are drawn overwhelmingly from among the lowest socioeconomic groups. As many as 77 percent of victims in my sample lived in shantytowns and the rest were only slightly better off. Virtually none came from the middle class (only four victims were middle class, of whom three were innocent bystanders who got in the way of loose bullets). This population is not only disadvantaged in dealing with the legal system generally, but is also vulnerable to intimidation and violence on the part of the police. No less than 85 percent of the cases in my sample show evidence of serious irregularities in the investigation, from the production of fraudulent autopsies, to the murder of witnesses, to threats against complainants. The "informational failures" I have been discussing are very often the direct result of additional violence and murder perpetrated by the police. The combination of a dominant and violent police force with a vulnerable population and a passive, if impartial, judiciary produces the near complete failure of the system to respond to police violence.

Buenos Aires, in contrast, has solved neither the normative nor the informational problem. An "open" institutional design in Buenos Aires during the 1990s—with political nominations and promotions, and low tenure security—led to the politicization of the judiciary and made it vulnerable to political and popular pressure.[12] To an even greater degree than in São Paulo, this pressure in general worked against aggressive prosecutions. Buenos Aires has seen provincial governors routinely call for the shooting of criminals—Ruckauf, for example, explicitly insisted that the solution to crime was to shoot criminals, supported by polls showing that more than half the population agreed that there was a need to put bullets into criminals.[13] It is no wonder then, that politicized judges and prosecutors are reluctant to convict in all but the most egregious cases.

Moreover, the police are adept at sabotaging investigations, so judges who are not too interested in convicting have plenty of cover for an acquittal. As in São Paulo, the same police force that commits the homicides is charged with investigating them, and can effectively use violence and intimidation of a vulnerable population to limit the information available about these cases. Whenever it seems that a prosecution might become serious, or when judges appear to need political cover, the police use their ascendancy over the victims and their position in the legal system to create a biased and unfair record.

The victims in Buenos Aires, however, can bring more resources to bear than those in São Paulo. In the first place, they are not so narrowly drawn from the most marginalized populations. There are fewer shantytown residents, more lower working class and middle class victims, in Buenos Aires than in São Paulo. Moreover, victims in Buenos Aires are more likely to have the substantial assistance of CORREPI and other legal aid organizations. This combination of greater resources and outside legal assistance produces a better factual record in a minority of cases. When this improved information is accompanied by political pressure organized by activist and neighborhood groups, the result is a conviction. The more political (relative to São Paulo) judges in Buenos Aires are especially susceptible to these pressures, so the combination of pointed political incentives and a better evidentiary record in a substantial minority of cases produces better results than in São Paulo, a 20% conviction rate versus roughly 5 percent. Still, forceful political action and outside legal assistance can only be a determining factor in a minority of cases, so the overall record still favors the police, who have both the political and material advantage.

In Salvador da Bahia, meanwhile, a monolithic political environment makes even a "closed" judicial design (virtually identical to São Paulo's) permeable to political meddling. Purportedly meritocratic appointment mechanisms were, during the period of the study, captured by political forces loyal to Antônio Carlos Magalhães, a leader of the Brazilian right. Judges I interviewed in 2000 agreed that political meddling in pending cases was relatively commonplace. And these pressures favor the police. Public opinion runs strongly in favor of extreme measures such as lynching suspects of crime. Official crime reports for Salvador in 1999 alone include 66 lynchings (not all of them ending in death). More than 41% of men and 38% of women in a 1997 survey agreed with the practice of "social cleansing" (*limpeza social*) (*A Tarde*, June 29, 2003). The overall political context is undoubtedly hostile to due process protections for suspects of crime, despite a lower overall homicide rate than São Paulo's. Judges (and prosecutors) respond to this political environment with a normative shift permitting nearly complete impunity for the police.

In Salvador, as in Buenos Aires and São Paulo, the police force that is responsible for most of the violations is the only official source of information, though in Salvador there is much less concern with secrecy—the police kill very openly, counting on the complaisance of the legal system. The lack of incentives to investigate means there is little opportunity to evaluate the informational capacity of the system, but all the indications are that this capacity is, if anything, lower than in São Paulo. When an investigation begins to take shape, as occurred in several cases involving murdered children or in a case in which the police were covering up a crime, the Military Police impose a virtual information blackout. They kill and intimidate witnesses and complainants, taking advantage of radical socioeconomic inequalities and the overall weakness of the criminal justice system. Not coincidentally, the practice of killing witnesses in this manner is known as a *queima de arquivo*—burning the files.

One case, for example, began when the police killed a witness to their criminal activity. The victims' parents were able to generate considerable public attention by joining with human rights groups, using the media, and meeting with opposition political leaders. The case ended with the additional murders of the victims' parents and three other witnesses. No convictions have resulted in any of the six cases.[14] When a prosecution threatens, then, the police are abundantly capable of preventing a conviction. In summary, Salvador has obviously not solved the normative challenge, and even if at some point it should, it would still face a formidable challenge in penetrating the wall of silence created by the police.

Uruguay, in contrast, has a normatively autonomous judicial system, free from outside pressures in individual cases. While the design of judicial careers is similar to that in Buenos Aires, and thus more open than in São Paulo to political pressures, a long-standing balanced and pluralistic political environment reduced partisan politicization and thus the ability of one party to meddle in individual cases (Brinks 2008). At least since the 1950s (except, of course, under military rule) appointments to the Supreme Court have either alternated between the two traditional parties or, with the rise of the new leftist coalition, have simply followed seniority. This is not to say that judges and prosecutors are politically insensitive. Rather, in both appointments and promotions they are evaluated by and have to please an array of actors representing the entire political spectrum, making them more autonomous than their peers in Buenos Aires from any one powerful party, but keeping them attuned to broad political currents.

As to Uruguay's informational capacity, in one sense context clearly trumps institutional design. As in all the other cases we have examined, judges and prosecutors do not have their own investigative staff. The police must assist with the investigation, and thus could pressure judges to be lenient, or limit the information available to them and to prosecutors. But in Uruguay exogenous political pressures tend in the direction of a more, not less, aggressive investigation of police homicides. This creates incentives for judicial actors to leave their offices and collect information with the means at their disposal, rather than waiting for the police to bring it in. These incentives also mean that Uruguay is the only place in which police officers await trial in detention, drastically reducing their opportunity to tamper with the evidence or intimidate witnesses. The political context helps overcome some of the same shortcomings in institutional design we observed in the other places.

On the other hand, in unintended ways, institutional design contributes to the positive outcome. Judges in Uruguay exploit some otherwise less desirable institutional traits to overcome their informational weakness. Uruguay is one of the last countries in the hemisphere to retain a purely inquisitorial criminal procedure, in which the same judge who conducts the investigation also adjudicates the case. This gives judges nearly prosecutorial endogenous incentives. The investigation and prosecution of the case is largely in their charge, and they can therefore resolve any doubts remaining after an investigation in favor of the prosecution. While in the abstract this prosecutorial bias raises the substantial due process concerns that have led many countries to abandon the inquisitorial model, in these cases in particular it redresses the resource imbalance between victims and the police. The result is apparent—a high conviction rate and, because the prosecution does not depend on the efforts of the victims' representatives, no evidence of socioeconomic inequalities in the outcomes.

Córdoba has also, on paper, solved many of these problems. It has an at least moderately independent judiciary that is the product of a political appointment process tempered by running judicial appointments through a public advisory committee. Advancement to a higher judicial position, which is common in Córdoba, depends on the same moderately political process. This explains judges' sensitivity to public demonstrations in favor of convictions. In contrast to Buenos Aires, what political influence there is does not have a strong tendency toward repressive police tactics. The governors of Córdoba since re-democratization through the end of the 1990s have been either moderate Radicals or Peronists, without a history of "*mano dura*" rhetoric. As a result, judges and prosecutors appear to take a relatively neutral stance except in those cases that provoke a public outcry, at which point they respond with more aggressive action.

The somewhat high level of informational failures in Córdoba can also be explained by a combination of institutional and contextual variables. Córdoba's criminal courts have taken important steps toward informational self-sufficiency with the creation of a judicial investigative police. This investigative police is technically separate from the operational police force most often implicated in the killings. Unfortunately, the actual development of the judiciary's investigative capacity lags somewhat behind the promise embodied in the formal structures. The investigative police force, according to prosecutors, was very weak throughout the 1990s and has not fully developed an independent investigative capacity. As a result, much of Córdoba's success is attributable to the investment of private resources into prosecutions. State investigators throw themselves into cases only if the cases have attracted a high level of political and public attention. In cases that do not generate demonstrations, the system continues to rely to a great extent on the victims' efforts in the production of information, leading to high levels of socioeconomic inequality.

Having reviewed the evidence at both the individual case level and the system level, it is time to turn our attention to the lessons we might derive from the experiences of these five cities. As the existing literature on legal transplants abundantly demonstrates, drawing general lessons from particular experiences is a dangerous enterprise. When the smoke had cleared after the collapse of the law and development movement (Trubek and Galanter 1974), it seemed only one principle was left standing: the wholesale transplantation of foreign legal solutions into new social, economic, and political contexts is bound to fail. Rodriguez, in this volume, argues the same point with respect to prescriptions for economic growth, and the conclusion seems sensible. Less clear, however, was what needed to be done to make any new—imported or domestically grown—legal arrangement work.

The findings summarized so far show once again that institutional solutions must be sensitive to the particularities of context, but such a conclusion is neither new nor especially helpful. If we cannot specify the particular institutional mechanisms needed in all countries, across different legal subject areas, we must at least attempt to specify some of the parameters to be considered in designing these mechanisms. The next section addresses these parameters and illustrates them with examples taken from particular cases. Most of this discussion rests on a very basic observation: new rights, like any new policy, create new winners and losers, and are not immediately self enforcing. We must, therefore, pay attention to the inequality of enforcement-related resources between those directly benefited or disadvantaged by the new arrangement. Where there is a significant imbalance, we must identify key state enforcement actors and motivate them to supply any deficiencies on the part of those directly interested. In addition, we must give these state actors the capacity to address violations of the policy, by crafting capabilities that are specific to the environment in which they must operate.

The first observation, then, is that reform must be comprehensive rather than punctual. Efforts to improve the functioning of legal systems have typically focused on one institution at a time, and have been criticized for that reason (Prillaman 2000). This research suggests that, in order to improve results, legal reform will have to take into consideration both the rule-crafting and the fact-finding dimensions of legal decision making, and that both require examining the relationship among the various actors in the legal system, as well as the broader social context. To be effective, legal reform must take into account the relationship between judges, prosecutors, the police, victims, private attorneys, and other legal actors, as well as the context in which they will operate.

To take just one example, after the *Carandiru* massacre, the *Candelárias* killings, and the videotaped abuses in *Favela Naval*, the human rights community and broader political movements in Brazil finally noted the level of impunity the Military Police enjoyed in the Military Justice system (Cano 1999). They correctly concluded that the problem there lay with judges who would not apply the correct rule and passed the *Lei Bicudo* transferring jurisdiction in cases of murder to the civilian justice system. My analysis suggests that reformers were indeed correct in supposing that civilian judges would apply a stricter standard, but failed to note the gross disparity of resources between competing claimants in the construction of the record. Reformers *incorrectly* assumed that civilian prosecutors could and would handle the investigation of these crimes and properly prepare the cases for trial. In fact, prosecutors rely too heavily on the police for information, receiving biased and incomplete information, and victims are too weak to supply the deficiency. As a consequence, the results did not improve as much as the reformers had hoped.[15] Fixing the rule of decision was not enough.

To improve results in actual cases, the *Lei Bicudo* needed also to redress this imbalance in the production of information. One not very satisfactory solution would have been to make these cases easier to prove. In civil cases involving inmates killed while in custody, for example, trial judges have reversed the burden of proof, requiring the state to demonstrate that the killing was justified. The result is, of course, a dramatic improvement in the outcomes. Civil awards in favor of a victim's survivors, based on a lower standard of proof, are by far more common than convictions, even in cases arising out of the very same facts.[16] But in a criminal prosecution, this "guilty until proven innocent" approach would be a rather egregious violation of conventional standards of due process. A broader rule holding superiors responsible for the levels of violence employed by subordinates (a sort of *res ipsa loquitur* presumption that high levels of violence are evidence of improper supervision) may tend in the same direction with fewer due process implications, and motivate supervisors to offer their subordinates additional incentives for compliance.

A better solution, as the Uruguayan case suggests, would be to improve the investigative capacity of prosecutors in this category of cases, while increasing their incentives to make use of that capacity. In São Paulo and Salvador especially, the number of killings of this nature (at least 10% of all homicides in a given year, and sometimes as many as 27%), to say nothing of the hundreds of other police abuses that take place on a daily basis, clearly justifies the creation of a specialized prosecutorial corps. In addition, since these prosecutors cannot count on the police for an investigation, they would need independent investigative capacity, and access to, for example, federal forensic scientists. If these prosecutors were evaluated on the strength of their performance in prosecuting police officers who commit abuses, they would also have the incentive to aggressively pursue these cases. Keeping this corps in the regular prosecutor's office (rather than inside the police force, as the *Corregedorias* currently are, or in a separate military justice system, as was the case before the *Lei Bicudo*) would not only harness the prestige and independence of the *Ministério Público*, it would help avoid the problem of an overly lenient enforcement agent responding to corporatist impulses.[17]

In general, the assumption has been that, when a particular law or policy does not enjoy broad popular support, the operators of official enforcement instances must be insulated from political pressure. This is the reasoning behind Central Bank independence, for example, and what allows prosecutors and judges in São Paulo to be as effective as they are in many areas. Indeed insulation gives São Paulo legal actors at least some effectiveness (once their informational problem is solved) in responding to police violence. Insulation alone is not sufficient, however. In addition, as Madison might have recommended, we must give these operators "the necessary constitutional means and personal motives" (Federalist No. 51, Hamilton, Madison, and Jay 1961) to vigorously enforce the law. If prosecutors' wealth, power, or prestige depends on providing an effective response to police violence, we might be more confident that they would use any means at their disposal to do so.

In short, if every incident of lethal use of force by the police triggered immediate oversight by a specialized prosecutorial task force, a prompt examination of the crime scene, access to federal forensic scientists, a witness protection plan, and accelerated trial times, the proportion of successful prosecutions would increase, and the incidence of violations might also drop.

For at least two reasons, however, we must look beyond sole reliance on state actors. As the comparison of the performance of private prosecutors with that of the independent prosecutors in São Paulo or the independent judicial police in Córdoba suggests, the most reliable advocates for a particular policy are the intended beneficiaries of that policy—especially if the policy is not broadly popular. Moreover, regardless of the effectiveness of prosecutors, as O'Donnell (1999a) has also pointed out, one of the crucial preconditions for an effective rule of law is the presence of multiple alternative sources of information concerning the conduct of lower level actors in the system (including individuals in society). To broaden the range of enforcement actors and harness more reliable enforcement action, the government can create enforcement structures that are accessible to the affected population, and give that population the legal and material tools to intervene directly in enforcement. For example, the impact of the private prosecutor in the cases I have examined is evident, and the figure could be strengthened, with additional support at state expense for those wishing to retain a private lawyer. Private causes of action for violations of legal rights are another way to give beneficiaries enforcement capacity.[18]

But to truly empower the likely victims of a violation, much more than passive receptivity to their claims is needed. When the victims are likely to be taken from the margins of society they will also need rights education, free legal assistance within the affected community, outreach through community groups, and proactive efforts such as contacting the relatives of known victims and informing them of their options. Clearly, in places like São Paulo and Salvador, or the shantytowns of Buenos Aires and Córdoba, the state cannot simply sit back and wait for victims or their relatives to contact an ombudsman or prosecutor. Perhaps the clearest lesson from the Uruguayan case is that, when the affected population is (predictably) underprivileged, affirmative action on the part of state actors is necessary.

This leads to a more general point: many of the proposed fixes for legal systems follow universal prescriptions, often applying them not only across areas of the law, but across countries. As noted by Rodriguez, effective solutions must be designed taking into consideration existing institutional strengths and weaknesses, and other local conditions. The results discussed here strongly suggest that different categories of cases require different enforcement structures, driven primarily by differences in the composition of the pools of competing claimants. Thus land disputes in Northeastern Brazil, which often pit wealthy landowners against small-plot peasant farmers, need to take into consideration the disparate capacity of each of these claimants to produce documentary evidence—genuine or not—in support of their competing claims. Rather than relying on an adversarial process and using legal documents as proof of ownership, an independent fact-finding agent akin to the Special Masters sometimes appointed by courts in the United States might be better designed to discover the truth. Land disputes in the commercial district of São Paulo, or in a *favela*, on the other hand, may require a rather different enforcement structure. The same is true for governance problems more generally—the key is to pay attention to the capabilities and incentives of the key actors, not simply to import "best practices" from other subject areas or other societies.

Importantly, reforms must address broader social imbalances or risk creating even further dislocation. New rights can appear to empower the victims of abuse, but enacting narrowly tailored individual rights protections without addressing the broader context leaves undisturbed the balance of power at the enforcement stage both outside and inside the legal system. So long as a new law (or newly enforced law) does not attempt to shift the balance of power in the social and political system too far from the current equilibrium, it can, over time, move society slowly in the desired direction. The further and the faster the law seeks to shift that balance, however, the more coercive and pervasive the enforcement structure needs to be—and the more ancillary changes will be required to make it effective.

At minimum, failing to address these social imbalances is a recipe for legal inequality. The disparate results across social classes in police prosecutions in Córdoba clearly illustrate the impact of victims' disparate resources. Córdoba's neutral stance and high quality legal system produce strikingly different results for different classes of citizens. I have described Uruguay as having a generally egalitarian and effective legal system. But even in Uruguay, lawyers who work with street children have described a condition of arbitrary power on the part of the police who interact with these children. While killings are rare, beatings and similar abuses are routine; moreover, they are generally accepted as permissible, and therefore do not produce an aggressive intervention on the part of judges or prosecutors. When the state adopts a neutral stance in a decidedly unequal context, the result is predictable.

At worst, enacting rights without addressing social inequalities can generate a great deal of violence, as seen most clearly in the case of Salvador. There the police have historically ruled the streets of the *favelas* with almost unbounded discretion; murders of street children were common and open. The 1990 *Estatuto da Criança e do Adolescente*, however, established new rights and created a new juvenile justice enforcement structure. If fully effective, this new law would have quite radically shifted the balance of power between street children and police officers. Indeed, in the early 1990s, observers detected an important improvement in the investigation and enforcement of children's rights against abusive policemen in Salvador.[19] But without a strong state presence and a pervasive enforcement mechanism, the police were able to create a new strategy for leaving the existing balance of power undisturbed: rather than counting on the courts to look the other way, they simply began to use their coercive power to force acquiescence on the part of the victims. To truly shift the balance, the state will have to invest resources in shoring up the capacity of claimants to resist this coercion.

In these cases, for example, there must be effective and proactive mechanisms in place to prevent stricter enforcement from leading to more violence against witnesses and complainants. A witness protection program is one component; speedy trials is another. Prosecutors and judges, as they currently do in Córdoba, must more aggressively prosecute obstruction of justice cases. Another measure, more problematic from a due process perspective, is erring on the side of caution in pretrial detention rulings. Only in Uruguay is it a common practice to hold accused police officers pending trial. This clearly raises due process issues, but the counterpart, apparent in every other case, is the capacity of the accused to terrorize witnesses and claimants. The courts need to acknowledge the danger and balance these two concerns in deciding pretrial release issues.

In conclusion, then, is there an institutional solution to the governance challenge of establishing an effective rule of law in the unequal societies of Latin America? In this chapter I examined the failure of the rule of law in an area that should be especially important to democracies—the arbitrary and unpunished killing of hundreds of people by the police. Underlying this failure of liberal democratic governance is, indeed, an institutional failure: the legal systems in Buenos Aires, São Paulo, and Salvador are unable to effectively oversee the actions of the police, because the institutions that compose them are too dependent on the police for information, or too willing to accept the popular verdict that these deaths are the acceptable price of an ongoing war against crime. The relevant institutions are not designed in such a way as to create the right incentives for the right actors or to give them the right capabilities. The solution, therefore, is at least in part an institutional one—reform police, prosecutorial, and judicial structures to align incentives with policy goals and create the resources that will produce more aggressive, higher quality prosecutions, as detailed above.

Unfortunately, these institutional prescriptions, like those extended to other governance failures, lose sight of a more fundamental problem. In the first place, as we have seen, the most reliable advocates for a given right or policy are its direct beneficiaries. And even the best designed enforcement mechanisms require some investment on the part of those who would engage them. To claim rights, resist coercion, and engage with enforcement agents requires self-assurance, knowledge, time, transportation, social networks of support, and many more resources that cannot be created by legislative fiat or individual institutional solutions. As a result, deep social inequalities and exclusion, such as affect shantytown residents in Córdoba, Buenos Aires, São Paulo, or Salvador, pose formidable obstacles to any institutional fix. Resolving inequality is a more difficult task than enacting legal changes and institutional reforms, and arguably a more important one.

Even more importantly perhaps, beneath many of the institutional failures are the political dimensions of the problem. In the case of police violence in particular, the politicization of violent crime leads to the failure of the electorate in cities like Buenos Aires, São Paulo, or Salvador to demand an end to police violence. In turn, this sociopolitical failure rests on a socioeconomic reality: large urban masses of the dispossessed and unemployed, and increasing levels of violent crime, lead even the most frequent victims of police violence to call for draconian police action. The social and economic conditions that give rise to a hostile political context—in this case, hostile to due process protections for the presumed criminal—are not amenable to quick institutional solutions. And the necessary deep institutional fixes will not be forthcoming in the absence of effective political movements that mobilize for an end to the problem.

What is needed for a complete response to police violence, then, is somewhat utopian: an improvement in the capabilities of rights bearers to mobilize and act in their own defense through the reduction of inequality, a solution to the problem of violent crime and political opportunism, the overall strengthening of the state and its legal system, and the restoration of faith in due process as part of an effective solution to crime, not part of the problem. That would be the strongest foundation on which these democracies could create the institutional structures to effectively tackle the problem of police violence, and move closer to delivering on their promise of full democratic citizenship, based on legal equality and freedom from fear. That is, at best, a long-term project. In the meantime, the more modest institutional proposals detailed above will have to await a propitious political moment.

Notes

1. The 2001 U.S. State Department Human Rights Report for Venezuela notes that the government claimed that 2000 criminals had been shot by the police in the first eight months of that year. That figure suggests an annual per capita rate of killings of 12.75 per hundred thousand, twice as high as Salvador's.

2. The alternative explanation, that convictions are so infrequent in São Paulo, for instance, because the police are more often legitimately shooting violent criminals in actual armed confrontations, is highly unlikely. In the first place, if the deaths were occurring in the course of armed confrontations that posed a legitimate danger to the police, we would expect at least a minimal correlation between the number of police killed in a given year and the number of civilians killed that year by the police. In fact, the correlation, for all the years available from the *Ouvidoria da Polícia* (1990–2002), is actually negative, though minuscule, at −0.042, and completely nonsignificant. Moreover, the imbalance between police casualties and civilian casualties is striking. The average annual number of police officers killed in the line of duty from 1990–2000 is just under 16, compared to about 750 civilians per year (www.ouvidoria-policia. sp.gov.br/pages/tabelas.htm); in 1999, the Ouvidoria reported a 40 to 1 ratio of police to civilians killed (Ouvidoria da Polícia 1999). Finally, the Ouvidoria found that there were 14 civilians killed for every one wounded, the exact opposite of the ratio of police officers killed to wounded, and the exact opposite of what we see in cities in the United States, for example. As Chevigny concludes, it seems clear that the São Paulo police rely on violence as a method of social control, and resort to executions as an alternative to prosecutions (1995).

3. We typically think of the law as defining permissible conduct rather than rules of decision, but conduct responds to individual rules of decision in particular circumstances, so this formulation is more general—it applies to legislatures in deciding the constitutionality of proposed legislation, to judges in applying the standard in a particular case, and to individuals in deciding whether to adjust their conduct to the legal norm.

4. Judge Antônio Carlos Malheiros (São Paulo Appellate Judge), interviewed by author, São Paulo, April 17, 2001.

5. Occasionally there is a specialized judicial police force that performs the investigative task for the courts, but in all the cases where it exists that I have examined, this police force remains closely tied, functionally and organizationally, to the regular police.

6. Given the number of victims in each city and the difficulty in obtaining complete information about the victims and the process in each case, the analysis is necessarily limited to a sample of cases. The period of data collection is 1990–2000, to the extent data was available. In Uruguay, I interviewed members of SERPAJ (*Servicio Paz y Justicia*), a prominent human rights group that works on issues of police violence and receives complaints from the public, searched the online archives of *El País* and *La Brecha*, and reviewed all available human rights reports on the country for the 1990s. Here I used all the reported cases. In Buenos Aires, I began with a list of victims put together by CORREPI, a police violence NGO, and supplemented it with searches of the online archives of *La Nación* and *El Clarín*. For Buenos Aires, I used all the cases listed by CORREPI for which there is outcome information. This almost certainly biases the sample in favor of more effectiveness. In São Paulo, I obtained lists of victims from the *Ouvidoria da Polícia*, an ombudsman organization that began work in 1996 and receives a report on every use of deadly force by the São Paulo police, and supplemented with searches of the *Folha de São Paulo* on line. I used 100% of the cases that were not dismissed outright, plus a random sample (about 20% of the total, weighted appropriately in the analysis) of cases that were dismissed. Again, this should bias the sample toward effectiveness, as it includes only the cases that triggered a formal follow up. In Córdoba, I obtained a list from CORREPI's sister organization there, and again did online searches in *La Voz del Interior*, the main regional daily based in Córdoba city. I included all the cases I found. Finally, in Salvador, I interviewed members of the state legislature's human rights commission, obtained the PT's reports on extermination groups, spoke with members of civil society groups (the *Commissão Justiça e Paz* of the Archdiocese of Salvador, *Tortura Nunca Mais*, the *Centro de Defesa da Criança e do Adolescente*, and Afro-Brazilian groups, for example), and searched the main daily, *A Tarde*'s, archives. In all cases I excluded those with substantial evidence of an armed confrontation. The result here is a nonrandom list strongly biased in favor of more effectiveness. In each case, any biases in the samples produce more conservative estimates of the extent of judicial failure. I used some care to ensure that this underlying distribution would be roughly comparable across cases. A more extensive discussion of sampling methods and data difficulties is available upon request or in my book (Brinks 2008).

7. We could speculate that the demonstrations mark cases of especially egregious police abuse, but the data do not support this conclusion. The cases of outright executions of a defenseless suspect do not generate more demonstrations, for example. In fact, demonstrations appear to be more common in cases of accidental shootings than in intentional ones.

8. For the impact of a private attorney to be attributable to normative rather than informational changes we would have to assume that the private attorneys

are somehow changing the incentives the judge faces in a given case, by bribing the judge, for example. My conversations with attorneys (and judges), my own review of the case files, and the trials I have observed suggest that what changes in the presence of a private attorney representing the victim is the quality of the prosecution's case, not the incentives for the judge.

9. Chevigny also reports that São Paulo police acknowledged to human rights investigators that "for the most part it was not the violent criminals who were being shot" (1995, 162).

10. *"O silêncio sorridente de São Paulo/ diante da chacina/ 111 presos indefesos."*

11. Interviews with Hélio Bicudo, São Paulo, March 27, 2001; Antônio Carlos da Ponte, São Paulo, April 2001; Luiz Eduardo Greenhalgh, São Paulo, April 30, 2001; Mário Papaterra, São Paulo, March 23, 2001; Norberto Joia, São Paulo, April 16, 2001.

12. A series of institutional and procedural reforms in both the provincial courts and federal courts of the city of Buenos Aires have substantially changed formal attributes and incentives. By the end of the 1990s, however, these reforms had had little or no impact on actual conduct in these cases.

13. El Cronista reported that a poll taken in the Buenos Aires area on September 8, 1999 found that 5.7% were more or less in agreement, 44.9% were in agreement, and 4.6% were strongly in agreement with this statement: "We have to pump bullets into criminals" ("hay que meterle bala a los delincuentes").

14. This case is described in detail in Brinks (2008).

15. Cano (1999) showed that the conviction rate in the Military Justice system in Rio de Janeiro was only 3%. My own results in São Paulo suggest that civilian judges have managed to improve this record only to about 6 or 7%.

16. This discussion is based on conversations with the *Promotora* in charge of assisting relatives of the victims of the *Carandiru* massacre, on an examination of judicial opinions and records tracking judgments in the several dozen civil cases that arose from that incident, as well as on discussions and review of files at the *Centro Santo Dias* in São Paulo.

17. This is not to suggest these prosecutions would ever be easy. In São Paulo, Salvador, and Córdoba we have seen just how difficult it is to wrest control of the facts from the front-line police forces, even if there is an investigative police force in place.

18. This recommendation corresponds broadly with what McCubbins and Schwartz (1984) described as "fire alarm" monitoring.

19. Valdemar Oliveira (Director, *Centro de Atendimento à Criança e Adolescente*), interviewed by author, Salvador, May 22, 2001.

References

Ames, Barry. 2001. *The Deadlock of Democracy in Brazil*. Ann Arbor: University of Michigan Press.

Amnesty International. 2005. *"They Come in Shooting": Policing Socially Excluded Communities*. New York: Amnesty International.

Barcellos, Caco. 1992. *Rota 66: A História Da Polícia Que Mata*. São Paulo: Editora Globo.

Barros, Robert. 2003. Dictatorship and the Rule of Law: Rules and Military Power in Pinochet's Chile. In *Democracy and the Rule of Law*, ed. José María Maravall and Adam Przeworski. Cambridge: Cambridge University Press.

Brinks, Daniel M. 2008. *The Judicial Response to Police Violence in Latin America: Inequality and the Rule of Law*. New York: Cambridge University Press.

Cano, Ignacio. 1999. O Papel Da Justiça Militar Na Investigação Das Mortes De Civis Pela Polícia No Rio De Janeiro [The Role of Military Justice in the Investigation of Civilian Deaths at the Hands of the Police in Rio De Janeiro]. *Polícia e Sociedade Democrática* 1(1).

Chevigny, Paul. 1995. *Edge of the Knife: Police Violence in the Americas*. New York: The New Press.

Dahl, Robert. 1957. Decision-Making in a Democracy: The Supreme Court as a National Policy-Maker. *Journal of Public Law* 6(2): 279–95.

Diamond, Larry, ed. 1999. *Democracy in Developing Countries: Latin America*. Boulder, CO: Lynne Rienner Publishers.

Dutil, Carlos, and Ricardo Ragendorfer. 1997. *La Bonaerense: Historia criminal de la policía de la Provincia De Buenos Aires*. Buenos Aires: Editorial Planeta.

Epstein, Lee, and Jack Knight. 1998. *The Choices Justices Make*. Washington, DC: Congressional Quarterly Press.

Faria, José Eduardo, ed. 1988. *A Crise Do Direito Numa Sociedade Em Mudança*. Brasília: Editora Universidade de Brasilia.

———. 1994. Os Desafios Do Judiciário. *Revista USP* 21: 46.

———. 1996. A Crise Do Poder Judiciário No Brasil. *Justiça e Democracia* 3(1): 18–64.

FORES, and Colegio de Abogados de Buenos Aires. 1999. Justicia y desarrollo económico (Trabajo Completo). In *CD-ROM with full report of investigation*. Buenos Aires: Consejo Empresario Argentino.

Galanter, Marc. 1974. Why the "Haves" Come Out Ahead: Speculations on the Limits of Legal Change. *Law & Society Review* 9(1): 95–160.

Hamilton, Alexander, James Madison, and John Jay. 1961. *The Federalist Papers*, ed. Clinton Rossiter. New York: Mentor (Penguin Books).

Hammergren, Linn. 1999. Fifteen Years of Justice and Justice Reform in Latin America: Where We Are and Why We Haven't Made More Progress. *http://darkwing.uoregon.edu/~caguirre/papers.htm*.

Helmke, Gretchen. 2002. The Logic of Strategic Defection: Court-Executive Relations in Argentina under Dictatorship and Democracy. *American Political Science Review* 96(2): 291–303.

Hojman, David E. 2004. Inequality, Unemployment and Crime in Latin American Cities. *Crime, Law and Social Change* 41: 33–51.

Holmes, Stephen. 2003. Lineages of the Rule of Law. In *Democracy and the Rule of Law*, ed. José María Maravall and Adam Przeworski. Cambridge: Cambridge University Press.

Holston, James, and Teresa P.R. Caldeira. 1998. Democracy, Law and Violence: Disjunctions of Brazilian Citizenship. In *Fault Lines of Democracy in Post-Transition Latin America*, ed. Felipe Aguero and Jeffrey Stark. Coral Gables, FL: North-South Center Press.

ISIS International. 2006. *16 Years of Progress, 16 Years of Challenges: The Campaign to Eliminate Violence against Women in Latin America and the Caribbean*. Santiago, Chile: ISIS International. www.isis.cl/temas/vi/activismo/Ingles/thecampaign.pdf.

Larkins, Christopher M. 1998. The Judiciary and Delegative Democracy in Argentina. *Comparative Politics* 31(July): 423–42.

Mainwaring, Scott. 2006. The Crisis of Democratic Representation in the Andes. *Journal of Democracy* 17(3): 13–27.

———. 2006. State Deficiencies, Party Competition, and Confidence in Democratic Representation in the Andes. In *The Crisis of Democratic Representation in the Andes*, ed. Scott Mainwaring, Ana María Bejarano, and Eduardo Pizarro, 295–345. Stanford: Stanford University Press.

Mainwaring, Scott, and Christopher Welna, eds. 2003. *Democratic Accountability in Latin America*. Oxford: Oxford University Press.

Maravall, José María, and Adam Przeworski, eds. 2003. *Democracy and the Rule of Law*. Cambridge: Cambridge University Press.

McCubbins, Matthew, and Thomas Schwartz. 1984. Congressional Oversight Overlooked: Police Patrols Versus Fire Alarms. *American Journal of Political Science* 28(1): 165–79.

Méndez, Juan E., Guillermo A. O'Donnell, and Paulo Sérgio Pinheiro, eds. 1999. *The (Un)Rule of Law and the Underprivileged in Latin America*. Notre Dame, IN: University of Notre Dame Press.

Miller, Jonathan. 2000. Evaluating the Argentine Supreme Court under Presidents Alfonsín and Menem (1983–1999). *Southwestern Journal of Law and Trade in the Americas* 7(Fall): 369–433.

O'Donnell, Guillermo A. 1999a. Horizontal Accountability and New Polyarchies. In *The Self-Restraining State: Power and Accountability in New Democracies*, ed. Andreas Schedler, Larry Diamond and Marc F. Plattner, 29–52. Boulder, CO. & London: Lynne Rienner Publishers.

———. 1999b. Polyarchies and the (Un)Rule of Law in Latin America: A Partial Conclusion. In *The (Un)Rule of Law and the Underprivileged in Latin America*, ed. Juan E. Mendez, Guillermo A. O'Donnell, and Paulo Sérgio Pinheiro, 303–37. Notre Dame, IN: University of Notre Dame Press.

———. 2001. Democracy, Law and Comparative Politics. *Studies in Comparative International Development* 36(1): 7–36.

———. 2004. Why the Rule of Law Matters. *Journal of Democracy* 15(4): 32–46.

Ouvidoria da Polícia. 1999. Pesquisa sobre o uso da força letal por policiais de São Paulo no ano de 1999. Ouvidoria da Polícia de São Paulo (on file with author).

Prillaman, William C. 2000. *The Judiciary and Democratic Decay in Latin America: Declining Confidence in the Rule of Law*. Westport, CT: Praeger Publishers.

Raz, Joseph. 1979. The Rule of Law and Its Virtue. In *Liberty and the Rule of Law*, ed. Robert L. Cunningham. College Station, TX: Texas A&M University Press.

Segal, Jeffrey, and Harold Spaeth. 2002. *The Supreme Court and the Attitudinal Model Revisited*. Cambridge: Cambridge University Press.

Shifter, M. 1997. Tensions and Trade-Offs in Latin America. *Journal of Democracy* 8(2): 114–28.

Stanley, Ruth. 2005. Controlling the Police in Buenos Aires: A Case Study of Horizontal and Social Accountability. *Bulletin of Latin American Research* 24(1): 71–91.

Stotzky, Irwin P., ed. 1993. *Transition to Democracy in Latin America: The Role of the Judiciary*. Boulder, CO: Westview Press.

Trubek, David M., and Marc Galanter. 1974. Scholars in Self-Estrangement: Some Reflections on the Crisis in Law and Development Studies in the United States. *Wisconsin Law Review*, 1062–105.

Ungar, Mark. 2001. *Elusive Reform: Democracy and the Rule of Law in Latin America*. New York: Lynne Rienner Publishers.

Van Cott, Donna Lee. 2000. *The Friendly Liquidation of the Past: The Politics of Diversity in Latin America*. Pittsburgh: Pittsburgh University Press.

Verbitsky, Horacio. 1993. *Hacer la Corte: La creacion de un poder sin control ni justicia*. Buenos Aires: Planeta.

Yashar, Deborah J. 1999. Democracy, Indigenous Movements, and the Postliberal Challenge in Latin America. *World Politics* 52(1): 76–104.

CHAPTER SEVEN

Political Institutions, Populism, and Democracy in Latin America

PATRICIO NAVIA AND IGNACIO WALKER

The end of the cold war coincided with the most widespread and successful wave of democratization that Latin America has experienced in its history. As the decade of the 1980s drew to an end, democracy was on the way to becoming "the only game in town." Yet, two decades after the auspicious transitions to democracy, the results of the democratic experience have been decidedly mixed. On the one hand, elections have been broadly recognized as the only legitimate mechanism to select authorities; on the other hand, in many countries and along many dimensions, the quality of democracy is less than satisfactory. Public levels of support for democracy are disturbingly low in some countries. In others, concerns about corruption, low levels of participation, and institutional designs not conducive to adequate accountability point to glaring deficiencies in the region's democracies. Two decades ago, the countries in the region prioritized making transitions to democracy possible. Today, the major challenge consists of ensuring democratic consolidation. Democracy has to be a self-sustaining system capable of producing concrete and positive results for its citizens. When its exercise strengthens institutions, democracy will be a virtuous cycle that produces concrete results and satisfies international standards. In that sense, democracy must be self-sustainable (Przeworski 2005).

To take up the challenges faced by the countries of the region, we address two major themes in this chapter. First, we discuss the elements of democracy. We lay out formal criteria that must be present in order for a system to be democratic. We advocate a minimalist definition, and

246 Variance in Success: Economics, Social Policy, and the State

discuss conditions that have to exist in democracies. In this theoretical-practical discussion, we explore one of the principal challenges in contemporary Latin America: the consolidation of democracy in a context conducive to populism. Democratic consolidation is undermined when populist leaders are legitimized in elections. In our discussion of this phenomenon, we stress the need to strengthen a "democracy of institutions" so as to minimize the possibility of a populist eruption. Because populism cannot be combated by limiting the electoral and participatory components of democracy, the best antidote to populism lies in strengthening democratic institutions.

Second, we broadly explore the quality of democracy in Latin America since 1990. In doing so, we analyze the recent evolution of Latin American democracies in the context of the economic reforms adopted beginning in the 1980s and into the 1990s. We analyze how the combination of weak institutions, the persistent inequality of income, wealth and opportunities, and the negative reaction to some of the more deleterious effects of the economic reforms of the Washington Consensus ultimately favored the appearance of populism. In analyzing the recent experience of various Latin American countries, we show how strong institutions and sound social and economic policies contributed powerfully to consolidating democracy in some countries. However, we argue that in other countries the combination of less well-consolidated democratic institutions promoted populist leaderships resulting in political and social policies detrimental to either sustained development or to combating poverty and inequality.

DEFINING DEMOCRACY

Democracy is a system in which parties lose elections (Przeworski 1991). As such, democracy is constituted by a set of complex rules and procedures. Following Przeworski's definition, democracies have four essential characteristics.

First, democracies are systems. That is, there are rules of the game that have been decided on in advance and are fairly stable over time. These rules guarantee that there is a relatively leveled playing field for all. The rules of the game, regardless of how they were established initially, are accepted by most (preferably all) relevant political actors. The rules are of course subject to alteration, but the procedures through which they can be modified have also been established *a priori*.

A second essential characteristic, following Przeworski (1991), who was inspired by Dahl's (1971) classic definition of democracy as competition among actors, is the existence of political parties. There is no stable democracy without political parties. Since contemporary democracies are essentially representative, political parties come to constitute principal vehicles for representation. In contrast to classic idealized definitions of direct participatory democracy, the complex systems of our modern societies favored the development of democracy based upon representation. Under democracy, electors entrust to their representatives the defense of their own interests and those of the country (Brennan and Hamlin 1999; Manin 1997).

Representative democracy cannot exist without political parties. Because of the information asymmetries that exist between those who govern and those who are governed, there must be incentives for representatives to build reputation. And there must be tools for voters to punish and reward authorities. Only when representatives run as members of political parties, voters can use information shortcuts and can reward or punish their past performance. Without parties, voters find it too costly to cast informed and meaningful votes in representative democracy.

In addition, political parties are an antidote to populist leadership. True, populism is almost the inevitable result of social and economic exclusion, especially in the context of weak institutions. Populist leaders promise to bring about inclusion. However, as with cholesterol, there is good and there is bad populism. After it successfully fosters social inclusion, a populist eruption should fade away. Yet, as populism is championed (almost by definition) by individual leaders rather than by political parties, it becomes the legitimizing force that helps keep the leader in power. Thus, if we understand populism as a likely outcome of social and economic exclusion, political parties advocating inclusion can win office and deliver on their promises without undermining democracy. But populist leaders promising inclusion will undermine institutions as they seek to fulfill their electoral promises.

Since the first half of the twentieth century, and as a result of demands for more social, economic, and political inclusion, populism has become a recurrent characteristic in the region (Cammack 2000; Di Tella 1997; Weyland 2004). Populism has been identified with the weakness of democracy, both as a cause and as a consequence (Conniff 1999; Dugas 2003; Hawkins 2003; Weyland 2001). But insofar as political parties are constituted adequately to represent the various strata of society effectively, there will be a diminished possibility of Latin America's continuing to experience the proliferation of populist leaders (Navia 2003; Walker 2006a).

The third component of Przeworski's definition of democracy is the holding of elections. Modern democracy is essentially representative (Manin 1997). In order for their representative components to function satisfactorily, democracies need elections. There exists a broad consensus on the necessity of holding regular, free, and informed elections that have reasonable eligibility requirements for candidates and mechanisms for guaranteeing universal suffrage as well as preventing fraud. However, there is less of a consensus on the mechanisms that accomplish these objectives. Nevertheless, although there is no universal formula for organizing legitimate elections, the quality of elections can be satisfactorily evaluated *a posteriori*. After an election, acceptance of the results by both winners and losers is the best evidence of the legitimacy of the electoral process.

The fourth component in this minimalist (but rigorous) definition of democracy is that elections are associated with uncertainty about the results. This constitutes both a requirement for democracy to function well and a test that it is functioning satisfactorily. When there is uncertainty as to the outcome, those involved know they must carry out a more arduous campaign—that they have to work harder—in order to triumph. The experiences of restricted democracies in which parties alternated in power and in which elections were not the determining factor in identifying who governed—and who would be left out—inevitably led the parties and the elite to ignore the electors. Such democracies evolved into systems with little transparency, and weak accountability.

The requirement for uncertainty in the electoral process cannot be limited only to its not being known in advance who is going to win an election. It is not enough to avoid the old custom in the Mexico governed by PRI, where elections (whose results were known before people voted) were "organized" by the party rather than held in a free and competitive manner. The component of uncertainty in the electoral process must also include an institutional design that makes such uncertainty serve the end of the voters' obtaining relevant information that will allow them to make informed decisions.

DEMOCRACY AS A SYSTEM OF INSTITUTIONS

Democracies are systems of institutions in which elections occupy a primordial space. But of course other components are also necessary for successful democratic consolidation. In democracy, the institutions constitute checks and balances that demarcate, limit, and restrain, but also facilitate and legitimize the exercise of power by democratically elected representatives (O'Donnell 1998).

Traditionally, democratic systems have been classified according to their specific characteristics. Thus, for example, we distinguish between presidential democracies and parliamentary democracies. Other classifications emphasize other criteria, like centralized, decentralized, or federal democracies. Others emphasize formal aspects of democracies, such as the attribution and distribution of powers between the executive and the legislative. Depending on their emphasis, there are different ways to classify and categorize democracies.

In Latin America, where presidential systems are the norm, various voices have questioned the suitability of maintaining presidential systems. Because they are said to be associated with greater stability and because they allow power to be less concentrated, parliamentary systems have often been pointed to as a suitable alternative (Linz and Valenzuela 1994a, 1994b). Other studies have focused on how particular sets of rules of the game affect the balance of power between the legislative and the executive, each set producing different results in the ability to reach agreements and enact laws (Alemán 2003, 2005; Alemán and Saiegh 2007; Cheibub, Przeworski, and Saiegh 2002, 2004). Some have pointed out that reforms contributing to decentralization can have positive as well as negative effects for democracy (Eaton 2004; Jones et al. 2002; Montero and Samuels 2003).

All these contributions analyze specific aspects of democratic institutions in isolation from other components. Thus, although these studies are helpful in shedding light on one dimension or other, they do not result in a model that explains the overall interaction of the whole system. Tsebelis has suggested a novel alternative that seeks to unify various criteria for classifying democracies (2002). Instead of identifying the various institutions according to their type and distribution of their powers, Tsebelis suggests that we can understand democratic institutions in terms of the veto players present within the system. Some democracies have more veto players than others. In some democracies (centralized, presidential, unicameral, those where the executive has vast powers in relation to the congress), the number of veto players is smaller than in those with decentralized systems, bicameral systems, those having a constitutional court, an autonomous central bank, strong local governments, and a president with fewer powers in relation to the legislative branch. In advancing an understanding of institutions as veto players, Tsebelis makes it possible to compare the degree of influence of seemingly quite different institutions on the decision-making processes.

In this chapter, we use Tsebelis's proposition to better understand a phenomenon that has existed historically in Latin American democracies: populism. Although it made its appearance in the 1930s and 1940s as it sought to incorporate the growing masses of urban workers (Conniff 1999; Di Tella 1965, 1997; Weyland 2001), populism has again become a recurrent phenomenon. Without entering into an extensive discussion about what constitutes populism and what political experiences may be considered populist (Barr 2003; Cammack 2000; Dornbush and Edwards 1992; Dugas 2003; Hawkins 2003; Knight 1998; Murillo 2000; Stein 1999; Szusterman 2000; Weyland 2001, 2003; Roberts 2007a, 2007b), for our purposes we define populism tentatively as the tendency of democratically elected leaders—usually presidents—to reduce the number of veto players in the political system.

Ours is consistent with other definitions of populism. Mayorga defines contemporary *populism* as "a pattern of personalistic and anti-institutionalist politics, rooted mainly in the appeal to and/or mobilization of marginalized masses" (2006, 134). Weyland sees it as "a political strategy through which a personalistic leader seeks or exercises government power based on direct, unmediated, uninstitutionalized support from large numbers of mostly unorganized followers" (2001, 14). Seeking to explain populism to a non-academic audience, Reid summarizes it as "two things: first, a brand of politics in which a strong, charismatic leader purports to be a saviour, blurring the distinction between leader, government, party and state, and ignoring the need for the restraint of executive power through checks and balances. Second, populism has often involved redistribution of income and/or wealth in an unsustainable fashion" (Reid 2007, 12). Most authors coincide in associating populism with a combination of high concentration of power in a single leader and weak institutional settings. In a context of weak institutions, the demand for redistribution seems to brew the emergence of populist leadership around a charismatic politician.

Accordingly, although populists may differ in the economic policies they adopt—some being considered "neoliberals" others more "traditional," and still others "neopopulists"—and on the emphasis they place on redistribution, they all share a propensity to reduce the number of veto players in the political system. Populist leaders are different from authoritarian leaders in that the former are legitimized electorally, time and time again, through relatively clean and competitive elections. Yet, they both prefer systems where the number of veto players is limited. This tendency often finds expression in conflicts between the democratically elected leaders and some institutions that "interfere"—for more or less legitimate reasons—with the new leaders' drive to carry out their programs and objectives (including their promises to bring about more inclusion).

INSTITUTIONS AND LEADERSHIPS

Because we understand populism as the tendency of democratically elected presidents to reduce the number of veto players in the political system, there is an obvious two-way relation between the initial strength of institutions and the emergence of successful populist leaders in Latin America. The stronger the institutions, the less likely a populist attempt is going to succeed.

The conditions of social and economic exclusion under which populism usually emerges might be present in strong or weak institutional settings. In the former, demands for redistribution might feed populist temptations, but the strong democratic institutions will process those demands for redistribution and constrain the populist's attempt to concentrate power. In the latter, demands for redistribution will conduce to concentration of power in the hands of the populist president who rises to power promising to end inequality.

To be sure, charismatic leadership capable of mustering voters is essential for electoral success. Good candidates have the ability to communicate their proposals successfully and to mobilize potential voters by using their personal appeal. To be able to win elections, candidates must have popular appeal. But in a context in which democratic institutions are weak, charismatic leadership has a tendency to evolve into populism. Because presidential candidates receive a mandate from voters, they are tempted to concentrate power in their own hands to fulfill their electoral promises. Because weak democratic institutions do not provide for adequate checks and balances to executive power, charismatic leaders successfully consolidate power and become populist presidents. Whether they implement expansive fiscal policies or adopt neoliberal policies, chief executives, in the absence of solid democratic institutions, tend to evolve into populist presidents when institutional constraints on their power are absent, or are weak.

By contrast, when solid democratic institutions exist, the popularity of a winning presidential candidate can be transformed into a force that can induce support and cooperation from the institutions that exercise veto power over the adoption of new public policies. The more popular presidents are, the better able they are to advance their legislative agendas. When a solid democratic institutional context exists, popular chief executives are less likely to get away with populist instincts.

Table 7.1 shows the interaction between the popularity of a president and the solidity of a nation's democratic institutions. Popular political leaders capable of demonstrating successful leadership qualities in the campaign and during their administration are more likely to become successful presidents if there is a context of solid democratic institutions. In contrast, they are more likely to face a populist temptation in a context of weak democratic institutions. On the other hand, unpopular presidents are often incapable of carrying out their agendas and fulfilling

TABLE 7.1

Interaction between Presidential Popularity and Strength of
Democratic Institutions

	Solid democratic institutions	Weak democratic institutions
Popular president	Government can fulfill campaign promises	Government faces populist temptation
Unpopular president	Government fails to fulfill campaign promises	Lack of legitimacy and risk of ungovernability

their campaign promises even when solid democratic institutions exist. The worst-case scenario is that in which solid democratic institutions do not exist and the president is unpopular. Under these conditions, there exists the risk of ungovernability.

In the following section, we explore the political evolution of Latin America from 1990 onward, in the context of the economic reforms adopted by most countries in the region. After discussing how these reforms were adopted, we analyze the emergence of recent populist regimes, and we compare these with what we define as non-populist regimes. Again, while the former are generally produced in weak democratic institutional contexts, the latter tend to appear in contexts of greater democratic and institutional strength. Finally, we argue that leadership matters: some leaders have contributed to consolidating democratic institutions while others have left a legacy of weakened democratic institutions.

THE NEOLIBERAL ECONOMIC REFORMS OF THE
NINETIES AND THEIR OUTCOME

The so-called "lost decade" (the 1980s) in Latin America was characterized by massive foreign debt and serious macroeconomic problems—including very high inflation and budget deficits—arising from the economic policies implemented by various governments, such as those of Raúl Alfonsín (1983–1989) in Argentina, José Sarney (1985–1990) in Brazil, and Alan García (1985–1990) in Peru, all occurring amidst transitions to democracy. Subsequently, in the 1990s the region experienced the introduction of numerous economic reforms commonly known as "neoliberal," and connected with what came to be known as the "Washington Consensus."

In face of those realities, principally the fiscal and inflationary dilemmas, the Washington Consensus advanced ten specific proposals: control of fiscal deficits, clear standards on priorities for public spending, tax reform, interest rates and exchange rates (both were to be left to the market), liberalization of trade, opening to foreign investment, privatization of state enterprises, deregulation, and strengthening of property rights.[1]

A number of Latin American governments implemented a good share of these measures in the nineties, in some cases with significant popular support, in the face of serious macroeconomic disequilibria and the possibility of widespread social disruption. Carlos Andrés Pérez (1989–1993) in Venezuela, Carlos Salinas de Gortari (1988–1994) in Mexico, a series of governments—although with differing emphases—in Bolivia between the administration of Victor Paz Estensoro (1985–1989) and that of Gonzalo Sánchez de Lozada (2002–2003), Carlos Menem (1989–1999) in Argentina, Alberto Fujimori (1990–2000) in Peru,[2] Fernando Collor de Mello (1990–1992) and Itamar Franco (1992–1994) in Brazil represented some of the exponents of these economic reforms carried out in the 1990s, at the very time when economic and political stability was required to facilitate the transition from authoritarian rule. And although there exists a wide variety of differences among these governments, we might also include in this category the governments of Luis Alberto Lacalle (1990–1995) in Uruguay, Violeta Chamorro (1990–1996) in Nicaragua, and Sixto Durán (1992–1996) and Abdalá Bucaram (1996–1997) in Ecuador, among others.

Although many of the policies advocated by the Washington Consensus, especially those in the fiscal domain, were to matters of common sense rather than to an actual or supposed "neoliberal" ideology—such as those meant to ensure orderly fiscal accounts, low inflation, and a manageable foreign debt, the outcomes of these reforms generally fell far short of their promised objectives. Indeed, from the "caracazo" (the riots in Caracas) of 1989, directed against the "neoliberal" reforms of Carlos Andrés Pérez in Venezuela, through the acts of repression that brought to an end the second administration of Gonzalo Sánchez de Lozada in Bolivia in October 2003 and which marked the beginning of the ascent to power of indigenous leader and coca farmer Evo Morales, a series of destabilizing situations occurred, culminating in some cases in the abrupt termination of administrations that, under a variety of circumstances, had earlier enjoyed significant popular support, as in the case of Carlos Menem in Argentina and Alberto Fujimori in Peru. After governing for a decade, both leaders ended up reviled and harshly criticized, especially when it came to corruption (in the case of Fujimori, he was later tried for human rights violations in Peru).

POPULIST AND NON-POPULIST RESPONSES

The neoliberal economic reforms of the nineties precipitated two types of response in the region: the populist (more visible) and the non-populist, less visible than the former perhaps but more important from the point of view that concerns us, that is, democratic consolidation in Latin America and the central question of institution building.

The neoliberal reforms of the nineties triggered large-scale disruption, especially in countries that were experiencing a pronounced incapacity on the part of their governing elites and traditional political institutions to respond effectively to the social demands of emerging or long-ignored sectors: working and middle-class sectors whose living conditions deteriorated; indigenous peoples and social movements, urban and rural, emerging with unusual force; unemployed sectors, mainly made up of young city dwellers, capitalizing successfully on the discontent became a driving force in the region.

Opposition has erupted with unusual force where neoliberal economic reforms were the most profound and the institutions (or the political elites) the weakest, as in Venezuela, Bolivia, Argentina, Mexico, and Peru. These include the populist or neopopulist reactions personified by Hugo Chávez in Venezuela (1998 to present), Néstor Kirchner (2003–2007) in Argentina, Evo Morales (2006 to present) in Bolivia, and also—in spite of their having been defeated in recent presidential elections—by Andrés Manuel López Obrador in Mexico and Ollanta Humala in Peru, to mention only some of the most emblematic exponents of this populist or neopopulist reaction. The government of Rafael Correa in Ecuador would appear to be headed in a similar direction, after the 2006 election that pitted a populist of the right (Noboa) against a populist of the left (Correa), in a country that had eight presidents in ten years.[3] All these leaders share a discourse of antiglobalization and antineoliberalism and of opposition to the IMF and the Washington Consensus. Their countries undertook neoliberal economic reforms in the nineties (under Carlos Andrés Pérez in Venezuela, Carlos Menem in Argentina, Gonzalo Sánchez de Lozada in Bolivia, Carlos Salinas de Gortari in Mexico, and Alberto Fujimori in Peru). These countries have weak traditional elites and weak political institutions, especially in regard to their ability to channel emerging social demands.

This reaction contrasts clearly with the non-populist response found in other cases in the region, chiefly under the administrations of Fernando H. Cardoso (1995–2003) and Luiz Inácio Lula da Silva (2003 to present) in Brazil; under the four Concertación governments in Chile headed by Patricio Aylwin (1990–1994), Eduardo Frei (1994–2000), Ricardo Lagos

(2000–2006), and Michelle Bachelet (2006 to present); and in Mexico, under the administrations of Ernesto Zedillo (1994–2000) and Vicente Fox (2000–2006). To these we might add the governments of Tabaré Vásquez (2005 to present) in Uruguay, Leonel Fernández (2004 to present) in the Dominican Republic—especially when we consider that his presidency was preceded by the dismal populist experience of Hipólito Mejía (2000–2004), Martín Torrijos in Panama, Antonio Saca in El Salvador—more to the right, along with that country's last three administrations, Álvaro Uribe in Colombia, and certainly the governments of Oscar Arias and Alan García, in Costa Rica and Peru, respectively.

The three cases mentioned as the most emblematic of this non-populist reaction (Brazil, Chile, and Mexico) are particularly interesting. After having been preceded by governments that implemented neoliberal economic reforms—in the case of Chile most markedly under the Pinochet dictatorship, with the policies of the "Chicago Boys"—the governments of these countries have introduced significant corrections of a more heterodox and less dogmatic kind. Moreover, in each case a process of institution building has raised a wall of containment against the neopopulist temptation.

The results of this process are especially evident in Chile, where a coalition of parties, rather than any particular president, endeavors to implement a strategy of "growth with equity," with a consistent critique of both neoliberalism and neopopulism, and within a framework which has sought to engender broad consensus. In Brazil, the basic continuity between the economic policies of Cardoso and Lula has provided stability to the political and economic process of the last decade, after the implementation, under the government of Itamar Franco in 1994, of the "Real Plan." Particularly worthy of attention is that President Lula, with his long experience as a union leader, has resisted the temptation to populism, thus contributing to relieve the anxieties of the international financial community and the Brazilian business community—no small matter in a country that experienced four external financial shocks under the two administrations of President Cardoso (1995–2002), and also contributing to the stability of the overall political process, which has been bolstered further by the re-election of "Lula" in October 2006. Lastly, the case of Mexico is worthy of attention not simply in terms of democratic consolidation but also for the remarkable transition to democracy between Ernesto Zedillo and Vicente Fox. The victory of Felipe Calderón of the National Action Party (PAN) and the defeat of Andrés Manuel López Obrador in the 2006 presidential election is another demonstration of how, despite everything—including the very narrow electoral margin between the two candidates and the pressing conditions of poverty, social inequality, and marginality—Mexico has political and institutional resources to resist the neopopulist temptation.

It is precisely these three cases that Javier Santiso takes up to develop his theory about changes that have taken place in Latin America in the last thirty years in his book, *Latin America's Political Economy of the Possible: Beyond Good Revolutionaries and Free Marketeers* (2006). In Santiso's view, leaving behind the utopias that have traversed the history of the region since the conquest and the countless experiments that have taken place since the 1950s, Latin America—the land of magic realism— has in its most recent history adopted a greater pragmatism. This new pragmatism is expressed not only in fiscal and monetary policies adopted in countries such as Chile, Brazil, and Mexico but also in the process of institution building, all of this leaving behind the extremes of the past.[4] These three cases, along with Uruguay, the Dominican Republic, Panama, and El Salvador, and quite possibly Costa Rica and Peru, fit the category of non-populist reactions that are based on a "democracy of institutions" qualitatively distinct from the "personalistic democracy" of Chávez, Kirchner, and Morales. With nuances and variations depending on the case, these experiences evince a more pragmatic neoliberalism that (with the possible exceptions of Colombia and El Salvador) is more heterodox and less dogmatic compared to the neoliberal reforms of the region in the 1990s.

To be sure, the case of Kirchner merits a special clarification. There are good reasons to include Kirchner as part of the populist responses to neoliberalism. First, *kirchnerismo* initially emerged and has consolidated within the tradition of Peronism. Peronism epitomizes Latin American populism. Second, there is still a strong element of concentration of power in the presidency under Kirchner. Third, there are weak democratic institutions in Argentina (Levitsky 2003). In that sense, we cannot speak of democracy of institutions properly when referring to the political system there. Yet, *kirchnerismo* should not be automatically equated to Chavez, and Morales, and so on and so forth. Argentina's democratic institutions have partially resisted the efforts by the executive to concentrate power. Thus, a democracy of institutions could easily reemerge in the future. The use of discretionary powers under the Kirchners' administrations has undoubtedly weakened democratic institutions, but much less so than in Venezuela or in Bolivia (where they were historically very weak).

Lastly, the cases of Paraguay, Nicaragua, Guatemala, and Honduras are "unfinished trajectories," somewhere between Democracies of Institutions and Personalistic Democracies, given their reactions, non-populist and populist, to the neoliberal reforms of the 1990s. Our classification agrees with that found in the meticulous work of Mainwaring and Pérez-Liñán (2006, 51) on post-1978 democracies in Latin America, in which these four cases are referred to specifically as examples of "stag-nation of semi-democratic regimes" in the region during the period in question. Figure 7.1 gives an account of what we have said previously.

The non-populist reactions, commonly associated with what we have called democracy of institutions, contrast with neopopulist responses, commonly associated with personalistic democracies. While the former are represented especially by cases such as Brazil, Chile, and Mexico (among others) this latter type—of institutional weakness, associated with the emergence of populist leaders—is reflected in particular in the path followed by the Andean countries.[5]

René Mayorga (2006, 133) maintains that what is involved in these Andean countries is not only a crisis of representation but also a crisis of governability, the latter being the cause of the former. In Mayorga's view, the institutions of representative democracy have been the major victims here. In this context, "neopopulism" becomes a viable "political regime" characterized by personalistic and anti-institutional policies, a govern-ment based principally on appealing to the marginalized masses and pos-sibly mobilizing them. Mayorga states, "In this regard, unlike historical populism, neopopulism is involved in the democratic game. It accepts the rules of democratic competition, but at the same time resorts to the higher quality and legitimacy of the leader, who presents himself as redeemer and embodiment of the people and the nation" (Mayorga 2006, 135).

Concerning what has been said up to here and what appears in Figure 7.1, we might stress the following points:

1. The region is not experiencing a general "leftist trend" of a neo-populist cut. Recent elections such as those of Álvaro Uribe in Colombia (2006) and Felipe Calderón in Mexico (2006)—and earlier, the election of Antonio Saca in El Salvador and the three presidents before him—run contrary to the claim. Second, we have not one, not two, but three lefts in Latin America, very different from one another: the Marxist left of Fidel Castro in Cuba, sec-tors within the Sandinista National Liberation Front (FSLN) in Nicaragua, and the Farabundo Martí National Liberation Front (FMLN) in El Salvador, the Chilean Communist Party, and nu-merous extra-parliamentary expressions in the region; the populist left of Chávez and Morales, which shows evidence of a growing convergence with the Marxist left; and the social democratic left, such of that of Lula in Brazil, Ricardo Lagos and Michelle Bache-let in Chile, Oscar Arias in Costa Rica, Leonel Fernández in the Dominican Republic, Martín Torrijos in Panama, or Alan García in Peru, in clear contradiction with the Marxist and populist left (Walker 2006b).

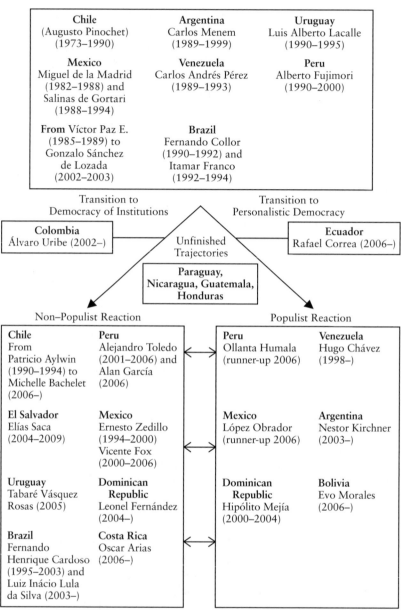

FIGURE 7.1 Neoliberal Economic Reforms and Populist and Non-Populist Reactions in Latin America

2. It is not true that there exists a general populist reaction in opposition to the neoliberal economic reforms of the 1990s. There does exist, along with a populist reaction, a non-populist path aiming at a democracy of institutions, different from the personalistic democracy of Chávez, Kirchner, or Morales. Along with its emphasis on institutions, the non-populist path also differs in that it has generally advocated a series of corrections to the neoliberal model, with heterodoxy taking priority over orthodoxy, so as to assure the sustainability of both the democratic institutions and economic and social reforms. In this context, non-populist reactions have had the know-how and ability to implement many of the economic reforms commonly associated with the Washington Consensus, without the ideological and dogmatic baggage of those reforms, at least in their original formulation.

3. Figure 7.1 shows us that once there has been a passage from the neoliberal economic reforms of the 1990s to the adoption of a non-populist path, it is very difficult to pass from there to a populist or neopopulist one. What is more, the electoral defeats in 2006 of López Obrador and Ollanta Humala, in Mexico and Peru respectively, show that democracies of institutions have significant popular support. And further, the passage from Hipólito Mejía to Leonel Fernández in the Dominican Republic demonstrates that there does indeed exist the reverse possibility of a trajectory from populism to non-populism.

4. Just as it has been said before, there also exist ambiguous, incomplete, and uncertain trajectories, such as those of Paraguay and some Central American countries such as Guatemala, Honduras, and Nicaragua.

5. Both forms of democracy (of institutions and personalistic, commonly associated with non-populist and populist paths respectively) are democratic forms of government and the governments that arise out of them are endowed with a formal democratic legitimacy. Nevertheless, in accord with what has been argued earlier, the democracy of institutions is the more functional in terms of the requirements for successful democratic consolidation.

BY WAY OF CONCLUSION

In this chapter we have adopted a procedural, minimalist definition of democracy, devoting our analysis to the tensions that arise between a democracy of institutions and one characterized by populist leadership and distinguishing between populist and non-populist paths followed after the neoliberal reforms of the nineties.

We have defined democracy, following Przeworski, as a system of institutions based on the irreplaceable action of political parties and the holding of free, periodic elections (representative democracy) with uncertainty as to the outcome. Following Tsebelis, we have defined populism tentatively as the tendency of leaders, usually presidents, to reduce the number of veto actors in the political system. We have amplified that by saying that while populist responses are generally produced in weak democratic institutional contexts, non-populist responses appear in contexts of greater democratic and institutional strength. Because we understand populism as personalistic leaderships that weaken institutions, there exists an obvious two-way interaction between the strength of the institutions and the appearance of personalistic leaderships in Latin America.

In our view, successful democratic consolidation is the product of the action of the institutions of representative democracy combined with the ability of the state to respond adequately to the demands of its citizens, especially in the socioeconomic realm.

Twenty-five years ago, only Venezuela, Colombia, and Costa Rica had free, fair, and orderly regular elections in Latin America. The authoritarian wave that took hold in Latin America has yielded to a democratizing wave that is making its way as never before in the history of the region. In a twelve month period (from late 2005 to late 2006), elections were held in Honduras, Chile, Bolivia, Haiti, Costa Rica, Colombia, Peru, Mexico, Brazil, Ecuador, Nicaragua, and Venezuela. These twelve elections were significant in quantitative and qualitative terms. The election for the first time of a union leader (in Brazil), an indigenous leader (in Bolivia), and a woman (in Chile and Argentina); the holding of the cleanest presidential and parliamentary elections ever held in the history of Haiti—an example of a "failed state" in the region; the transition to democracy that has taken place in Mexico between Ernesto Zedillo and Vicente Fox (2000–2006) after seventy years of PRI hegemony; the widening of universal suffrage in terms hitherto unknown—all these are examples of the new democratic reality in the region.

At the same time, these gains take place in a social-economic context marked by the widespread reality of poverty, social inequality, exclusion, and marginality, which much of the time leads to the new reality of electoral democracy coexisting with deep skepticism with respect to the institutions of representative democracy, which are perceived as weak and remote. In spite of a period of unprecedented economic growth in 2004, 2005, 2006, and 2007 throughout Latin America, fluctuating between an annual 4 and 5%, more than 200 million people subsist below the poverty line, and Latin America remains the most unequal region in the world.

Consolidating a stable and vigorous democracy includes establishing solid institutions and a strong state that are capable of responding to accumulated social demands, especially those among the most neglected sectors of the population (Birdsall, de la Torre, and Menezes 2008). On an institutional level, there exists a general trend toward the establishment of strong presidentialism, with a significant degree of concentration of power in the executive, a development not accompanied by an increase in responsiveness to the demands of citizens. Along with this strengthened presidentialism, which is certainly related to the broad discrediting of parliaments and parties, there exists a trend toward a fragmented multipartism, with an ensuing difficulty of building stable governing coalitions. Many of the traditional bi-party systems of the region no longer exist (those in Uruguay, Colombia, Venezuela, Costa Rica, Nicaragua, among others), and fragmented multipartism has reached a truly alarming state in Brazil, Ecuador, Colombia, and Peru.

This fragmentation is possibly connected to a lack of agreement between different electoral majorities represented by the executive and the legislative, the problem of "double legitimacy." Under a presidential form of government, both the president of the republic and the legislature are directly elected by the people and thus both can claim to base their support on the popular will. Such a situation can easily lead to tensions between the two branches of the state as well as to a marked difficulty in forming stable majority coalitions for governing, all of which impacts democratic consolidation negatively. Along with the challenges at the institutional level, we find serious deficiencies in terms of the (in)effectiveness of states to respond to the growing, unsatisfied demands and expectations of their populations. This gap leads to a deepening of the problems of democratic (un)governability found on the institutional level. This is connected, for example, with the serious problems states face in designing, determining, and implementing public policies, and also generally goes along with the non-existence of technical personnel or a political-institutional design that would provide coherence and continuity to policies. Accordingly, it should not surprise us that in the last twenty years there have been fourteen governments in the region that did not finish out their terms of office.[6] The subsistence of abrupt and unexpected government collapses confirms the difficulties faced by a region that has advanced significantly in achieving democratic consolidation. In that process, we have argued that the interaction of populist leadership with the strength of democratic institutions constitutes a decisive variable to explain populist and non-populist responses to the neoliberal reforms adopted since the 1990s.

Notes

1. These measures are contained in Williamson (1990), which, together with his *The Progress of Policy Reform in Latin America* (Washington, DC: Institute for International Economics, 1990), constitutes the foundation for the Washington Consensus.

2. Weyland (2003) refers to Menem and Fujimori as examples of "neoliberal populists," based on the synergies and affinities between economic liberalism and political populism, especially at the beginning of the nineties. At that time, the introduction and implementation of drastic neoliberal economic reforms paved the way to personalistic and plebiscitary leaders. This dynamic diminished in intensity in subsequent years.

3. Rafael Correa competed in the presidential election without having a single candidate for parliament, under the assumption (and the promise) that he would call a constituent assembly, a feature commonly associated with personalistic, populist, and plebiscitary democracy.

4. "The region's economies have propelled one of the most remarkable reform processes of their history, in tandem with a generalized movement toward democracy. Although incomplete and imperfect, this synchronized dual movement of economic reforms and a transition to democracy is very encouraging. To a large extent, this political and economic shift has been accompanied by an epistemic change. The reform policies enacted reflect a more pragmatic approach, a political economy of the possible" (Santiso 2006, 4).

5. This reality is precisely the subject of *The Crisis of Democratic Representation in the Andes* (Mainwaring, Bejarano, and Pizarro 2006), which recounts the crisis of democratic representation in Venezuela, Peru, Bolivia, Ecuador, and Colombia, one characteristic of which is the emergence of political outsiders with an anti-establishment discourse, whose rise is usually accompanied by a collapse of party systems. It is pointed out in this work that the delegitimization and decay of the party systems and the discrediting of the parliaments, in the wider context of the deterioration of the institutional channels of democratic representation, has "paved the way for plebiscitarian forms of representation in which populist presidents displace parties as the primary vehicles of expressing the popular will.... Thus, it might be argued that personalistic, plebiscitarian representation is simply displacing more institutionalized democratic representation" (Mainwaring et al. 2006, 30).

6. Fernando de la Rúa, Argentina (2001); Fernando Collor de Mello, Brazil (1992); Hernán Siles Suazo (1985), Gonzalo Sánchez de Lozada (2003) and Carlos Mesa (2005), Bolivia; Abdalá Bucarán (1997), Jamil Mahuad (1999), and Lucio Gutiérrez (2005), Ecuador; Jorge Serrano Elías, Guatemala (1993); Jean-Bertrand Aristide, Haiti (2004); Raúl Cubas Grau, Paraguay (1999); Alberto Fujimori, Peru (2000); Joaquín Balaguer, Dominican Republic (1994); and Carlos Andrés Pérez, Venezuela (1993).

References

Alemán, Eduardo. 2003. Legislative Rules and the Amending Process: Theory and Evidence from Argentina, Chile and México. In *The Annual Meeting of the American Political Science Association*. Philadelphia Marriott Hotel, Philadelphia.

———. 2005. The Origins of Presidential Conditional Agenda-Setting Power in Latin America. *Latin American Research Review* 40(2): 3–26.

Alemán, Eduardo, and Sebastián Saiegh. 2007. Legislative Preferences, Political Parties and Coalition Unity in Chile. *Comparative Politics* 39(3): 253–72.

Barr, Robert R. 2003. The Persistence of Neopopulism in Peru? From Fujimori to Toledo. *Third World Quarterly* 24(6): 1161–78.

Birdsall, Nancy, Augusto de la Torre, and Rachel Menezes. 2008. *Fair Growth: Economic Policies for Latin America's Poor and Middle-Income Majority*. Washington, DC: Center for Global Development and Inter-American Dialogue.

Brennan, Geoffrey, and Alan Hamlin. 1999. On Political Representation. *British Journal of Political Science* 29(1): 109–27.

Cammack, Paul. 2000. The Resurgence of Populism in Latin America. *Bulletin of Latin American Research* 19(2): 149–61.

Cheibub, Jose A., Adam Przeworski, and Sebastián Saiegh. 2002. Government Coalitions under Presidentialism and Parliamentarism. *Dados-Revista De Ciencias Sociais* 45(2): 187–218.

———. 2004. Government Coalitions and Legislative Success Under Presidentialism and Parliamentarism. *British Journal of Political Science* 34(4):565–87.

Conniff, Michael, ed. 1999. *Populism in Latin America*. Tuscaloosa, AL and London: University of Alabama Press.

Dahl, Robert A. 1971. *Polyarchy. Participation and Opposition*. New Haven, CT: Yale University Press.

Di Tella, Torcuato. 1965. Populism and Reform in Latin America. In *Obstacles to Change in Latin America*, ed. C. Véliz. London: Oxford University Press.

———. 1997. The Transformations of Populism in Latin America. *Journal of International Cooperation Studies* 5(1): 47–78.

Dornbush, Rudiger, and Sebastian Edwards. 1992. *The Macroeconomics of Populism in Latin America*. Chicago: University of Chicago Press.

Dugas, John C. 2003. The Emergence of Neopopulism in Colombia? The Case of Alvaro Uribe. *Third World Quarterly* 24(6): 1117–36.

Eaton, Kent. 2004. Designing Subnational Institutions: Regional and Municipal Reforms in Postauthoritarian Chile. *Comparative Political Studies* 37(2): 218–44.

Hawkins, Kirk. 2003. Populism in Venezuela: The Rise of Chavismo. *Third World Quarterly* 24(6): 1137–60.

Jones, Mark P, Pablo Spiller, Sebastián Saiegh, and Mariano Tommasi. 2002. Amateur Legislators-Professional Politicians: The Consequences of Party-Centered Electoral Rules in a Federal System. *American Journal of Political Science* 46(3): 656–69.

Knight, Allan. 1998. Populism and Neo-Populism in Latin America, Especially Mexico. *Journal of Latin American Studies* 30: 223–49.

Levitsky, Steven. 2003. *Transforming Labor-Based Parties in Latin America: Argentine Peronism in Comparative Perspective.* New York: Cambridge University Press.

Linz, Juan J., and Arturo Valenzuela, eds. 1994a. *The Failure of Presidential Democracy I: Comparative Perspectives.* Baltimore: John Hopkins University Press.

———. 1994b. *The Failure of Presidential Democracy II: The Case of Latin America.* Baltimore: John Hopkins University Press.

Mainwaring, Scott, Ana María Bejarano, and Eduardo Pizarro, eds. 2006. *The Crisis of Democratic Representation in the Andes.* Stanford, CA: Stanford University Press.

Mainwaring, Scott, and Aníbal Pérez-Liñán. 2006. Latin American Democratization Since 1978: Democratic Transitions, Breakdowns, and Erosions. In *The Third Wave of Democratization in Latin America: Advances and Setbacks*, ed. Frances Hagopian and Scott Mainwaring, 14–59. Cambridge: Cambridge University Press.

Manin, Bernard. 1997. *Principles of Representative Government.* Cambridge: Cambridge University Press.

Mayorga, René. 2006. Outsiders and Neopopulism: The Road to Plebiscitary Democracy. In *The Crisis of Democratic Representation in the Andes*, ed. Scott Mainwaring, Ana María Bejarano and Eduardo Pizarro Leongómez. Stanford, CA: Stanford University Press.

Montero, Alfred, and David Samuels, eds. 2003. *Decentralization and Democracy in Latin America.* Notre Dame, IN: University of Notre Dame Press.

Murillo, María V. 2000. From Populism to Neoliberalism: Labor Unions and Market Reforms in Latin America. *World Politics* 52.

Navia, Patricio. 2003. Partidos políticos como antídoto contra el populismo en América Latina. *Revista de Ciencia Política* 23(1): 19–30.

O'Donnell, Guillermo. 1998. Horizontal Accountability in New Democracies. *Journal of Democracy* 9(3): 112–26.

Przeworski, Adam. 1991. *Democracy and the Market.* Cambridge: Cambridge University Press.

———. 2005. Democracy as an Equilibrium. *Public Choice* 123(3–4): 253–73.

Reid, Michael. 2007. *Forgotten Continent (The Battle for Latin America's Soul).* New Haven, CT: Yale University Press.

Roberts. Kenneth. 2007a. Latin America's Populist Revival. *SAIS Review* 27(1).

———. 2007b. Repoliticizing Latin America: The Revival of Populist and Leftist Alternatives. *Democratic Governance and the "New Left," Woodrow Wilson Center Update on the Americas*, Woodrow Wilson International Center for Scholars, Washington, DC, November.

Santiso, Javier. 2006. *Latin America's Political Economy of the Possible: Beyond Good Revolutionaries and Free-Marketeers.* Cambridge, MA: MIT Press.

Stein, Steve. 1999. The Paths to Populism. In *Populism in Latin America*, ed. Michael Conniff. Tuscaloosa and London: University of Alabama Press.

Szusterman, Celia. 2000. Carlos Saúl Menem: Variations on the Theme of Populism. *Bulletin of Latin American Research* 19(2): 193–206.

Tsebelis, George. 2002. *Veto Players: How Political Institutions Work*. Princeton, NJ: Princeton University Press.

Walker, Ignacio. 2006a. Democracia en América Latina. *Foreign Affairs en Español* 6(2).

———. 2006b. Qual é o caminho da globalização, da democracia e da esquerda na América Latina? *Política Externa* 15(2): 21–32.

Weyland, Kurt. 2001. Clarifying a Contested Concept: Populism in the Study of Latin American Politics. *Comparative Politics* 34(1): 1–22.

———. 2003. Latin American Neopopulism: Neopopulism and Neoliberalism in Latin America; How Much Affinity? *Third World Quarterly* 24(6): 1095–115.

———. 2004. Neoliberalism and Democracy in Latin America: A Mixed Record. *Latin American Politics and Society* 46(1): 135–57.

Williamson, John. 1990. *Latin American Adjustment: How Much Has Happened*. Washington, DC: Institute for International Economics.

PART TWO

Country Cases: Explaining Success

CHAPTER EIGHT

Democratic Governance in Chile

ALAN ANGELL

☾

Effective governance does not have to be, by definition, democratic. There are examples of prolonged and, at certain periods at least, relatively effective authoritarian governance—the Mexican PRI or Pinochet's Chile come to mind in Latin America, and Singapore or South Korea in Asia. So what do we mean by democratic governance? Is this just another variant of the concept of governance or can we argue that in some ways the democratic form is superior? Are social and economic policies more effective and more sustainable when they are associated with democratic governance?

In his definition of *effective governance*, Michael Coppedge (2001, 7) stresses the need for stability, order, and legitimacy. However, to define not just effective governance but democratic governance we should add accountability and transparency.[1] Regimes that are democratic have, in theory at least, better mechanisms for making policies in a way that because they are based upon consent, can be imposed without coercion and are more likely to be sustained beyond changes of government. Moreover, democracies, again in theory, can ensure that policies are applied correctly and have mechanisms to control corruption and the abuses of executive power through an active opposition, a congress with powers to investigate, an independent and vigilant judiciary, and a free press. Critics should not fear sanctions.

We also need to incorporate the notion of societal accountability (Smulovitz 2003). Social rights should depend not only on what the center thinks is good for the people, but what the people want and are able to demand through their elected representatives, or through the courts.

Of course, it can be argued that few democracies meet these demanding criteria, and that democratic governments are prone to clientelism and populism. But not all are, and not all (if any) authoritarian governments are free of these distortions. Indeed, an independent judicial system that can check populist temptations is obviously more possible to construct under democracy. This chapter argues that Chile has made considerable advances in constructing governance that is both effective and democratic.

If we compare governance between various countries of Latin America then we need to consider the starting point of each newly established or re-established democracy—and there is no doubt that the starting point has been very varied. Chile was, of all the transition countries, the only one relatively well placed to construct democratic governance. This places an obvious limitation on the extent to which we can draw lessons for comparative purposes.[2] However, I would also argue that if we are trying to explain why since 1990 Chile has a good record of governance, then we need to go back not to the Pinochet reforms but much earlier.

GOVERNANCE BEFORE 1973

It is often assumed that the modern efficient state was a creation of the Pinochet years. My argument is to the contrary—that the Pinochet regime was able to implement a program of far-reaching reforms in part because there was a relatively efficient and consolidated state before 1973. This long tradition of state efficiency and political institutionalization provided a beneficial inheritance both to authoritarian and democratic regimes after 1973.[3] Even the military government, paradoxical as it may seem, felt constrained by the prevailing legalism of the Chilean state, and impelled to provide a judicial explanation and justification of what they were doing—as is illustrated by Robert Barros' account of the 1980 Constitution.[4]

If conventional historiography tends to downplay the extent of repression and political conflict in post-independence Chile, nevertheless there was a strong, perhaps dominant, basis of legality and constitutionalism.[5] The nineteenth century saw fewer internal conflicts than in most if not all other Latin American republics. The Constitution of 1833 lasted until 1925. Political parties early established a near monopoly of political representation (Scully 1992). Regional pressures were weak in the face of a highly centralized state. The judiciary was relatively independent. Since the 1920s the Contraloría General has performed a critical role of audit, scrutiny, and control over executive action at all levels, thereby helping to legitimate the constitutional system and central authority.[6] Even under General Pinochet the Contraloría served as a force for probity in the public administration on routine matters, including the local sector— though it was forced to bend to the dictator's will on key constitutional issues and was incapable of exercising scrutiny over the corrupt financial dealings of Pinochet and his family.

President Aylwin expressed his belief in the centrality of institutions in Chilean development in these words:

> You cannot overemphasize the tradition of institutionalization in Chile—this is fundamental. Cardinal Silva used to refer to the soul of Chile being its love for its institutions. This is true at the popular level as much as the elite level. And closely associated with this is a tradition of solving disagreements through discussion and negotiation. Of course, it went horribly wrong in 1973 but the consequence of that trauma and the dictatorship that followed was to reinforce the need for a return to the respect for institutions.[7]

Central to our argument is the proposition that the state achieved a relative degree of independence from political forces. It was never colonized by a personalist movement such as Peronism in Argentina, or by dominant parties as in Venezuela. It was, in the phrase used by Navia and Walker in this volume, "a democracy of institutions." The state was able to develop a system of social welfare which, though far from perfect, brought benefits to the middle and working class sectors in a way that was relatively free from clientelistic practices.[8] The state was also capable of running large-scale development agencies like CORFO that made an important contribution to industrial and economic development. When nationalized, the copper mines under CODELCO were also reasonably well managed. The Chilean tax system collected taxes with relatively low levels of evasion.[9] The police were markedly less corrupt or partial than in other republics. Even the military was not normally a threat to the civil order except in special circumstances such as in 1924 or 1973.

Historians sometimes use the concept of path-dependence to explain long-term historical developments. This can be overly deterministic, implying that it is difficult to take other directions. The very fact of a brutal dictatorship from 1973 to 1990 makes it difficult to push the argument too far for Chile. But I would argue that effective governance had solid and deep-rooted foundations—perhaps along with Uruguay the best start in Latin America for the task of post-authoritarian reconstruction—and that there was also a strong attachment to democracy and to the institutions of democracy that were an asset to the post-Pinochet governments. This brief and oversimplified historical account is important in trying to understand how Chile has achieved a high level of democratic governance since 1990. It is easier to resume good democratic practices than it is to invent them afresh.

It is sometimes assumed that the incoming democratic government in 1990 had such a favorable inheritance from the Pinochet government that it was all plain sailing. In fact the new government faced a host of difficulties.

Not least were the difficulties on the economic front. Undoubtedly there were reforms during the Pinochet period that were of benefit to the macroeconomy. These are well known and hardly need further comment. Yet Pinochet's government left office in 1990 with the economy in a far from healthy condition. The short-term legacy was increasing macroeconomic disequilibrium. In a burst of populist expenditure targeted at the plebiscite of 1988 and the elections of 1989, real demand rose by an unsustainable 22% in the period 1988–1989; inflation for the period September 1989 to January 1990 on an annualized basis rose to 31.5%, and though exports rose by 20% in the same period, imports rose by an alarming 46% (Ffrench-Davis 1991).[10]

The economic growth of 1988–1989, therefore, rested on precarious foundations. It was based upon using underutilized capacity, but investment to increase capacity was inadequate. The growth of new investment in the economy was only 15.4% per year in the 1981–1989 period compared with 20.2% per year in 1961–1971. The Pinochet government cut social expenditure, contributing to an already serious problem of poverty which in 1987 affected 45.1% of the population (of which 17.4% were in extreme poverty). All this plus the adverse effects on international prices of the Gulf War made macroeconomic management very difficult for the new government. Moreover, the Pinochet government had tied up state funds to deprive the Aylwin government of freedom of action. An estimated US $2 billion in the Copper Stabilization Fund on which the Aylwin government was counting as a cushion against likely future falls in copper prices, had already been spent by the Pinochet government to repay the bad debts accumulated in the Central Bank when it bailed out the financial sector from the collapse of 1982–1983.

The constitutional and political system also imposed real constraints on the incoming government. The Constitution of 1980 gave the state a limited role, but with authoritarian controls over democratic processes. The military, in the original version, was given a tutelary role over the political system. Congress lacked powers to perform an adequate regulatory and monitoring role over the executive. There were nine designated senators in the Senate, four of whom were nominated directly by the military. The Constitution safeguards private property rights against the state and gives the courts extra powers to ensure that the free-market economy remains intact. The Constitution is difficult to reform—only in 2005, after fifteen years of trying, was there agreement to abolish the designated senators, increase congressional investigatory powers, and increase the authority of the President over military appointments. During the first eight years after the return to democracy, the Right enjoyed a veto power over legislation though a combination of Pinochetista designated senators, and an electoral system that benefited the Right (and also the Concertación, though to a lesser extent).[11]

Pinochet intended that when the Constitution came into force in the 1990s, he would be chosen as President until 1997. But in a plebiscite held in October 1988, Pinochet lost by 55% of the vote against 43% in favor and had to call for a free election for the presidency to be held in December 1989. Nevertheless, the 43% of the vote that he obtained was testimony to the extent of support that he still enjoyed, even if part of that vote is discounted because of the fear of opposing the military regime.

Pinochet's strategy after the October plebiscite defeat was to safeguard his own position by insisting upon his constitutional right to remain as Commander-in-Chief of the army whoever won the elections in 1989. His aim was a military free of civil interference in internal matters such as promotions, and enjoying a privileged budgetary position for equipment, salaries, and pensions. The military budget could not be reduced below its 1989 level in real terms, and the obligatory 10% of the share of copper sales of the state corporation CODELCO assured it a considerable sum for arms purchases.[12] Pinochet also sought to make impossible any trials of members of the armed forces for human rights abuses.

Constitutional amendments in 1989 removed some of the objectionable parts of the constitution. But the outgoing government also passed laws to restrict future governments—the *leyes de amarre*, (literally, the binding laws), intended to limit the discretionary power of the incoming government.[13] One law granted security of tenure in the public sector, so that the incoming government had few posts at its discretion. Another law prohibited the incoming congress from investigating the activities of the Pinochet government. Members of the Supreme Court were offered handsome payments to retire to make way for equally conservative but considerably younger judges.

So the Aylwin government took office with a constitution much of which it rejected, an electoral system which was not of its choice, an armed forces over which it had relatively little formal control, a judiciary which had been an unquestioning loyal ally of the outgoing government, an entrepreneurial class confident in its ability to mobilize the political Right if that were necessary, and a hostile media. On the other hand, its own supporters expected a great deal, including the restitution of many social and economic rights. Yet the new government was a coalition of forces that had come together only fully in the late 1980s. Previously the major parties—the Christian Democrats, the Socialists (several varieties), and the Communists—had been engaged in recriminations over responsibility for the coup and how to confront the Pinochet regime. These parties had never collaborated before—indeed had been hostile to each other since the 1960s.

It is important to stress these economic difficulties, an unfavorable constitution, the untried political coalition, and a Right with veto power, as all of these factors demanded of the new government very considerable tactical skill and vision to combine positive policy outcomes with strengthening of democratic practices. Far from an easy ride, it is clear that the government faced major challenges. How well did it do?

DEMOCRATIC GOVERNANCE IN CHILE SINCE 1990: ECONOMY AND SOCIETY

Economic Growth

Growth in Chile accelerated after the economic crisis of 1982–1983 when the Pinochet government adopted more flexible policies with greater state intervention.[14] Chile also enjoyed high copper prices from the mid-1980s. GDP grew annually on average by 7.5% between 1983 and 1993, and by 4.4% between 1993 and 2003—the slower performance is explained by the recession of 1999–2001, but growth recovered by 2005–2006 to levels from 5% to 6%.[15] In per capita terms Chile grew by 4.2% annually from 1990–2005. At the end of the Pinochet regime the GDP was only 58% greater than in 1973: after fifteen years of democratic governments it had grown by 126.4% (Meller 2006, 92). Total GDP, expressed in constant US$ of 2000, grew from US $30.4 billion in 1983 to US $68.3 billion in 2003. In terms of Purchasing Power Parity, the estimate for total GDP in 2007 was US $234.4 billion and for GDP per capita (PPP) US $14,440—higher than Argentina with US $13,000 or Costa Rica with US $13,500.[16] Exports grew at 10.3% per year between 1983 and 1993, and 8.4% between 1993 and 2003. In terms of constant US$ of 2000, exports rose in value from US $5.8 billion in 1983 to US

$18.7 billion in 2003. Exports as a proportion of GDP rose from 24% in 1983 to 34.5% in 2003—not far short of the economic performance of the legendary Asian tigers. By 1996, public investment was only 16% of the total and private investment was 84% (Rodríguez and Serrano 1998). International debt as a proportion of GDP has fallen from 90.7% in 1983 to 49.1% in 2003. Democratic governments concluded a number of important bilateral trade deals with the United States, South Korea, and the EU. These agreements are important not just for trade relations but for their impact on the political and international standing of the government. All this was achieved with a gradually declining inflation rate which between mid-2005 to mid-2006 was 3.7%.[17]

De Gregorio (2005, 42) argues that in matters of fiscal policy, Chile is one of the most responsible countries in the world. Moreover, by maintaining the relatively small size of government, the composition of government expenditure has favored growth—he estimates that the size of government in Chile is 5% of GDP lower than would be expected for a country of its size of income.

Social Welfare

But have the benefits of growth been so badly distributed that the majority of the population has seen no substantial improvement in incomes and welfare? The answer clearly is no. On many indicators Chile ranks favorably with the OECD countries—life expectancy in 2005 was 78.3 years (compared with a Latin American average of 71), infant mortality was 10 per 1000 births (compared with the Latin American average of 28), and illiteracy is down to 4% of the population (compared with the Latin American average of 11%). On the composite index of human development prepared by the UNDP (2007) on a 0–1 scale, in 2005 Chile was rated 0.867—marginally lower than Argentina but almost the same as Portugal and above Costa Rica. Seventy percent of Chileans now own their own houses—an increase of 10% since 1990; house ownership levels are the same across all socioeconomic strata; and 43% of homes were bought with state assistance. Of the houses, 81% are classified as of good quality and only 7% of poor quality.[18] Chileans also participated in technological innovations. The number of fixed lines and mobile telephones per 1000 people rose from 358 in 1999 to 659 in 2002; and the number of internet users rose from 625,000 in 1999 to 3.6 million in 2002 (World Bank 2004).

Governments after 1990 emphasized growth as the major objective, but this was also seen as the best way to deal with poverty and to improve equity. Real wages increased by 3.3% per year in the ten years after 1990, the minimum wage increased by 17% in real terms between 1989 and 1991 alone, and employment grew by 1.7% per year in the same period. The minimum wage by 1998 was equivalent to 45% of the average salary of unskilled workers—and this rose to 60% by 2003 (De Gregorio 2005, 70). At the end of the Pinochet period, the minimum wage in 1989 was 30% less than it was in 1980, whereas under the Concertación governments it grew in real terms 5% annually. Huber and Stephens in this volume estimate that minimum wage legislation increased the earnings of about a quarter of the labor force sufficiently to keep themselves and a spouse above the poverty line. Unemployment fell to a low of 6.1% in 1997, increased to around 9% in 2001, and fell to a little over 7% by 2006. The government introduced an unemployment insurance system in which by mid-2005 some three million workers were enrolled. According to Mainwaring and Scully in the introduction to this volume, by 2005 Chile had the highest percentage of jobs in the formal sector in Latin America, and registered the largest increase of such jobs of any country in Latin America between 1990 and 2005. Nevertheless it needs to be stressed that average earnings are still very low—only US $250 per month in 2005 (Meller 2006, 95).

There was a massive increase in social expenditure. Investment in public hospitals and primary care units increased from US $10 million to US $100 million in the Aylwin period (though for a variety of reasons performance overall was less satisfactory). Social expenditure on health increased by 9.4% per year from 1990 to 2000, and on education by 10.6% per year over the same period. The government in 2005 began a system—known as *Plan Auge*—which offered protection to all Chileans for 25 major illnesses, regardless of income.[19] Housing subsidies rose by 160% in the decade, targeted at low income and rural families. As Mainwaring and Scully point out in their introduction, Chile showed an impressive increase in the number of students enrolled in secondary education—the highest proportion in Latin America.

The government's skillful handling of social expenditure is shown by the tax reform of 1990, based upon cooperation with the political Right which accepted an increase in taxation as a price to pay to sustain the economic model, and, presumably, to extract future concessions from the government. The reform symbolized to the population that the government was serious about equity issues, for the tax increases were linked to social spending. The timing was very effective—one of the first major measures of the government.[20] It showed that the new government could negotiate with the Right without abandoning its commitment to social equity.

Chile is exceptional in Latin America for the extent of the reduction of poverty. Overall poverty fell from 45.1% of the population in 1987 to 20.6% in 2000, and those in extreme poverty from 17.4% to 5.7% (four times lower than the regional average of 20%).[21] Despite the recession of 1999, overall poverty continued to decline to 13.7% in 2006 and extreme poverty to 3.2%.[22] Costa Rica also had a poverty rate of 20% in 2000, but it was only 26% ten years earlier. The Latin American average fell from only 48% at the start of the period to 44% at the end. Chile has by far the lowest rate of child malnutrition in Latin America, with only 1.9%: the next lowest was Costa Rica with 6.1%, and the rate in Argentina in the mid-1990s was 12.4% (UNDP 2004, 119).[23] However, how much further Chile can progress in poverty reduction remains to be seen. Foxley (2004, 1) emphasizes that the first stage of poverty reduction is relatively easy—60% of the reduction was due to economic growth and the remainder to social policies. But thereafter it is not so easy. The real problems now reside in the precariousness of employment and in unequal opportunities of access to such basic services as health and education (Muñoz 2007, 37). Unless higher expenditure on health and education translates into better performance—and the results have been disappointing—then the anticipated benefits to equity will not be realized. Moreover, though it is relatively easy to reach those who are just below the poverty line, there remains a hard core of extremely poor for whom social policies are very difficult to reach (as in all countries). It remains to be seen how well the initiative started by the Lagos government—Chile Solidario, a family-centered project—performs in this respect.[24]

If the intention of the government was that the quality of the reforms should match that of expenditure, the results have been disappointing.[25] In education there were imaginative and successful attempts to target the poorest schools in the P900 program, and a wider program of reform of the primary and secondary sector, MECE Básica and MECE Media.[26] Yet the results in terms of educational achievement indicators have been lackluster, either through inefficient expenditures, inequality, or a combination of the two (De Gregorio 2005, 71). No doubt the reforms were more difficult to implement than thought, not least because of the resistance of the labor force in those sectors, and the benefits have taken longer to emerge than hoped. The Lagos government announced a major initiative to restructure the Ministry of Education in order to make it much more decentralized. Teachers, on the other hand, are strong advocates of centralization. Another controversial reform that is running into difficulties is the attempt to introduce performance evaluation, and corresponding sanctions and benefits, for teachers. How these reforms work out remains to be seen.[27] They face the major obstacle of the inheritance of the Pinochet era three-tier educational system of fee-paying

private schools, state-funded private schools, and municipal schools almost guaranteed to reproduce and reinforce social inequality.

DEMOCRATIC GOVERNANCE IN CHILE SINCE 1990: INSTITUTIONS AND POLITICS

Governance

A World Bank Governance Project created a series of indicators to measure the quality of governance using as criteria political stability, government effectiveness, regulatory quality, rule of law, control of corruption,
and voice and accountability. Table 8.1 shows that Chile is above the
Latin American average; overall, it performs better than the next rated
country in Latin America, Costa Rica, is clearly superior in governance
to Italy, and is not ranked as very inferior to the United States or UK
(Kaufmann, Kraay, and Mastruzzi 2007).

Moreover, on all but one indicator Chile has improved since 1998.
Hence voice and accountability went up in the period 1998–2006 from
67% to 87.5%; political stability from 71.5% to 77.4%; government
effectiveness from 87.4% to 87.7%; regulatory quality fell marginally
from 92.4% to 91.7%; rule of law rose from 85.5% to 87.6%; and control of corruption from 86.3% to 89.8% (Kaufmann, Kraay, and Mastruzzi 2007).

The World Economic Forum measures the competitiveness of national
economies—including indicators such as the quality of public services
and of macroeconomic policy. In the 2007 survey, Chile was ranked 26
in the international comparisons—higher than Spain at 29, Costa Rica
at 57 and Uruguay at 75.[28] Another survey conducted by the Adenauer
Foundation constructs an Index of Democratic Development. On a 1 to
10 scale, with 10 equivalent to a high level of democratic development,
in 2007 Chile scored a remarkable 10.360 (followed by Costa Rica with
9.706 and Uruguay with 9.384).[29]

These are all very impressive achievements. In a relatively brief period,
Chile has constructed a system of democratic governance superior on
these indicators to any other country in Latin America, and on a par
with many of the most developed countries.[30] This has been achieved
with a high level of political stability and predictability. Few governing
coalitions have received such a stable vote in a comparable period of time
since the elections in Chile from 1989. Electoral results for the Chamber
of Deputies since 1989 show some variation in the voting for individual
parties inside the coalitions, a slight decline in the vote for the governing

TABLE 8.1
Governance Indicators

Governance indicators	Year	Chile	Costa Rica	Italy	Latin America and the Caribbean	United Kingdom	United States
Voice and accountability	2006	87.5	74.0	86.5	51.6	92.8	83.7
Political stability	2006	77.4	79.8	56.3	37.7	61.1	57.7
Government effectiveness	2006	87.7	65.4	67.3	43.2	94.8	92.9
Regulatory quality	2006	91.7	63.9	74.1	45.4	98.0	93.7
Rule of law	2006	87.6	64.8	60.0	35.4	93.3	91.9
Control corruption	2006	89.8	67.0	64.1	42.0	93.7	89.3

Source: Kaufmann, Kraay, and Mastruzzi (2007)

Percentile Rank (0–100)

Readers who are puzzled by the low scores on political stability for the UK and the United States are referred to the methodology paper to accompany these tables: Kaufmann, Kraay, and Mastruzzi, *Governance Matters VI: Governance Indicators for 1996–2006*, July 2007, World Bank Policy Research Working Paper 4280.

Concertación, and a rise in the vote for the Right. Overall, however, the vote for the Concertación has varied from a high of 57.8% in the 1993 Presidential elections to a low of 45.6% in the first round of the Presidential elections in 2005 (when the government candidate faced tough opposition from two strong right wing candidates). Overall electoral volatility in comparative terms is very low indeed. Signs of political *desencanto* or *desgaste* may be shown by the public opinion polls, but the electoral evidence shows far less evidence of any serious disenchantment.[31]

Taxation

The democratic governments inherited an efficient tax system (as indeed did the Pinochet government—though it reformed the tax system with the introduction of the VAT).[32] The Aylwin government was determined to lower the rate of tax evasion, firstly, by improving the agency's operating procedures and increasing the level of expertise, and, secondly, by making the system more transparent, simple, and impartial. Outside experts were recruited, and special performance bonuses were introduced. A fully merit-based system of recruitment and promotion was implemented to reduce clientelistic practices in the hiring of staff.

A major innovation—producing both efficiency gains and savings—was the reduction of paperwork by use of the Internet to make tax payments.[33] The Director of the SII (Servicio de Impuestos Internos) claimed in 2001 that Chile was more advanced in its use of the internet for tax purposes than the United States, France, Spain, or Germany.[34] Almost three-quarters of a million of the country's two million corporate and individual taxpayers use the internet for tax purposes. The SII also pioneered the use of information on general financial transactions of taxpayers to provide a more accurate picture of real earnings (against the opposition of the political Right and business groups as an invasion of privacy). The SII used opinion polls to see what complaints were made about their procedures, and implemented improvements which reduced tax evasion. As Sánchez (2005, 244) points out, "no less than 94.4% of Chilean taxpayers in 1992 considered that evading taxes constituted a serious transgression and 73% of them declared themselves scared of the powers of the SII."

The results have been impressive. Tax evasion levels fell from 30% of potential revenues in 1990 to 18.3% in 1993—a figure which has been more or less constant since then (compare this with Argentina at 31.5% or Peru with 68.2%). Evasion on income tax was reduced from almost 50% to 40% in the same period. Evasion overall was by 1995 very similar to Canada (23%) or Spain (26%). By 1999 the additional revenue gained that year as a result of lower tax evasion, compared with the rate of evasion in 1991, was more than US $1 billion. Tax revenues as a proportion of GDP rose from 15.1% in 1990 to 18.8% in 2005. This is, of course, much lower than the 30 to 40% of the developed countries, but Chile has proportionately far fewer taxpayers, as given the inequality of income, 82% do not pay direct taxes (Muñoz 2007, 113–14).

There are problems with the tax system in Chile. Some sectors of the economy (agriculture, mining, and transport) and some regions enjoy a preferential tax regime, income tax is still very complex, and the differential between personal and business taxes too great (Sánchez 2005, 336).[35] Mario Marcel, the head of the Budget Office during the Lagos government, points out that of the top 5% of income earners only half pay tax at the proper level; the rest use various devices to pay at the 17% rate rather than the top rate of 40%.[36]

For our purposes, nevertheless, the tax system does illustrate the achievements of democratic governance in Chile. Taxation is a crucial element in the relationship between a state and its citizens. If citizens trust the fairness of the tax system, and the ends to which taxation is used, then a vital building bloc of good governance is created. An equitable and efficient system improves the quality of democracy, provides resources for growth, and enhances social justice.

Corruption

The issue of corruption has recently received much attention in Chile—as it has throughout Latin America. According to Alfredo Rehren, the Contraloría investigated 241 cases of corruption at the local level in 1993–1994. Public enterprises such as Chile's huge Copper Corporation (CODELCO), the Concón Oil Refinery, a water and sewage plant in Valparaíso, the Maritime Corporation, and the Port Authority have been accused of corruption. Services such as the National Housing Service, the Sports and Recreation Direction, the National Emergency Office in the Ministry of Interior, the Military Hospital, the National Police's Retirement Service, and the Office for the Return of Political Exiles also faced accusations of corruption (Rehren 2004, 32).

Rehren (32) lists recent cases, including corruption in the Ministry of Public works diverting funds to increase salaries in the Ministry, a scandal involving the transfer of government bonds from the Chilean Development Agency (CORFO) to a private investment corporation, and most notorious of all, the removal of congressional immunity from six deputies for involvement in bribery. His explanation is based upon the persistence of traditional clientelistic structures, and, more importantly, upon a new and powerful entrepreneurial class able to make use of the market economy to maximize its influence over the political elite.

However, while this points to corruption at the higher levels of the state bureaucracy, he also quotes data showing that most Chileans, in terms of their daily encounters with the Chilean bureaucracy and social services, do not experience corrupt practices (Rehren 34). This is supported by the Latinobarómetro finding that while most Chileans considered corruption to be a major problem, on the other hand, when asked about the probability of successfully bribing a judge, a police officer, or a civil servant, only 20%, in two cases, and 19%, in the other, thought that was likely. These were the lowest rates in Latin America—in Mexico the responses were 58%, 65%, and 55% (and the figures for Argentina were not much lower). Presumably when Chileans express concerns about corruption, this is directed at politicians and not at the institutions of the state. In the survey of Transparency International for 2007, which measures subjective perceptions of the misuse of public office for private gain, Chile is ranked 22 out of 179 countries, with a score of 7 on a 1 to 10 scale, only two places behind the United States. In Latin America, Uruguay is ranked 25, Mexico is ranked at 72, and Argentina at 105, with a score of 2.9 on the index.[37]

The system of financing elections by contributions that were neither registered nor limited was clearly an area that did lead to corruption in fact if not in law. However, a 2004 law attempts to control private donations (and to introduce a system of partial state funding). The law came into effect for the municipal elections in 2004, but the real test will be how it performs in the future and how far it is reformed to take account of its deficiencies.[38] This is a notoriously tricky area in which efforts to regulate effectively have defeated policy makers in the most advanced countries.[39]

Corruption exists in all countries. At least in terms of scale, in Chile it does not seem to be a serious threat to the political system, and public rejection of corruption is strong. Moreover, governments have made efforts over the years to control corruption—the latest of which was a Commission on Transparency and Probity created by President Lagos in January 2003 to begin a major governmental overhaul to fight corruption, many of the recommendations of which have been made into laws.

Current concerns about corruption need to be put into historical context. It is now clear that the dictatorship, in spite of its initial image of a tough but honest regime, was in fact highly corrupt at the top level, not least of course Pinochet himself, with an estimated US $27 million accumulated in the Riggs Bank amongst others in the United States, using false passports. This is not the only case, however. An earlier and massive scandal involved fraud by directors of Enersis (a privatized electricity supply firm) to the Spanish company Endesa. The sums involved amounted to over US $200 million, and the Supreme Court (July 2005) confirmed fines of US $66 million against those involved—principally José Yuraszeck, a major contributor to the finances of the UDI.[40] In addition, a group of Concertación deputies produced a report claiming that the loss to the state, due to the way that the privatizations were conducted during the Pinochet government, amounts to US $2,500 million.[41] The disclosure of corruption under the Pinochet regime and not least by the dictator himself strengthens the argument that democratic governance is better at discovering and prosecuting corruption than dictatorship.

Executive-Legislative Relations

One of the major political problems for governance in Latin America has been the unsatisfactory relationship between executive and Congress.

The optimum position is one in which behavior is co-operative, where the legislature acts as an effective check on executive action and participates constructively in the framing of public policy. At first sight it might seem that Chile is not at this point. The Constitution gives the President excessive powers—regarded by some in theory as one of the most powerful presidencies in the world (though the Constitution also restricts the scope of the state and government more than in many other constitutions in Latin America).

Peter Siavelis (2002, 81) argues that the overall political context has modified excessive executive power, and that the party system, the extent of Presidential support in Congress, and the political context of the transition have meant in practice that the informal influence of Congress is much greater than the constitutional provisions would suggest. Crucial in orchestrating good relations between President and Congress in the transition period of the Aylwin presidency was the Secretaría General de la Presidencia (SEGPRES), responsible for two-way contact between both branches and making the relationship one of persuasion rather than conflict.[42] Moreover, the prevailing political consensus made the President's task in important policy areas rather easier—for example, Siavelis (100) writes that "there was a consensus amongst legislators that without centralised budgetary control in the executive branch, particularistic spending initiatives of individual legislators could break the national budget." Congress has also acquired greater power, including a 1997 protocol giving it access to better information to consider the budget.[43] Nevertheless, there is a long way to go before Congress assumes the role that many congressional representatives feel is its due. A proposal to create a powerful Budget Office—even though it was supported by the Finance Committee of both chambers—was never approved (Montecinos 2003, 39).

Formal constitutional rules are not necessarily a guide to the real power of particular institutions—constitutional conventions can alter the spirit if not the letter of the constitution. The legitimacy of the democratic process in Chile has strengthened as government and opposition have bargained over issues comparable to those in other democracies—how to reform the health system, the appropriate level of taxation, and how to deal with crime. The government has obtained far less than it wanted in many areas—labor law reform for example, but that is part of the process of bargaining in any democratic society. The process of "normalization" of political life was assisted by the high degree of internal unity of the governing coalition and the relative lack of substantive disagreement with the opposition. Samuel Valenzuela (1998, 195) writes that "though the continuity of the 1980 Constitution has not been broken, the transformations have been significant, and the recreation of previous institutional practices has been so extensive, that one can say that there has been a transition, not yet finished, towards the recreation of a fundamental legal framework for the practice of democracy." This argument is strengthened by the constitutional reforms of 2005.

John Carey's data shows a high level of re-election of incumbents in both chambers of the legislature—in the 1993 and 1997 elections "around three-quarters of incumbents have been re-nominated for the Chamber within the same coalition, and three-fifths have won re-election (2002, 234, 253). Carey concludes that:

Chile's Congress is re-establishing itself as an unusually professionalized and technically competent legislature. Politicians endeavour—generally successfully—to build careers through re-election to Congress.... Much of the substantive oversight and policy-making work of the legislature is, moreover, delegated to a set of standing committees and stable membership on these committees... which means that these intra-legislative institutions are accumulating substantial policy expertise (253).

The work of congressional representatives is organized at the level of the governing coalition, rather than at the level of the individual parties. The two major institutions of the lower house—the *mesas directivas* and the committees—are organized by the two coalitions. This gives an additional weight to the proceedings of Congress even though the constitution allocates it a very subordinate role.[44] These patterns of behavior are important, and tend to become the norm. A president using excessive executive powers, or a Congress in which the Right was totally obstructive, would seriously undermine governance in Chile. This is not to say that constitutional reform is irrelevant, but the fact remains that since 1990 President and Congress have cooperated in the task of governing Chile in a democratic fashion.

DEMOCRATIC GOVERNANCE SINCE 1990: THE DEFICITS

If the previous analysis is correct, it is still only part of the story. There are aspects of democratic governance in Chile that have come under increasing scrutiny, and criticism.

Equity and Income Distribution

If poverty reduction has been dramatic, the same cannot be said for income distribution. There are questions raised about the government's commitment to equity given the unequal distribution of income.[45] Income distribution in Chile is one of the most unequal in Latin America—not least because of the enormous increase in earnings of the top 1% or less of the population (Palma 2002). Yet the widely quoted GINI coefficient—0.57 in 1990, 0.58 in 2000, and down to 0.54 in 2006—needs to be put into context.[46] Chile has long had a pattern of very unequal income distribution; in the early 1950s the coefficient was 0.44 and it rose to 0.5 in 1968 and fell only a little in the Popular Unity years to 0.47 in 1971 (Thorp 1998, 380). The worst deterioration occurred during the Pinochet years, and it takes a long time to counter the entrenched inequality that built up during those years. Moreover, in the period since 1990 the relationship between the various quintiles has not varied significantly, which suggests that all the various social strata have improved their living standards in a relatively proportional way.[47]

What is very marked in Chile, however, is the concentration of income in the top decile and even more in the top 1% of income earners. Between 1987 and 2003, the share of income going to the top 1% rose from 12% to 14.1%, and the share of income going to the top decile in 2006 was 46%—in comparison, this same decile took an average of 25% in the OECD countries and 30% in the United States.[48]

Apart from the share going to the top decile, income distribution in Chile looks very similar to that of the OECD countries. Moreover, the effect of social policies on inequality has also to be taken into account. In 1996 the World Bank calculated that there was a monetary income differential of 1 to 20 between the top and bottom quintiles of the population (World Bank 2006). However, if the redistributive effect of social expenditures is taken into account, then the income differential for the same quintiles fell to 1 to 11. A calculation for 2006 for the same quintiles puts the income differential at 1 to 7 (Muñoz 2007, 29).

Women suffer more than men from the pattern of inequality. Over two million women work only in the home and contribute to no pension scheme, but even worse off are the half a million who live in single-parent households, who cannot hope to share the pension of a partner. It is true that younger women are much more likely to have paid employment, but those over 35 have very low levels of participation. And at any educational level, women earn less than equally qualified men—and this inequality is highest at the level of those with most education.[49] In an estimate by the World Economic Forum of the gender gap in 2007 measuring economic participation, economic opportunities, political power, educational opportunities, and quality of life, Chile comes 86 out of 128 countries and scores 0.648 on the scale (where 1 is equality). Costa Rica is ranked 28 with a score of 0.701 (the most equal country is Sweden with a score of 0.814).[50] As Foxley points out in this volume, in the lowest quintile of incomes only one woman in five has access to a job, whereas in the top quintile it is one out of two.

Normally such an unequal income distribution has negative consequences on growth. However, in Chile this has not been the case, and De Gregorio (2005, 69–70) attributes this to effective social expenditures and to solid institutions. Yet even if these considerations modify the negative effects of inequality, it still remains a serious problem. Presumably one of the theoretical merits of neoliberal economies is the creation of a genuine capitalist culture in which employment opportunities are based upon merit, and in which monopolistic practices do not damage the process of economic decision making. But there is little doubt that economic power is highly concentrated in Chile, and it seems likely that the structure of privilege impedes the development of those small and medium-sized enterprises regarded as of crucial importance to the creation of employment.[51] Moreover, in social terms the exodus of the wealthy from the state sector in health and education—even in policing, to some extent, with the development of private security agents—creates a social dualism which imposes barriers to social mobility.[52] The prevailing system of income distribution is clearly unpopular with the Chilean population—in the Latinobarómetro survey for 2007 only 10% of those questioned considered the system to be just.

An important area of social dualism and inequity in Chile lies with the individual pension system introduced by the military government. The system has been much admired and regarded as a model for other countries, but such praise seems misplaced. Pension reform normally involves complex political bargaining, but Chile's pension law was imposed by an authoritarian state with none of the public debate and scrutiny that would have taken place in a democracy. The enthusiasm of advocates of the system has been excessive, as Carmelo Mesa-Lago suggests.[53] Coverage is less than the previous system, and there is still the need for state-funded pension support for those who fall outside. Moreover, of those who are in the scheme, a large proportion is not contributing actively, as shown in Chapter 5 by Huber and Stephens. The combination of these two factors means that the private pension funds (AFPs) are covering less than half of the country's workforce.[54] The fiscal cost of the transfer to the private system in the mid-1990s was about 3.4% of GDP annually. The AFPs are paying relatively few pensions so far; the test will be in years to come. Moreover the administrative costs are very high—representing the largest single item of costs, equivalent to 30% of the total. Another criticism, made by the ILO, of the Chilean scheme, is that there is no redistributive element in the Chilean pension scheme, generally regarded as an important component of pension arrangements.

President Bachelet made pension reform a major issue in her proposed policy initiatives. According to her advisors the system will run into a major crisis after 2010 when many more contributors will become recipients. Under consideration are automatic state pensions for those over 65 who are not covered, or not covered adequately, by the AFPs, a campaign to reduce their administrative costs and make them more competitive, and a campaign to create incentives for independent workers to become members of the scheme.[55]

An Overcentralized State

Decentralization was not high on the agenda of the new government, even though the free election of local authorities clearly was, and the government fought hard to secure those elections, held for the first time in 1992. But the decentralized system agreed upon after hard bargaining with the Right was very modest in Latin American terms. The incoming government wished, for good reasons at the start of the transition, to secure and maintain strong central political and fiscal control. Although the Pinochet government had transferred many functions to the municipalities and the regions, this was still combined with central control, and is best seen as deconcentration rather than decentralization.

In reality, there was little pressure for real decentralization to offset these centralizing tendencies. Regional sentiment is very weak, and there is nothing comparable in Chile to the regional identities in Colombia.[56] Nor were the cities outside Santiago hotbeds of local identity. Decades of centralized government, reinforced by the fierce authoritarianism of the Pinochet government, had produced tacit consent to the doctrine that "the man in Santiago knows best." Hence the form of decentralization adopted is a uniform standard structure that does not allow for regional and local differences—which certainly exist geographically and in economic terms, even if public perception of them is weak.[57] Regional governments are appointed and not elected. Municipal governments have very little real power and practically no fiscal autonomy. This system may have been felt necessary in order to maintain political control and perhaps even more so to prevent any of the fiscal problems that have affected decentralization elsewhere. But it hardly created much enthusiasm for local government or fostered local participation.[58]

In a speech to mayors during the electoral campaign of 2005, Bachelet agreed that centralization of power in Chile was exaggerated and that the coordination between local and central authorities was not adequate, and proposed a municipal reform to increase the power of local authorities to make them real local governments.[59] Yet whether this pledge will be enforced with sufficient determination on the part of the government, and whether the opposition accepts the need for reform, remains to be seen.

Decline of the Party System?

There is considerable criticism of the party system in Chile.[60] Commentators often assume (explicitly or implicitly) that parties since 1990 have to be measured against an earlier period of mass, participatory parties, when ideological and programmatic differences were clear and hotly debated not just by party elites but also by ordinary members. In other words, they were truly parties of masses and not parties of elites more concerned to control than to express popular sentiment. By contrast, since 1990 there is much comment that parties are elitist, detached from the concerns of ordinary people, nonparticipatory and unpopular.

But is this picture of the past accurate? It is difficult to be authoritative in the absence of detailed studies of party organization and behavior, in contrast to the many studies of party ideology. Undoubtedly the parties did have deep social roots, there was fierce electoral competition, and there were pronounced ideological differences. At least there was in the period 1964 to 1973. But was this period typical or not?[61] Probably not—and that period was exceptional not just in Chile but in many parts of Latin America and indeed in the world (remember the events of 1968, for example). If we look to earlier periods of Chilean party history, we have a different picture. Had there been reliable polls in, for example, 1946 to 1958, it is not obvious that the level of public trust or confidence in the parties would have been very different from those of today. There was massive rejection of the parties in the election of 1952, even though the desertion was temporary. There was also much greater electoral volatility as parties like the Partido Agrario Laborista rose and declined, or the Christian Democrats suddenly moved from small minority to almost majority status. In other words, it is very misleading to contrast parties today with a model of parties based on an unusual period in Chilean party development.

There is concern in Chile about declining electoral participation. In the most recent Presidential election of 2005–2006, abstention of registered voters was 13.11%—higher than the 5.27% in 1993 or the 10.05% in 1999, though the null and blank votes were low, at 2.16% and 0.66%, respectively.[62] Electoral participation has been declining in Chile since 1988, when of the potential electorate of just over 8 million voters, an extremely high proportion, 92.2%, was registered. By 2005, registered voters were 78.71% of the potential electorate. Yet, as Marta Lagos points out, this is still considerably higher than the 69.08% registered to vote in the most competitive election of the turbulent years of the Popular Unity government—the congressional election of 1973 (2005, 17). Of the potential electorate in 2005–2006, 69.15% participated. This figure is still relatively high in comparison with other countries, and hardly gives grounds for grave doubts about the stability of Chilean democracy. Moreover, there is little increase in voting for anti-party movements or new parties (this may be partly explained by the rigidities of the electoral system), though there is concern about the low level of voter registration amongst the potential first-time voters—as indeed there is in most countries.

Undoubtedly there have been changes in the party system. It would have been remarkable if the experience of exile and clandestine activity for seventeen years had not changed them. Parties have become more centralized and controlling, and the widespread consensus around the free-market model has reduced the scope of political debate to seeming technicalities rather than rival policies, let alone different ideologies. But it is also important to stress that this change is a worldwide trend observable in most of the developed countries and Latin America. In other words, there are global influences as well as national ones here. Comparing the data on trust in parties of the Eurobarometer with that of the Latinobarómetro for 2002, Chile occupies a middle position (12%) between the low of 4% level of trust in parties in Argentina to the (not very) high of 36% in Holland and Denmark. The level of trust in parties in Chile is not very different from that in France or Britain. Partisan identification is also declining worldwide (Angell 2003a).

Despite mistrust of parties and of politicians, the electorate continues to give overwhelming support to the governing coalition. This coalition has successfully fought and gained over 50% (or very close) of the vote in a plebiscite, four presidential, five congressional, and three municipal elections, has witnessed an unprecedented successful period of economic growth, and dealt with complex political issues such as justice for human rights abuses. And complementing the role of parties of the Concertación as agents of government has been the role of the parties of the Right as agents of opposition. Increasingly, those parties have come closer to the government in the most controversial of matters—that of human rights, or the trials of General Pinochet—while continuing to bargain with the government over more mundane matters of government. The Right offers a plausible alternative government to that of the existing one—without this being perceived as a threat to democratic governance. Democracy in Chile, in a way not typical of Latin America, is party democracy.

Yet the concern over the health of parties is not without foundation. A great deal of concern over elitism, lack of participation, and excessive infighting derives from the effects of an electoral system that was imposed by the dictatorship and was not the choice of the democratic governments. Jaime Gazmuri, a leading Socialist senator, has argued that unless there is electoral reform, there is a real danger that the existing system will destroy the party system. He argues that the tension between the interests of the parties and that of the coalitions is creating serious problems that are more and more difficult to manage—shown, for example, in the disputes over the choice of congressional representation for the 2005 elections.[63] It is also clear that the electoral system depresses voter interest. If it is obvious that each constituency will, with very few exceptions, return one member for the government and one for the opposition, the incentive to vote is clearly lessened (FLACSO 2006).

But what system should it be? Carlos Huneeus (2004) argues strongly that Chile needs to reestablish the proportional representation system:

This system best suits the political diversity of the country, and it has a historical legitimacy chosen in the past as the best method for the kind of multi-party system that Chile had. It is also the best system to promote democracy as it allows for the expression of political pluralism, and by creating a more competitive electoral system it allows for the participation of all parties, both those now in existence and those that might form in the future.

Opponents of this point of view will argue that the PR system was in part responsible for the crisis of democracy in the 1970s, and there is truth in this. But those were times of intense political mobilization and ideological division, very different from the consensus-based politics of the present time. Moreover, it is not difficult to devise a PR system that does not lead to a proliferation of small parties—by having a 3% or 5% barrier to entry to Congress—or one that encourages parties to form coalitions—by holding simultaneous elections for President and Congress. Such a system would encourage participation, allow representation of small but important expressions of political opinion, and subject politicians to stronger pressures from civil society. No electoral system is perfect. All involve a trade-off between securing effective representation and securing stable government.[64] All systems need to be chosen to reflect specific realities and on those grounds Huneeus' arguments are convincing—but implementing such a reform is a major challenge. The prospects are not very promising and there will be resistance to change and not just from the Right. The Socialists and the PPD would, for example, suffer a loss of support if parties further to the left had a real chance of gaining political representation.

If Governance Is So Good in Chile, Why Do the Opinion Polls Show Such Negative Findings?

Asked in 2006 if they thought that democracy was preferable to any other form of government, 56% of Chileans agreed that it was—up from 50% in 2002.[65] The 2006 figure was just below the Latin American average of 58% (and way below the 75% of Costa Rica or the 76% of Uruguay).[66] Preference for an authoritarian government in some circumstances was the choice of 19% of respondents and the same number thought that it made no difference if the government was democratic or authoritarian. Asked in 2007 if they were very, or more or less, satisfied with the way that democracy worked in Chile, only 36% agreed—though this was an increase from the 23% of 2001 (when the country was recovering from recession). In Latin America, satisfaction with democracy was expressed on average by 29% of respondents, and even the best rated country, Costa Rica, had only 48% satisfied (a fall from the 75% of 2002). Confidence in the institutions of government was also low. In 2006, only 27% of Chileans expressed confidence in the judiciary, 36% in Congress, and in 2007, 20% expressed confidence in parties—compared with 15% in 2001. The executive was more highly regarded—when President Lagos left office in 2006, as many as 64% of Chileans approved of him, making him the third most highly rated president in Latin America.

Chileans are not very impressed with their economic model. In 2002, only 19% expressed satisfaction with the way that the market economy functioned in their country—below the Latin American average of 24%. However this rose to 36% in 2004, reflecting the recovery of growth, but fell to 30% in 2007. Of course the explanation for this economic discontent might well be that of rising expectations—Chileans have been accustomed to growing prosperity and are demanding more. Privatization was not very popular—only 33% of Chileans in 2007 thought that it had been beneficial to the country. In contrast, when Chileans are asked of which enterprise they have a high opinion, then the state enterprises—CODELCO, BancoEstado—come out on top. The much-vaunted private pension scheme, the AFPs, is not popular.[67]

Chileans do not trust each other very much. Asked in 2002 if one could trust in the majority of people, only 13% of Chileans agreed—the fourth lowest level of trust in Latin America (with Brazil the lowest with only 3% and Uruguay the highest with 36%).[68] In another survey combining happiness with life satisfaction scores, although Chile was ranked medium high, it was well below the levels of, for example, Colombia, El Salvador, or Venezuela (Ingelhart 2004). But one needs to be cautious with this data as we lack similar findings for the past and do not know, for example, if this has been a persistent trait.

Is public mistrust of politicians necessarily harmful for democracy? Or is it beneficial? There would hardly be societal accountability in a democratic system unless there were levels of discontent that led society to scrutinize what politicians were doing and why certain policies were adopted. Chileans are now more educated, more accustomed to improvement, and it is quite natural that this leads not to contentment but to demands for more. Should we minimize the critical perceptions of the workings of democracy in Chile, and write them off as a healthy expression of democratic discontent? Should we be concerned for the survival of the political system as a legitimate stable force? Or should we accept that these attitudes point to deficiencies in the political system, and with the quality of democracy, that can to some extent be remedied? What is important is that citizens have satisfactory outlets for the institutional expression of discontent—such as the existence of an effective political opposition, separation of powers, effective scrutiny of executive actions, and the rule of law. It is when these conditions are not present that discontent becomes a threat not just to the government but to the political system as a whole. If we accept that those conditions are present, then discontent in Chile is different from that in, for example, Venezuela, which led to the collapse of the party system and the regime, or from that in Bolivia which led to the resignation of President Sánchez de Lozada.

The skeptics come predominantly from the Right. Asked in 2003 if they were satisfied with democracy in Chile, those sympathetic to the Christian Democrats registered an approval rating of 55%, for the PS 62%, and for the PPD 42%. On the Right, the figures were, for the UDI, 27% and for RN, 21%. Asked if democracy was the best system for a country like Chile, the supporters of the Concertación gave approval varying between 87% and 93%, but for supporters of both parties of the Right it was only 52%. For many Chileans, the government of the Concertación and the democratic system have become, more or less, the same thing. If this perception exists, then the low support expressed for democracy by the Right both as a system and as a practice is understandable. As Huneeus (2003, 118) points out, it is not that in Chile there are fewer democrats than in other countries, but that there is a substantial group—some 20 to 30%—who remain nostalgic for the days of the dictatorship, and who see democracy as government by the anti-Pinochet forces.[69] Initially, elements of the Right would also have feared that voting for the Concertación might signal a return to the politics of the Allende period but it is doubtful if many now hold that belief.

There exists a general perception that the major beneficiaries of the economic model are the wealthy business sectors—and that the poor are poor because of lack of opportunities and not because of lack of effort.[70] When a government has managed to reduce poverty very considerably, when most people feel relatively secure economically, and feel confident about the country's future economic performance, then attention tends to shift to relativities. The public is becoming increasingly aware not just of income inequities, but of inequities in other aspects of state provision, whether it is the conditions of employment, education, health, or even the law.[71] These issues were the theme of the electoral campaign of Michelle Bachelet for the Presidency, and her electoral platform offered an agenda revolving around the issues of extending social rights and enhancing equity.[72]

ASSESSING THE QUALITY OF DEMOCRACY IN CHILE

While claims for the efficiency of governance can be sustained, there are still questions over the extent to which Chile can be considered to have created a fully democratic system. How far has Chile overcome the obstacles to democracy contained in the Constitution of 1980 and the commitment of sectors of the Right to maintaining that Constitution?

The issue symbolizing the difficulties facing the new government at the time of the transition was human rights. Resolving this issue was important for the legitimacy of the democratic government. No attempt to achieve justice with reconciliation is ever going to be fully satisfactory, but it can be argued on a number of grounds that the government has achieved a great deal. The number of former military officers arrested, on trial, or being investigated for human rights abuses is way above those of any other country of Latin America. In 2005, 94 former members of the military were convicted of human rights violations, with an additional 405 cases on trial, and 600 cases were under investigation, representing a total of 1,240 victims.[73]

Not only was there a Commission in 1991 to investigate disappearances and summary executions, but with much effort in 2004 the Lagos government was able to create a commission to investigate torture. Reparations have been made, trials continue, the attempts to bring Pinochet to justice were never ending up to his death, the Courts are much more inclined to take an active role than earlier, new interpretations challenge the Amnesty Law of 1978, and the Army has admitted culpability and has apologized. The Lagos period saw a major revision of the views of the past. The Valech Commission on Torture in 2004 produced such undeniable evidence of horrific brutality on such a massive scale than only the hard-line Pinochetistas could ignore it. Cheyre, the Commander in Chief of the Army, undertook a series of initiatives to express genuine repentance for the abuses that took place under Pinochet. Pinochet's reputation, already fairly low, became even lower with mounting evidence of fraud and illicit enrichment. These developments were unimaginable ten years ago, and strengthen the argument that if one essential element of democracy is the rule of law, then Chile has gone a long way toward that.

President Bachelet herself was a victim of human rights abuses—her father, an Air Force general, was tortured and died after the coup, and Bachelet and her mother were both twice arrested and tortured. There was little reference to these episodes in the campaign, but her background undoubtedly struck a chord with many Chileans with their own memories of human rights abuses. As Alex Wilde puts it, "Bachelet in her very person incarnated both the painful past and a positive way of dealing with it for a core group of voters—a powerful combination."[74]

Another aspect of concern for Chilean democracy was the entrenched power of the military and the possibility of the military exerting influence beyond that acceptable in a democratic system. Yet this concern has diminished as Pinochet as head of the army was replaced by successors who took major steps towards improving relations with the government, accepting a subordinate role, admitting and apologizing for human rights violations, and ridding the armed forces of officers suspected with good reason of such abuses. Moreover the constitutional reforms of 2005 give the President the power previously absent to appoint and dismiss the heads of the various branches of the military. Military-civil relations have now assumed a form compatible with a democratic system (though the military enjoys certain budgetary privileges that still need reform).

If there is a deficit of major concern it is that of the need to extend and deepen rights (including a freer choice of parties and candidates than that offered by the existing electoral system). There are restrictions on the investigatory powers of the press and media that protect the state too much. If the courts are more active in correcting the injustices committed by the authoritarian regime, they are less active in pursuit of rights in other areas such as censorship, recognition of international law rulings, or the rights of the Mapuche.[75] The "rights revolution" that has influenced court behavior in many parts of Latin America has had much less impact in Chile.[76]

There has been much criticism of Chile for the lack of access open to the public on the activities of the state. According to the Latin American

Director of Transparency International, there is much to praise in Chile, such as a strong attachment to legal norms, and much lower levels of abuse of public office for private gain than in other countries of Latin America. On the other hand, "Chile has neither a tradition nor a culture of access to information;" and "the authorities prefer to keep things secret, are not in favour of granting access to information, and have no culture of transparency."[77]

Yet there has been a promising development in the broadening of rights symbolized by the election of a woman, Michelle Bachelet, as President in 2006 with an agenda precisely to make Chile more participatory and democratic. In her own words in her victory speech after the result of the second round, "Chile needs a new politics for new citizens. The fact that I am here is symbolic of a Chile that is more open, more tolerant, and more active. Let us create opportunities for this desire to participate."[78] And she has given strong support to demands for greater transparency and accountability.[79]

Indigenous groups have become vocal in their demands for respect for their rights—especially to retain control of their ancestral lands. Bachelet promised to create a Subsecretaria Nacional de Asuntos Indígenas, more powerful than the previous institution dealing with the indigenous people, CONADI, and with higher status. The various indigenous groups, mostly Mapuche, are a small minority of the population and are internally divided. But they have suffered from a combination of indifference and insensitivity on the part of the central government, and were prosecuted as "terrorists" under laws inherited from the Pinochet regime. More than four hundred Mapuche have been prosecuted for illegal protests since 1990. A real test of the government's commitment to the extension of rights will be the way that it deals with the demands of the Mapuche.

Bachelet started her term of office with the advantage, thanks to the constitutional reform of 2005, of being the first President to have a majority in Congress. She also inherits a buoyant macroeconomy and an efficient state apparatus. But her term of office has been reduced from the previous six years to only four with no re-election. Much also depends on how far the Right is prepared to be cooperative, as much more than a simple majority is necessary for important measures of reform. But her task became more difficult again when she lost her congressional majority when in 2007 Senator Adolfo Zaldívar was expelled from the PDC and a number of deputies followed him.[80] Moreover, the spectacular initial failure of the reform of the public transport system in Santiago—the Transantiago—seriously weakened the standing of the government, even if it many ways it was an inheritance of the previous government.

LESSONS FROM THE CHILEAN EXPERIENCE

If Chile has been as successful as I have argued, then it might seem obvious that the country has much to teach the rest of Latin America about how to achieve that result. This, however, ignores crucial factors. One is that the very different starting point for the post-authoritarian governments meant that problems differed from country to country. Another factor complicating the task of making recommendations is that the high level of resource endowment of Chile, the relatively small and relatively well-educated population, and the long history of state and political institutionalization are all conditions conducive to successful reform but not conditions common to many other Latin American countries.

Social and economic reform is partly about the design of the reform, but much more about the politics of implementation, and that is contingent upon the specific political and institutional structure of each country. President Sánchez de Lozada may well have been right that the proposed pipeline for gas exports from Bolivia through Chile was fundamental for economic growth. Unfortunately, his misreading of the political situation meant that not only did he lose the pipeline but also his post.

It is immensely difficult to reform certain institutions, such as the police, for example. Even countries with relatively high levels of economic development are unable to reform police forces so that they become agents of law and order rather than part of the problem of criminality—consider Argentina or Mexico. But it is not just a question of corruption, it is also, and perhaps more importantly, a question of efficiency and the level of public trust in the police. Even an honest police force could fail on those two scores. No doubt the Chilean Carabineros could offer many useful lessons to the police forces of other countries, but whether they were adopted or not would depend largely upon the will and ability to reform in the host country. Similarly, it would be a benefit for any country in Latin America to have an institution like the Chilean Contraloría General, but it stretches the imagination to think how it could be copied and even more how it could survive uncorrupted in most countries of Latin America. The same point could be made about the Central Bank—compare the way in which it has maintained its autonomy from the government with, for example, the similar institution in Argentina. There are, however, certain aspects of the Chilean experience that one would most certainly not recommend as a positive lesson (though they might be useful negative ones). One is the Chilean Constitution and another is the Chilean electoral system, and until recently the system of party and electoral finance had nothing to commend it.

It is increasingly clear that without an effective legal system, democracy remains shallow, and the cost of economic transactions is increased. The faults of many existing legal systems are not difficult to diagnose and the design of reform is not especially complicated. Yet millions of dollars of expenditure by the IFIs have produced at best marginal improvements in countries that already had reasonable judicial systems—like Costa Rica—and arguably have worsened the state of judiciary in countries with corrupt judiciaries, such as Honduras (Faundez and Angell 2005). One common recommendation is to adopt a more modern criminal procedure code. Chile has recently introduced a major reform in its criminal procedure code which was introduced initially in the provinces and then in mid-2005 in Santiago as well. It is hoped that this simpler system of oral-based, adversarial procedures will promote greater access and equity. Whether it works well or not depends greatly on the overall political and judicial environment and that can be hostile as well as favorable. This underlines another difficult aspect of policy reform: the nature of the interrelationship, and even the interdependence, of various institutions. A reformed criminal procedure code depends for its success not only on the design of the reform and the abilities of the judges, but also upon the police, the prisons, and the resolve of politicians not to interfere in judicial matters.

It is relatively easy to list the conditions for successful democratic governance that Chile has met. It is not so easy to extrapolate from that success to draw lessons. There are plenty of blueprints that can be drawn up from the Chilean experience but implementation depends upon the local institutional and political structure and that will be very different. I assume that Argentine tax experts are as equally well-trained and capable of devising an efficient tax system as their counterparts in Chile, and an interchange of expertise might benefit both countries. But whereas the Chilean tax system is insulated from short-term political interference and enjoys both respect and autonomy, this is clearly not the case in Argentina.

I am conscious that the conclusion of this chapter about lessons is rather skeptical, not to say negative. But this is based upon the belief that what matters most is not what a country has to teach another, but the receptivity of the country that needs to learn the lesson. As Rodríguez argues in this volume, there is no one-size-fits-all policy for development. What determines receptivity to reform is a complicated matter—the historical legacy, the strength of the reform movement, the condition of the economy, and the level of state and political institutionalization. Unless, however, the conditions are right for learning lessons, then it is unlikely that the most perfect of reform design will prosper.

Notes

I would like to thank Malcolm Deas, Julio Faundez, Alfredo Joignant, Carlos Huneeus, Lucas González, Peter Siavelis, David Sugarman, and especially, Samuel Valenzuela for their helpful comments on this paper.

1. Samuel Valenzuela's detailed comments on this section and others have been incorporated into the text at so many points that I would like to express my gratitude in general. Alfredo Joignant has pointed out that my definition is rather restricted and that the debate on social capital has opened another way of approaching the definition. The concept is obviously more complex than I have indicated but for the purposes of this case study it seemed necessary to limit the definition.

2. This point was made to me by Guillermo O'Donnell.

3. Indeed, the history of Chile in the nineteenth and the first part of the twentieth century in terms of a relatively stable constitution and gradual development of democratic institutions compares very favorably with many European countries.

4. Barros (2002, 4) writes that "autocratic institutional self-limitation was possible because the collective organization of the dictatorship denied any single actor the authority to shape rules at their discretion."

5. This interpretation of Chilean history has been challenged by another school, emphasizing the brutality of repression of popular movements, the neglect of the Mapuche people, the suppression of the Communist party for ten years after 1948, the privileges that went to the upper class, and the restricted nature of democratic participation. And the coup itself showed how fragile the system was when faced with the intense strains of that period.

6. Chile is probably the only country in Latin America where the municipal governments regularly send their accounts to be audited every month by the *Contraloría*.

7. President Aylwin, interviewed by author, Santiago, December 2001. A similar argument is offered by Góngora (1981, 5). He writes that in Chile, "el Estado es la matriz de la nacionalidad: la nación no existiría sin el Estado, que la ha configurado a lo largo de los siglos XIX y XX." For a discussion of the way in which democratic government developed in Chile through a gradual process of extension of the suffrage from the 19th century onwards see Valenzuela (1985). An interesting discussion of the centrality of the state for the development of democracy is found in González and King (2004).

8. See Arellano (1984) and Valenzuela, Tironi, and Scully (2006) for an account of the development of social policies in Chile.

9. The Chilean tax bureau, the *Servicio de Impuestos Internos*, was founded in 1902—and the average tenure of its director is six years, which is much longer than the comparable Latin American figure. Sánchez (2005, 234), a student of the subject, concludes that, "historically speaking, corruption within the Chilean tax agency has not been systematic or generalized but episodic."

10. For an article placing the Pinochet government in longer term economic perspective see Ffrench-Davis and Múñoz (1990).

11. After the first eight-year term of the designated senators, the majority of the new ones were appointed by the democratic government.

12. Expenditure on the military during the Pinochet regime on one calculation was the highest in Latin America (outside Cuba) as a percentage of GDP and continued to be so during the democratic governments—though in Chile the police was included in the military budget as were the generous military pensions paid by the only part of the pension system that remained in state hands. Figures of military expenditures are difficult to calculate because many items appear in the budgets of other ministries—military hospitals under those of the Health Ministry, and subsidies for defense industries under economic development (Lahera and Ortúzar 1998, 15–30).

13. For details, see Angell and Pollack (1990).

14. A much more critical view of the record of the government is offered in Allamand (2007). This is a sustained attack on the policies of the *Concertación* by one of the most able of Chilean politicians, and he makes many good points. Yet his alternative policies look simply like improvements of the existing ones. If this most intelligent of politicians is unable to offer a tempting alternative to the electorate, this may help to explain why the Right has been unable to defeat the government in any election since 1989. In one opinion poll, though the level of identification with the government fell from 38% in October–November 2005 to 26% in October–November 2007, that for the Right fell in the same period from 22% to 16% (CEP 2007).

15. *El Mercurio*, Santiago, February 8, 2005. The growth rate per capita in Chile in the 1990s was 4.8% whereas the Latin American average was 1.8%; and the rate in the Asian tiger economies plus China was 4% (De Gregorio 2005).

16. The PPP figures are from the CIA World Fact Book on www.cia.gov.

17. Which De Gregorio (2005, 38) argues is based on three factors—the independence of the Central Bank, a sound fiscal policy, and high levels of growth.

18. Figures from *La Tercera*, March 31, 2005, quoting the figures of the Ministry of Planning (MIDEPLAN).

19. Huber and Stephens in Chapter 5 discuss the system and also illustrate the problems that governments face in Chile when radical reforms are watered down by the Right in Congress.

20. A rather more muted appraisal is found in Boylan (1996). But she concedes that "this reform played a crucial role in soldering the fragile rule-making environment at the delicate moment of regime change" (29).

21. The data in this and the following paragraph are largely drawn from Foxley (2004). Chile achieved the UN Millennium Development Goal to cut poverty by half ten years ahead of schedule. Some legacies of the Pinochet government were positive, including a much improved database and effective targeted programs such as those towards mothers and young children.

22. Official figures from the CASEN survey of the government, available at www.mideplan.cl/casen.

23. In the United States, the poverty rate in 2005 was estimated at 12.7% (though the United States uses a different measure of poverty, which lowers the rate compared with the method used in Chile).

24. According to President Lagos in his "State of the Nation" address in May 2005, of the 225,000 families in extreme poverty, already 180,000 families are

incorporated into the program. The full text of the speech is published in *El Mercurio*, May 22, 2005.

25. For a careful analysis of the social policies of the Lagos government, see Castiglioni (2006).

26. For an (overoptimistic) account of these programs, see Angell (2003b).

27. The results are not encouraging. Of the evaluation of teachers' performance in 2006, 40% of teachers in the municipal sector were classified as having a low standard, and 3.8% as unsatisfactory—though only one was forced into retirement. The government is to offer help to those teachers who require it (*La Tercera*, March 29, 2006).

28. Reported in *The Economist*, October 16, 2004.

29. Available on the website www.idd-lat.org.

30. Presumably, relatively low levels of crime can also be used as an indication of governance. In Chile the mortality rate caused by intentional injury in 2000 was 4.5 deaths per 100,000 inhabitants. In Colombia it was 70, in Honduras 154, in Mexico 14, and in Costa Rica it was 6.2 (UNDP 2004, 112).

31. The vote is compulsory in Chile, but registering to vote is voluntary. So it is unlikely that high participation rates are explained by the obligation to vote.

32. This section relies upon the excellent Oxford thesis of Omar Sánchez (2005). Another institution worthy of study is the *Dirección de Presupuesto* which plays an important role in securing the efficient and transparent functioning of the ministries. I am grateful to Carlos Huneeus for this point.

33. It says a lot about the efficiency of the tax system—and about Chileans— that the most visited website in Chile is that of the tax office.

34. Sánchez (2005, 245) quoting from a February 21, 2001 interview in *El Mercurio* with Javier Etcheberry.

35. However, a royalty tax on the mining sector was agreed in 2005.

36. "Economia y Negocios," *El Mercurio*, October 22, 2005.

37. Figures are available at www.transparency.org.

38. For a discussion of the new law see Mujica (2004). The new law establishes a limit on campaign expenditures depending on the nature of the election and the size of the constituency; it establishes three different kinds of private financing with strict regulations on size; and also introduces a limited system of state funding depending on the size of the vote in the last election. Nevertheless, there are many forms of campaign expenditure that are not covered by the law, and there are still great disparities in the amounts spent by different parties and candidates in the elections in 2004. Moreover, the *Servicio Electoral* has very limited capacity to monitor expenditures.

39. This is dealt with in Casas (2003). For a study of the effects of party finance in Chile, see Garretón (2005).

40. Details from *La Tercera*, July 8, 2005.

41. *La Tercera*, July 25. 2005.

42. Montecinos (2003, 8) summarizes the role of SEGPRES: "charged with ensuring fluid relationships between a cohesive executive branch, Congress, political parties and social organizations, SEGPRES became the core of what many called the 'transversal party', a vast network of economists and other policy experts.... This powerful agency managed to integrate the political and economic

dimensions of government by facilitating agreements regarding the legislative agenda, evaluating the implementation of the government programme, and scrutinizing the technical and political viability of all policy and legislative proposals." After the Aylwin presidency, this role was taken over by the Ministry of the Interior under José Miguel Insulza.

43. Manzetti (2008), reviewing the various changes in this area, concludes that "by the late 1990s Congress had made considerable strides in diminishing the iron control which the executive enjoyed early in that decade over the budget process." This work includes a comprehensive account of the lack of accountability and the resulting fraud under the Pinochet administration.

44. Baldez and Carey (2002, 130), in a careful study of the budgetary process in Chile, argue that the way the process is structured prevents Congress from processing clientelistic measures into the budget, and hence underpins the executive policy of running a fiscal surplus. However they also conclude that though congress has no formal role in drafting the budget, there is congressional input at this stage, especially for the governing coalition.

45. This is one of the themes examined in Winn (2004).

46. Official figures from the *Encuesta Casen* (2007).

47. This discussion draws on Muñoz (2007, 27–29). This work is a balanced and informative evaluation of economic policies in Chile since 1990.

48. Muñoz (2007, 28).

49. Alejandro Saez Rojas, "Todavia el sexo débil," *El Mercurio*, October 30, 2005.

50. Karen Poniachik, "Donde Chile saca mala nota," *El Mercurio*, October 30, 2005, and at www.weforum.org.

51. I owe this point to Julio Faundez.

52. Huneeus (2005) makes a strong case for broadening the issue of inequality to the political and social spheres as well as that of income. He argues that the issue is essentially about the power structure and argues for the need to strengthen social organizations such as the trade unions.

53. Mesa-Lago (1996, 77–78) suggests too that it may be something of a misnomer to regard the scheme as purely private: membership is compulsory, the funds are strictly regulated and supervised, there are heavy state subsidies and transfers, and state guarantees in the event of bankruptcy.

54. Barrientos (1996, 319) writes that "the personal pension scheme has proved unattractive to workers in the flexible labour force for whom it was designed to be especially attractive. Pension coverage probabilities are low or negative for workers in the informal sector, for younger workers, and for married women...it is unlikely that in their present form personal pension plans will substantially increase their coverage of the labour force."

55. "Las Primeras Decisiones de Bachelet," *La Tercera*, July 31, 2005.

56. For a discussion of decentralization in Chile, see Angell, Lowden, and Thorp (2001).

57. This form of decentralization contrasts sharply with the Spanish or Venezuelan form that has seen individual negotiations between the provinces and the central government within the framework of a permissive constitution.

58. When asked by the author why decentralization in Chile was so timid,

President Aylwin replied: "It is not at all timid. The problem is that Chileans are timid in the use they are making of the possibilities for decentralization. The laws are there—but we need not just laws but a change of mentality." Interview by author, December 2001.

59. Report in *El Mercurio*, October 29, 2005.

60. This section draws extensively on Angell (2003a) and Angell and Reig (2006).

61. For a similar argument, see Bermeo (2003). As she writes of the years before the coup: "the changes ...that look like polarization were usually not the result of vote switching but the results of changes in electoral laws and changes in the tactics of the party elites" (139).

62. Null and blank votes were relatively low in Presidential elections—the highest combined total was 5.52% in 1993 and the lowest was 2% in 2000. In congressional elections not concurrent with presidential ones, the figures rose to 17.65% in 1997, and fell to 12.65% in 2001 (Lagos 2005).

63. Interview in *La Tercera*, August 2, 2005. The tensions were further shown when in 2008 the Christian Democratic Party expelled one of its leading figures, Senator Adolfo Zaldívar, for failing to observe the party line on an important vote in the Senate. Five deputies followed him out of the party, thereby eliminating the government's majority in Congress.

64. The argument that the binominal system was necessary to ensure political stability might have had some validity at the onset of the transition but hardly seems a relevant argument for today. An excellent book that brings together opponents and supporters of the system is Huneeus (2006).

65. This section draws upon Angell (2005).

66. The data in this section is all taken from the annual reports of the *Latinobarómetro* at www.latinobarometro.org.

67. Hence a vast majority—78%—oppose the privatization of BancoEstado or of CODELCO or of the postal service; while in 2003 only 29% expressed confidence in the privatized pension scheme, the AFPs, and 19% in the private health providers ISAPRES; 56% agreed with the proposition that taxation is necessary for the state to make adequate provision of the basic social services (Huneeus 2005, 150–54).

68. CERC polls indicate that in 2003 only 13% expressed general levels of trust in other people, compared with Canada and the United States with 38% and India with 39%. One possible explanation is the lingering division over Pinochetism and the effects of living under that dictatorship for so many years. The Chilean dictatorship was characterized by its high level of organization, including surveillance over its citizens in a way that resembled the Stasi in the former GDR. It was prudent in the Pinochet years not to trust too many people. The persisting presence of Pinochet under democracy was a reminder of those times, and may well have helped to sustain the culture of mistrust that grew up after the 1973 coup. However, as Samuel Valenzuela has pointed out, the meaning of "trust" can vary between countries (personal communication with author).

69. Huneeus (2003) is an essential book not just for the wealth of information it contains but also for its acute political analysis. If the Right had a minimalist conception of democracy, some on the Left had a maximalist conception—a

yearning for the good old days, and this attitude is also reflected in negative perceptions of democracy.

70. In the United States, surveys show that about 41% think that the poor are such because of factors outside their control and 43% because of lack of personal effort. In Chile over 60% think it is because of factors outside the control of the poor (Huneeus 2003, 138).

71. Ninety percent of Chileans think that there is not equality before the law (Huneeus 2003, 158).

72. On the elections of 2005–2006, see Huneeus, Berríos, and Gamboa (2007). It is ironical that the first major confrontation the new President faced were massive protests from secondary school students in June 2006 demanding free bus fares, elimination of fees for taking university exams, and a recentralization of education from municipal control.

73. David Sugarman drew my attention to the report of the human rights organization FASIC, www.fasic.org/doc/bal2005.htm.

74. Personal communication with author, February 26, 2006. A close advisor of Lagos, Ernesto Oddone, argues that Lagos defeated fear—referring to the fear that had characterized the Pinochet period and still lingered on in democracy. *La Tercera*, March 12, 2006.

75. I owe this point to David Sugarman who also expresses concern about the extent to which the courts may be overly sensitive to pressure from the government, and about tensions between the various levels of the court system.

76. For a discussion of this issue, see Faundez (2005).

77. Interview of Alvaro Rodriguez Vial with Silke Pfeiffer, "Chile: nada que esconder y nada que mostrar," *El Mercurio*, October 23, 2005.

78. Cited in *El Mercurio*, January 16, 2006.

79. Bachelet has indicated that among the first measures she wishes to promote as priorities are regulation of the lobby, access to information, open declaration by public functionaries of their assets, improvement in the auditing system in ministries and public enterprises, and the promotion of codes of ethics in the public administration. But the difficulties she faces with opposition from the Right is shown in the fate of the government report on reform of the electoral system—without the support of the Right it is impossible to make more than marginal changes.

80. Two articles that assess the new government at mid-term are Huneeus (2008) and Mardones (2007).

References

Allamand, Andrés. 2007. *El Desalojo: Porqué la Concertación deber irse el 2010.* Santiago: Aguilar.

Angell, Alan. 2003a. Party Change in Chile in Comparative Perspective. *Revista de Política* 23(2):88–108. Santiago: Instituto de Ciencia Política, Universidad Católica.

———. 2003b. The Politics of Education Reform in Chile. In *Social Policy Reform and Market Governance in Latin America*, ed. Louise Haagh and Camilla Helgoe. London: Macmillan.

————. 2005. Facts or Perceptions: A Paradox in the Interpretation of Chilean Democracy. In *La política chilena: Entre la rutina, el mito y el modelo*, ed. Manuel Alcántara and Leticia Rodríguez. Salamanca: Edicions Bellaterra.

————. 2007. *Democracy after Pinochet: Politics, Parties and Elections in Chile*. London: Institute for the Study of the Americas.

Angell, Alan, Pamela Lowden, and Rosemary Thorp. 2001. *Decentralizing Development: The Political Economy of Institutional Change in Colombia and Chile*. Oxford: Oxford University Press.

Angell, Alan, and Benny Pollack. 1990. The 1989 Elections in Chile and the Politics of Transition to Democracy. *Bulletin of Latin American Research* 9(1):113–35.

Angell, Alan, and Cristobal Reig. 2006. Change or Continuity: The Chilean Elections of 2005/6. *The Bulletin of Latin American Research* 25(4):481–502.

Arellano, José. 1984. *Políticas sociales y desarrollo: Chile 1924–1984*. Santiago: CIEPLAN.

Baldez, Lisa, and John Carey. 2002. Budget Processes and Fiscal Restraint in Post-transition Chile. In *Presidents, Parliaments and Policy*, ed. Stephan Haggard and Mathew McCubbins. Cambridge: Cambridge University Press.

Barrientos, Armando. 1996. Pension Reform and Pension Coverage in Chile. *Bulletin of Latin American Research* 15(3):309–22.

Barros, Robert. 2002. *Constitutionalism and Dictatorship: Pinochet, the Junta and the 1980 Constitution*. Cambridge: Cambridge University Press.

Bermeo, Nancy. 2003. *Ordinary People in Extraordinary Times*. Princeton: Princeton University Press.

Boylan, Delia. 1996. Taxation and Transition: The Politics of the 1990 Chilean Tax Reform. *Latin American Research Review* 31(1):7–32.

Carey, John. 2002. Parties, Coalitions and the Chilean Congress in the 1990s. In *Legislative Politics in Latin America*, ed. Scott Morgenstern and Benito Nacif. Cambridge: Cambridge University Press.

Casas, Kevin. 2003. Paying for Democracy in Latin America: Political Finance and State Funding for Parties in Costa Rica and Uruguay. D.Phil. thesis, Oxford University.

Castiglioni, Rosana. 2006. Cambios y continuidad en política social. In *El Gobierno de Ricardo Lagos*, ed. Robert Funk. Santiago: Universidad Diego Portales.

Centro de Estudios Públicos (CEP). 2007. *Encuestros Nacionales*. Santiago: Chile.

Coppedge, Michael. 2001. Party Systems, Governability and the Quality of Democracy in Latin America. Conference paper. Buenos Aires: Universidad de San Andrés.

De Gregorio, José. 2005. Crecimiento económico en Chile: Evidencia, fuentes y perspectivas. *Estudios Públicos* (Centro de Estudios Públicos, Santiago) 98.

Encuesta, Casen. 2007. www.mideplan.cl/casen.

Faundez, Julio. 2005. Democratisation through Law: Perspectives from Latin America. Special issue, *Democratization* 12(5).

Faundez, Julio, and Alan Angell. 2005. Reforma judicial en América Latina: El rol del Banco Interamericano de Desarrollo. *Sistema Judiciales* (Santiago) 4(8).

Ffrench-Davis, Ricardo. 1991. Desarrollo económico y equidad en Chile: Herencias y desafíos en el retorno a la democracia. *Colección Estudios Cieplan* (Santiago) 31(March).

Ffrench-Davis, Ricardo, and Oscar Múñoz. 1990. Desarrollo económico, inestabilidad, y desequilibrios políticos en Chile. *Colección Estudios Cieplan* (Santiago) 28(June).

FLACSO. 2006. *Programa de gobernabilidad, una reforma necesaria: Efectos del sistema binominal.* Santiago: FLACSO.

Foxley, Alejandro. 2004. *Successes and Failures in Poverty Eradication: Chile.* Washington, DC: World Bank.

Garretón, Manuel. 2005. Exploring Opacity: The Financing of Politics in Chile. In *Money, Elections and Party Politics: Experiences from Europe and Latin America,* ed. Carlos Malamud and Eduardo Posada-Carbo. London: Institute of Latin American Studies.

Góngora, Mario. 1981. *Ensayo histórico sobre la noción de Estado en Chile en los siglos XIX y XX.* Santiago: Editorial Universitaria.

González, Francisco, and Desmond King. 2004. The State and Democratization: The United States in Comparative Perspective. *British Journal of Political Science* 34(2):193–210.

Huneeus, Carlos. 2003. *Chile, Un País Dividido.* Santiago: Catalonia.

———. 2004. *Binominalismo: Sistema con pecado original que debe der denunciado y reemplazado.* Informe 424, October 15. Available at www.asuntospublicos.ced.cl.

———. 2005. *Las desigualdades en el Chile de hoy: Una aproximacion política.* Available at www.asuntospublicos.cl.

———. 2006. *La reforma al sistema binominal en Chile: Propuestas para el debate.* Santiago: Catalonia.

———. 2008. *El gobierno de Michelle Bachelet a mitad de camino.* Anuario del Instituto Elcano. Madrid: Instituto Elcano.

Huneeus Carlos, Fabiola Berríos, and Ricardo Gamboa, eds. 2007. *Las Elecciones Chilenas de 2005.* Santiago: Catalonia.

Ingelhart, Ronald. 2004. *Subjective Well-Being Rankings of 82 Countries.* Available at www.worldvaluessurvey.org.

Kaufmann, David, Aart Kraay, and Massimo Mastruzzi. 2007. *Governance Matters: Governance Indicators for 1996–2006.* Washington, DC: World Bank.

Lagos, Marta. 2005. *Participación electoral 1952–2005.* Chile: MORI.

Lahera, Eugenio, and Marcelo Ortúzar. 1998. Military Expenditures and Development in Latin America. *CEPAL Review* 65(August):15–30.

Manzetti, Luigi. Forthcoming. *Democratic Governance and Financial Crises in Emerging Markets.* University Park, PA: Pennsylvania State University Press.

Mardones, Rodrigo. 2007. Chile: Todos íbamos a ser reinas. Special issue, *Revista de Ciencia Política* (Santiago):79–96.

Meller, Patricio. 2006. Consideraciones económicas en torno al gobierno de Presidente Lagos. In *El gobierno de Ricardo Lagos,* ed. Robert Funk. Santiago: Universidad Diego Portales.

Mesa-Lago, Carmelo. 1996. Pensions Systems Reform in Latin America: The Position of the International Organizations. *CEPAL Review* 60(December).

Montecinos, Veronica. 2003. Economic Policy Making and Parliamentary Accountability in Chile. *Democracy, Governance and Human Rights Programme* 11 (December). UNRISD: Geneva.

Mujica, Pedro. 2004. *Ley del gasto electoral en su debut: Sus deficiencias y una propuesta.* Available online at www.asuntospublicos.org.

Muñoz, Oscar. 2007. *El modelo económico de la Concertación.* Santiago: Catalonia.

Palma, Gabriel. 2002. The Kuznets Curve Revisited. Unpublished manuscript. University of Cambridge.

Rehren, Alfredo. 2004. Political Corruption in Chilean Democracy. *Harvard Review of Latin America* (Spring).

Rodríguez, Jorge, and Claudia Serrano. 1998. Cómo va el proceso de descentralización. In *Construyendo opciones,* ed. René Cortázar and Joaquín Vial. Santiago: CIEPLAN.

Sánchez, Omar. 2005. The Political Economy of Tax Policy in Chile and Argentina. D.Phil thesis. Oxford University.

Scully, Timothy. 1992. *Rethinking the Center: Party Politics in Nineteenth and Twentieth Century Chile.* Stanford, CA: Stanford University Press.

Siavelis, Peter. 2002. Executive-Legislative Relations in Chile. In *Legislative Politics in Latin America,* ed. Scott Morgenstern and Benito Nacif. Cambridge: Cambridge University Press.

Smulovitz, Catalina. 2003. How Can the Rule of Law Rule? In *Democracy and the Rule of Law,* ed. Jose Maria Maravall and Adam Przeworski. Cambridge: Cambridge University Press.

Thorp, Rosemary. 1998. *Poverty, Progress, and Exclusion.* Washington, DC: Inter-American Development Bank.

UNDP. 2004. *Democracy in Latin America: Towards a Citizens Democracy.* New York: United Nations.

———. 2007. *Human Development Report.* New York: United Nations.

Valenzuela, Samuel. 1985. *Democratización via reforma: La expansión del sufragio en Chile.* Buenos Aires: Ediciones del Ideas.

———. 1998. La Constitución de 1980 y el inicio de la redemocratización en Chile. In *Crisis de representatividad y sistemas de partidos políticos,* ed. Torcuato di Tella. Buenos Aires: Grupo Editor Latinoamericano.

Valenzuela, Samuel, Eugenio Tironi, and Timothy Scully, eds. 2006. *El eslabón perdido: Familia, modernización y familia en Chile.* Santiago: Ediciones Taurus.

Winn, Peter, ed. 2004. *Victims of the Chilean Miracle: Workers and Neoliberalism in the Pinochet Era, 1973–2002.* Durham, NC: Duke University Press.

World Bank. 2004. *World Development Indicators Database.* Washington, DC: World Bank.

———. 2006. *World Development Indicators Database.* Washington, DC: World Bank.

CHAPTER NINE

Limits to Costa Rican Heterodoxy:
What Has Changed in "Paradise"?

MITCHELL A. SELIGSON AND
JULIANA MARTÍNEZ FRANZONI

With a population of approximately four million, a minuscule land area that can easily be overlooked on a world map, and an economy that is one-sixth of Pittsburgh's, there is a lot that can be learned from the Costa Rican experience of the impact of high quality governance on democratic stability and the risks of losing it. During the second half of the 1980s and the 1990s, this little country that by the 1970s had already achieved the status of being known as the "Switzerland of Central America," was able to maintain an enviable record of preserving democratic liberties while continuing to produce improved levels of economic and social performance at a time when civil wars and major upheavals were commonplace in the Central American region. Nonetheless, not all was well in "paradise." Gini coefficients have shown gradual yet systematic increases, voting turnout has declined sharply, highly visible corruption scandals have shaken public confidence in government, and once steady economic growth has become more volatile. By documenting economic, social, and political outcomes and tracing policy decisions and the policy-making motivations that lie behind them, we address the reasons behind these changes and are able to speculate on prospects for the future.

Our research design, although focusing on one single country, is comparative in that it looks at multiple public policies, and traces them over four presidential administrations. Those administrations include two terms by each of the major political parties that have alternated in office since the late 1970s—the social democratic, National Liberation Party (PLN), and Christian democratic, United Social Christian Party (PUSC).

We begin our analysis by reviewing Costa Rica's "Golden Age," which preceded the severe economic crisis of the early 1980s. We then describe what we believe to be aptly termed a "critical juncture" (Collier and Collier 1991; Mahoney 2001) of the early 1980s, when political leaders chose a specific road to structural adjustment. We then describe the major structural reforms implemented between 1986 and 2002, based on what were actually a series of piecemeal structural reforms. The chapter then addresses the economic, social, and political outcomes that have made the Costa Rican case an excellent example of democratic governance—as defined by Mainwaring and Scully in the introduction to this volume as the sustained capacity of democratic governments to implement effective policies for a country's political, social, and economic welfare and to facilitate economic advancement, provide citizen security, address serious social problems, and maintain a reasonably high quality of democratic practice.

That section looks at key economic indicators of governance (targeted at stability, growth, and distribution), selected social indicators (namely, poverty, infant mortality, and life expectancy), and selected indicators of political performance (namely, electoral participation and system support, drawn from a series of public opinion surveys). Finally, the chapter addresses the challenges and limitations of democratic governance as they have emerged over the past two decades.

FROM THE GOLDEN AGE TO THE ECONOMIC CRISIS

The Costa Rican Golden Age of growth and modernization occurred between 1950 and 1970 to 1975 (Solís 1992). During that period the country undertook a series of innovative social experiments—of more than two decades—through which it constructed and advanced the social welfare state in a relatively underdeveloped tropical country (Sandbrook et al. 2007). It relied both on the private sector and direct public intervention in strategic areas such as banking, infrastructure, utilities, energy, and the production of selected goods (Mesa-Lago 2000). The outcomes were an impressive series of accomplishments in terms of growth and economic diversification, social development, and the consolidation of a political regime based on representative democracy with a competitive party system, along with a deep respect of human rights (Seligson 1980; Booth 1989, 1998; Rovira 2000). From the early 1950s until 1979, Costa Rica's growth rates consistently ranked among the highest in Latin America; reductions in the proportion of the population living in poverty were impressive, as were improvements in income distribution; infant mortality dropped considerably; and health indicators improved markedly.

Two primary development strategies were the signatures of the period. The first, outwardly oriented, relied on the traditional exports of coffee and bananas. In contrast, industrialization policy followed a largely inwardly oriented strategy, based on import substitution industrialization, carried out under state tutelage.[1] The one exception to the traditional economic policy was increases in exports to the Central American region, stimulated by the emergence and rapid expansion of the Central American Common Market. That expansion of exports, however, was quickly attenuated by an international war (the so-called "Football War" between El Salvador and Honduras), followed by the outbreak of civil wars in several of the countries. Gradually, the role of the state increased, eventually expanding to become an "entrepreneur state," as reflected in the creation of state enterprises clustered under the overall direction of Costa Rican Development Corporation, CODESA. Unfortunately, CODESA became a key factor in both the disruption of the long-standing state-private sector alliance and later—through its unwise investment decisions and inefficiency—contributed importantly to what would become Costa Rica's most serious economic crisis of the twentieth century (Mesa-Lago 2000).

Import substitution had long-lasting and nationwide effects. Among other factors, it promoted a transition from a purely agrarian economy to one that stressed secondary and tertiary activities in an urban setting. By the end of the 1970s, the country had developed an impressive (for Central America) network of national and international communication facilities, ports, and airports that linked the country with the world, and provided an extensive range of financial and commercial services (Ulate 2000).

Throughout those years, Costa Rica built a broad and complex set of institutions tasked with the responsibility of implementing progressive social policies that encompassed an ever-larger portion of the country's population. Importantly, much of the expansion was targeted at rural areas, where most of the poor have traditionally lived. Between 1958 and 1962, 70% of all public investment was directed toward energy and transportation, while 25% went to social policy (Solís 1992). Social investment targeted universal free elementary and secondary education (including the rural regions); universal access to health care through integrated services of social insurance and social assistance for the poor; the high coverage of pensions among the labor force, which integrated contributory and non-contributory social assistance programs; low-cost subsidized housing; and antipoverty programs, which preceded by a full decade the promotion of safety nets elsewhere in Latin American during the 1980s (Mesa-Lago 2000). As anthropologist Mark Edelman has noted, "the reach of state and public-sector institutions into even the most remote areas contributed to diminishing the urban-rural gap and to creating a nearly universal national sense of belonging and shared national identity among the citizenry" (Sandbrook et al. 2007).

Public investment paid off. Between 1950 and 1980 infant mortality dropped from 87.2 to 28.6 per 1,000 and life expectancy increased from 55.6 to 72.6 years (Asociación Demográfica Costarricense 1984). Social insurance improved coverage from 21% in 1949 to 51% in 1971. At the same time, however, the state's participation in the GNP increased from 10% in 1961 to 22.5% in 1976, and state personnel expanded from 17,000 in 1950 to 40,000 in 1962 and reached 70,073 in 1974. In 1976, public jobs surpassed the private secondary sector as did the state's contribution to the domestic national product (Solís 1992). The growing state delivered increasing levels of vital services to the population and its own success made its further growth—beyond employment generation—almost inevitable. Eventually, however, with perhaps inevitable inefficiencies in state-run enterprises and as the world moved toward a neoliberal paradigm, the state's growth needed to be reined in. However, it became increasingly difficult to dismantle the institutional apparatus due to its success in providing increasing levels of wellbeing and its consequent growing popular support. As a result, both the public and the political class worked to "preserve its *modus operandi* (with eventual reforms) rather than to promote drastic changes to it" (Rovira 2000, 508; authors' translation).

A hallmark of this period of Costa Rica's Golden Age is that with the exception of two periods (1958–1962 and 1966–1970), the National Liberation Party (PLN) held the reins of political power. While it drew inspiration from social democratic ideals, in many ways it was a traditional party, with a strong emphasis on caudillista, pragmatic politics, and an effort, only somewhat successful, to become trans-class in its electoral base (Hernández 2007). However, up until the economic crisis of the early 1980s, the PLN was first and foremost a reformist party that stressed measures such as economic diversification with a strong role for the state, the redistribution of income, the building of a robust middle class, and the expansion of social insurance and education (Rovira 1990).

However, Costa Rica's success rested on a substantial vulnerability: in the 1970s, as foreign investment gradually diminished as a result of the broader world economic crisis, it increasingly relied on foreign borrowing, primarily commercial bank loans with variable interest rates (Vargas Solís 2002). A sharp drop in coffee prices coupled with the oil price shocks of 1973 and 1979 had a powerfully negative impact on the country's balance of payments, especially given the continued heavy reliance on coffee exports, and the absence of domestic oil or gas production. The result was the onset of a financial crisis that began with the dual catalysts of increases in oil prices and decreases in coffee prices, but was also rooted in the limitations of the export agriculture model that had served the country so well, for so long (Rojas Bolaños 1981). The external crisis provoked an internal crisis since the state sector had grown so large by the late 1970s, and demanded such large amounts of resources, that it was in danger of collapsing. In effect, the Golden Age came rather suddenly to an end; as one observer put it, this was "the end of the *fiesta*" (Feinberg 1984).

The 1980s heightened social and economic discontinuities within a context of political continuity. Indeed, between 1978 and 1982 the Costa Rican GNP plummeted by 16%; unemployment, which had historically remained below 5%, increased to 9.4%; inflation soared from an average of 7.8% in 1976–1979 to 81.8% in 1982; broad sectors of the middle classes suddenly found themselves impoverished; growth dropped from an average of 6.2% (between 1950 and 1980) to –3% between 1980 and 1982; and by the early 1980s the fiscal deficit was 14% of the GNP (Seligson and Muller 1987). The overall result was that the carefully built social safety net rapidly unraveled (Céspedes et al.1984; Rovira 1987; Solís 1992).

At the darkest moment of the crisis, however, the PLN—the same party that had run the country for two decades—managed to lead the country out of the crisis (Solís 1992) and throughout the 1980s, the party was able to successfully reform the model it had created (Mesa-Lago 2000). Reinvention and reformism—rather than a complete restructuring—were key in the country's, and particularly the PLN's, dealings with the crisis which was the most serious since the depression of the 1930s.

Fortunately for Costa Rica, it found itself in an unusually advantageous geopolitical position with respect to U.S. foreign policy interests in the region. The civil wars in El Salvador and Guatemala, and the Sandinistas' rule in Nicaragua, placed Costa Rica in a privileged position in terms of its ability to attract U.S. support, and Costa Rica became a favored client of the U.S. foreign assistance. In the immediate post-crisis years of 1983–1985, U.S. aid amounted to 35.7 percent of the Costa

Rican government's budget, one-fifth of export earnings and about 10 percent of GDP (Sandbrook et al. 2007). Never before (or since) has Costa Rica been the recipient of such largess.

One United States' Agency for International Development (USAID) report refers to this support as Costa Rica's "Sandinista windfall" (Fox 1998). In return for this "windfall," USAID insisted on the state taking measures to auction off CODESA's companies, to foster currency reforms, to establish private-sector banks and non-traditional export enterprises, and to create private institutions—from agricultural schools to export promotion offices—that competed with (and frequently undermined) state and public-sector agencies. In exchange, Washington sought, with some success, to enlist Costa Rica as an ally in its war against the Sandinistas in Nicaragua (Honey 1994).

Undoubtedly, geopolitical conditions gave Costa Rica leverage; however, they also made the country unusually dependent on foreign—or more specifically, U.S.—policy. This dependency had an impact on the domestic balance of political power in terms of rival images of the proper role of the state. As Edelman notes, "the scale of this U.S. aid, as well as the way disbursements were tied to the fulfillment of specific reforms, greatly strengthened those sectors of the elite sympathetic to neoliberalism and hostile to the social-democratic model" (Sandbrook et al. 2007). Thus, the economic crisis of the early 1980s not only demonstrated the limits of the state-led agricultural export economy, but it also shifted the domestic political equation to allow for the emergence of a different approach to the political economy.

DOMESTIC FILTERING AT A
CRITICAL JUNCTURE

Critical junctures have been defined as decision points when a particular option is adopted from among two or more alternatives and which produce a policy legacy (Mahoney 2001). Once a given path is selected, the range of possible outcomes narrows considerably. Mahoney, an astute observer of Central American political development has noted, "Critical junctures increase the probability that countries will follow particular paths of development... (they) have this effect because they lead to the formation of institutions that tend toward persistence and that cannot be easily transformed" (Mahoney 2001, 114). We argue that between 1982 and 1984 Costa Rica confronted a classical critical juncture: distinct alternatives presented themselves, and political leaders could have pushed for more radical change. Yet, unlike the theory's predictions, where a critical choice is made and one alternative—or path—is definitively selected over another, Costa Rica chose a moderate, balanced response to the crisis. These decisions led the country onto a successful path to democratic governance based on piecemeal structural reforms that continued rather than disrupted the mixed economic model of the previous decades. In short, rather than a critical juncture leading to a critical decision, it led to the British-style response of "muddling through." Consequences of that choice are discussed next.

In the early 1980s, Costa Rica's economic situation was fragile and under increasingly heavy international pressure to promote a clear break with the past and to embrace pro-market policies (Clark 2001). Additionally, the Sandinista revolution politically divided Costa Ricans between those who favored U.S. intervention in Nicaragua, which had been promoting the so-called "Contra" war, and those who believed that Costa Rica should remain neutral. In 1982, after four years of a Social-Christian administration, the social-democratic PLN regained the presidency and Luis Alberto Monge took office (1982–1986). The PLN won with overwhelming electoral support, gaining 33 out of 57 legislative seats, or 57% of all legislators—an unprecedented record in the period since 1953, exceeded only when Figueres Ferrer received 60% (Rovira 1987). President Monge thus operated with an electoral and legislative mandate.

Once in office, Monge immediately made a political move that had strong and long-lasting effects. He reached out to Social Christian leaders and passed legislation that enabled the opposition parties to be grouped under one party—the United Social Christian Party.[2] Politically, the outcome was a solid bipartisan system that led the country through the period of post-crisis stabilization during the first half of the administration and then into a series of gradual structural reforms from the second half of the administration that continued throughout the 1990s and into the twenty-first century. Economically, the outcome changed direction from a social democratic style to one strongly influenced by neoliberalism (Rovira 2000). However, in terms of social policy, the result was to maintain the institutional apparatus, that is, the policies and programs that had been established in previous decades.

After stabilization was achieved, the United States started withdrawing financial assistance. USAID, the International Monetary Fund (IMF), and private lenders established cross-conditionality measures that promoted economic liberalization (Rovira 1987). A cartoon by the famous Argentinean Quino (Figure 9.1), adapted and published in a Costa Rican newspaper, illustrated public perceptions of what was happening to Costa Rica's Golden Age. Domestically, key political and economic

FIGURE 9.1 Costa Rican Concerns over the Impact of the IMF on Its Democracy

Polémica. 1983. ¿"Podrá sobrevivir la democracia costarricense"? Número 12, Noviembre–diciembre, pages 13–29.

actors became divided between pro-market and anti-market reforms, but pro-market actors became increasingly stronger. Social protests involved only small groups of people; collective bargaining weakened; strikes in banana plantations failed; and unions in the private sector were dismantled (CEPAS 1990a).[3]

In 1984, the Minister of Public Security publicly announced that there were threats to overthrow the government (Hidalgo 2003). At the peak of the political crisis, prompt decisions prevented the threat from going any further and Monge called for the resignation of key members of his cabinet. Changes favored conservatives but also pursued equilibrium between conflicting geopolitical and economic agendas (CEPAS 1984; 1990b).[4] The coexistence of these differing economic development viewpoints was the trademark of the Costa Rican approach to economic reforms that took place over the following twenty years. However, pro-market reformers prevailed, as could be seen by the strong role played by cabinet member and later central bank president, Dr. Eduardo Lizano, a well-known economist and intellectual of pro-market reforms in the years that followed. Ultimately, development strategy changed its direction from the former social democratic path into the newer neoliberal one. However, ideological differences between both parties lessened considerably and mostly revolved around the *pace* rather than the *direction* of change (Rojas Bolaños 1992).

U.S. economic support and internal debt helped to cushion the fiscal emergency, but neither source served to move the country toward radical adjustment. Although international and geopolitical factors were important, it was the social-democratic policy legacy that created the conditions for a negotiated and piecemeal resolution to the crisis. Former social democratic president Daniel Oduber (1970–1974) played a key role, as did social and productive sectors that were a result of protectionism and the entrepreneur state. Even the Costa Rican business associations (Union of Chambers and the Chamber of Industry), which immediately supported pro-market reforms, showed concerns with liberalization (Fernández 1992).

Although the government could have chosen a more radical path toward liberalization, it did not, and this is a key puzzle in the Costa Rican case. Instead, the country departed from international prescriptions and, at times, intense pressure, and determined a *sui generis* way to deal with structural adjustment. The Monge Administration initiated this piecemeal approach to democratic governance.[5] From that point on, the logic of path-dependent policy style unfolded. For instance, in 1990 Calderón sought to implement radical adjustment measures but was unsuccessful due to a lack of sufficient political support (CEPAS 1990a).[6] We argue that the decisions made by the Monge administration closed off future options to radical reform, at least for the two decades (and possibly longer) that followed. In that sense, this period had aspects of being a "critical juncture."

In the following sections, we outline the reforms that were pursued after Costa Rica stabilized from the crisis of the early 1980s. We attempt to show that the initial decision not to embark upon a "shock therapy" approach led to a systematic process of gradual reforms, but, more recently, has also faced serious limitations.

POLICY REFORMS, 1986–2002: SELECTIVE, PIECEMEAL, AND CONTRADICTORY

Once the critical juncture had passed, there was tight interaction between actors supporting pro-market reforms, and those resisting it. This interaction took place "in the context of a representative democracy with a tight bipartisan electoral competition" (Rovira 2004, 321). The formula involved civil coexistence of paradigms and mutual veto powers.

The outcome was neither radical adoption nor radical rejection. Domestic factors filtered out international pressures and explain how a tiny country diverged from international policy prescriptions, despite powerful external pressures to do otherwise, and led to policy changes that both complied with and departed from the Washington Consensus. The outcome resulted in domestic margins of maneuver rather than lockstep convergence with regional trends.

Conventional wisdom among Costa Rican experts is that the reforms were either "heterodox" (Rovira 2004) or "hybrid" (Sandbrook et al. 2007). In our view, while we accept these definitions, we believe that a more precise qualification of heterodoxy involves the following three features:

1. *Piecemeal solutions*, that is, incremental changes rather than radical transformation, across all public policies considered;
2. *Contradictory trajectories in policy design* between primary policy areas, economic, on the one hand, and social and institutional, on the other. While reforms maintained the fundamental position of state intervention, they also furthered the role of the private sector, thus reducing the public sector resources and capacities.
3. *A selective, deliberate ordering of reforms*, in which policy makers made decisions in terms of which policies would be pursued first, those that would be undertaken at a later date, and those to be left unreformed, vis à vis a more comprehensive agenda for policy reform.

Table 9.1 summarizes primary policy reforms pursued between 1986 and 2002. As the table shows, structural adjustment policies were fairly similar, despite the passage of four presidential administrations and two parties alternating in office (Mesa-Lago 2000): Arias (PLN, 1986–1990), Calderón (PUSC, 1990–1994), Figueres (PLN, 1994–1998), and Rodríguez (PUSC, 1998–2002). Administrations of the neoconservative United Social Christian Party pushed the mixed model closer to the market (Mesa-Lago 2000), as, by that time, did the PLN.

Economic Reforms

The country selectively adopted policy prescriptions packaged under the "Washington Consensus." None of the reforms listed involved shocks. Each subsequent administration made a steady but selective turn towards a neoliberal developmental style: trade was liberalized and new agencies related to the export-led model were created. Change was hybrid in that it maintained most of the pre-existing institutional landscape, combined with the new one. The dismantling of the ISI-related rules, expectations, and agencies was piecemeal, although the creation of the new,

TABLE 9.1

Costa Rica: Prescriptions by the Washington Consensus and Implemented Reforms, 1986–2002

Policy dimensions	Economic		Social	
	Washington consensus	Costa Rican policy reform	Washington consensus	Costa Rican policy reform
Fiscal and monetary policy	Fiscal discipline through drastic reduction of public expenditures Stabilization	Reduction was not drastic but reflected reduced institutional capacities for traditional productive sectors (e.g., agriculture) Micro devaluations	Fiscal discipline through drastic reduction of social expenditures, particularly of universal programs	Expenditures increased and their sectoral composition changed with pensions growing and health care declining
Sectoral policies	Liberalization of trade	Trade rapidly and almost completely liberalized with heavy public subsidies to counteract the previous anti-export bias	Withdrawal from social protection and other programs targeted at the population at large	Growing role of targeted programs yet persistence of services with universal coverage, equitable access and funding (e.g., education and health care)
	Financial liberalization	The Central Bank withdrew from programming credit. Private banking grew rapidly with heavy public subsidies; public banking accounts for 70% of all domestic business. "Bank Reserves" dropped but interest rates did not.	Targeting of social expenditures (safety nets)	
State reform	State downsizing and transformation to eliminate institutions of the ISI era; creation of regulatory agencies	*First generation reforms were not accomplished: almost no agencies were privatized and most services remained public* *Downsizing and marginalization* Creation of new agencies that strengthen regulatory capacities (even prior to the international spread of second generation reforms) as well as those related to foreign trade and investment	State downsizing and transformation to eliminate institutions of the ISI era, and creation of regulatory agencies	The institutional landscape underwent substantial changes as public agencies take on new functions such as the regulation of private actors. Public agencies remained strongly involved in funding and social service delivery. Yet, the *de facto* reforms withdrew state support from areas such as planning and agriculture.
Labor market reform		Change has been mild and more *de facto* than formal	Decentralization	Very little

Italics indicate departures from the Washington Consensus.

Source: Estado de la Nación (1994, 1995, 1996, 1997, 1998, 1999, and 2000); CEPAS (1990b).

export-related agencies was faster and more systematic. The neoliberal turn deepened the entrenchment of a mixed rather than Chilean-style heavily privatized market economy (Mesa-Lago 2000).

Nevertheless, gradual and methodical economic liberalization was successful and foreign investment steadily grew. In 2003, Costa Rica had 2.3 times more foreign investment than in 1991 (and without the sharp fluctuations that took place in other countries of Latin America), and exports amounted to three times more dollars than in 1991. In 1990, economic openness corresponded to 73% of the GNP, and only 3.8% came from free trade zones. By 2003, however, openness reached 95.4%,[7] of which 30% came from export processing zones (Zona Franca) (Estado de la Nación 2004). The diversification of production and export supply was remarkable: in 2003 the territory devoted to five nontraditional agricultural products was 50% more than the area devoted to bananas, which—along with coffee—was the traditional economic base of the country (Estado de la Nación 2004).

Liberalization was also successful in the financial sector. Reforms to the Organic Law of the Central Bank that were approved in 1995 allowed the participation of private banks, which between 1990 and 2003 grew at an average annual rate of 38%, almost twice as much as public entities. Still, without considering mostly private offshore operations, public entities prevailed: their share of the market declined only slightly, from 67% in 1993 to 56% in 2002 (Estado de la Nación 2004). Public banks responded to tough private competition with modernization and increased efficiency, but also with cutbacks in their noncommercial, developmental services. The price of survival of public banking rested upon partially eliminating one of its traditional missions—affordable credit for micro- and small businesses. In addition, transaction costs for finance are the highest in Latin America (twice as high as Chile's), and taxes are the lowest. This clearly shows that—as one of the main benefactors of the neoliberal turn promoted during the period—the financial sector has declined to share the profits with society at large.

Liberalization was state-led. State intervention played a key role in supporting nontraditional exporters and the financial sector, allegedly to counteract previous anti-export bias. Exporters received huge subsidies through a tax credit program (CATs) which was dismantled in 2000. Beginning in the mid-1980s, exporters also received tax exemptions on raw materials, semi-processed goods, machinery, and equipment, as well as exemptions from income generated in export activities. Export processing zones provided export enterprises with these and other facilities, as well as streamlined customs inspections and complete exemption from taxes on assets and capital repatriation, and municipal assessments and licenses (Clark 2001; Sandbrook et al. 2007). Meanwhile, the Central Bank withdrew from credit programming but, at the same time, heavily subsidized the growth of a private financial sector through monetary policy such as the lowering of financial reserves.

The state did not accomplish first generation institutional reforms. Almost no agencies were privatized and most services remained public. *De facto* reforms, however, were more profound: marginalization as well as financial and personnel cutbacks undermined agencies such as those related to agriculture and planning. Some examples of governmental cutbacks are the Ministries of Agriculture and Livestock, and MEIC— Economy, Industry and Trade, whose budget and personnel were slashed by 50%. During this period the state ceased central planning of any kind (Estado de la Nación 2004). Meanwhile, new agencies related to foreign trade and the financial sector were put in place—e.g., the Ministry of Foreign Trade (Comercio Exterior, COMEX), the Promoter of Exterior Commerce (PROCOMER), and three superintendencies of Stock, Finances, and Pension Funds, respectively. Most of the new institutional landscape pursued regulation rather than service funding and provision, and the private sector played a key role.

Heavy state intervention for trade promotion and financial liberalization was as much a "Tico-style" trademark as was gradualism. As well, no matter how uncomfortable its coexistence with the old institutional setting, by the end of the 1990s everything required by the new model was already in place. Agencies and stakeholders developed under the ISI were largely bypassed, financially and otherwise. They decreased in quality as well as capacity but were not significantly threatened, which was particularly evident in institutions related to the agricultural sector. In sum, in terms of economic reforms, Costa Rica embraced neoliberalism in a piecemeal and selective fashion.

Social Reforms

To a large extent, foreign investors moved to Costa Rica for its well-developed infrastructure and highly educated, healthy work force. Thus, some of the dynamism of the new model can be attributed to legacies of the social-democratic welfare state (Sandbrook et al. 2007), which were maintained during the adjustment period (Huber 1996). We summarize below the primary developments in social policies and the key areas of resistance to the neoliberal turn.

Social policies underwent reforms in key areas such as pensions, education, and health care. However, such reforms were hybrid: health care and pensions continued to be universal and based on principles of equity and solidarity. What changed were policy instruments in these areas, which showed an increased reliance on mixed market, quasi-market, and state-directed modalities. Pensions, for example, continued to be organized around collective funds but incorporated individual accounts as well. Health care continued to be universal, yet reorganized through measures that sought to transform both managerial practices and the attention models. The creation of the Basic Health Teams (Equipos Básicos de Salud, or EBAIS, for their acronym in Spanish) experienced remarkable success in expanding coverage, particularly among low-income groups (Vargas and Li 2002).[8] Education was a priority: between 1990 and 2003 both the number of educational personnel and schools doubled. Over 90% of all children and adolescents enrolled in primary and secondary education attend public schools. Public housing expanded at an annual rate of 4%, virtually the same rate at which households grew. A key policy tool was the housing bonus which was among the most important targeted policies. Unfortunately, the program became very much entangled with clientelistic politics.

Levels of public investment persisted and even increased during the period, increasing from 14.5% of the GDP in 1990 to 18.2% in 2002. Per capita investment, however, has not managed to match the pre-economic crisis levels that were achieved during the 1970s (Estado de la Nación 2004). In addition, sectoral composition changed, with education and pensions growing and health care declining. Public investment in education went from 3.8% in 1990 to 5.9% in 2003, slightly below the constitutionally mandated 6% level. As a proportion of all educational expenditures, basic education increased from 55% in 1990 to 70% in 2003. Growth in university enrollments were largely absorbed by private institutions, which during the decade grew in number from 8 to 50. Targeted programs were stressed, but social investment lost ground during the period. Most resources accessed by the poor came from nontargeted, universal programs, particularly education.

Formally, there was no withdrawal from social protection and other universal programs targeted at the population at large. However, the performance of the public sector is not what it once was. Middle class emigration to the private sector reflects difficulties in access, timing, and quality of services. A move to the private sector even has been observed in health care services, which are insurance-based and mandatory for salaried and non-salaried workers. Therefore, many individuals are funding public services, while also paying for out-of-pocket private services (Martínez Franzoni and Mesa-Lago 2003). As well, individuals often make an illegal payment for public services in order to skip waiting periods and receive more sophisticated or urgent care, such as surgery

(Martínez Franzoni 2005). It is evident that Costa Rica's social welfare institutions have suffered (Sandbrook et al. 2007).

For the most part, agencies in charge of funding and implementing social policies were left untouched. Newly created institutions focused mostly on supervisory roles while previous agencies concentrated on funding and service provision. Maintaining the social-democratic take on social policy reflected the endurance of most policy instruments, combined with new private components (such as mandatory and complementary individual accounts for salaried workers and the larger role of private providers) and new supervisory roles (such as with pensions and health care). At least formally, the institutional and programmatic landscape for social policies looked similar to the pre-reform era.

In summary, the state continued to perform a central role in funding and providing social services. A protective state role persisted from previous decades, yet with a greater role of private business (reflected in health care and pensions) and productive orientation (reflected in education and welfare programs). Policies show persistence of primary institutions and increased private and market participation.

Overall, in terms of social policies, reforms were piecemeal, selective, and embedded within a social-democratic ideology.

Political and Institutional Reforms

Parallel to the Tico-style neoliberal turn in economic policy and the social-democratic persistence in terms of social policy, legislation protecting civil, political, and social rights increased considerably during the period, as did specific mechanisms to enforce these rights. The outcome was a deep institutional reform around an improved "politics of recognition" as termed by Nancy Fraser (2003).

Institutional changes added to "one of the most remarkable features of the Costa Rican political system: the degree to which it gives important policy-making responsibilities to a set of autonomous institutions" (Lehouq 2004, 145). Over one hundred autonomous agencies are responsible for providing services such as health-care, pensions, telecommunication, and electricity. Overall, these institutions "control monies rivaling the central state apparatus (the three branches of government plus the Supreme Tribunal of Elections)" (145).

Indeed, during the period considered, an Ombudsman agency was created, along with public audiences and other mechanisms that protect consumers. Social rights were strengthened for children and women as well as for those living with disabilities or AIDS. Political rights were improved for women and other underrepresented populations such as indigenous and Afro-Caribbean groups. The Constitutional Chamber (the *"Sala constitucional"*), created in 1989, increased individual and collective opportunities for due processes and appeals. Institutional changes made the Executive lose ground to the Judicial Power (particularly the Constitutional branch) and to horizontal accountability agencies (more specifically, the Comptroller General of the Republic—the primary agency for horizontal accountability that oversees all agencies' budgets, with the exception of the central government—as well as the Regulatory Agency of Public Services, or ARESEP—the agency in charge of establishing public tariffs).

A primary outcome of institutional reforms has been the discord between a well-developed pro-rights body of laws and insufficient state capacities and resources to adequately enforce them. The state has increasing obligations yet shrinking resources necessary to meet those obligations. The broadening of state duties has not been accompanied by an equally broadened tax-base. Therefore, technical and institutional capacities have weakened, the gap between expectations and reality has increased, and both have led to frustration among the population that continues to seek state support (Estado de la Nación 2001).

The reasons for this increasing gap revolve around capacities and resources. State personnel declined from 17% of the economically active population in 1990 to 14% in 2003 and public investment also dropped. Institutions that did not lose personnel were those in charge of health care, education, and pensions.

Moreover, the Costa Rican state has never stopped growing. Between 1990 and 2003, 117 new agencies were created, far more than the 66 agencies created during the 1970s. However, while before the 1980s agencies tended to be large and aimed at service delivery, after 1980 they were smaller and mainly focused on regulation. Examples of smaller or regulatory agencies are PROCOMER, SUGEF, SUPEN, Puestos de Bolsa, Operadoras Pensiones, Consejo de Viabilidad/Consejo de Concesiones, Tribunal Aduanero, and the Tribunal Ambiental.

In general, in terms of institutional and political policy, reforms were selective, piecemeal, and consistently broadened civil and social rights as well as the formal mechanisms necessary to enforce them, which, in practical terms, were largely ineffectual.

Overall Implications

The fiscal deficit has been the Achilles' heel of the period. Taxes amount to 13% of the country's GNP. Ironically, one of the most developed states of the Latin American region ranks among the most poorly funded.

Old and new public expenditures reflect a growing fiscal deficit. In 2003, debt service absorbed a quarter of the government's budget

(Estado de la Nación 2004). While the average fiscal burden between 1985 and 2001 was 11.5% (excluding social security, it amounted to 5%), trade liberalization provided incentives to exporters along with a drop in import tariffs. It was difficult to rectify the problem of higher public expenditures and lower income, as the most dynamic sectors were exonerated from the fiscal effort. The most successful businesses, such as INTEL, work as an enclave—more similar to the banana enclave than to the political economy of coffee, which is much more effective in terms of income distribution. On the social policy side, pension regimes funded by the national budget were shut down, yet the government had to honor previous pension commitments. Debt services continued to grow and were funded by internal debt, therefore pushing interest rates higher and making the debt service 20.5% of all central government expenditures (Sauma and Sánchez 2003).

In summary, the overall developmental style that Costa Rica has followed is characterized by an imbedded tension between the neoliberal turn of economic policy, the social-democratic resistance of weakening social policy, and the expansion of civil and social rights acknowledged by the political reform with a deterioration of state capacities that emerged throughout the process. The result has been neither solid interventionism nor sound regulatory institutions, producing neither an effective nor an indifferent state.

"Winners"—chiefly exporters, importers, the financial sectors, and top professionals—have consolidated throughout the period, but so have "losers" in their capacity to resist the neoliberal turn. Losers were mainly peasants, farmers, and businesses that target the domestic market, as well as public servants. While during the first half of the 1990s these sectors, through civil society organizations, did protest, it was in the second half of the 1990s that protests became effective, as shown by the veto of the privatization of the electricity and telecom market in 2001, as well as by public demonstrations that paralyzed the country for a week in 2004.

ECONOMIC, SOCIAL, AND POLITICAL PERFORMANCE

According to Mainwaring and Scully (see the introduction to this volume), "Democratic governance is the capacity of democratic governments to implement policies that enhance a country's political, social, and economic welfare while governing democratically. Successful democratic governance means that governments succeed in maintaining a reasonably high quality of democratic practice, protect citizen rights, help their countries advance economically, provide citizen security, and help address the serious social problems (poverty, income inequalities, poor social services) that afflict, albeit to very different degrees, Latin American countries." The challenge this research project has posed to both authors is how to address these economic, social, and political issues as a whole, and their impact on democratic stability. By looking at their interactions, and placing them in an international context, the present study hopes to draw political lessons for decision makers. The specific question is, how successful was Costa Rica in the domestic filtering of international pressures? In the next section, we focus on economic, social, and political dimensions of Costa Rica's performance. Figure 9.2 summarizes the key economic and social indicators we address next.

Stability and Satisfactory Economic Growth, Although Disproportionate and Concentrated in Few Hands

Economic performance can be assessed in terms of stability, growth, and distribution. Macro-economic stability was the primary goal of structural adjustment, but results were modest: inflation was irregular, unstable, and, except for 1993, was in the two-digit figures (see Figure 9.2). Dollarization became worrisome: it increased from only 4% of all credit in 1991 to 56% in 2003, increasing the risks of external shocks.

In terms of growth, between 1994 and 2003, Costa Rica had the highest average rate of growth for Latin America (4.3%), along with Chile. The total value of exports increased considerably, from US $1.676 billion in 1991 to US $5.277 billion in 2002, due to increases in the value generated by export-processing zones. A second achievement was the promotion of a more diversified export structure. New exports such as flowers, tilapia, and beef increased substantially, while traditional exports such as coffee and bananas declined. By the year 2000, there were more than 3,342 products being exported, and 53% of all export value was concentrated in seven products (pineapples, electronic circuits, textiles, bananas, coffee, medicines, and medical equipment) (PROCOMER 2001).

And yet, according to official data presented in Figure 9.3, only 2.33% of all domestic businesses are exporters (a total of 1,745 companies) while the rest, mostly micro, small, and medium-size businesses, produce for the domestic market (Castillo and Cháves 2001; PROCOMER 2003).

In addition, as shown in Figure 9.2, growth was volatile and followed a stop-and-go pattern (Sauma and Sánchez 2003; Estado de la Nación 2004). The nature of the irregular growth patterns, with constant sharp cycles, was due to the sources of the growth. Throughout the 1990s nontraditional agricultural products boomed, while in the late 1980s

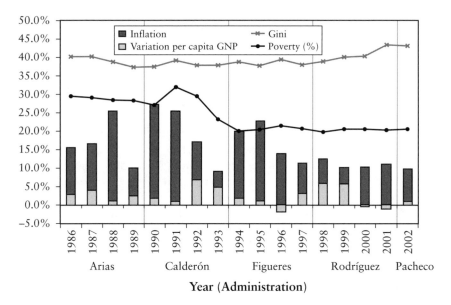

FIGURE 9.2 Costa Rica: Social and Economic Performance by Selected Indicators, 1986–2002
Source: Estado de la Nación (1994–2002)

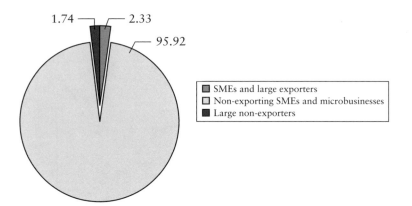

FIGURE 9.3 Costa Rica: Number of Productive Units according to Size and Market
Source: Castillo and Cháves (2001); PROCOMER

textiles flourished and in the early 1990s tourism provided the spark to growth. In other years, the economy underwent a series of virtual recessions, such as the one that occurred during the second half of the 1990s, until the arrival of INTEL, which made a major investment by building a microchip assembly plant in 1998. Again, in the year 2000, the economy entered another slump, largely due to the international retrenchment in high technology businesses.

A partial explanation of the cyclical nature of growth is the weak link that exists between foreign investment and the domestic economy: on average between 2000 and 2003 foreign business purchased 3.2% of all their inputs and 2.4% of all their exports in Costa Rica (Estado de la Nación 2004). Ironically, the weakness or absence of productive chains between foreign and local economies has protected the economy from crisis such as that of the electronics industry in 2000 and 2001.

Addressing distribution as the third dimension of economic performance, the above information helps explain why the external sector determines the country's GNP as well as how the income generated has been distributed. Indeed, the Gross National Income is not necessarily the best indicator to measure how economic activity affects citizen well-being. However, the Net National Income (NNI) which is GNP minus purchases to external factors, such as repatriation of profits, provides such a proxy measure of well-being (Estado de la Nación 1999). Figure 9.4 presents the 1991–2003 trends for both GNP and NNI and shows the gap between the two. While GNP reflects booms and busts in terms of foreign investment (primarily INTEL's), the NNI indicates variations

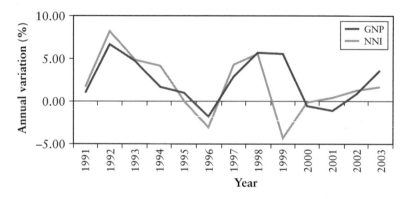

FIGURE 9.4 Costa Rica: Annual Growth, Per Capita, 1991–2003
Source: Estado de la Nación (2004)

in the economic resources available to the population. Noteworthy, 1999 was a year in which foreign investment did very well, yet Costa Ricans did quite poorly.

The lack of interaction between dynamic external sectors and the rest of the economy is also reflected in taxes and job creation. Most foreign investment operates under special regimes, which enjoy considerable tax exemptions. The trivial component of domestic purchases means the primary contribution these businesses make to the country's economic performance is related to jobs. However, less than 3.5% of the economically active population is currently working in export zones and a macroeconomic success story such as INTEL employs only a relatively small number of workers. Exports directly employ 359,282 people out of the 1,640,387 economically active population (INEC 2003), and even the most optimistic estimations report 30% of the economically active population if indirect jobs created by export markets are considered. That is, most Costa Ricans depend on jobs related to the domestic market. In fact, after two decades of launching an economic strategy revolving around liberalization, foreign investment, and exports, 94.8% of all Costa Rican business primarily targets the domestic market (Estado de la Nación 2001).

Human Development with Increased Inequality

Despite the unprecedented crisis of the early 1980s, the worst since the Great Depression years, by the mid-1990s Costa Rica's long-standing success in developing human capacity placed it at the top of Latin America for most social indicators. According to the Human Development Index (HDI) by the United Nations Development Program (UNDP), Costa Rica ranks in the "high" category of human development—at number 45—in the world, along with Argentina (34), Chile (43), Uruguay (46), Cuba (52), Mexico (53), and Trinidad and Tobago (54). Although the methodology for the index has changed over time, using the unchanged estimation shows that Costa Rica increased from .745 in 1975 to .834 in 2002. The country does best in terms of social accomplishments, more specifically health, while it does worse than countries with a similar ranking in the HDI in terms of income per capita.

At the beginning of the new century, the average life expectancy of Costa Ricans is the highest in Latin America, at 78.6 years. The country's infant mortality is the second lowest in the region, after Cuba's and tied with Chile (10 per 1,000). A decline in secondary education in the 1970s and 1980s was remedied in part, and the coverage it had had twenty years before (60%) was restored; however, only 3.6 out of every 10 youths actually finish high school (Estado de la Nación 2004). Contributory pensions cover less than half of the economically active population; 45 percent are covered primarily through one contributory program, Disability, Old Age, and Death (known as "IVM" for its acronym in Spanish). Housing remains a troubling issue and approximately 300,000 housing units, a third of the national total, are in a serious state of disrepair (Estado de la Nación 2004). Overall, we can say that the country is doing well in terms of living conditions that reflect prior long-term investment (e.g., life expectancy), yet not so well in terms of living conditions that reflect current social investment for the future. In addition, families have still not recovered the purchasing capacity that they had prior to the economic crisis of the 1980s, although this has been partially compensated with a housing bonus targeted at the poor.

The reason for this pattern is straightforward; during the last decade (particularly during the second half of that decade) social investment has not compensated for greater inequality, as shown in Figure 9.2. Primary inequality has increased with surprising rapidity. In household surveys conducted in 1988 and 2004, the Gini coefficient for primary income went from 0.31 to 0.48 (Trejos 2006). Over the same period, social expenditure became only slightly more progressive, and that shift did not compensate for the growing inequality. As a result, overall income inequality moved from a Gini of 0.37 in 1988 to 0.40 in 2004. Although Costa Rica remains as the second most egalitarian country in Latin America after Uruguay, for the first time since inequality data were gathered on the country, there has been an increase toward rapid income concentration.

Since then, however, it has increased, surpassing 0.40 in 1999, at which point it has remained above ever since. Poverty showed a dramatic drop until the mid-1990s, when it stabilized at around 20 percent, where it has remained resistant to further declines. In relative terms, and also shown in Figure 9.2, the poor have remained the same, both in terms of profile and proportion of the population. In absolute numbers, however, the poor have increased, reaching 750,000 in 2003.

Indeed, for reasons mentioned above, employment shows the worst performance of the period: in 2003, unemployment was 6.3%, the highest over the past two decades. Underutilization of the labor force reached 15%, compared to 10% in 1990. The reason is simple: nontraditional export-oriented agriculture and tourism have not compensated for the large number of jobs lost in other sectors, such as traditional agriculture (e.g., basic grains). As a result, informal jobs currently grow faster than formal ones (6.7% and 5.3% each year, respectively). There is increased polarization of the labor market, with fewer formal and high-quality jobs and large numbers of people who are worse off (Pérez Saínz et al. 2004).

In many ways, the country is currently enjoying the positive effects of long-term investment, particularly in health and social protection. Inequality, however, has increased and social policy has faced serious difficulties in offsetting its effects.

Democratic Endurance with Growing Electoral Skepticism and Exit

Costa Rica has had a competitive party system for over one hundred years, and its democracy has been uninterrupted since the 1940s, the longest of any country in Latin America. In comparative terms, Costa Rica remains as one of the—if not *the*—most legitimate political system in all of Latin America. Surveys carried out by the Americas Barometer of the Latin American Public Opinion Project (LAPOP), while not including every country in the region, show that Costa Ricans are more likely than citizens of other countries to believe in the legitimacy of their regime. Using a five-item scale of system support (with each item scored on a 1 to 7 basis, standardized to a mean of zero and a standard deviation of one), the results shown in Figure 9.5 clearly depict this point. The figure shows that not only is Costa Rica high on political legitimacy compared to other countries in Latin America, but also that support is independent of the country's level of wealth and social development (the "controlled" bar shows the level of system support when controlled by GNP per capita and infant mortality rates, as well as presidential popularity).

While Costa Rica remains a legitimate political system in the eyes of its citizens, its legitimacy has, in fact, been eroding. This erosion can be measured in two ways. Consider first the evidence presented in Figure 9.6, which draws on the recent LAPOP surveys conducted in Costa Rica, along with the archival files from the LAPOP project.[9] In the archival files, two of the five items that comprise the legitimacy scale shown above are presented in detail for the period beginning before the economic crisis of the 1980s, continuing through the Monge administration's stabilization program, and ending in 2004. The first question asks: "To what extent do you believe that the basic rights of Costa Ricans are protected by the political system?" The second question asks, "To what extent are you proud of the Costa Rican political system?" As can be seen in Figure 9.6, the opinions of Costa Ricans have declined for both items (and for the five-item scale as a whole, even though the scale is not show here).

The second indication is in the area of voting abstention. Since 1998, electoral turnout has been declining, with a changed profile for those

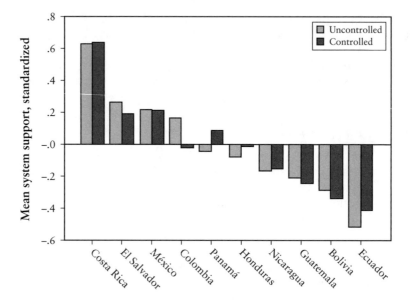

FIGURE 9.5 Political Legitimacy: Costa Rica in Comparative Perspective
Source: Americas Barometer from the Latin American Public Opinion Project (LAPOP), Vanderbilt University

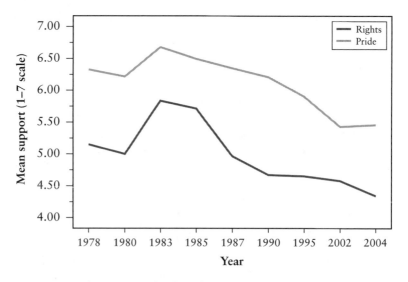

FIGURE 9.6 The Erosion of Political Legitimacy in Costa Rica, 1978–2004
Source: Latin American Public Opinion Project (LAPOP), Vanderbilt University

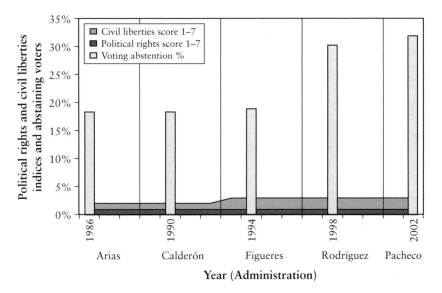

FIGURE 9.7 Costa Rica: Political Performance, 1986–2002
Source: Freedom House, Tribunal Supremo de Elecciones

who do not vote, due to the combination of political and economic factors underlying electoral abstention (see Figure 9.7). The former appears to be due to discontent with politics and politicians and reflects a way of protesting; the latter reflects social and economic exclusion and indicates disinterest (Raventós and Fournier 2005). In addition, in 1998—for the first time since the elections of 1986—no presidential candidate met the 40% threshold and a presidential run-off was carried out (Lehouq 2004). Shortly after the 1998 election, Seligson (2002) interpreted electoral results as an indication of the decreasing support to the political system. So far, this interpretation remains unchallenged, while new evidence has corroborated it (Lehouq 2004).

We argue that a contributing factor to this decline is that since 1994 no party has had a Congressional majority and Congressional performance has been poor: approximately one-half of all legislation passed took between one to three years to be approved (Estado de la Nación 2004). The result is the growing gap between promises made by parties during their electoral campaign and the agenda they pursue once in office. This may well explain the loss of confidence in politics and politicians. In addition, there is a departure between elites in favor of neoliberal reforms and masses of citizens who, to varying degrees, appreciate and remain attached to benefits derived from welfare state institutions. Finally, many voters do not support the neoliberal path since past state policies clearly provided significant subsidies to investors, a literate, healthy workforce, and a well-developed infrastructure, all of which facilitated a new insertion in the global economy.

In addition to its electoral manifestations, discontent has also been noticed on the street. Protests, which in the 1980s drew primarily on specific constituencies affected by economic adjustment measures (public employees, small farmers), have grown since the mid 1990s to include a broader range of constituencies (Raventós and Fournier 2005). Manifestations of the new wave of popular discontent emerged in 1995, when a month-long strike and major protests occurred after the government of José María Figueres Olsen (son of former president José Figueres) attempted to shut down the teachers' pension fund. In 2000, the magnitude of the earlier protest was overshadowed by weeks of road blockades and large demonstrations throughout the country in reaction to Legislative Assembly's approval (in the first of three required debates) of a measure that would have eventually privatized the Costa Rican Electrical Institute (*Instituto Costarricense de Electricidad*, ICE), which generates and distributes electricity and operates the telephone system. Again, in 2004, trucks and taxis led by a coalition of business and workers against the privatized car inspection blocked major roads throughout the country and financial loss amounted to millions of dollars in just a few days. Approval of the Free Trade Agreement between Dominican Republic, Central American and the United States (DR-CAFTA) has taken over four years,[10] with massive protests in 2006 and the first half of 2007, and finally a referendum in October of 2007, at which point it was finally approved. The approval of approximately thirteen complementary laws needed for CAFTA to be implemented, however, is still taking place in Congress as late as April 2008.

Will these indications of unease disappear? Whether analyzing electoral turnout or social protests, evidence suggests that Costa Rican democratic arrangements are facing a precarious situation. However, to date, democratic channels have proved extremely capable of coping with conflict in a peaceful manner.

THE UNCLEAR FUTURE

The payoff of the political bargain that was struck in the mid-1980s seems to have come to an end. Costa Rican heterodoxy has made the country socially, economically, and politically successful over the past twenty years, although that success has brought discord between the winners and losers of the turn towards economic liberalization. The relative strength of supporters and opponents of economic liberalization has also led to the coexistence—rather than actual hybridization—of two ideological projects. These projects are reflected in economic policy strongly influenced by a neoliberal project; social policies entrenched in social-democratic ideals that carried over from the Golden Age; and the expansion of recognized civil, political, and social rights—from gender equity to environmental issues. Tensions among these trends have been strong and increasingly stressed by the sustained deterioration of state capacities. The overall outcome has been a decreasing performance of the "Tico" approach to democratic governance.

In 1987, social scientist Jorge Rovira claimed that the structural damage caused by the 1929 crisis was only resolved some twenty years later in 1948. Early in the twenty-first century, we could be witnessing the resolution of the crisis of the 1980s by entering a new critical juncture, that is, a decision point when a particular option may be adopted from two or more alternatives, any of which will have long-term consequences in policy legacies to come. It is hard to predict how this critical juncture will be solved.

Notes

1. Throughout the period, the outwardly oriented strategy was accompanied by agricultural and industrial tariff barriers.

2. It allowed the new party to access the political debt (i.e., the campaign finance funds) from the previous election.

3. By 1986, the situation had begun to change: unions, mainly based in the public sector, were preparing to confront structural adjustment. For example, middle class workers in the public sector demanded wages and improved working conditions (CEPAS 1990a, 16–17).

4. The Minister of Security was a former business representative and well-known anti-communist, founder of the paramilitary anti-Sandinista movement, "Costa Rica Libre." A left-wing PLN member took over the Ministry of the Presidency. Juan Manuel Villasuso, a social-democrat, became Minister of Planning and Economic Policy. He supported an export-oriented strategy, yet stressed the active role of government in sectoral support (rather than only macroeconomic support). At the same time, leading the Central Bank was Eduardo Lizano. As director of the Central Bank in both PLN and PUSC administrations, he embodied the beginning of the end of paradigmatic differences between the PLN and the other parties (by 1984, already grouped under the PUSC).

5. According to Barahona, Güendell, and Castro (2005), this measure to overcome the crisis was consistent with the social pact that took place after the 1948 Civil War and gave way to the Second Republic.

6. He announced fiscal balance within eighteen months. Lizano stated that fiscal balance was easier to achieve than reactivating the economy (CEPAS 1990a).

7. Measured as the sum of exports and imports of goods and services as a percentage of GNP (Estado de la Nación 2004, 404).

8. EBAIS made it possible to standardize and expand primary care services throughout the entire country.

9. For a monograph-length treatment of this and related findings from the 2004 survey see Vargas-Cullell, Rosero-Bixby, and Seligson (2005).

10. The agreement was signed by all Presidents involved in 2004 and, since then, ratified and come into effect into all countries.

References

Asociación Demográfica Costarricense. 1984. *Mortalidad y fecundidad en Costa Rica.* San José: Asociación Demográfica Costarricense.

Barahona, Manuel, Ludiwg Güendell, and Carlos Castro. 2005. Política social y reforma social "a la tica": Un caso paradigmático de heterodoxia en el contexto de una economía periférica" en UNRISD. *Política pública y desarrollo* 20.

Booth, John A. 1989. Costa Rica: The Roots of Democratic Stability. In *Democracy in Developing Countries: Latin America*, ed. Larry Diamond, Juan Linz, and Seymour Martin Lipset. Boulder, CO: Lynne Rienner Publishers.

———. 1998. *Costa Rica: Quest for Democracy.* Boulder, CO: Westview Press.

Castillo, Geovanny, and Luis Fernando Cháves. 2001. *PYMES: Una oportunidad de desarrollo para Costa Rica.* San José: Fundes Costa Rica.

CEPAS. 1984. Las presiones del gobierno. *Costa Rica: Balance de la situación* 9:3–7.

———. 1990a. 8 años de análisis de la realidad nacional. *Costa Rica: Balance de situación* 38(November-December).

———. 1990b. ¿Se justifican las medidas de shock? *Costa Rica: Balance de la situación* 35(April–May):10–11.

Céspedes, Víctor Hugo, et al. 1984. *Estabilidad sin crecimiento.* San José: Academia de Centroamérica.

Clark, Mary. 2001. *Gradual Economic Reform in Latin America: The Costa Rican Experience.* Albany: State University of New York Press.

Collier, Ruth Berins, and David Collier. 1991. *Shaping the Political Arena: Critical Junctures, The Labor Movement, and Regime Dynamics in Latin America.* Princeton, NJ: Princeton University Press.

Estado de la Nación. 1994. *Primer informe estado de la nación en desarrollo sostenible.* San José: Programa Estado de la Nación.

———. 1995. *Segundo informe estado de la nación en desarrollo sostenible.* San José: Programa Estado de la Nación.

———. 1996. *Tercer informe estado de la nación en desarrollo sostenible.* San José: Programa Estado de la Nación.

———. 1997. *Cuarto informe estado de la nación en desarrollo sostenible.* San José: Programa Estado de la Nación.

———. 1998. *Quinto informe estado de la nación en desarrollo sostenible.* San José: Programa Estado de la Nación.

———. 1999. *Sexto informe estado de la nación en desarrollo sostenible.* San José: Programa Estado de la Nación.

———. 2000. *Séptimo informe estado de la nación en desarrollo sostenible.* San José: Programa Estado de la Nación.

———. 2001. *Octavo informe estado de la nación en desarrollo sostenible.* San José: Programa Estado de la Nación.

———. 2004. *Décimo informe estado de la nación en desarrollo sostenible.* San José: Programa Estado de la Nación.

Feinberg, Richard. 1984. Costa Rica: The End of the Fiesta. In *From Gunboats to Diplomacy: New U.S. Policies for Latin America,* ed. Richard Newfarmer. Baltimore, MD: John Hopkins University Press.

Fernández, Álvaro. 1992. Hitos y dirección del proceso de aperture comercial. *Costa Rica: Balance de situación* (segunda época),10(1):103–128.

Fox, James. 1998. *Real Progress: Fifty Years of USAID in Costa Rica.* USAID Program and Operations Assessment Report, Vol. 23. Washington, DC: Center for Development Information and Evaluation, USAID.

Fraser, Nancy. 2003. Social Justice in the Age of Identity Politics: Redistribution, Recognition, and Participation. In *Redistribution or Recognition? A Political-Philosophical Exchange,* ed. Nancy Fraser and Axel Honneth. London: Verso.

Hernández, Gerardo. 2007. Dinámicas del sistema de partidos políticos y del cambio institucional en el régimen electoral de Costa Rica, 1952–2002. Ph.D. dissertation, El Colegio de México, Centro de Estudios Sociológicos.

Hidalgo Capitán, Antonio Luis. 2003. *Costa Rica en evolución: Política económica, desarrollo y cambio estructural del sistema socioeconómico Costarricense (1980–2002).* San José: Universidad de Huelva / Editorial de la Universidad de Costa Rica.

Honey, Martha. 1994. *Hostile Acts: U.S. Policy in Costa Rica in the 1980s.* Gainesville, FL: University Press of Florida.

Huber, Evelyne. 1996. Options for Social Policy: Neoliberal versus Social Democratic Models. In *Welfare States in Transition: National Adaptations in Global Economies,* ed. Gøsta Esping-Andersen, 141–91. London: Sage Publications.

INEC. 2003. Regular Household Survey Data. www.inec.go.cr.

Lehouq, Fabrice. 2004. Costa Rica: Paradise in Doubt. *Journal of Democracy* 16(3):141–54.

Mahoney, James. 2001. Path-Dependence Explanations of Regime Change: Central America in Comparative Perspective. *Studies in Comparative International Development* 36(1):111–41.

Martínez Franzoni, Juliana. 2005. Salud en Costa Rica: Una década de reformas y mercantilización de servicios. Paper prepared for the conference *Latin American Perspectives on Public Health,* University of Toronto, May 5–7.

Martínez Franzoni, Juliana, and Carmelo Mesa-Lago. 2003 *Las reformas inconclusas: Pensiones y salud en Costa Rica.* San José: Fundación Ebert.

Mesa-Lago, Carmelo. 2000. *Market, Socialist and Mixed Economy: Chile, Cuba and Costa Rica.* Baltimore, MD: Johns Hopkins University Press.

Pérez Sáinz, Juan Pablo, Katharine Andrade-Eekhoo, Santiago Bastos, and Michael Herradora. 2004. *La estructura social ante la globalización: Procesos de reordenamiento social en Centroamérica durante la década de los 90.* San José, Costa Rica: FLACSO/CEPAL.

PROCOMER. 2001. *Estadísticas de Exportación.* www.procomer.com.

———. 2003. *Estadísticas de Exportación.* www.procomer.com.

Raventós, Ciska, and Marco Fournier. 2005. *Abstencionistas en Costa Rica ¿Quiénes son y por qué no votan?* San José: Editorial de la Universidad de Costa Rica.

Rojas Bolaños, Manuel. 1981. Las perspectivas de la crisis en Costa Rica. In *Crisis en Costa Rica: Un Debate,* 8:20–30. San José: Cuadernos Centroamericanos de Ciencias Sociales.

———. 1992. El momento político y la contienda electoral. *Costa Rica: Balance de la situación* (segunda época), 10(1):13–35.

Rovira Mas, Jorge. 1987. *Costa Rica en los años ochenta.* San José: Editorial Porvenir/CRIES.

———. 1990. Costa Rica: Elecciones, partidos políticos y régimen democrático. *Polémica* 11 (segunda época), (May–August):44–60.

———. 2000. Comentarios a la reforma económica y los problemas sociales. In *Reforma económica y cambio social en América Latina y el Caribe. Cuatro casos de estudio: Colombia, Costa Rica, Cuba, México,* ed. Mauricio Miranda, 557–70. Cali: TM Editores, Pontificia Universidad Javeriana Cali.

———. 2004. El nuevo estilo de desarrollo nacional de Costa Rica 1984–2003 y el TLC. In *TLC con Estados Unidos: Contribuciones para el debate,* ed. María Flores Estrada and Gerardo Hernández, 309–46. San José: Universidad de Costa Rica.

Sandbrook, Richard, Marc Edelman, Patrick Heller, and Judith Teichman. 2007. *Social Democracy in the Global Periphery: Origins, Challenges, Prospects.* Cambridge: Cambridge University Press.

Sauma, Pablo, and Marco Sánchez. 2003. *Exportaciones, crecimiento económico, desigualdad y pobreza: El caso de Costa Rica.* San José: Isis.

Seligson, Mitchell A. 1980. *Peasants of Costa Rica and the Development of Agrarian Capitalism.* Madison and London: University of Wisconsin Press.

———. 2002. Trouble in Paradise: The Erosion of System Support in Costa Rica, 1978–1999. *Latin American Research Review* 37(Spring):160–85.

Seligson, Mitchell A., and Edward N. Muller. 1987. Democratic Stability and Economic Crisis: Costa Rica 1978–1983. *International Studies Quarterly* 31:301–26.

Solís, Manuel. 1992. *Costa Rica: ¿Reformismo Socialdemócrata o Liberal?* San José: FLACSO.

Trejos, Juan Diego. 2006. ¿A quién beneficia el gasto público social en Costa Rica? Paper prepared for the IV Jornada anual de la Academia de Centroamérica (December). San José.

Ulate, Anabelle. 2000. Reformas recientes en Costa Rica: Un desafío para el empleo y el crecimiento con equidad. In *Empleo, crecimiento y equidad: Los retos de las reformas económicas de fines del siglo XX en Costa Rica*, ed. Anabelle Ulate, 15–74. San José: Editorial de la Universidad de Costa Rica/ CEPAL.

Vargas, Mauricio, and Sandra Li. 2002. Informe final de consultoría para la CCSS: Desarrollo de una propuesta para fortalecer los niveles de complejidad desde una perspectiva de red de servicios. (November). San José. Mimeo.

Vargas-Cullell, Jorge, Luis Rosero-Bixby, and Mitchell A. Seligson. 2005. *La Cultura política de la democracia en Costa Rica, 2004*. San José, Costa Rica: Centro Centroamericano de Población (CCP).

Vargas Solís, Luis Paulino. 2002. *Liberalización y ajuste estructural o la autodestrucción del neoliberalismo*. San José: Editorial Universidad Estatal a Distancia.

CHAPTER TEN

Structural Reform and Governability: The Brazilian Experience in the 1990s

FERNANDO HENRIQUE CARDOSO

At the beginning of the 1990s, many political scientists, economists, and other observers shared the opinion that a combination of anachronistic ideas and flawed institutions blocked the path to necessary reforms that would allow Brazil to control inflation and resume growth. While the discussion regarding reforms advanced—although not without resistance—in sectors of the universities, the state techno-bureaucracy, the business community, and the media, politicians generally remained ideologically aligned with the national statism that the Constitution of 1988 had enshrined in its provisions regarding public administration and economic order. In day-to-day politics, old clientelistic and populist practices reemerged in the shadow of the democratic institutions established by the new Constitution. With regard to macrodecisions, the design of political institutions simultaneously weakened the parties and made the passage of the President's initiatives through Congress difficult. In this perception, this situation ultimately threatened to reproduce the pattern of conflict between the Executive and Legislative branches that had set the stage for the 1964 coup, although the threat in the early 1990s was that of a slow death via ungovernability rather than a sudden institutional breakdown.[1]

In 1989, Fernando Collor de Mello's victory in the first presidential election held since 1960, in which the candidate represented a practically nonexistent party, the PRN,[2] placed in bold relief the premature exhaustion of the Brazilian parties that had led the transition to democracy.

The PMDB (Party of the Brazilian Democratic Movement), which had galvanized the opposition to the authoritarian regime and had elected an ample majority to the Constituent Assembly in 1986, broke apart during the debates surrounding the new Constitution from 1987–1988. In the 1990 election the PMDB's share of seats fell to one-fifth of the Chamber of Deputies, although it maintained a plurality of seats in the Senate.[3]

The backdrop to Collor's impeachment under accusations of corruption in December 1992 consisted of the failure of his attempt to bring down inflation "with a single shot" (a monetary shock that included the freezing of bank deposits) and the lack of support for the proposals for reform that he had submitted to Congress. Hyperinflation and weakened governability evinced symptoms of a sort of historic trap that drained the nation's energy, exasperated society, and led to deep pessimism with regard to the recently-established Brazilian democracy.

The widespread and vibrant, yet peaceful, character of the protests against Collor in 1992 and the respect for constitutional procedure resulting in his replacement by Vice President Itamar Franco reinstilled confidence in the democratic process. Itamar, an experienced politician, formed his Cabinet with a broad multi-party coalition as its foundation, a strategy that guaranteed more consistent support in Congress. The diminished tension in the political environment, however, did not bring economic relief. Fueled by price and salary indexing, inflation continued to accelerate, sapping external investment and discouraging investors within Brazil as well. When I became Finance Minister in May of 1993, three Ministers had preceded me in only five months, and the monthly inflation rate registered 30 percent. In addition, political tensions had returned, this time centering on corruption in Congress, regarding the distribution of budgetary resources. The scandal resulted in the removal of several officials, including some high-profile congressional leaders.

Under these conditions, it is understandable that the proposal to attack head-on the "country's three biggest problems: inflation, inflation, and inflation," as I emphasized during my induction ceremony as Minister, was received with skepticism, despite good will among the media, the business community, most of Congress, and the public at large. With a President legally in office but without the legitimacy of the ballot box (in Brazil, as in the United States, the candidate to the Vice Presidency is not voted into office individually) and with Congress mired in a painful self-questioning, the general consensus was that political conditions were unfavorable for taking on such a battle. Nor did time allow for a careful elaboration of a comprehensive stabilization plan, since general elections, including the presidential election as per the recently amended constitution, were scheduled for October 1994. Little more than a year remained before the campaigns would tie politicians to their more narrow bases of electoral support, making impossible the requisite plenary session for passing any complex legislation.

The success of the "Plano Real"[4] (Real Plan) and the results it produced seemed to contradict, or at least relativize, the diagnoses that emphasized the political obstacles to economic stabilization and reform. Despite the limited time permitted by the electoral calendar, we were able to assemble a competent technical team in the Ministry of Finance—a vital prerequisite for a Minister who (as in my case) is not an economist—to devise an innovative strategy for economic stabilization, combining both orthodox and unorthodox measures. My previous experience as a member of Congress proved helpful in order to secure the political support to implement this strategy in such a short period.

THE REAL PLAN

Lax fiscal policies had undermined the credibility of previous attempts at stabilization during the presidencies of José Sarney (1985–1990) and Collor de Mello (1990–1992). The first stage of what became the Real Plan was a set of measures designed to address this fiscal imbalance, including spending cuts in the federal budget; the partial freeing-up of revenue tied to predetermined expenses by constitutional provisions; a new tax on financial transactions, including check discounting; and the renegotiation of the states' debts, several of which were in arrears or nearly so. Although admittedly insufficient to assure long-term fiscal balance, these measures were presented to the President, to Congress, and to the public as a first step in attacking the structural causes of inflation. By proposing them, the government sent a clear message that it would not repeat the discredited practice of anti-inflationary "shocks," and demonstrated its determination to dissolve the unholy union between inflation and the Treasury, a union that had become the trademark of the Brazilian fiscal regime.[5] By approving the measures, Congress demonstrated that it was possible to create consensus for subsequent reforms. For the financial community, these factors, combined with negotiations that released Brazil from a moratorium on foreign debt in October 1993, created the confidence needed for successful stabilization.

The monetary stage of the Plan consisted of dismantling the price and salary indexing that had become widespread in the 1980s and had fostered, through inertia, a culture of inflation, as past inflationary rates determined the base for future inflation. The innovative and most daring aspect of this phase was using the index as its own antidote, much like the homeopathic principle *similia similibus curantur* ("like cures like"). The Real Unit of Value (URV), a daily indicator introduced by the government in February 1994, functioned as a reference point for the spontaneous adjustment of contracts and prices prior to the introduction and circulation of the new currency on July 1, 1994. This prevented lawsuits between private agents as well as against the government for the annulment of contractual rights and obligations before and after the stabilization plan. As a result, the National Treasury was not subjected to the types of disputes that sprang up under previous stabilization plans. Only one aspect of the Real Plan was invalidated by the courts, with comparatively minor consequences. This legal armor-plating was a key element in inspiring confidence in the plan.

Upon its introduction to the market on July 1, 1994, the *real* was valued on par with the U.S. dollar, although it was not tied legally to the dollar as was the Argentine peso under the Cavallo Stabilization Plan of 1991. The fact that the *real* was not pegged legally to the dollar had important implications for the eventual consolidation of Brazilian stability. It allowed the transition, five years later, to a floating exchange rate with considerable turbulence but without a financial collapse.

Inflation, which had risen to 47% per month on the eve of the currency change, fell to less than 3% per month after 30 days and subsequently remained steady at approximately 1% per month.[6]

The first polls after I left my position as Finance Minister to run for President in May 1994 projected me to win about 15% of the vote. Lula (Luiz Inácio da Silva), the Workers' Party candidate who was the front-runner, enjoyed 40% in these early surveys. However, in October, I won the presidential election in the first round with 54.3% of the official vote. The hope awakened by the Real Plan was the driving force behind my candidacy. It also provided a bond holding together the multiparty coalition with which I ran and which I later attempted to broaden as President. Although my platform was not limited to combating inflation, the effort to consolidate stabilization—or to "secure the *real*," as the public put it—became the basic obligation in function of which my government sought support in Congress and in society, and upon which ultimately my administration would be judged.

Controlling inflation was not the end but rather the beginning of a process, as my collaborators and I did not tire of repeating. We knew that changes initiated in a climate of near-euphoria would take time and would require persistent and consistent effort in order to achieve lasting results. Our strategy anticipated the beneficial effects of stabilization and postponed the costs of reforms necessary to consolidate the stabilization. A neoclassical economist would have recommended the opposite: pay the price now and reap the benefits later. As a reader of Machiavelli, I envisioned in this inversion of conventional economic logic a political opportunity to win over the unorganized majority that stood to gain from the reforms and to neutralize opposition from well-organized minorities. We did not overlook the risk of "reform fatigue." However, we wagered that the relief provided by the drop in inflation would sharpen Brazilians' perceptions of secular societal ills and spur demand for further advances. We walked on the razor's edge between two collective sentiments:

1. the unleashing of aspirations inspired by the changes we had initiated, and
2. frustration over the time and the funds needed to accomplish the change.

STABILIZATION AND STRUCTURAL REFORM

We had a clear sense of the way forward. The general vision and several of the more specific measures on our reform agenda during my first term (1995–1998) and a considerable part of the second (1999–2002) already were outlined in papers that document the planning stages of the Real Plan.[7] The road ahead, however, "is created as one walks it," with many stones and unforeseen curves.

Our point of departure was the conviction that hyperinflation, fiscal imbalance, foreign debt, and economic stagnation that had dragged along since the 1980s signaled the end of one cycle of development in Brazil, without the foundations in place for the succeeding cycle. Conjunctural causes, including volatility in the foreign oil market and the repercussions of errors and oversights of successive governments, were partly responsible for the crisis. However, the fundamental cause was the bankruptcy of the centralist, interventionist state founded by the dictatorship of Getulio Vargas (1937–1945) and strengthened by the military governments of 1964–1985. After 50 years (1930–1980) of strong growth—but also of income concentration and social marginalization—this model of state-led development had exhausted its capacity to drive industrialization through public investment, protectionism, and subsidies to the private sector.

If Brazil remained on the margin of international currents related to the expansion of trade, investment, and technology, then lasting economic stability and sustained growth would be impossible. In spite of the crisis, many Brazilian companies had managed to modernize their methods of management and production, if not their capital stock. Unlike the public sector, private industry was not excessively indebted. While surprised by the trade liberalization promoted by the Collor administration, the private sector generally proved capable of handling increased exposure to international competition.

In order to make its economy more competitive, the country needed a new model for the state. What was needed was not the great protagonist of national development, as in the past, nor the minimalist neoliberal state, but the "necessary state," as we preferred to call it: one with more brains and nerves than a bureaucratic body, capable of responding in time to the opportunities and turbulence of global capitalism. We needed a state oriented toward the coordination and regulation of private initiative rather than to direct intervention in the economy. And equally important, we needed a state capable of fulfilling the promises of democracy without burdening the very beneficiaries of those promises—workers, retirees, the poor—with the weight of an inflationary "tax."

Extensive and detailed to the extreme,[8] the Constitution of 1988 was—and to a large extent still is—a contradictory document. Forward-thinking in its recognition and guarantees of the fundamental rights of citizens, as well as generous in its vision of social rights, it also contains provisions linked to the special interests of the Vargas state, rooted deeply in the traditional patrimonialism of Brazilian political culture.

The 1988 Constitution maintained public sector monopolies in the oil and telecommunications industries. In mining and shipping, the Constitution did not grant state monopolies, but it gave exclusive rights of exploitation to domestic firms. The consequence of both these measures was paralysis or insufficient investment. Investment was also inadequate in the state electric companies. With the state in a full fiscal crisis, we needed to eliminate or loosen these constitutional constraints and establish rules to involve the private sector, including foreign capital, in the efforts to expand the productivity of these sectors. Otherwise, bottlenecks in infrastructure would thwart the resumption of economic growth.

The Constitution guaranteed to civil servants highly favorable pension arrangements in terms of age requirements, years of service, and contributions as well as the value of retirement packages. Workers in the private sector affiliated with social security had fewer perks, but they also had guaranteed and/or expanded benefits. With increases in expenditures exceeding the capacity to generate revenue, both public and private pension systems began to show growing deficits that would burden society as a whole, either through increased taxes, inflation, or by pressure on interest rates. Increases in contributions from the payroll in the private sector, a palliative measure to contain the expansion of the deficit, would lead to an increase in the size of the informal sector, leaving a large portion of workers without social security protection. As a result, despite the promise of universal coverage, a highly stratified, inequitable, and ultimately unsustainable social security system emerged.

Civil servants still received benefits by the extension of guarantees typically limited to judges, such as lifetime employment and no salary reductions. These guarantees were extended to all civil servants, including the large number of temporary workers. These provisions complicated ambitious efforts to modernize public administration, and they made the growth of personnel expenditures for the civil service within the three levels of government—federal, state, and municipal—practically uncontrollable.

Correcting these distortions was necessary both for reasons of economic efficiency as well as social equity. Consequently, we sought to redress these problems through constitutional amendments to articles on state monopolies, the definition of a national company, social security, and public service. We submitted those amendments to Congress in the months immediately following the inauguration of the government on January 1, 1995.

For the public in general, the discussion of reforms became confusing with demonstrations and counter-demonstrations related to the constitutional amendments. These amendments were an important part, but only a part, of the government reforms carried out in the subsequent years.

A BATTLE ON SEVERAL FRONTS

The consolidation of economic stability involved a battle on several fronts. Financial authority at a number of levels—federal, state and local—was renegotiated arduously until a legal limit to the future indebtedness of the states (as well as some prefectures of midsized and large cities) was agreed upon. These states and municipalities were also induced to settle up their accounts and guarantee the payment of loans for debts assumed by the federal government. In this process, several state-owned banks, used by their respective governments for the uncontrolled emission of debt, were closed or privatized.[9]

The battle to align states, municipalities, and the federal government itself in the search for fiscal sustainability intensified from 1999 on, after the introduction of a floating exchange rate and a plan to limit inflation. In May 2000, as a culmination of this effort on the normative plane, Congress approved a Law of Fiscal Responsibility, applicable to the three levels of government, with strict new limits on the assumption of debt and the expansion of personnel and other permanent positions.

The private banks suffered, with varying intensity, the impact of the loss of inflationary revenue that they were accustomed to collect from unremunerated deposits. A program to restructure and fortify the banking system strengthened controls over weakened banks while limiting the losses of the depositors and, most importantly, avoiding the devastating effects of a chain-reaction crash. Federal financial institutions also were restructured and capitalized. These steps prepared the country to confront the external financial crises of the second half of the 1990s more effectively.

The removal of most non-tariff barriers and the reduction of tariffs on imports had already taken place, as I mentioned above, under the Collor administration. With the *real* stable and pegged to the U.S. dollar, trade liberalization became a reality. In contrast to what many had predicted, this trade opening did not lead to a dismantling of the substantial industrial capacity created in Brazil during decades of import substitution. Despite localized difficulties, Brazilian industry as a whole responded well to the liberalization, taking advantage of the favorable exchange rate to import machinery and technologically advanced equipment. It benefited from the expansion of the internal market and maintained basically the same level of complexity and sector integration as before.

At the same time, the state had to do its part to support the resumption of growth under the new conditions that resulted from the liberalization of the economy. The publicly owned National Bank of Economic and Social Development (BNDES) increased its expenditures by nearly five hundred percent between 1994 and 1998, exceeding the level of 20 billion *reals* per year. The presence of a financing vehicle on such a scale, without equal in other emergent countries, was decisive for the productive restructuring of the private sector.

Governmental agencies that were either neglected or nonexistent in a closed economy had to be created or strengthened in areas such as the promotion of exports, the regulation of competition, the protection of livestock-farming, intellectual property rights, and support for innovation. Their design helped to clear the way for a considerable expansion of Brazilian exports, including both commodities as well as manufactured products, following the fiscal reforms in early 1999.

The entrance of private initiative in the sectors of infrastructure required a new legal regime for the concession of public services and the creation of something unprecedented in the organization of the Brazilian state: regulatory agencies with legal authority and political independence designed to protect the rights of consumers when dealing with service providers. Several such agencies were created in the wake of the constitutional amendments regarding oil, electricity, and telecommunications.

Last but not least, institutional vehicles of the state needed to be re-crafted to deliver on the promises of universalization of social rights. New rules for the participation of the federal, state, and municipal governments in financing primary education and public health were established through constitutional amendments, and a Fund for Combating Poverty was created. The criteria for the expenditure of these resources represented a step forward with regard to the equity of public spending. They were targeted to benefit primarily the poorest and most vulnerable sectors of the population, which had traditionally been short-changed in the distribution of benefits from social programs. Broad changes in the conception and execution of essential programs in these areas improved the efficiency of spending, devolving resources and initiative capacity to the states and municipalities, in partnership with actors in civil society.

Not all of the reforms were completed to the extent originally proposed. The social security and public administration reforms had limited effects. The knots we hoped to untie did loosen up, but still, they suffocated the Brazilian state and hindered economic growth. After the policy window of the inflation crisis had passed, corporatist interests managed to rearticulate themselves within society, the political parties, and Congress to bar new changes. A constitutional amendment proposed by the Lula administration, during his first term in office, for Civil Service pension reform, was approved—with the support from PSDB, currently an opposition party—but has not yet been regulated, remaining simply as an unkept written promise.

Limited as they were, the reforms we accomplished have functioned well enough to sustain the stability of the economy over the last years. I am perhaps not the best judge of their success, nor can I guarantee that there will not be reversals. Even though they do not constitute the unshakeable foundation of a new model of development, they at least defined the general contours of such a model.[10]

The reform agenda was extensive and complex and constituted an intense agenda for the legislature. Between 1995 and 2002, the Brazilian Constitution was amended 35 times; 36 if we include the amendment that made possible the fiscal adjustment in preparation for the Real Plan in 1993.[11] Each of these amendments required the approval of three-fifths of all members (including the absent and abstentions) in both the Chamber of Deputies and the Senate, in two rounds of voting in each chamber. Because the regulations of the Chamber of Deputies allowed (and continue to allow, within certain limits) that any party call for separate votes on individual parts of a proposition, the qualifying quorum of three-fifths had to be achieved on hundreds of different votes. More than five hundred complementary laws, ordinary laws, and presidential decrees ("medidas provisórias") of some relevance were approved during the same period.

To the best of my knowledge, in no other Latin American country did the reform process require such an effort of consensus building in the legislative arena. In Chile, Pinochet's reforms dispensed with the Congress's seal of approval. In Argentina, privatization, deregulation, and efforts to reduce the size of the state were carried out in large part through legislative delegation to the Executive branch. In retrospect, that such political consensus was necessary may have worked to Brazil's advantage. The Argentine shortcut to reform seems to have resulted in weaker rather than stronger institutions. The torturous Brazilian path may have provided a more solid political foundation for reform.

The entire legislative agenda mentioned above was processed within a fundamentally unaltered political-institutional setting, with the same actors and the same rules of the game, or almost the same, which supposedly had previously posed insurmountable obstacles to reform. The question that arises is: How was it possible to move this agenda forward while avoiding what was considered the "mother of all reforms"— namely, political reform?

THE FALLACY OF POLITICAL PRECONDITIONS

I have alluded to the exceptional political circumstances—Collor's impeachment, the lack of direct electoral legitimacy behind his replacement, a Congress mired in a scandal of corruption—that justified skepticism regarding the chances for the success of a frontal attack on inflation at the moment when I became Minister of Finance. Paradoxically, these very circumstances made the Real Plan possible. Where analysts saw only the lack of political preconditions, in fact a window of opportunity had opened. Under normal circumstances, the groups that benefited from the inflationary process and the fragmentation of the state, including factions within Congress, the private sector, and the state bureaucracy itself, would have positioned themselves more effectively to defend their interests. The nearly complete disorganization of traditional political forces helps explain how they allowed themselves to be defeated—or persuaded, it doesn't matter—by a Minister and his small group of close advisors and sympathizers in the government, with the backing of the President of the Republic, with very hesitant support from parties other than my own, the PSDB.

Another decisive factor combined with the momentary weakness of traditional political forces: society's generalized exasperation with years of living with the gnawing effects of hyperinflation. With prices rising almost every day and accumulating average increases above 20 percent per month, practically no one escaped. All were in some way adversely impacted: salaried workers, retirees, and those living on pensions, because of the accelerated corrosion of the buying power of their fixed incomes; the self-employed and small-scale entrepreneurs without access to the banking system, because of the devaluation of their scant cash assets; the upper middle class and businessmen, because of the immense difficulty of calculating, planning, and investing in a hyperinflationary environment, even given indexed financial applications.

Any credible proposal to attack inflation would tend to achieve, in these circumstances, broad societal consensus, taking precedence over other, eventually divergent and even conflicting interests. This consensus, reinforced by the means of mass communication, ended up influencing those who made decisions in the government and in Congress. Our efforts to "sell" the Real Plan were directed, therefore, in toward the government and the Congress as well as out toward the broader political arena, in order to convince the larger Brazilian society. I dedicated myself obsessively to both tasks, first as Minister, and later as a candidate to the Presidency.

Credibility was a critical prerequisite in a country that had suffered the consequences of the failure of successive stabilization plans in the previous years. We benefited at the start from the good will of the media, most businesspeople, other organized sectors of society, and from a Congress that, although skeptical of our prospects for success, valued the seriousness of our proposals and the competence of our team. Aware of the importance of maintaining and broadening this trust, we decided that there would be no surprises nor promises too difficult to keep: each step of our strategy of stabilization would be announced in advance and explained to the public at large, with the clear message that our efforts did not consist of a unilateral *act* of government, but rather of a *process* whose results depended on the continued convergence of the efforts of the government, Congress, private economic agents, and society as a whole.

Many times we were close to losing this battle of trust. Over the course of months there were increases in society's woes due to the acceleration of inflation, pressure for measures with greater impact in the government itself, and resistance from parties and leadership that saw in the eventual success of the plan of stabilization the frustration of their own political aspirations.

The change of currency to the *real*, with the substitution of all money in circulation, helped convince the public: the *real* became the symbol in which society's expectations for change were crystallized. Even before the introduction of the new currency into circulation, the parties and political leaders began to pick up a change in the spirit of society. The perception that this could drive a successful presidential campaign facilitated winning support for our proposals in Congress.

This is how the breakthrough came about: launched under the stigma of a "lack of political preconditions," the Real Plan ended up being its own precondition for the realignment of political forces favorable to reforms.

Almost by exasperation, the old order of things gave way to a new situation. Victory in the 1994 presidential election conferred upon me the opportunity and the responsibility to anchor this new situation to an institutional foundation, carrying forward the extensive agenda of reforms that were necessary to "secure the *real*" and to keep hope in our success alive.

TESTING THE LIMITS OF A COALITIONAL PRESIDENTIAL SYSTEM

The initial success of stabilization benefited from a momentary opportunity, but the consolidation of stability took eight years of persistent efforts. Progress throughout this period depended on a political strategy based on two principles:

1. securing a stable majority in Congress by dividing power in the Executive branch among the parties of the governing coalition, and
2. the presence of presidential leadership to rally support for the reforms from government forces and the allied parties as well as from the public and organized sectors of society.

I witnessed the crises that led to the resignation of President Jânio Quadros in 1961 and the overthrow of President João Goulart in 1964, and I participated, as a Senator, in Collor's impeachment in 1992. The lesson from each of these episodes was clear to me: the worst mistake presidents can commit is imagining that they have a mandate to govern alone. In order to fulfill their promises to the electorate, they need Congress. And to obtain a majority in Congress they need to build alliances, because the Federation's heterogeneity and the peculiarities of the Brazilian system of proportional representation produce a fragmented partisan picture in which no party holds a majority by itself.[12] With these lessons in mind, I undertook an alliance of my party, the PSDB (Party of

Brazilian Social Democracy), with the PFL (Party of the Liberal Front) and the PTB (Brazilian Labor Party) during the presidential campaign of 1994. Later, the PMDB and the PPB (Brazilian Progressive Party) entered into the governing coalition. This broad coalition provided the support of more than the three-fifths of Deputies and Senators required to approve constitutional amendments.

An inevitable tension exists between the roles of the President as the elected representative of the majority of the nation and as the speaker for the parliamentary majority. Without alliances presidents do not govern. But if they "give in" to Congress, they also cannot govern in the sense that they cannot execute their program. The question is: Why build alliances—only to remain in power, or to attain larger goals?

The larger goals set limits on the concessions that presidents can make to their allies and to their own party. If presidents cannot identify and preserve the parts of the Executive branch essential to the realization of their project, they can end up naming the wrong people to key positions. In our case, the area of the economy, including ministries and federal financial institutions, and the most important posts in the social arena, beginning with education and health, were not subjected to partisan considerations. The privatization of state industries took off the table dozens of administrative positions that traditionally had been partisan bargaining chips. The introduction of formal procedures for selecting regional and intermediary public sector managers in areas such as social security, agrarian reform, and environmental protection had the same effect. Nonetheless, with other positions left open to nominations from coalition parties, it was possible to reconcile political criteria to satisfy coalition demands with technical competence and align them with the objectives of the government.

Members of the opposition and other critics of the government decried what they considered to be a "steamroller" in a Congress greased by the distribution of public sector posts and budgetary funds to political allies. In fact, the opportunities for political appointments had diminished for the above reasons, just as the space for so-called "parochial amendments"[13] had decreased after the scandal involving members of the Budget Commission in 1993. If the clientelistic use of positions and funds were the key to the government's legislative majority, it would be impossible to explain how we won broad support for a long period of time, with an ambitious and complex legislative agenda, while relying less on clientelism and patronage than previous governments.

The political support for the reforms also depended—maybe more than it should have—upon a combination of the appreciated exchange rate and a relatively loose fiscal regime. The weak dollar forced deflation at a fast pace, which rendered the government—and those associated with it—popular. The fiscal regime gave rise both to the expansion of essential social policies and to the accommodation of budgetary pressures from government allies.

But in my view the key to a working majority was something else: it was the project itself, in the name of which the government built alliances and sought support in Congress. Common sense might suggest that the more the government asks for from Congress in terms of legislative output, the higher the price it needs to pay in its negotiations with the parliamentary base. The experience of my eight years as president shows the opposite: the consistency of the government's legislative agenda with its principal commitment to "securing the *real*," rather than making its work more difficult, facilitated the task—which nevertheless proved arduous—of attending to the specific demands of its partisans and allies, within reasonable limits.

Support from the streets does not substitute for the support of the parties. Without stable alliances among the parties, it would have been difficult for the government to overcome the 1999 currency crisis, which coincided with the beginning of my second term, when the sustainability of that commitment appeared to be compromised. The combination of tactical flexibility to negotiate and renegotiate a parliamentary majority with the strategic resolve to defend the essential points of the reform agenda allowed us to endure the inevitable highs and lows of presidential popularity while maintaining both the majority and the government's program.[14]

GOVERNABILITY REVISITED

The years of economic stability and the advance of reforms that began with the Real Plan diminished concerns regarding (un)governability but did not dampen theoretical and practical interest in the question. If the institutions remained basically the same, what other conditions could explain our ability to overcome the impasse perceived at the beginning of the 1990s? More importantly: did the preponderance and permanence of these other conditions justify declaring victory over—and not merely a temporary truce around—the impasse?

The first question widens the focus of the analysis of governability from the strictly institutional level to the political plane in a broader sense, including ideologies and social forces that contribute to the decision-making environment in the Executive and Legislative branches.

Beginning with ideologies: I mentioned above the relative delay of the discussion of reform among the political class in the 1990s. In fact, rather than specific resistance to change from one group or another, there was a lack of clarity among the political forces in general regarding the direction of the changes—a conceptual fog that sometimes obscured, and other times mixed with, institutional bottlenecks that prevented decision making.

The politicians were not the only latecomers in understanding the need for reform. In Brazil, as throughout the world, an important pocket of intellectuals continued to argue on behalf of a basically statist vision—labeled as leftist, socialist, nationalist, progressive—even after this vision was questioned by the collapse of the Soviet Union and the acceleration of capitalist globalization. Surprising alliances sprung up among these fellow travelers. In the discussions on fiscal reform, for example, the traditional budgetary populism of politicians, summed up by the phrase "spend and the money will appear," was often aided by the pseudo-Keynesian arguments of economists revered by the left.

The critique of this statist vision matured, however, during the five years between the promulgation of the Constitution and the Real Plan. Initially taking place outside the political system, the debate between specialists (mainly economists) of some university centers, high-ranking officials of the federal administration, and research centers linked to business entities celebrated a new vision of Brazil and its place in the world as well as a strategy for development consistent with this vision. Collor de Mello embraced some of these proposals in the name of a vague "modernity." His meteoric passage through office shook up the political world and opened up the discussion of reform in the media. By taking presidential intervention in the political scene and in economic life to the extreme, he quite possibly left behind a demand for leadership that, without regressing to a vision of the past, could reestablish confidence in an agenda for change that would not prove traumatic.

When a worsening of the crisis following Collor's impeachment tested the limits of society's tolerance of hyperinflation and lowered resistance to change in Congress, there was a sufficiently mature alternative agenda to offer to the country.

My contribution as a hybrid intellectual/politician was to serve as an interpreter and liaison between the government, the parties, and Congress, on one hand, and the reformist sectors in the universities, the techno-bureaucracy, and the business community, on the other.

My personal reflection on these themes had advanced during the work of the Constituent Assembly. A speech that I gave in January, 1988, entitled "The Crisis and National Options," anticipated much of what we did or attempted to do with the Real Plan: less protectionism and more technological development; less corporatism and greater permeability of the state to the demands and the participation of civil society. I criticized the insensitive defenders of the state monopolies as well as those who considered any intervention by the state to be a threat to the market economy. Nationalization versus privatization, I said, was a false problem when reduced to a matter of principle, without taking into consideration the limits and possibilities of state action and private initiative appropriate to each sector.

It was too late to try to change the direction of the Constituent Assembly. My party, the PSDB, was launched in July 1988 following the splintering of the PMDB. The PSDB's program incorporated many of the new ideas. Later, when the Real Plan's window of opportunity opened, the conversation with the reformist sectors provided us an intellectual critical mass and the public backing that we needed to move forward.

With the fog dissipated and the alternative path defined, resistance to change appeared, headed by a parliamentary opposition that was small but fierce and an important segment of the union movement, based mainly among the civil service and employees of state businesses.

The debate over reform never amounted to a schism in society. While this could have happened, the government limited its objectives rather than feeding polarization that could potentially fray the seams of democracy. Several times, however, on the eve of contested votes in Congress, I appealed publicly to the sectors that favored the government's proposals. I did so not to constrain the Congress, but rather to counterbalance pressure from the other side and to legitimize the vote that the majority was willing to give—even, at times, without much enthusiasm, as was the case with social security reform.

The interplay of presidential leadership, Congress, and organized sectors of society would leave out the overwhelming majority of the population, and therefore would have limited consequences, if not for another political resource fundamental in today's world: public opinion mediated and produced by means of mass communication.

Brazil is a country with proportionally few readers, but with a number of TV viewers and radio listeners that includes practically the entire population. The broadcasting of information by these two vehicles—radio and television—is reasonably pluralist and independent. The political force of the masses informed by the electronic media was felt for the first time in the massive campaign for "direct presidential elections now," in 1984, an event that marked the end of the military regime. Every important political event since then bears their mark, from the indirect election of Tancredo Neves to the Presidency in 1984 to Collor's impeachment, from the Cruzado Plan (the failed economic stabilization plan of 1986) to the Real Plan, passing through periodic elections along the way.

Mass television and radio profoundly alter the democratic use of power. It is not enough to be voted in, even by tens of millions of people, or to be vested with legal authority. Legitimization of decisions requires a never-ending effort to explain your reasons and to sway public opinion. Collor, before me, and Lula, my successor, have assumed the role of the Media President, each in his own way. My training as a professor prepared me for this role—if not well, in any case better than for the role of a speaker at campaign rallies. I turned time and again to the media, as Minister and later as President, to explain and sustain before the public each step of the Real Plan and the reform agenda.

In sum, three factors outside the political-parliamentary arena created conditions favorable to beginning the decisive reform process:

1. the emergence of a vision for the development of the country that provided an alternative to the old national statism,
2. the accumulation of a critical mass in favor of this vision among organized society, and
3. the virtual but powerful presence of public opinion mediated by mass communication. The function of presidential leadership was to make these potential conditions converge in favor of the reforms, neutralizing the resistance of traditional political actors.

AWAITING POLITICAL REFORM

It is more difficult to respond to the second question posed above—can we declare victory, or is this a mere temporary suspension of the political impasse? The process of reform, of any reform, slowed in Lula's government. Several facts, however, work against the hypothesis of a relapse to the syndrome of ungovernability.

First, there has been an unmistakable shift in the country's ideological center of gravity. Although national statism may be alive in some sectors of the parties, intellectual circles, and the state apparatus, it has lost much of its past appeal, to the extent that today it represents perhaps more a "mentality" than a vision for the future.

Congress is an indicator of this shift. Contrasted with the fierce resistance to our proposals for fiscal adjustment in 1993, leading up to the Real Plan, the Law of Fiscal Responsibility was approved with relative ease in 2000. The constitutional amendment proposed by Lula's government that included additional modifications to the social security system for civil servants was approved much more easily than that which I proposed in 1995, in part because in 1995 Lula and the PT were part of the frontline opposition to the reform.

The most tangible sign of transformation was the about-face of Lula and the PT, previously the most hardened critics of my government's economic program, in continuing along the same general lines of my policies, beginning with a commitment to fiscal austerity. The PT leadership directed this about-face by making a *tabula rasa* of the opinion of the party's rank and file. Looking in from the outside, it is possible to notice at times pronounced exaggerations, and at others, hesitation in the management of fiscal and monetary policies by Lula's team. Nevertheless the PT government has maintained a rejection of past commercial protectionism and budgetary populism.

In some ways this transformation has reduced the political drama of reform. It is true that there is fatigue in Congress and in society itself. But it is no longer a matter of breaking down one model of government and creating the foundation for another in its place. The work ahead consists of providing continuity for changes in accord with a new model that, for better or for worse, is delineated—although far from complete. Concepts such as privatization, commercial liberalization, and fiscal responsibility have already faced judgment. The political cost of specific measures in these areas will diminish from this point forward. And, at least in theory, openings will appear in the agenda for other topics that progressed little during my administration, such as tax and judicial reform, as well as political reform.

There are also signs of cultural transformation apparent in the preservation of political stability. The alternation of power on the three levels of government, culminating in Lula's election as President in 2002, reinforced the commitment of the different groups and parties to the regularity of the democratic process. This serves as a brake against the inclination to allow conflicts to grow unchecked, ultimately undermining institutional stability.

Finally, although the bases of the presidential system of government and the electoral system have not been modified, some incremental changes have affected Executive–Legislative balance.

1. The reduction of the presidential term from five to four years in the 1993 constitutional revision aligned the presidential term with that of the Deputies. This tends to facilitate the coordination of the agendas of the Executive and the Legislative branches, diminishing the potential for conflict between the two powers.
2. The constitutional amendment of 1997 that permitted the reelection of the President for a second consecutive term increased, in principle, presidential capacity to press for changes over time and to maintain the support of the majority in Congress for their agenda.

3. The President's capacity to enact provisional executive decrees (a presidential decree that becomes invalid if not confirmed by Congress) was restricted in 2001, but not to the point of impeding the use of this recourse in clearly relevant and urgent cases, such as the ones that put the Real Plan into effect.

The political reforms proposed at the beginning of the 1990s were different and broader. There was discussion about changing both the system of government to parliamentarism and the system of proportional election in the Chamber of Deputies. But the proposal of a parliamentary system, to which the PSDB was committed, was defeated in the Constituent Assembly, and again in a plebiscite held in 1993, when more than 60% of the electorate voted to maintain a presidential system. And the substitution of an open list proportional system encountered, and continues to encounter, the Deputies' objections to the different alternatives—single member districts, a mixed district vote, and a proportional vote with a preordered party list.

As President, I stimulated a discussion of electoral reform in Congress but did not want to involve the government in defending a specific proposal. I feared that the discussion would not culminate in a timely fashion and would end up blocking the legislative agenda. The fact that economic reforms have progressed indicates that this decision was correct, but it does not mean that the political-institutional obstacles to this crucial process were negligible. Proof of this includes the excruciatingly slow and tortuous trajectories of some proposals, particularly that of social security reform, which dragged out throughout my entire first term.

The Brazilian institutional design encourages the political interaction between the President and Congress toward a false coalitionist presidential system. The representation of the coalition parties in the ministry gives some stability to the parliamentary base of the government but does not guarantee that their projects will pass. Pressure from coalition partners to expand their "space" in the Executive branch by getting more cabinet and high-level positions and to obtain other benefits is constant. One way to exert pressure is to create difficulties in the legislative process. At times the leaders of the governing coalition parties compromise with the opposition. At other times the second-tier congressional leaders—the so-called "lower clergy"—rebel against their party leaders. When conflicting interests and pressures from different sectors of society are added to this mix, pushing through legislation of interest to the government becomes a marathon with hurdles.[15]

The political difficulties faced by President Lula's government brought back to the table the discussion of political reform, but with different implications. The *legitimacy* of political representation, as much as or more so than *governability*, constitutes a key concern.

There are no signs of an impasse between the Executive and Legislative branches, at least not in relation to the legislative process, as even the government's most controversial proposals, such as the new round of social security reform, had support from the opposition. Concern over the fragmentation and lack of discipline among the parties reemerged following the disclosure of the less-than-orthodox methods of cooptation of political allies by the current government and its party.[16]

The proportional system with an open list, by introducing life-or-death competition between candidates of the same party for a better place on the electoral list, tends to make electoral campaigns more expensive and has a corrosive effect on party unity. Above all, it weakens the relationship between representatives and their constituents. Generally it is difficult for voters to know whom they elected as Deputy, and even to remember for whom they voted, when hundreds of candidates vie for votes in the same super-district that each state represents. Scandals over undeclared campaign contributions create a cloud of suspicion over campaign financing, ultimately calling into question the legitimacy of the legislators' mandates.

The alternatives to the proportional system with an open list seem more favorable to the transparency of the electoral process and to accountability of representatives to their constituents. The great difficulty lies in convincing the parties and each deputy that these alternatives do not jeopardize their chances for future electoral success. Small parties fear being obliterated by the majority principle of single member, simple plurality districts. Many deputies fear the manipulation of party lists by regional political bosses, both in the proposal for a proportional system with closed party lists and in a mixed proportional system.[17]

Another appropriate concern with respect to the proportional system with closed party lists is that they could strengthen the party leadership too much, to the detriment of the renovation of political representation or narrowing the President's room to maneuver when attempting to attain a majority in the legislature. Fragmented and undisciplined parties turn creating a legislative majority into a Sisyphean trial. Smaller, rigidly led parties can be consistent with governability under parliamentarianism. In a presidential system, however, they could either facilitate the building of a majority or make it even more difficult by contributing toward an impasse rather than concentrating on the legislative process.

The best possible outcome of this array of alternatives is not a matter of theory but rather of historic opportunity. Large-scale political reforms are almost always the result of large crises. In Brazil in the 1990s, under very specific historical circumstances, squeezed by the crisis facing the old model of government and exasperated by the inflationary process, we did what was perhaps the most difficult: we initiated a process of structural reform within a political-institutional milieu that did not favor large-scale changes.

Perhaps under less dramatic circumstances, with a lighter legislative agenda, an opening for institutional engineering that until now has been missing will appear. Such an opening could result from a consensus among politicians, or from the mobilization of public opinion in favor of more transparent rules and more predictable results.

POSTSCRIPT: LESSONS ON DEMOCRATIC REFORMS

The overview on the ups and downs of democratic governance in Latin America offered by this book suggests some additional reflection on aspects of the Brazilian experience compared to that of our neighbors.

Brazil, like other Latin American countries, opened its economy driven by the crisis, more than by promises of growth. The accumulated impact of external shocks originated from oil and interest rates drove the country into a long period of stagnation and inflation, while capitalism was being reorganized globally during the 1980s. The reluctance of the Brazilian political class to believe that the global market was a way out of the crisis was proportional to the success of the previous autarchic and state-led model that gave the country fifty years of extraordinary growth and enabled the establishment of a large industrial complex, like no other in Latin America.

Finally, after the "lost decade" of the 1980s, the perception that commercial and financial isolation would lead Brazil to be technologically behind in a globalized world prevailed. Congress backed the reduction of import taxes and also the elimination of non-tariff barriers during Collor's administration as of 1990. In 1993, we ended a seven-year period of default on the external debt. In 1994, we controlled inflation and liberalized the exchange rate. In 1995, we opened the telecommunication, electrical power, oil, and maritime sectors to foreign capital. These measures were followed by a broad set of reforms designed to make the opening process compatible with stability, as well as to make the structures of the state suited to its new role as coordinator, more than a direct promoter of development.

However, it took more than ten years before economic growth started to respond more vigorously to the change of economic paradigm. Some see this as the proof that the prescriptions of the Washington Consensus failed. Others, conversely, attribute this poor economic performance to the insufficiency of reforms carried out under my administration, and to the loss of drive for the reform agenda shown under Lula's.

The discussion on the efficacy or inefficacy of one-size-fits-all development policies means very little to me. Not only must the choices on this matter be country-specific, as stated by Francisco Rodríguez (Chapter 3), but also the Brazilian experience—in this sense, similar to that of so many other countries—shows that, in fact, choices *are necessarily* country-specific: made in the heat of the historical moment, at the mercy of the ever-changing blowing winds of the world economy, under very particular internal political junctures, in light of the common view that the political leadership formed regarding the challenges and opportunities for the development of their countries within their context.

The more general conditions of the development of capitalism limit what is possible. Autarchic development is no longer an option in the era of instant information and a transnational productive chain. The participation in international flows of commerce and finance limits, to a certain extent, the range of choices available to governments. Inflation constantly on the rise and the unilateral breach of contracts obviously do not facilitate integration. However, the real possibilities for integration vary enormously.

José De Gregorio draws attention to an obvious but essential factor that differentiates countries, that is, the size of their domestic economies (Chapter 2). The occupation of niches in the global market tends to be simpler (but not necessarily easier) for small countries. Sixteen million Chileans can prosper by combining technological and logistical excellence to a relatively small set of exports. One hundred ninety million Brazilians will not. For countries such as Brazil, Mexico, Colombia, and Argentina, with large urban populations, diversified production bases, and important domestic markets, neither the return to the position of supplier of commodities nor the specialization in a small range of services or products are feasible options. Therefore, the rise of China means both a solution and a problem for those countries—a short-term solution due to the fact that the global demand for raw materials and food is picking up steam, but a mid-term problem, due to the fierce and increasing competition posed by Chinese manufacturers.

Both the definition and implementation of specific development strategies within this context have involved a slow process and, in my view, still an open one. Autarchy is surely out of the question. As for statism, not so much. My idea of the role the state should play in terms of development coincides with that of Alejandro Foxley (Chapter 4), but it is impossible to dismiss, as mere statistical outliers, the signs of strengthening of the state in several Latin American countries. The visions about the future of the region may come to vary not between capitalism and socialism, as occurred during the Cold War, or between dependence and autarchy, as in most of the twentieth century, but rather between different versions of liberal capitalism (or showing a trend towards social democracy, as I would prefer) and state capitalism. These are very distinct "roads to development," although they compete in the search for opportunities of integration in the global market. To some extent, this disjunctive is present in Brazil, where there have been attempts to reinvigorate forms of direct state intervention in infrastructure services, despite the insufficiency of public funds to finance the heavy investments required by the energy and transportation sectors, notably.

Once again, the abstract discussion of the virtues and flaws of each model seems to me out of focus. Liberal capitalism has historical development credentials beyond dispute in the Western world. The contemporary state capitalism found in places such as China, Russia, and Korea have proven to be aggressive and successful strategies, both in terms of domestic growth as well as in terms of access to external markets. However, as I see it, the gist of the matter does not lie in economic growth rates or indexes of human well-being, although they are both important. What is at stake is the *quality of the development*: what kind of society we are and what kind we wish to become. This involves not only levels of wealth but also values, satisfaction of material needs, and strengthening of cultural identities.

That is why I understand the importance of institutions in much the same way as other authors in this book, from different perspectives. Institutions are important not because of a specific effect on economic performance or public policies, but rather because of patterns of relationship that may modify or be reproduced within a society.

According to this point of view, the nationalization movements in Latin America can be very worrisome because of what lies under the promises of strengthening the domestic economy. On the one hand, the return to forms of authoritarianism and paternalism—with or without the explicit rupture of representative institutions, however, denying them popular support. On the other hand, the demoralization of the judicial institutions, which were fragile to begin with, in many cases denying democracy what is its very essence, that is, the sentiment that all people are equal under the law.

Other countries, with different cultures, under other circumstances, traded individual freedoms for domestic development with some level of success, in strictly economic terms at least. Latin America, despite seeing itself as occupying a marginal place in the Western world, is far too much a westerner—even if a part of the Far West, so to speak—to successfully reproduce this kind of transaction.

Mainwaring, Scully, and Cullell (Chapter 1) show that a healthy democracy, the individual liberty and judicial guarantees, the improvement of social indicators, and good economic performance walk hand in hand in our part of the world. So do bad results. This is an empirical correlation that does not apply to other regions, warn the authors. However, it can serve as a warning to our "neo-nationalizers." By dishonoring the democratic institutions to claim themselves as the sole supporters of the national and popular interests, they risk denying their fellow citizens both the freedom and the sustainable perspectives of development.

Our calling as a region—my personal faith—goes in the opposite direction, that of the pursuit of development with freedom, or development as freedom, in the words of Amartya Sen.

Notes

1. The opinions of Brazilian and North American specialists brought together by the University of Miami and the Fundação Getulio Vargas in late 1991 are representative of this vision. See Marks (1993).

2. Editors' note: The PRN (Party of National Reconstruction) was created by Collor de Mello as a vehicle for running for president in 1989. In the 1990 congressional elections, the PRN won only 40 of 503 lower chamber seats and 2 of 27 senate seats. It virtually disappeared after Collor de Mello's impeachment in 1992.

3. In 1990, elections were held for only one-third of the seats in the Senate.

4. Editors' note: The Real Plan was the economic stabilization plan introduced in 1994.

5. The implicit rule of this marriage was that the nominal expansion of revenue and the erosion of the real value of projected expenses guaranteed *a posteriori* a balanced budget, or something close to it, sparing the government and Congress the inconvenient task of negotiating *a priori* priorities and spending cuts.

6. Editors' note: According to the Economic Commission for Latin America and the Caribbean, Brazil's consumer inflation rate was 2489% in 1993. It declined to 22% by 1995, 9% in 1996, and 4% in 1997.

7. See the expositions of the motives for the Plan for Immediate Action, from July 1993, and of the measure that introduced the *real*, from July 1994. Both can be consulted on the following page from the Ministry of Finance's website: http://www.fazenda.gov.br/portugues/real/realhist.asp.

8. Editors' note: The 1988 Constitution runs a few hundred pages long in most editions.

9. Editors' note: For background on the state debts and state banks, see Abrucio (1998).

10. Mauricio Font spoke of a "structural realignment" to refer to the transformations in Brazil during this period (2003). For a balance sheet of reforms by Brazilian specialists, some of whom were active participants in their realization, see Giambiagi, Guilherme Reis, and Urani (2004).

11. The text of the Brazilian Constitution, including all amendments to date, can be consulted on the Presidency of the Republic's webpage: www.planalto. gov.br/ccivil_03/Constituicao/Constitui%E7ao.htm.

12. For the characterization of the Brazilian institutional system prior to 1964 as a "coalition presidential system," see Abranches (1988).

13. Editors' note: "Parochial amendments" are narrow, clientelistic budgetary amendments, designed to benefit members of congress and their constituents. They are roughly analogous to congressional earmarks in the United States.

14. See Graeff (2000).

15. See Mainwaring (1999).

16. Editors' note: The Lula government has been embroiled in some corruption scandals involving paying members of Congress for their legislative support.

17. Editors' note: In mixed proportional systems, some members of the assembly are elected in single-member districts while others are elected in multimember districts with proportional representation. See Shugart and Wattenberg (2001).

References

Abranches, Sérgio. 1988. Presidencialismo de Coalizão: O Dilema Institucional Brasileiro. *Dados* 31(1):5–33.

Abrucio, Fernando Luiz. 1998. *Os Barões da Federação: Os Governadores e a Redemocratização Brasileira*. São Paulo: Hucitec/Departamento de Ciência Política, USP.

Font, Mauricio. 2003. *Transforming Brazil: A Reform Era in Perspective*. Lanham, MD: Rowman & Littlefield.

Giambiagi, Fabio, José Guilherme Reis, and André Urani, eds. 2004. *Reformas no Brasil: Balanço e Agenda*. Rio de Janeiro: Editora Nova Fronteira.

Graeff, Eduardo. 2000. The flight of the beetle; Party politics and decision making process in the Cardoso government. Transl. Ted Goertzel. Paper prepared for the 5th Congress of the Brazilian Studies Association, Recife (Brazil), June. Available at: http://www.crab.rutgers.edu/~goertzel/flightofbeetle.htm.

Mainwaring, Scott. 1999. *Rethinking Party Systems in the Third Wave of Democratization: The Case of Brazil*. Stanford, CA: Stanford University Press.

Marks, Siegfried, ed. 1993. *Political Constraints on Brazil's Economic Development; Rio de Janeiro Conference edited proceedings and papers*. Coral Gables, FL: North-South Center Press.

Shugart, Matthew Soberg, and Martin P. Wattenberg, eds. 2001. *Mixed-Member Electoral Systems: The Best of Both Worlds?* Oxford: Oxford University Press.

PART THREE

Conclusion

CHAPTER ELEVEN

Democratic Governance in Latin America: Eleven Lessons from Recent Experience

SCOTT MAINWARING AND TIMOTHY R. SCULLY

☾

The third wave of democratization in Latin America began thirty years ago in the Dominican Republic. What have we learned about democratic governance in these three decades? And what does this volume teach us about democratic governance? We address these questions in this concluding chapter. These three decades have prompted many revisions in how social scientists and policy makers perceive democratic governance, but there have been few efforts to systematize lessons about the political aspects of democratic governance.

In this chapter, we present eleven conclusions about democratic governance based on contemporary Latin America. As is often the case in the social sciences and the policy world, research and debate generated as many questions and doubts as clear answers. Accordingly, we also highlight some of the unresolved critical debates related to these eleven conclusions. These conclusions represent our synthesis of major lessons that stem from recent Latin American experience. They are not necessarily shared by all of the authors in this volume, but the volume gives rise to these conclusions. Given our disciplinary backgrounds as political scientists, we focus on political aspects of democratic governance.[1]

1. *In most countries, creating effective democratic governance has proven far more difficult than most analysts anticipated in the early 1990s.* At that time, the Soviet Union had just collapsed. Many countries in

Latin America, the post-Soviet region, and Africa were experiencing political liberalization, and many were transitioning to democracy. These processes of regime change generated optimism among some scholars regarding future prospects for democracy. Expressive of this line of thinking, Francis Fukuyama's (1992) *The End of History and the Last Man* heralded the worldwide triumph of the ideal of liberal democracy. In another book that captured the optimism expressed in some circles, Di Palma (1990) argued that political craftsmanship could overcome the obstacles to democracy.

The early 1990s were also a period of optimism regarding Latin America's economic prospects. Most leading economists at that time expected that the market-oriented reforms that were well under way in most countries would catapult the region out of the dismal performance of the 1980s. Sebastian Edwards's 1995 book, *Crisis and Reform in Latin America: From Despair to Hope*, was an illustrative example, though it was more measured in its expectations than some work at that time.

Many analysts were aware that building democracies that governed effectively was going to be difficult in Latin America and in most countries that have undertaken regime transitions since 1978. Nevertheless, as several chapters (Mainwaring, Scully, and Vargas Cullell; Brinks; and Huber and Stephens) in this book show, the path toward building democracies that govern effectively has proven even more difficult than we imagined. If our yardstick is simply the survival of competitive political regimes, Di Palma (1990) was right to explicitly express optimism in his assessment of prospects for democracy. However, the difficulties in building democracies that function well have been great. In Latin America, many countries have remained stuck at low-quality democracies, with inadequate protection of rights and weak mechanisms of intrastate accountability. Guatemala, Paraguay, and Venezuela are semidemocratic, with even more serious limitations in democratic practice. Only three countries, Chile, Uruguay, and Costa Rica, are high quality democracies with generally solid rule of law, protection of rights, free and fair elections, and effective mechanisms of accountability of state agents. (See Table 11.1 for Freedom House scores in 2007.)

Chile alone has sustained a high rate of economic growth and of poverty reduction. Most countries in the region experienced almost no per capita growth between 1982 and 2002. Beyond Latin America, many countries that in the early 1990s appeared poised to undergo transitions to competitive political regimes have instead degenerated into competitive authoritarian regimes. Many democracies have failed to win the support of large numbers of citizens.

TABLE 11.1

Level of Democracy, State Capacity, and Satisfaction with Democracy in Latin America

	Combined Freedom House score, 2008	Rule of law, 2007	Control of corruption, 2007	Regulatory quality, 2007	Satisfaction with democracy, 2008
Argentina	10	−0.52	−0.45	−0.77	34
Bolivia	8	−0.96	−0.49	−1.18	33
Brazil	10	−0.44	−0.24	−0.04	38
Chile	12	1.17	1.35	1.45	39
Colombia	7	−0.57	−0.28	0.21	44
Costa Rica	12	0.44	0.39	0.49	44
Cuba	1	−0.79	−0.21	−1.63	No data
Dominican Republic	10	−0.55	−0.65	−0.15	47
Ecuador	8	−1.04	−0.87	−1.09	37
El Salvador	9	−0.68	−0.13	0.20	38
Guatemala	7	−1.11	−0.75	−0.15	27
Haiti	5	−1.42	−1.28	−0.86	No data
Honduras	8	−0.86	−0.69	−0.22	24
Mexico	9	−0.58	−0.35	0.39	23
Nicaragua	7	−0.84	−0.78	−0.40	39
Panama	11	−0.20	−0.34	0.39	35
Paraguay	8	−0.97	−0.96	−0.57	22
Peru	9	−0.71	−0.38	0.20	16
Uruguay	12	0.49	0.96	0.16	71
Venezuela	6	−1.47	−1.04	−1.56	49

Sources: Freedom House scores: www.freedomhouse.org. We inverted the combined score for civil liberties and political rights. Twelve is the best combined inverted score; zero is the worst.

Rule of law: Daniel Kaufmann, Aart Kraay, and Massimo Mastruzzi, "Governance Matters VII: Aggregate and Individual Governance Indicators, 1996–2007," The World Bank, June 2008, pp. 91–93. Available at www.worldbank.org.

Control of corruption: Kaufmann et al. (2008: 94–96).

Regulatory quality: Kaufmann et al. (2008: 88–90).

Satisfaction with democracy: Corporación Latinobarómetro, Informe 2008, p. 107. Available at www.latinobarometro.org.

In the greater sweep of the history of democratization, countless attempts at building effective democracies failed. In contrast to the past, however, very few competitive political regimes in Latin America have suffered overt breakdowns. A new pattern has emerged in the third wave of democratization in Latin America. Governmental instability has been rampant, but even weak competitive regimes have rarely succumbed to breakdowns (Pérez-Liñán 2007; Valenzuela 2004). Democratically elected presidents or their constitutional successors have resigned under pressure or been ousted in Argentina (1989, 2001, and 2002), Haiti (1991), Brazil (1992), Venezuela (1993), Guatemala (1993), Ecuador (1997, 2000, and 2005), Paraguay (1999), Bolivia (2003 and 2005), and Haiti (1991, 2004). But the only clear breakdowns of competitive regimes occurred in Peru in 1992 and in Haiti in 1991 and 2004.

This combination of glaring deficiencies in achieving effective democratic governance and the ongoing persistence of competitive regimes is unprecedented in the world history of democracy. In no other region and at no other time have competitive regimes survived as long as they did in Latin America in the 1980s and 1990s in the face of grinding poverty and poor government performance. This phenomenon of competitive regimes that endure despite poor governance ran counter to the expectations of most policy makers and social scientists well into the 1990s (Mainwaring 1999b). For democratic leaders and citizens of the region, the foremost question is no longer how to avoid democratic breakdowns or erosions—although these issues are certainly not off the table—but rather how to promote effective governance under competitive regimes.

What is less immediately obvious is why it has been so difficult to build high quality democracies. First, as O'Donnell (1993, 1999) has forcefully underscored, in much of Latin America, state weakness has been a major obstacle to building decent democracies. Weak states cannot enforce rights, and where citizens cannot claim their legally enshrined rights, democracy is impaired. Weak states cannot deter corruption, and indeed they serve as a fertile breeding ground for it. In this volume, Daniel Brinks advances similar reasoning.

Second, gross social inequalities and poverty make it difficult for large numbers of individuals to participate effectively in politics. Formal political rights have expanded greatly in the post-1978 wave of democratization, but poverty and huge social chasms undercut the capacity of poor people to be full-fledged democratic citizens. These individuals are more susceptible to clientelistic exchanges that hamper building an effective, high-quality democracy (UNDP 2005). Evelyne Huber and John Stephens write about related issues in this volume.

Third, some powerful political actors are ambivalent or worse about further democratization. While almost all actors in contemporary Latin America express rhetorical support for democracy, governing elites often resist being bound by democratic checks and balances. Rather than accept these constraints, they undermine democracy. Some presidents such as Hugo Chávez justify undermining liberal democracy ostensibly in the name of direct democracy. Others such as Alberto Fujimori in Peru (1990–2000) and Carlos Menem in Argentina (1989–1999) claimed that weakening and eliminating checks and balances was needed to remove sclerotic self-interested actors and to deal with grave crises. Powerful local and regional elites often subvert democracy, preferring to rule in unfettered fashion (Gibson 2005; Hagopian 1996; O'Donnell 1993).

Finally, the initial economic conditions for most competitive regimes in Latin America in the post-1978 period presented difficult challenges. In the aftermath of the great debt crisis of 1982, most Latin American countries suffered through extremely high inflation and prolonged economic stagnation. These parlous economic circumstances coupled with the pains of adjusting to marked oriented approaches to economic development crippled most of the new democracies for an extended time.

2. *The volume underscores the tremendous diversity of outcomes in contemporary Latin America.*   This point goes against a common tendency to understate diversity and overgeneralize for the region. Most Latin American countries converged around three macro trends in the 1980s and 1990s: toward competitive political regimes, toward more open and stable economies, and toward mediocre government performance. These convergences have sometimes overshadowed the diversity in the region. We developed this theme at length in Chapter 1. Given these variations in regime performance, scholars and policy makers make generalizations about success in democratic governance for the region as a whole at peril.

Four other chapters in this volume underscore the diversity in outcomes. In Chapter 5, Evelyne Huber and John Stephens show that Argentina, Chile, Costa Rica, and Uruguay stand out from the rest of Latin America in terms of their social policies and results. Poverty is much lower in these four countries than in the rest of the region. Inequalities are not as pronounced in Argentina, Costa Rica, and Uruguay as elsewhere. Adult literacy rates are highest in these three countries and Chile. The social gap between these four countries and the poorest ones is very substantial.

In Chapter 6, Daniel Brinks underscores stunning differences in how effective states are at discouraging police homicides and at prosecuting those responsible for them. On a per capita basis, police commit more than sixty times as many homicides in the city of Salvador, Brazil than in Uruguay. Conviction rates of police who kill are more than ten times greater in Uruguay than in Salvador. Combining these two effects, the police are more than 600 times greater to kill and get away with it in Salvador than in Uruguay. As Brinks argues, these data underline dramatic differences in the efficacy and evenness of the rule of law.

In Chapter 7, Patricio Navia and Ignacio Walker call attention to sharp cross-national differences in the strength of political institutions and the prevalence of populism in the region. Finally, in Chapter 8, Alan Angell underscores the resounding success Chile has experienced since 1990 along most dimensions of democratic governance. This success story stands in sharp contrast to the experience in many other countries.

3. Market-oriented economic policies are necessary but not sufficient for success in today's global economy. This perspective is consistent with mainstream thinking at the Inter-American Development Bank and the World Bank and among many leading economists today (Birdsall and de la Torre 2001; Forteza and Tomassi 2005; Kuczynski 2003; Naím 1994, 2000; Williamson 2003). What our volume offers relative to this mainstream thinking is 1) intelligent nuancing of this perspective by the three prominent economists who wrote chapters; and 2) some fruitful disagreements among them.

The broad policy parameters that José De Gregorio proposes in Chapter 2 are consistent with market-oriented policies. He argues that trade openness, especially in small economies, is more likely to promote economic growth (see also Alcalá and Ciccone 2004; Edwards 1995, 115–69) and to reduce poverty. In this sense, he agrees with the earlier prescription of the Washington Consensus, but he adds the important caveat that "good institutions are needed for trade liberalization to be effective in promoting growth" (see also World Bank 2005, 131–53).

Francisco Rodríguez is less sanguine that market-oriented policies will pave the road to a bright economic future. He argues in Chapter 3 that it is not clear that the policies prescribed by the Washington Consensus foster growth. He concludes that "development thinking should be specific to a country's institutional and structural characteristics and that thinking about a 'list' of policy prescriptions to apply to a broad group of developing economies is methodologically erroneous." He advocates relying "on local, case-specific knowledge for designing growth strategies. One size does not fit all in terms of policy reform, and not recognizing this is likely to lead to frequent missteps in the search for economic growth." He questions the econometric support for claims that trade

openness is favorable to economic growth (see also Rodríguez and Rodrik 2001; Rodrick et al. 2004) and argues that good policies are highly
context dependent (see also Rodrik 2003).

Rodríguez's chapter challenges mainstream economics in two respects. First, he questions conventional growth regressions, which are
the basis of De Gregorio's chapter and of much conventional wisdom in
growth economics. But he does so not from an anti-quantitative bias or
from normative predilections that animate some critics of mainstream
economics, but rather on the basis of careful econometric analysis of
the assumptions that go into growth regressions. Second, few prominent
economists would go as far in eschewing general policy prescriptions and
arguing that good policy is case specific.

Notwithstanding differences between De Gregorio and Rodríguez,
they converge on some important themes. De Gregorio, who supports
trade openness, nevertheless shows that on average, it produces scant
to modest growth benefits. In his Table 2.4, the effect of trade openness
on growth is marginal. He estimates that if Latin America had the same
trade openness as the world average, per capita growth would have been
an additional 0.2% per year higher than it was.[2] Insufficient openness
therefore accounted for only a small part of Latin America's underper-
formance. Moreover, whereas some earlier advocates saw trade openness
as unequivocally beneficial, for De Gregorio, it generates higher growth
only if a country has solid institutions (see also Rodrik et al. 2004).

Some parts of the Latin American left have pointed to the tepid
results of the 1990s and the early part of this decade as proof that
market-oriented approaches do not work. However, in the aftermath
of the debt crisis of the 1980s, Latin American countries had no alternative but to implement stabilization policies in order to tame raging
inflation. Moreover, as the 1980s and the 1990s wore on, countries
that maintained statist nationalistic policies and ignored the tenets of
the Washington Consensus fared poorly economically. Examples include Argentina from 1983 to 1989, Bolivia from 1982 to 1985, Brazil
from 1985 until 1990, and Peru from 1985 to 1990. Like Alejandro
Foxley, Patricio Navia and Ignacio Walker, and José De Gregorio in
this volume, we believe it is very unlikely that statist economic policies
will pave the way toward a brighter future. Modern economies are too
complex, and markets are too powerful, for highly statist approaches
to be successful.

To some observers, the phenomenal growth performance of the Venezuelan economy since 2004 might suggest that highly statist policies can
succeed. However, it is unlikely that President Chávez can sustain this
strong record. The very high growth rates in these years were fueled by

a dramatic increase in oil prices. The high growth in 2004–2005 also represented compensation for the sharp economic downturn in 2002–2003,[3] but this compensatory effect is probably exhausted.

Arguing that a general orientation toward the market is necessary for success does not mean that reliance on the market always succeeds or is always the best course of action. No credible evidence supports this viewpoint, and there is evidence to the contrary, including the chapter by Francisco Rodríguez in this volume (see also Rodrik 2000). For example, as De Gregorio notes, financial liberalization does not always produce beneficial results; some markets do not work efficiently and require regulation. Contrary to the facile assumption of some observers who decry Chile's putatively neoliberal policies, Chile's post-1990 success can be attributed in part to a strong state. Also contrary to this assumption, Chile has one of the highest percentages of tax revenue as a share of GDP in Latin America.[4]

If an orientation toward the market is crucial in today's world economy, the Latin American experience underscores that it is not sufficient (Easterly 2001; Easterly and Levine 2003; Rodríguez, this volume; Rodrik et al. 2004; Williamson 2003). The mediocre economic performance that most countries experienced in the aftermath of profound market-oriented reform until 2003 highlighted this point. Many countries that undertook sweeping economic reforms faltered in the late 1990s and early this decade (e.g., Argentina 1999–2002, Bolivia 1999–2002, Peru 1998–2001, Mexico 1995 and 2001–2003). Well after deep market-oriented economic reform in most of Latin America, the region suffered from a prolonged economic stagnation from 1998 to 2002. The earlier optimism that the Washington Consensus provided a recipe for success faded (Easterly 2001; Williamson 2003). This tepid growth performance shattered the brief-lived hegemony of the "Washington Consensus," and it raised new and difficult questions about how to foster growth and social improvements in an era of globalization. Our volume does not resolve these important issues,[5] but it presents a fascinating portrait of the current state of the debate.

4. The quality of institutions is important for effective democratic governance. This theme, which echoes much recent work in economics, cuts across the chapters of De Gregorio, Rodríguez, Foxley, Brinks, Navia and Walker, and Angell, among others. For De Gregorio and Rodríguez, quality institutions help foster economic growth. Foxley argues that an effective state is key for economic growth. Brinks shows that effective institutions (especially the police and courts) help protect citizens' lives, ensure citizen rights, and prosecute police wrongdoing. Angell claims that one of the pillars of Chile's post-1990 success is its long legacy of solid institutions.

Our volume poses more questions than definitive answers about the impact of institutions. In particular, it raises questions about which institutions are most important for democratic governance, how to build those institutions, and how economists have measured the effects of institutions.

In recent years, many prominent economists have emphasized the importance of institutions in fostering economic growth (Acemoglu et al. 2001; Easterly and Levine 2003; Hall and Jones 1999; Knack and Keefer 1995; North 1990; Rodrik 2000, 2003; Rodrik et al. 2004; Spiller and Tomassi 2003).[6] The World Bank (2002, 2005) has also emphasized institutions in its recent publications. But the recent work in economics on institutions does not take us very far because it is not clear in this work which institutions are important. For example, Nobel Prize winner Douglass North argued that institutions "are the underlying determinant of the long-run performance of economies. . . . Third World countries arepoor because the institutional constraints define a set of payoffs to political/economic activity that do not encourage productive activity" (1990, 107, 110). He defines institutions in a very expansive way as "the rules of the game in a society or, more formally, the humanly devised constraints that shape human behavior" (3). He explicitly includes both informal and formal constraints in his conception of institutions. "Codes of conduct, norms of behavior, and conventions" (36) are thus institutions. With this expansive definition, the argument that institutions are the main long-run determinants of economic growth is nebulous. Cultural norms and formal institutions both count as institutional factors that could explain differences in development outcomes. Yet it is one thing to say that a central bank's norms regarding financial transactions (or electoral rules, to take another example of a formal institution) affect development outcomes and quite another to claim that cultural norms influence them. Many cultural norms are far less susceptible to change than formal institutions through policy intervention. North's definition encompasses so much that it dilutes the potentially interesting claim that institutions are the main long run determinant of growth.

Most of the interesting recent quantitative work by renowned economists uses blunt and questionable measures of institutions that fail to give us leverage in understanding what institutions affect growth. Acemoglu et al. (2001) use settler mortality rates as an instrument for institutional quality. Settler mortality rates, however, intrinsically have nothing to do with institutional quality, and they tell us nothing about which institutions produce beneficent effects.[7] To measure institutional quality, Easterly and Levine (2003), Dollar and Kraay (2003), and Rodrik et al. (2004) use Kaufmann et al.'s (2003, 2005, 2006) scores, which measure perceptions of the rule of law, control of corruption, voice and accountability, regulatory quality, political stability, and government effectiveness.

Kaufmann et al.'s measures provide very useful information about how actors perceive important governance issues, but they are not measures of institutional quality. None of their six measures are institutions as North (1990) and most economists define institutions, nor can they be taken as reasonable proxies for institutions. Their measures are instead likely to be *effects* of institutions.[8] In short, the focus on the effect of institutions on economic growth is promising, but we need a better way to disaggregate and measure institutions.

Although our volume does not definitively resolve which institutions are most important for good governance, it offers some partial answers by calling attention to the importance of the state and of institutionalized party systems. These partial answers give some specificity to the institutional black box. In their chapter, Navia and Walker push the emphasis on institutions in another direction, namely, to counterpose solid institutions to populist political leadership, which is based on an unmediated direct relationship between a political leader and his/her followers. We agree with them that populism is one of the great temptations and challenges for democracy in Latin America (see also Viola and Leis 2007).

5. *Effective states are important for successful democratic governance.* A capable state is important for successful democratic governance. Without an effective state, neither democracy nor development will flourish. An effective state is important for democracy because the state must protect citizens, uphold their rights, and oversee fair and free elections (Linz and Stepan 1996, 16–37; Mainwaring 2006; O'Donnell 1993). An effective state is important for development because the state must provide decent public education, regulate some arenas of the economy, create an infrastructure that enables investors to make good use of natural and human resources, combat corruption, and ensure property rights, among many other functions (Foxley, this volume; Evans 1995; Evans and Rauch 1999; Fukuyama 2004; Kucyznski 2003; Naím 1994; Wolff and Castro 2003, 198–208).

These observations seem commonplace today. But consider the conventional wisdom that prevailed from the mid-1980s through the mid-1990s. State bashers were so eager to shrink the state that they failed to appreciate how important it is for democracy and for economic performance. Many reforms in the 1990s dismantled the state rather than striving to build a more efficient and effective state (Naím 1994). This anti-state bias still holds considerable sway in some policy circles in Washington. Relearning how important the state is for democracy and development has been one of the fundamental lessons of the third wave.

In most of Latin America, parts of the state are highly deficient. As Thomas Hobbes wrote in his classic, *Leviathan*, published in 1651, the state's primordial task is to protect citizens to ensure that life does not turn into a "solitary, poor, nasty, brutish, and short" free-for-all. In most countries of the region, the state has performed this task of protecting citizens poorly, as Daniel Brinks forcefully underscores in this volume. Crime rates are a huge problem in most Latin American countries. The Pan American Health Organization (2006, 7) reported that in the 1980s, homicides accounted for 11% of all deaths in Guatemala, compared to 0.03% in England. By this measure, homicides were a staggering 360 times more frequent in Guatemala than in England. Criminal gangs have displaced the state in the shantytowns of many cities. The police enter these areas infrequently and at their own peril unless the gangs have bought them off.

In much of the region, legal systems are precarious, inefficient, and corrupt, a point underscored by Brinks. States are not capable of, and in many cases are not interested in, enforcing equal rights for all citizens (Brinks 2008; Dodson and Jackson 2003; O'Donnell 1999). States' regulatory capacity in most countries is poor, and public investments in infrastructure have lagged. In addition, as Huber and Stephens note in this volume, states' ability to protect and enable citizens through social policy is fragile in most countries.

Calling attention to the state's importance for democracy and development helps frame the way social scientists and policy makers think about issues.[9] It is a contrast to some thinking about the state in the 1990s.

Three of the governance indicators developed by Daniel Kaufmann and his colleagues (2007) at the World Bank—their measures for rule of law, control of corruption, and regulatory quality—provide useful measures of perceptions of state capacity (see Table 11.1). According to these measures, most Latin American states exhibit some areas of pronounced weakness. Of the twenty Latin American countries, in 2007, only Chile scored at least half a standard deviation higher than the world mean on regulatory quality, while seven scored at least half a standard deviation worse than the world mean. For rule of law, only Chile and Costa Rica scored at least a half standard deviation above the world mean, and fifteen Latin American countries scored at least a half standard deviation below the world mean. In control of corruption, only Chile and Uruguay were more than a half standard deviation above the world mean; eight countries were more than a half standard deviation below it.

One contributing factor to state deficiencies in many countries is inadequate tax revenue. According to recent estimates, nine Latin American countries had tax revenue below 15% of GDP for the central government: El Salvador (14.2%), Panama (14.2%), Costa Rica (13.6%), Ecuador (13.4%), Paraguay (13.0%), Venezuela (12.6%), Mexico (11.0%), Guatemala (9.8%), and Haiti (9.7%). Costa Rica compensates for the low tax share of the central government with significant tax revenues for other levels of government; total tax revenues accounted for 20.5% of GDP in 2005 (CEPAL 2008). The other countries, however, have weak *total* (i.e., central government plus other levels of government) tax shares. To place these numbers in comparative perspective, the average total tax revenue for fifteen European Union countries circa 2003 was 40.6%. The U.S. and Japan, both low taxation countries, allocated 26.4% and 25.8%, respectively, of GDP to total taxes. Tax revenue as a share of GDP was even substantially lower in most Latin American countries in 1990 than today. High taxes are not necessary for democracy and development,[10] but at very low levels of tax revenue, the state cannot function adequately.

Privatizing some parts of the state was desirable in the 1980s and 1990s, but other parts of the state needed more resources and attention: education and health, the police, the judiciary, regulatory agencies, and infrastructure, among others (Naím 1994). As Foxley argues in his chapter in this volume, states can help to generate an environment conducive to creativity, entrepreneurship, investment, and the development of human resources—all key pillars of economic growth and social opportunities. States must possess sufficient flexibility to respond to opportunities and build effective national networks capable of meeting the rapidly changing challenges of the global market. And as Huber and Stephens argue in their chapter, state policies are crucial in reducing poverty and creating human capital (see also Birdsall and Székely 2003; Valenzuela 2006).

Underscoring positive effects of an effective state, of course, does not mean that all state action is beneficial. States can be predatory, and they can create perverse incentive systems that lead to bad collective outcomes. The desire to avoid these pernicious consequences, however, should not blind social scientists and policy makers to the importance of state building. State *building* reduces opportunities for predation by creating stronger mechanisms to thwart it.

Saying that the state is important does not resolve one of the great questions facing contemporary Latin America: how to build an effective state. This issue needs further research, but two conclusions are clear. First, having adequate tax revenue is a necessary but not sufficient condition for an effective state. This conclusion does not suggest a blanket prescription of increasing taxes and expenditures in all low revenue countries. In the poor countries of Latin America, patrimonial practices and public sector corruption are pervasive (Guevara Mann forthcoming; O'Donnell 1996). A significant portion of tax revenue ends up enriching politicians and their allies rather than promoting public investment and goods. Under these circumstances, greater tax revenue does not produce commensurately greater public goods. Second, in agreement with Navia and Walker, populism—understood as an unmediated relationship between a political leader and the masses—and state building are in mutual tension (see also Viola and Leis 2007). Populist leaders typically focus on political expedience and on cultivating popular support, not on the difficult choices and technical expertise that build a more effective state.

Social scientists and policy analysts have devised innovative suggestions for enhancing state efficacy in social policy (Birdsall and Székely 2003). We know less about how to develop more functional legal systems and police forces, two parts of the state that in most of Latin America perform poorly. As Brinks notes in his chapter in this volume, these parts of the state are crucial for citizen rights and well-being. We also know relatively little about how to construct the political conditions that make for more effective states.

In this volume, Alejandro Foxley makes a forceful case for the state's role in development. In their chapter on social policy, Huber and Stephens also call attention to the state's fundamental importance in fostering good collective outcomes. Daniel Brinks does likewise in his chapter on the rule of law. Alan Angell attributes Chile's success largely to the strength of its state institutions.

6. Institutionalized party systems facilitate effective democratic governance. The fact that parties are indispensable actors in mass democracy has long been established. The specific idea that party system institutionalization is important in effective democratic governance is a product of the third wave of democratization.

An institutionalized party system has four characteristics (Mainwaring 1999a; Mainwaring and Scully 1995; Mainwaring and Torcal 2006). First, patterns of interparty competition are relatively stable. Second, most voters develop relatively stable attachments to parties. Third, parties acquire legitimacy as the vehicles for accessing state power. Finally, party organizations acquire some solidity; parties are not merely the appendages of personalistic political leaders.

Institutionalized party systems offer three benefits for democratic governance. First, they provide structure to democratic politics in the electoral arena. The same parties are the main electoral contenders over a period of time, and this stability generates moderate predictability in how political actors behave and in the range of policy choices. This situation makes it more difficult for anti-party political outsiders to come to power. Anti-party political outsiders are less bound by the existing formal institutions and the rules of the game. Indeed, most are hostile to those formal institutions and rules of the game. Their hostility to the rules of the game often entails violating or encroaching upon democratic practice and constraints. Their political style also makes radical policy shifts and erratic leadership more likely. Under these circumstances actors are more likely to function with a short-term logic that is inimical to deal making and coalition building.

Weakly institutionalized or fluid party systems pave the path for populist politicians, who characteristically degrade other institutions and weaken democratic governance. Fluid party systems introduce more uncertainty regarding electoral outcomes. The turnover from one party to others is higher, the entry barriers to new parties are lower, and the likelihood that personalistic anti-system politicians can become the head of government is much higher. Such uncertainty proved inimical to democracy until the 1980s, when the end of the Cold War reduced the stakes of political conflict and facilitated the post-1989 expansion of democracy and semi-democracy in the world. Even in the post-Cold War context, the personalism in weakly institutionalized party systems has paved the way toward authoritarianism (e.g., President Alberto Fujimori in Peru in 1992) or toward the erosion of democratic or semi-democratic regimes (e.g., President Hugo Chávez in Venezuela since 1999) (Mayorga 2006; Tanaka 2006).

Second, institutionalized parties are also the primary actors within legislatures (Aldrich 1995). They foster greater accountability of political leaders to the party, and they are associated with stronger legislatures and the advantages that they provide for democracy. Although autocrats often claim that stronger parties and legislatures are a hindrance to governance, they are an asset for *democratic* governance. Parties organize support for and against policy proposals in the legislature. Organizing legislative support through parties is the most efficient way to govern democratically in anything but a very small legislature.

Third, moderately institutionalized party systems provide structure to democratic politics. This structuring of democratic politics, and the fact that most parties have strong incentives to preserve the democratic rules of the game, generates some incentives for actors to develop longer time horizons. Weak parties and populist leaders are less bound by the rules of the game. According to O'Donnell (1994) and Tanaka (2005), under these circumstances actors are more likely to function with a short-term logic that is inimical to deal making and coalition building.

Two chapters suggest the importance of institutionalized party systems. Navia and Walker argue that a crucial difference between the more successful cases of democratic governance and the less successful cases is that the former rest on stronger democratic institutions, including party systems. In his chapter on Chile, Angell argues that solid institutions including the party system underpin that country's success in the post-1990 period.

7. No set of formal institutions is clearly superior to others for ensuring successful democratic governance. In the 1980s and 1990s, some pioneering works argued that specific formal political institutions have decisive and consistent advantages over others for democratic governance. Yet two decades of impressive cumulative learning about political institutions have not produced easy recipes about the "best" institutions or institutional combinations. The impact of formal political institutions such as electoral rules, nominating procedures, and presidentialism on macro level outcomes such as economic growth and the efficacy of social policy are more conditional and less clear than many political scientists anticipated (see also IDB 2005).

Formal political institutions have important effects on democracy. Political scientists have examined the effects of electoral rules (Ames 2001; Pizarro 2006), federalism (Jones 1997; Samuels 2003; Stepan 2001, 315–61), nomination rules (Moreno et al. 2003), formal presidential powers (Carey and Shugart 1998; Figueiredo and Limongi 1999; Shugart and Carey 1992; Shugart and Mainwaring 1997), and the number of veto players (Ames 2001; Haggard and McCubbins 2001; Tsebelis 2002) on different aspects of democratic politics. These works have generated an impressive cumulative knowledge about the effects of political institutions. This emphasis on formal political institutions as a key to development has influenced some of the international financial institutions, especially the Inter-American Development Bank (2000, with the International Institute for Democracy and Electoral Assistance, 2002).

Juan Linz's work (1994) on the perils of presidentialism is a prominent example of work that argued for the decisive superiority of some formal institutions over others. Linz argued that presidentialism was inimical to stable democracy and that parliamentary systems were better equipped to foster democratic consolidation. Some of his arguments have ongoing merit, but today there is less agreement that presidentialism is clearly inferior in supporting stable democracy. One reason for the declining consensus about the perils of presidentialism is that all countries in Latin America have retained presidential or quasi-presidential systems, and yet there have been only three full breakdowns of competitive political regimes since 1978: Peru in 1992 and Haiti in 1991 and 1999. In addition, some scholars argued that the virtues and defects of presidentialism depend on how it interacts with other institutional arrangements (Cheibub 2007; Shugart and Carey 1992; Shugart and Mainwaring 1997).

Most scholars who work on political institutions in Latin America today offer more tempered arguments about the effects of presidentialism than Linz (1994) did. In a similar vein, whether institutional systems with multiple checks of balances or one in which a majority can easily set new policies is better depends on how well the system is functioning (Tsebelis 2002). If a system with powerful checks and balances is functioning well, then having multiple powerful veto players has advantages because it is more difficult to overturn effective policies. But if the system is limping along and producing poor policy results, then a multiplicity of powerful veto players is likely to thwart necessary reforms.

We are skeptical that reforming formal political institutions is the primary key to success and failure in contemporary Latin America.[11] Many institutional reforms that were intended to enhance democracy, especially its participatory aspects, have had deleterious effects on governance capacity. For example, the Colombian constitution of 1991 opened what had been a restricted democracy by creating new channels of participation and opening political competition. The new constitution achieved these meritorious objectives, but it paid insufficient attention to state building and facilitated the erosion of Colombia's traditional parties and the growing "atomization" of the party system (Bejarano and Pizarro 2005; Pizarro 2006).[12]

Electoral laws cannot explain major differences in governmental success from one administration to the next when there has been no major change in the institutional rules of the game—for example, from the innovative and partly successful Sánchez de Lozada government in Bolivia (1993–1997) to the succession of failed governments between 1997 and 2005,[13] or from the poor performances of three governments between 1985 and 1993 in Brazil to the more successful governments of Fernando Henrique Cardoso (1995–2003) and Lula da Silva (2003–present).

In his contribution to this volume, Fernando Henrique Cardoso makes a compelling argument that electoral reform was not a necessary condition to realize more success in Brazil (see also Tanaka 2005). According to Cardoso and contrary to the conventional wisdom in Brazil in the early 1990s, it was not essential to first undertake institutional reform in order to tame inflation. Cardoso argues instead that at times windows of opportunity present themselves (sometimes as a result of a crisis), allowing political leaders the autonomy and capacity to implement lasting reform. He may be leaning here on what Hirschman (1963) called a "blessing in disguise." Cardoso argues that hyperinflation provided the opportunity for real reform by creating a widespread desire to defeat inflation and willingness to bear the costs of doing so if a credible stabilization plan emerged.[14]

The impact of formal institutions such as electoral rules, nominating rules, presidents' constitutional powers, and federal arrangements on macro level outcomes is mediated by other factors. Moreover, formal political institutions do not always have the consequences that one would anticipate based on deductive reasoning (Helmke and Levitsky 2006; Levitsky and Murillo 2005; O'Donnell 1996; Weyland 2002a). For example, Hagopian, Gervasoni, and Moraes (2009) show that Brazilian politicians have become more party-centric over time despite many formal political institutions that favor an individualistic orientation (see also Figueiredo and Limongi 1999). Helmke and Levitsky (2006) present many other examples in which informal institutions counteract the effects of formal political institutions.[15]

8. *Successful democratic governance is context dependent.*   Many factors combine to produce success or failure in democratic governance. Latin America's recent experience leads to the conclusion that it is the specific combination of these factors—rather than discrete individual policies or specific formal institutions—that is important. Changing discrete policies or formal institutions in an effort to reproduce successful cases therefore does not ensure success. Indeed, depending on the context, it can even lead to failure. However, our emphasis on context specificity does not preclude the idea that some policies, practices, and institutions are more likely to foster success than others.

This emphasis on context runs contrary to the prevailing wisdom in the early 1990s. Most proponents of the Washington Consensus envisioned general policy descriptions that would spur economic growth. One cannot simply prescribe success for one country based on what has worked in another, or for that matter based on what has worked for a large number of countries on average (that is, based on quantitative results). Success depends on the institutional context and other country-specific factors.

The volume raises fascinating and contentious questions as to whether and how much social scientists can draw generalizable (as opposed to context specific) conclusions about democratic governance. Francisco

Rodríguez, Evelyne Huber and John Stephens, and Alan Angell force-fully develop arguments about context specificity in this volume (see also Rodrik 2003). Francisco Rodríguez writes skeptically about the feasibility of drawing general lessons in economic policy making. He argues that we cannot be confident that even such a basic idea as open markets are beneficial for economic growth. He asserts that policy success is highly contingent upon context. Growth regressions in economics violate crucial econometric assumptions, making it impossible to draw any conclusions about the beneficent effects of some policies over others. Huber and Stephens affirm that the same social policies have different effects in different contexts. Angell claims that other countries cannot easily reproduce Chile's success in contemporary Latin America because the political and institutional conditions that made for Chile's success are unique. What worked in Chile might not work in another context.

An emphasis on context specificity is in partial tension with the Washington Consensus of the early 1990s.[16] At the time, advocates of market-oriented economic reform generally believed that the path to success consisted of following some presumably generalizable policy prescriptions.

Nineteen years after Williamson (1990) published his influential work on the Washington Consensus,[17] the optimism that even some quite general policy prescriptions would pave the way toward success has faded. A striking expression of this change in orientation is the IDB's recent volume (2005), *The Politics of Policies: Economic and Social Progress in Latin America*, which expressed deep skepticism about generic policy prescriptions. A 2005 World Bank publication similarly emphasized that effective policy is context dependent. North (1990), Rodrik et al. (2004), Rodrik (2000, 2003), and Rodríguez (this volume) make converging arguments, as did Hirschman (1963, 1971) decades ago.

We wonder, however, whether the pendulum has shifted too much toward emphasizing context specificity in some recent work (e.g., IDB 2005). As De Gregorio argues in his chapter, it would be a mistake to retreat completely from the idea that some policies are more likely to succeed than others. A cookie-cutter model, by which it is easy to export success from one country to the next, is clearly misleading. Nevertheless, success in democratic governance is not entirely idiosyncratic; some policies and institutions are more likely to succeed than others.

Recognizing that the path to success is context dependent is compatible with arguing that some kinds of policies and institutions are more likely to produce success than others, or that successful democratic governance is not entirely context dependent or idiosyncratic. The past twenty-five years of efforts to build democracy and foster development suggest some broad lessons and orientations, even if the specific applicability of these broad orientations depends on context. Several chapters in this volume exemplify a fruitful combination of attention to context and awareness that some policies have been more likely than others to produce success in most contexts. For example, José De Gregorio's chapter points to some broad policy directions that are more favorable to success than other approaches. His evidence shows that trade openness *on average* provides a boost to economic growth (see also Alcalá and Ciccone 2004). This does not imply that trade openness in every country will favor greater economic growth; De Gregorio comments that the benefits of openness accrue mainly to countries with solid institutions. Foxley advocates a central role for both the market and the state in promoting economic growth, and in this respect, he shares with De Gregorio a view that some broad policy orientations (market-orientation, for example) are more likely to be successful than others. Most of Williamson's (1990) ten tenets of the Washington Consensus remain sound policy principles today, especially if they are combined with his additional suggestions (2003) published thirteen years later (see also Birdsall and de la Torre 2001).

Clearly, there are no easy recipes for successful democratic governance. A critical challenge for scholars and policy analysts is to discern what broad lessons can be distilled about successful democratic governance and when such seeming lessons are in fact context dependent and should not be generalized. The debate about how much one can generalize and how much is context specific runs throughout this volume.

9. Historical legacies shape the prospects for the subsequent success of democratic governance. However, countries also have opportunities to break from the past and to establish new regime dynamics. Both of these points appear in far bolder relief today than was the case before the 1990s. The first point runs counter to analyses in the early 1990s that exaggerated the role of political craftsmanship and leadership (e.g., Di Palma 1990). These voluntaristic approaches understated the effects of unfavorable historical legacies such weak states and stark inequalities. The second point stands in contrast to work that saw Latin America as mired in an authoritarian Iberian culture (Wiarda 2001), and it also diverges from strong versions of path dependent arguments.

The power of historical legacies to shape current success is witnessed by the three countries that today enjoy the highest levels of democracy in Latin America—Chile, Costa Rica, and Uruguay. These three countries had the strongest and longest democratic heritages as of 1973. After periods of harsh military rule in Chile (1973–1990) and Uruguay

(1973–1984), both countries rejoined Costa Rica as high-level democracies. The past history of institutionalized party systems, functional states, and a more democratic political culture enabled both countries to rebuild democracy after authoritarian rule. This outcome was not preordained. The military regimes in Chile and to some degree Uruguay attempted to radically change the political systems. In the years shortly after the transition to democracy (1990) in Chile, some analysts believe that the negotiations that made a transition possible would shackle the new democracy. Yet in relatively short order, both countries rebuilt democracy. Effective leadership and effective policies (especially in Chile) contributed to this positive outcome, but the previous democratic regime built a democratic capital that facilitated the path. No other country in Latin America except Costa Rica has succeeded equally at building high-level democracy.

Other countries' political regimes exhibit both profound change and yet some notable limits to change in their political regimes. With the exception of Cuba, in the post-1978 wave of democratization, the Latin American countries with strong authoritarian heritages have established competitive and reasonably free and fair elections. But they have not created high-quality democracies, established the rule of law successfully, or reined in corruption. The past patrimonial nature of many states under authoritarian rule has impeded the development of high-level democracies. This group of countries with pervasive authoritarian pasts until at least the 1980s includes El Salvador, Nicaragua, Paraguay, Guatemala, and Haiti.

Some other countries have escaped negative historic legacies of political regimes. After more than half a century (1930–1983) of shifting between unstable authoritarianism and unstable democracy, Argentina has developed a stable democratic *regime*, notwithstanding periodic episodes of *governmental* instability, most notably in 2001–2002, and despite the authoritarian instincts of the Kirchners.

Conversely, a successful past does not always set the stage for successful democratic governance today. From 1958 until the late 1970s, Venezuela had a stable and relatively vibrant democracy. Poor economic performance, corruption, and internecine leadership battles weakened Venezuela's democratic regime, ultimately making possible the election of Hugo Chávez in 1998 (Coppedge 2005). Chávez, in turn, has deliberately undermined Venezuela's democratic institutions. The unraveling of Venezuela's democracy could not have been predicted based on the earlier solidity of its institutions.[18]

The parallel question that our volume raises is how easy or difficult it is for countries to overcome negative legacies and embark on a more positive trajectory. Alan Angell weighs in forcefully on the side of emphasizing the impact of historical legacies, averring that Chile's history of democracy has been favorable for building high-quality democracy in the present. An extensive prior history of democracy is favorable to building solid institutions and to fostering a democratic political culture.

Although we agree with Angell's argument for the Chilean case, we are not full-fledged enthusiasts of all path dependent claims about political regimes. With so many profound discontinuities, the story of political regimes in Latin America is not one of clear path dependence. If we were writing in 1973, when Chilean democracy was in crisis and broke down, or in 1983, when the military regime was well entrenched despite a severe recession, it would have been impossible to foresee Chile's post-1990 success in democratic governance. Countries sometimes veer in unexpected and unpredictable directions. The analyses by Cardoso on Brazil and Seligson and Martínez on Costa Rica in this volume illustrate this perspective. Cardoso helped steer Brazil from the four-digit inflation of 1989–1994, with imposing social, political, and economic costs, to economic stability. Path dependent arguments usually do not consider such leadership effects and other contingent factors. Social scientists and historians look to the past to understand the present, but often they do so in ways that understate the role of choice, leadership, chance, and tipping points. History is deeply contingent. In his analysis of Brazil, Fernando Henrique Cardoso fruitfully underscores these elements. Leaders and their decisions or their lack of decisive action can alter a country's trajectory (Linz 1978; O'Donnell and Schmitter 1986; Stepan 1978; Tanaka 1998).

10. *In the post-1990 period in Latin America, in most countries, success in some dimensions of democratic governance has been associated with success in the others. Conversely, countries that have performed poorly in some dimensions have done poorly in most others.* This lesson is surprising in light of some earlier literature on development and the contemporary experience in the post-Soviet region. Much of the literature has emphasized that good outcomes do not always go together and that countries often face steep tradeoffs among development goals. Some analysts believed that democracy might be inimical to economic growth, or that authoritarian regimes were better at fostering growth. Most economists believed that there were tradeoffs between economic growth and social programs. Sylvia Hewlitt's (1980) book on Brazil, *The Cruel Dilemmas of Development*, and the admonition that the idea that "All Good Things Go Together" is false (Packenham 1973, 123–29), are expressive of the emphasis on tradeoffs that characterized the literature (Huntington 1968).

One explanation for this felicitous combination in contemporary Latin America might have to do with building a solid state, which in turn supports stronger democracy and better economic results (Rodrik 2000). Another plausible explanation is that better economic and social results have served as a bulwark for democracy, supporting a high level of democracy. Conversely, countries with a low level of democracy have also had worse performance in economic growth, job creation, and education. One plausible explanation for this pernicious combination is that weak democratic institutions fuel widespread clientelism, corruption, and patrimonialism, with negative consequences for democracy and economic and social performance.

Tradeoffs among different outcomes certainly exist in principle and in many real world situations. In post-1990 Latin America, however, as we show in Chapter 1, high levels of democracy have gone hand in hand with better performance in economic growth, control of corruption, rule of law, job creation, poverty reduction, and improvements in access to secondary education.[19]

11. *Effective democratic governance does not always satisfy popular aspirations.*[20]   It does not always generate enduring popular support; moreover, governments that govern poorly can capture popular support. The third wave has given us a much deeper appreciation of this point. The literature in political science did not anticipate how large the gap between government performance and citizen response can be.

Chile is an example of a country that has done well on objective measures but has not satisfied its citizens, as Alan Angell shows in his chapter in this volume. Notwithstanding Chile's successes, in the 2007 Latinobarómetro public opinion survey, only 36% of Chileans stated that they were mostly or very satisfied with democracy. Only 46% of Chileans stated that democracy is always preferable to other forms of government. This figure is considerably lower than the one for Uruguay (77%), Costa Rica (76%), Argentina (74%), the Dominican Republic (71%), and Venezuela (70%), and it is lower than the Latin American average (56%). Many Chileans do not express satisfaction with the economic model that has produced the most growth in Latin America, lowered poverty at a rate far faster than any other country in the region, and produced one of the highest growth rates in the world (Angell 2006). Confidence in parties is low.

Chilean dissatisfaction with democracy in the face of many impressive results points out a paradox of democracy. Democracy is a moving target. When democratic governments succeed at a series of tasks, this success generates new expectations and demands, and in some cases even new rights. Citizens might take for granted the successes of the recent past and demand new accomplishments and orientations.

In a similar vein, President Alejandro Toledo of Peru (2001–06) had a respectable performance in terms of most objective indicators, but his public opinion ratings were dismal until the last few months of his term. The economy grew at a rapid rate from 2002 until 2006, averaging slightly above four percent per capita per year—Peru's most sustained growth in four decades. Inflation was consistently low (below 4% per year all five years). Average real wages increased slightly, and urban unemployment decreased slightly. The rates of poverty and indigency declined from 54.8% and 24.4%, respectively, in 2001 to 44.5% and 16.1%, respectively, in 2006.[21]

Despite these policy successes, throughout almost his entire term, Toledo's approval rating was below 15% and as low as 8%. After an initial plunge in his approval rating, followed by four years of poor ratings, it rose above 15% only in January 2006, six months before the end of his term. For years, Peruvians debated whether he would be able to make it to the bitter end of his term. Based on the country's positive economic and decent social indicators, it is difficult to understand why he was so unpopular during most of his term. In the final six months, his approval shot up from 13% (January 2006) to 33% (July 2006).[22]

Venezuelan President Hugo Chávez represents a contrasting example of a leader who has produced at best mediocre results for his country in social and economic terms and who presided over the systematic erosion of Venezuela's democracy (Coppedge 2005). Yet Chávez has captured strong support among the poor and has won multiple electoral victories. He won the 2006 presidential election by a landslide margin, with 63% of the vote. His attacks on the oligarchy, his identification with the poor, his social programs aimed at the poor (although inefficient technically), and his personal charisma and background as a poor Venezuelan are crucial factors in explaining his electoral appeal. Most poor voters in Venezuela believe that Chávez is democratic and is committed to their cause. He has also benefited enormously from surging oil prices; it is impossible to explain his popular support based solely on cultural/symbolic/personalistic appeals and social programs. Yet at the same time, it is impossible to explain his popular appeal based on the quality of democratic governance. Some other populist leaders in Latin America have similarly won widespread popular support despite substandard governing performance; Juan Perón, president of Argentina from 1946–1955 and 1973–1974 is a prominent example.

Many theoretical approaches to politics assume that good government outcomes satisfy voters. Fiorina's seminal work (1981) on retrospective voting, for example, posits that citizens vote on the basis of government performance. Lipset's (1960, 64–70) classic work rests on the similar view that ultimately democratic legitimacy hinges on government performance. The work on economic voting also suggests that economic performance has a major impact on voting (and presumably on public opinion). Yet in Latin America, some presidents with good economic performance have had low approval ratings, and vice versa. Our book shows that in contemporary Latin America, the relationship between successful democratic governance and popular support is less clear-cut than the literature has posited. Populist leaders can mobilize broad support and legitimacy despite poor performance. Citizens may vote for governments that govern poorly, and they may view as legitimate governments that perform poorly.

Conversely, in a region of so much poverty and inequality, it is easy to politicize governmental failures of even relatively successful governments. Remarkably, for eighteen Latin American countries, better Freedom House scores for 2008 and higher scores for rule of law and regulatory quality in 2007 according to Kaufmann et al. (2008) had no correlation at conventional levels of statistical significance (even at $p < .10$) with satisfaction with democracy in the Latinobarómetro 2008. (Refer back to Table 11.1 for the data.) Control of corruption was correlated with citizen satisfaction with democracy at .45 ($p < .07$ in a 2-tailed test). At the country level, performance on crucial procedural dimensions of democratic governance thus has little to no discernible impact on citizen satisfaction with democracy.

Identity politics, expressive politics, and presidents' personalistic appeals sometimes trump performance-based voting (Silveira 1998). Political outsiders can cultivate popular support by creating mechanisms that seem to empower hitherto marginalized people. Poor people who have suffered indignities at the hands of the elite or of state bureaucrats can embrace the idea that the established system needs profound change, even if this change does not bring about promised improvements in living conditions.

The quality of democratic governance is important to citizens, but it is not all-important. Citizens also understandably care about other issues. Political leaders can use symbols and create leadership styles that win popular support even in the absence of effective governance. This tension between effective democratic governance and popular appeal gives rise to the pervasive tension between institutionalized representation and populism that Navia and Walker analyze in their chapter. As we look toward the second decade of this century, this tension has emerged as one of the great issues in Latin American politics.

Notes

We are grateful to Wendy Hunter, James McGuire, Aníbal Pérez-Liñán, Tim Power, Jaime Ros, Ignacio Walker, Kurt Weyland, and an anonymous reviewer for helpful comments.

1. For influential syntheses about effective economic policies, see Birdsall and de le Torre (2001); Kuczynski and Williamson (2003).

2. However, De Gregorio's comparison of Latin America with East Asia indicates a larger benefit to trade openness. Along similar lines, Lora et al. (2003) argue that market-oriented economic reforms "have had a positive but modest effect on growth" (p. 15).

3. According to the World Development Indicators, per capita GDP in Venezuela fell 11% in 2002 and another 9% in 2003 before increasing 16% in 2004 and 7% in 2005. Source: World Bank 2007.

4. In 2005, Chile's central government revenue was 18.8% of GDP, the fourth highest in Latin America behind Brazil (25.8% in 2004), Uruguay (23.8%), and Nicaragua (20.1%). Data from CEPAL. Source: www.cepal.org/ilpes/.

5. This is the central issue in Birdsall and de le Torre (2001) and Kuczynski and Williamson (2003). José De Gregorio's and Alejandro Foxley's chapters in this volume address these questions.

6. See Glaeser et al. 2004 for a dissenting view.

7. Acemoglu et al. (2001) do not claim that they are measuring institutional quality; they use settler mortality rates to instrument institutional quality. Although this procedure makes for the best estimating techniques in econometrics, it does not allow them to address which institutions foster growth.

8. Kurtz and Shrank (2007) offer some converging assessments.

9. A generation ago, Evans, Rueschemeyer, and Skocpol (1985), Skocpol (1979) and Stepan (1978) argued for more attention to the state in political science. Except for the literature on state failure, their call has not been heeded frequently.

10. Of course, high taxes can be a drag on economic growth. Many analysts believe that this is true in Brazil today.

11. Writing on the advanced industrial democracies, Roller (2005, 280) comes to a similar conclusion.

12. For elaborations of this general point in other contexts, see Mainwaring 2006; Tanaka 2005.

13. Some important institutional changes in Bolivia were enacted under the first Sánchez de Lozada government, but these reforms were not primarily responsible for the deterioration in democratic governance.

14. For a converging view, see Weyland (2002b), who argues that deeper crises in Latin America generated the willingness to accept the sacrifices needed for far reaching economic reform.

15. Along similar lines, Kitschelt and Wilkinson (2007) argue that formal political institutions do not account for differences in patterns of democratic representation and accountability.

16. The quest for generalizable policy prescriptions taps into larger debates in the social sciences about the desirability and feasibility of broad generalization. Some social scientists have asserted that generalization is at the core of social science. For example, Bates (1997, 166) argued that "social scientists seek to identify lawful regularities, which...must not be context bound." Along similar lines, Ferejohn and Satz (1995) claimed that social science should rest on universal laws. Other scholars (e.g., Green and Shapiro 1994) argue that the search for universal laws can be a hindrance to social science. Consistent with our view that successful democratic governance is context dependent, social scientists must be aware of the fact that causal patterns can differ according to context.

17. Along similar lines, Edwards (1995, 41–66) spoke of "a new Latin American consensus." His characterization of this consensus converged with Williamson's. Like Williamson, Edwards expressed optimism that market-oriented economic reform would pave the way to more robust economic growth.

18. Karl (1997) argues that oil dependence created vicious cycles that were difficult to avoid. Coppedge (1994) argues that a rigid party system and tight party control of democracy help explain the combination of stable democracy after 1958 and low quality democracy. However, Venezuela's pre-1993 trajectory did not make an erosion of democracy inevitable or even likely.

19. Virtuous feedbacks exist on some issues in a broader comparative framework. On a large-N scale, a higher level of democracy is associated with lower volatility in rates of economic growth (Przeworski et al. 2000; Rodrik 2000). Rodrik (2000) also argues that a higher level of democracy is favorable to better income distribution.

20. We are indebted to Kurt Weyland for underscoring this point.

21. Data on growth and inflation come from the Economic Commission for Latin America and the Caribbean (ECLAC) 2007: *Preliminary Overview of the Economies of Latin America and the Caribbean 2007*, Tables A-3 and A-22. Data on poverty come from the Economic Commission for Latin America and the Caribbean, Social Panorama of Latin America 2007 (Briefing Paper), p. 11. Both sources on line at www.eclac.cl/publicaciones/default.asp?idioma=IN.

22. National survey data from Apoyo. See *Opinión Data* Year 6 No. 78 (July 17, 2006), p. 2. Data courtesy of Charles Kenney.

References

Acemoglu, Daron, Simon Johnson, and James A. Robinson. 2001. The Colonial Origins of Comparative Development: An Empirical Investigation. *American Economic Review* 91(5):1369–1401.

Alcalá, Francisco, and Antonio Ciccone. 2004. Trade and Productivity. *The Quarterly Journal of Economics* 119(2):613–46.

Aldrich, John H. 1995. *Why Parties? The Origin and Transformation of Political Parties in America*. Chicago: University of Chicago Press.

Ames, Barry. 2001. *The Deadlock of Democracy in Brazil*. Ann Arbor: University of Michigan Press.

Angell, Alan. 2006. Hechos o percepciones ciudadanas? Una paradoja en la evaluación de la democracia chilena. In *Chile: Política y modernización democrática*, ed. Manuel Alcántara Sáez and Leticia M. Ruiz Rodríguez, 165–98. Barcelona: Edicions Bellaterra.

Bates, Robert. 1997. Area Studies and the Discipline: A Useful Controversy? *PS: Political Science and Politics* 30(2):167–68.

Bejarano, Ana María, and Eduardo Pizarro. 2005. From "Restricted" to "Besieged": The Changing Nature of the Limits to Democracy in Colombia. In *The Third Wave of Democratization in Latin America: Advances and Setbacks*, ed. Frances Hagopian and Scott Mainwaring, 235–60. Cambridge: Cambridge University Press.

Birdsall, Nancy, and Augusto de la Torre. 2001. *Washington Contentious*. Washington, DC: Carnegie Endowment for International Peace and Inter-American Dialogue.

Birdsall, Nancy, and Miguel Székely. 2003. Bootstraps, Not Band-Aids: Poverty, Equity, and Social Policy. In *After the Washington Consensus: Restarting Growth and Reform in Latin America*, ed. John Williamson and Pedro-Pablo Kuczynski, 49–73. Washington, DC: Institute for International Economics.

Brinks, Daniel M. 2008. *The Judicial Response to Police Killings in Latin America: Inequality and the Rule of Law*. Cambridge: Cambridge University Press.

Carey, John M., and Matthew S. Shugart, eds. 1998. *Executive Decree Authority*. Cambridge: Cambridge University Press.

CEPAL. 2008. Available at http://websie.eclac.cl/sisgen/ConsultaIntegrada.asp ?idAplicacion=6&idTema=140&idioma=i.

Cheibub, José Antonio. 2007. *Presidentialism, Parliamentarism, and Democracy*. Cambridge: Cambridge University Press.

Coppedge, Michael. 1994. *Strong Parties and Lame Ducks: Presidential Partyarchy and Factionalism in Venezuela*. Stanford, CA: Stanford University Press.

———. 2005. Explaining Democratic Deterioration in Venezuela Through Nested Inference. In *The Third Wave of Democratization in Latin America: Advances and Setbacks*, ed. Frances Hagopian and Scott Mainwaring, 289–316. Cambridge: Cambridge University Press.

Di Palma, Giuseppe. 1990. *To Craft Democracies*. Berkeley, CA: University of California Press.

Dodson, Michael, and Donald W. Jackson. 2003. Horizontal Accountability and the Rule of Law in Central America. In *Democratic Accountability in Latin America*, ed. Scott Mainwaring and Christopher Welna, 228–65. Oxford: Oxford University Press.

Dollar, David, and Arat Kraay. 2003. Institutions, Trade, and Growth. *Journal of Monetary Economics* 50(1):133–62.

Easterly, William. 2001. The Lost Decades: Developing Countries' Stagnation in Spite of Policy Reform 1980–1998. *Journal of Economic Growth* 6(June):135–57.

Easterly, William, and Ross Levine. 2003. Tropics, Germs, and Crops: How Endowments Influence Economic Development. *Journal of Monetary Economics* 50(1):3–39.

ECLAC (Economic Commission for Latin America and the Caribbean). 2007. Social Panorama of Latin America 2007 (Briefing Paper). Online at www.eclac.cl/publicaciones/default.asp?idioma=IN.

———. 2007. Preliminary Overview of the Economies of Latin America and the Caribbean 2007. Online at www.eclac.cl/publicaciones/default.asp?idioma=IN.

Edwards, Sebastian. 1995. *Crisis and Reform in Latin America: From Despair to Hope*. New York and Oxford: Oxford University Press.

Evans, Peter. 1995. *Embedded Autonomy: States and Industrial Transformation*. Princeton, NJ: Princeton University Press.

Evans, Peter, and James E. Rauch. 1999. Bureaucracy and Growth: A Cross-National Analysis of the Effects of "Weberian" State Structures on Economic Growth. *American Sociological Review* 64(5):748–65.

Evans, Peter B., Dietrich Rueschemeyer, and Theda Skocpol, eds. 1985. *Bringing the State Back In*. Cambridge: Cambridge University Press.

Ferejohn, John, and Debra Satz. 1995. Unification, Universalism, and Rational Choice Theory. *Critical Review* 9(1–2):71–84.

Figueiredo, Argelina Cheibub, and Fernando Limongi. 1999. *Executivo e Legislativo na Nova Ordem Constitucional*. Rio de Janeiro: Eitora Fundação Getúlio Vargas.

Fiorina, Morris P. 1981. *Retrospective Voting in American National Elections*. New Haven, CT: Yale University Press.

Forteza, Alvaro, and Mariano Tomassi. 2005. *Understanding Reform in Latin America*. Documento No. 22/05 (November). Departamento de Economía, Facultad de Ciencias Sociales, Universidad de la República.

Fukuyama, Francis. 1992. *The End of History and the Last Man*. New York: Free Press.

———. 2004. *State Building: Governance and World Order in the 21st Century*. Ithaca, NY: Cornell University Press.

Gibson, Edward. 2005. Boundary Control: Subnational Authoritarianism in Democratic Countries. *World Politics* 58(1):101–32.

Glaeser, Edward L., Rafael La Porta, Florencio López-de-Silanes, and Andrei Shleifer. 2004. Do Institutions Cause Growth? Unpublished.

Green, Donald, and Ian Shapiro. 1994. *The Pathologies of Rational Choice Theory*. New Haven, CT: Yale University Press.

Guevara Mann, Carlos. Forthcoming. *Forsaken Virtue: Reelection, Rent-Seeking, and the Search for Immunity in Panama's Assembly Members*, Notre Dame, IN: University of Notre Dame Press.

Haggard, Stephan, and Mathew D. McCubbins, eds. 2001. *Presidents, Parliaments, and Policy*. Cambridge: Cambridge University Press.

Hagopian, Frances. 1996. *Traditional Politics and Regime Change in Brazil*. Cambridge: Cambridge University Press.

Hagopian, Frances, Carlos Gervasoni, and Juan Andrés Moraes. 2009. "From Patronage to Program: The Emergence of Party-Oriented Legislators in Brazil." *Comparative Political Studies* 42(3): 360–91.

Hall, Robert E., and Charles I. Jones. 1999. Why Do Some Countries Produce So Much More Output per Worker than Others? *The Quarterly Journal of Economics* 114(1): 83–116.

Helmke, Gretchen, and Steven Levitsky, eds. 2006. *Informal Institutions and Democracy: Lessons from Latin America.* Baltimore: Johns Hopkins University Press.

Hewlitt, Sylvia. 1980. *The Cruel Dilemmas of Development: Twentieth Century Brazil.* New York: Basic Books.

Hirschman, Albert O. 1963. *Journeys Toward Progress.* New York: Twentieth Century Fund.

———. 1971. *A Bias for Hope: Essays on Development and Latin America.* New Haven, CT: Yale University Press.

Huntington, Samuel P. 1968. *Political Order in Changing Societies.* New Haven, CT: Yale University Press.

Inter-American Development Bank. 2000. *Development Beyond Economics: Economic and Social Progress in Latin America.* Washington, DC: Inter-American Development Bank.

———. 2005. *The Politics of Policies: Economic and Social Progress in Latin America.* Washington, DC: Inter-American Development Bank and the David Rockefeller Center for Latin American Studies, Harvard University.

Inter-American Development Bank, and the International Institute for Democracy and Electoral Assistance. 2002. *Democracies in Development: Politics and Reform in Latin America.* Washington, DC: Inter-American Development Bank.

Jones, Mark P. 1997. Federalism and the Number of Parties in Argentine Congressional Elections. *The Journal of Politics* 59(2): 538–49.

Karl, Terry Lynn. 1997. *The Paradox of Plenty: Oil Booms and Petro-States.* Berkeley, CA: University of California Press.

Kaufmann, Daniel, Aart Kraay, and Massimo Mastruzzi. 2003. Governance Matters III: Governance Indicators for 1996–2002. The World Bank, Policy Research Paper 3106 (August). Available at http://econ.worldbank.org.

———. 2005. Governance Matters IV: Governance Indicators for 1996–2004. The World Bank, Policy Research Paper 3630 (June). Available at http://econ.worldbank.org.

———. 2006. Governance Matters V: Aggregate and Individual Governance Indicators for 1996–2005." World Bank, Policy Research Paper 4012 (September). Available at http://econ.worldbank.org.

———. 2007. Governance Matters VI: Aggregate and Individual Governance Indicators for 1996–2006. World Bank Policy Research Paper 4280 (July). Available at http://econ.worldbank.org.

Kitschelt, Herbert, and Steven I. Wilkinson. 2007. Citizen-Politician Linkages: An Introduction. In *Patrons, Clients, and Policies: Patterns of Democratic*

Accountability and Political Competition, ed. Herbert Kitschelt and Steven I. Wilkinson, 1–49. Cambridge: Cambridge University Press.

Knack, Stephen, and Philip Keefer. 1995. Institutions and Economic Performance: Cross-Country Tests Using Alternative Institutional Measures. *Economics and Politics* 7 (3): 207–27.

Kuczynski, Pedro-Pablo. 2003. Reforming the State. In *After the Washington Consensus: Restarting Growth and Reform in Latin America*, ed. Pedro-Pablo Kuczynski and John Williamson, 33–47. Washington, DC: Institute for International Economics.

Kuczynski, Pedro-Pablo, and John Williamson, eds. 2003. *After the Washington Consensus: Restarting Growth and Reform in Latin America*. Washington, DC: Institute for International Economics.

Kurtz, Marcus J., and Andrew Schrank. 2007. Growth and Governance: Models, Measures, and Mechanisms. *The Journal of Politics* 69(2): 538–54.

Latinobarómetro (Corporación Latinobarómetro). 2007. Latinobarómetro Report 2007. Available at www.latinobarometro.org.

Levitsky, Steven, and María Victoria Murillo. 2005. Theorizing About Weak Institutions: Lessons from the Argentina Case. In *Argentine Democracy: The Politics of Institutional Weakness*, ed. Steven Levitsky and María Victoria Murillo, 269–89. University Park, PA: Pennsylvania State University Press.

Linz, Juan J. 1978. *The Breakdown of Democratic Regimes: Crisis, Breakdown, and Reequilibrium*. Baltimore: Johns Hopkins University Press.

———. 1994. Democracy: Presidential or Parliamentary. Does It Make a Difference? In *The Failure of Presidential Democracy*, ed. Juan J. Linz and Arturo Valenzuela, 3–87. Baltimore: Johns Hopkins University Press.

Linz Juan J., and Alfred Stepan. 1996. *Problems of Democratic Transition and Consolidation: Southern Europe, South America, and Post-Communist Europe*. Baltimore: Johns Hopkins University Press.

Lipset, Seymour Martin. 1960. *Political Man*. Garden City, NY: Doubleday and Company, Inc.

Lora, Eduardo, Ugo Panizza, and Myriam Quispe-Agnoli. 2003. Reform Fatigue: Symptoms, Reasons, Implications. Paper presented at the conference Rethinking Structural Reform in Latin America, Federal Reserve Bank of Atlanta. Inter-American Development Bank, Research Department.

Mainwaring, Scott. 1999a. *Rethinking Party Systems in the Third Wave of Democratization: The Case of Brazil*. Stanford, CA: Stanford University Press.

———. 1999b. The Surprising Resilience of Latin America's Elected Governments. *The Journal of Democracy* 10(3):101–14.

———. 2006. State Deficiencies, Party Competition, and Confidence in Democratic Representation in the Andes." In *The Crisis of Democratic Representation in the Andes*, ed. Scott Mainwaring, Ana María Bejarano, and Eduardo Pizarro, 295–345. Stanford, CA: Stanford University Press.

Mainwaring, Scott, and Timothy R. Scully. 1995. Party Systems in Latin America. In *Building Democratic Institutions: Party Systems in Latin America*, ed.

Scott Mainwaring and Timothy Scully, 1–34, 477–82. Stanford, CA: Stanford University Press.

Mainwaring, Scott, and Mariano Torcal. 2006. Party System Institutionalization and Party System Theory After the Third Wave of Democratization. In *Handbook of Political Parties*, ed. Richard S. Katz and William Crotty, 204–27. London: Sage Publications.

Mayorga, René. 2006. Outsiders and Neopopulism: The Road to Plebiscitary Democracy. In *The Crisis of Democratic Representation in the Andes*, ed. Scott Mainwaring, et al. Stanford, CA: Stanford University Press.

Moreno, Erika, Brian F. Crisp, and Matthew S. Shugart. 2003. The Accountability Deficit in Latin America. In *Democratic Accountability in Latin America*, ed. Scott Mainwaring and Christopher Welna, 79–131. Oxford: Oxford University Press.

Naím, Moisés. 1994. Latin America: The Second Stage of Reform. *The Journal of Democracy* 5(4): 32–48.

———. 2000. Washington Consensus or Washington Confusion? *Foreign Policy* 118: 87–103.

North, Douglass C. 1990. *Institutions, Institutional Change and Economic Performance*. Cambridge: Cambridge University Press.

O'Donnell, Guillermo. 1993. On the State, Democratization, and Some Conceptual Problems: A Latin American View with Glances at Some Post-Communist Countries. *World Development* 21(8): 1345–69.

———. 1994. Delegative Democracy. *Journal of Democracy* 5(1): 55–69.

———. 1996. Illusions about Consolidation. *The Journal of Democracy* 7(2): 34–51.

———. 1999. Poliarchies and the (Un)Rule of Law in Latin America: A Partial Conclusion. In *The (Un)Rule of Law and the Underprivileged in Latin America*, ed. Juan E. Méndez, Guillermo O'Donnell, and Paulo Sérgio Pinheiro eds., 303–37. Notre Dame, IN: University of Notre Dame Press.

O'Donnell, Guillermo, and Philippe Schmitter. 1986. Tentative Conclusions about Uncertain Democracies. Part 4 of Transitions from *Authoritarian Rule: Prospects for Democracy*, ed. O'Donnell, Schmitter, and Laurence Whitehead. Baltimore: Johns Hopkins University Press.

Packenham, Robert A. 1973. *Liberal America and the Third World: Political Development Ideas in Foreign Aid and Social Science*. Princeton, NJ: Princeton University Press.

Pan American Health Organization. 2006. Guidelines for the Design, Implementation, and Evaluation of Epidemiological Surveillance Systems on Violence and Injuries. Available at www.paho.org/.

Pérez-Liñán, Aníbal. 2007. *Presidential Impeachment and the New Political Instability in Latin America*. Cambridge: Cambridge University Press.

Pizarro Leongómez, Eduardo. 2006. Giants with Feet of Clay: Political Parties in Colombia. In *The Crisis of Democratic Representation in the Andes*, ed. Scott Mainwaring, Ana María Bejarano, and Eduardo Pizarro, 78–99. Stanford, CA: Stanford University Press.

Przeworski, Adam, Michael Alvarez, José Antonio Cheibub, and Fernando Limongi. 2000. *Democracy and Development: Political Institutions and Well-Being in the World, 1950–1990*. Cambridge: Cambridge University Press

Rodríguez, Francisco, and Dani Rodrik. 2001. Trade Policy and Economic Growth: A Skeptic's Guide to the Cross-National Evidence. In *NBER Macroeconomics Annual 2000* (15), ed. Ben S. Bernanke and Kenneth Rogoff, 261–338.

Rodrik, Dani. 2000. Institutions for High-Quality Growth: What They Are and How to Acquire Them. *Studies in Comparative International Development* 35(3): 3–31.

———. 2003. Introduction: What Do We Learn from the Country Narratives? In *In Search of Prosperity: Analytic Narratives on Economic Growth*, ed. Dani Rodrik. Princeton, NJ: Princeton University Press.

Rodrik, Dani, Arvind Sukbramanian, and Francesco Trebbi. 2004. Institutions Rule: The Primacy of Institutions over Integration and Geography in Economic Development. *Journal of Economic Growth* 9(2): 131–65.

Roller, Edeltraud. 2005. *The Performance of Democracies: Political Institutions and Public Policies*. Oxford: Oxford University Press.

Samuels, David. 2003. *Ambition, Federalism, and Legislative Politics in Brazil*. Cambridge: Cambridge University Press.

Shugart, Matthew Soberg, and John Carey. 1992. *Presidents and Assemblies: Constitutional Design and Electoral Dynamics*. Cambridge: Cambridge University Press.

Shugart, Matthew Soberg, and Scott Mainwaring. 1997. Presidentialism and Democracy in Latin America: Rethinking the Terms of the Debate. In *Presidentialism and Democracy in Latin America*, ed. Scott Mainwaring and Matthew Shugart, 12–54. Cambridge: Cambridge University Press.

Silveira, Flávio Eduardo. 1998. *A Decisão do Voto no Brasil*. Porto Alegre: EDIPUCRS.

Skocpol, Theda. 1979. *States and Social Revolutions: A Comparative Analysis of France, Russia, and China*. Cambridge: Cambridge University Press.

Spiller, Pablo T., and Mariano Tomassi. 2003. The Institutional Foundations of Public Policy: A Transactions Approach with Application to Argentina. *The Journal of Law, Economics, and Organization* 19(2): 281–306.

Stepan, Alfred C. 1978. *The State and Society: Peru in Comparative Perspective*. Princeton, NJ: Princeton University Press.

———. 2001. *Arguing Comparative Politics*. Oxford: Oxford University Press.

Tanaka, Martín. 1998. *El espejismos de la democracia: El colapso del sistema de partidos en el Peru, 1980–1995*. Lima: Instituto de Estudios Peruanos.

———. 2005. *Democracia sin partidos: Peru, 2000–2005*. Lima: Instituto de Estudios Peruanos.

———. 2006. From Crisis to Collapse of the Party Systems and Dilemmas of Democratic Representation: Peru and Venezuela. In *The Crisis of Democratic Representation in the Andes*, ed. Scott Mainwaring, et al. Stanford, CA: Stanford University Press.

Tsebelis, George. 2002. *Veto Players: How Political Institutions Work.* Princeton, NJ: Princeton University Press.

UNDP (United Nations Development Programme). 2005. *Democracy in Latin America: Towards a Citizens' Democracy.* New York: United Nations Development Programme.

Valenzuela, Arturo. 2004. Latin American Presidencies Interrupted. *The Journal of Democracy* 15(4): 5–19.

Valenzuela, J. Samuel. 2006. Democracia familiar y desarrollo: Chile y Suecia desde 1914. In *El eslabón perdido: Familia, modernización y bienestar en Chile,* ed. J. Samuel Valenzuela, Eugenio Tironi, and Timothy R. Scully, 97–136. Santiago: Taurus.

Viola, Eduardo, and Héctor Ricardo Leis. 2007. *Sistema Internacional com Hegemona das Democracias de Mercado: Desafios de Brasil e Argentina.* Florianópolis: Insular.

Weyland, Kurt. 2002a. Limitations of Rational Choice Institutionalism for the Study of Latin American Politics. *Studies in Comparative International Development* 37(3): 57–85.

———. 2002b. *The Politics of Market Reform in Fragile Democracies: Argentina, Brazil, Peru, and Venezuela.* Princeton, NJ: Princeton University Press.

Wiarda, Howard J. 2001. *The Soul of Latin America: The Cultural and Political Tradition.* New Haven, CT: Yale University Press.

Williamson, John. 1990. What Washington Means by Policy Reform. In *Latin American Adjustment: How Much Has Happened?,* ed. John Williamson, 1–20. Washington, DC: Institute for International Economics.

———. 2003. An Agenda for Restarting Growth and Reform. In *After the Washington Consensus: Restarting Growth and Reform in Latin America,* ed. Pedro-Pablo Kuczynski and John Williamson, 1–19. Washington, DC: Institute for International Economics.

Wolff, Laurence, and Claudio de Moura Castro. 2003. Education and Training: The Task Ahead. In *After the Washington Consensus: Restarting Growth and Reform in Latin America,* ed. Pedro-Pablo Kuczynski and John Williamson, 181–212. Washington, DC: Institute for International Economics.

World Bank. 2000/01. *World Development Report: Attacking Poverty.* New York: Oxford University Press.

———. 2002. *World Development Report 2002: Building Institutions for Markets.* New York: Oxford University Press.

———. 2005. *Economic Growth in the 1990s: Learning from a Decade of Reform.* Washington, DC: The World Bank.

———. 2007. *World Development Indicators.* Online.

CHAPTER TWELVE

Postscript: Democratic Governance in Latin America

JOSÉ MIGUEL INSULZA

After fifteen years of predominantly democratic rule in our region, we face a dual challenge. If we want the citizens of Latin America to continue believing in and supporting democracy all over the continent, we must, first, improve the stability and quality of democratic governments and, second, deliver the benefits of democracy to the vast majority of Latin Americans.

The past several years have brought promising news in terms of economic activity in Latin America and the Caribbean. GDP has grown an average of 5% between 2004 and 2007, its strongest growth in twenty-five years, despite rising energy costs.

As a result of this economic growth, poverty has been reduced in the region, according to data from CEPAL, from 48.3% of the population in 1990 to 34.1% in 2007. The strong growth performance during these years was supported by a generally favorable external environment, and also by positive developments at the domestic level. Externally, the region benefited from robust global growth, vigorous growth in international trade, higher commodity prices, lower international interest rates, and spreads on emerging markets at historical lows. At the domestic level, we saw greater resilience to domestic and external shocks due to strengthened fiscal positions (in contrast to previous growth episodes, where large capital inflows financed the expansion of public and private spending); more proactive monetary policy targeted at containing inflation; and greater flexibility in exchange rates.

However, daunting challenges still lie before us. Unemployment continues at unreasonably high levels in many countries, the region's foreign debt burden remains a threat, and foreign investment is lower than expected. Though there are some signs of improvement, many in the region wonder if Latin American economies will, this time, be able to sustain this period of growth and if, this time, this growth can reach the large numbers of people who still remain at the margins of our societies.

There exists a pervasive sensation that we have been here before. At the beginning of the nineties, after a series of important reforms that allowed for much stronger fiscal situations, lower inflation, smaller state expenditures, and opening to trade and foreign investment, several countries in the region experienced a promising period of economic growth. Coupled with the recovery of democracy that took place in the southern cone, these developments gave way to a wave of optimism. For a short period of time we felt that this was really a new beginning.

Unfortunately, Latin America's economies were not able to withstand the changes of fortune that took place toward the end of the 1990s, and our economies again went through hard times. We discovered, yet again, that we still have a long way to go as a region to achieve rates of development that will lead us down the path of sustained growth. And, perhaps most importantly, many came to realize that, despite the proliferation of democracy and economic reform, the benefits of material progress continued to elude the poor.

At the beginning of this century an atmosphere of uncertainty pervaded many sectors. Studies have revealed that in several countries the prevailing feeling was of insecurity: people were more afraid of losing their jobs, uncertain of their immediate future, afraid of illness, felt increasingly less protected, and even felt that their children might be worse off than they themselves had been. More recently other surveys, including the Latinobarómetro, have found that many citizens of this region felt that democracy had not delivered what they hoped, leading in some cases to a questioning of the value of democracy itself.

Small wonder, if you consider that this region had nearly 225 million poor at the close of the first decade of the twenty-first century; nearly 100 million of them extremely poor, which means that they live with less than a dollar a day. Latin America is, as one contributor to this volume, Fernando Henrique Cardoso, once said, not the poorest region in the world, but the most unfair. Indeed at the other extreme, less than 5% of the population brings home more than 25% of the region's income.

This is what makes this period so crucial for Latin America and the Caribbean. On one hand, there have been important accomplishments in relative terms. Where less than two decades ago we had mostly dictatorships, we now have democracies; where there was war, there is mostly peace (except in Colombia); respect for human rights has increased substantially; and considerable economic reforms have allowed countries in the region to gain ground in terms of macroeconomic stability. But on the other hand, many of these democracies are still weak, reforms are incomplete, crime has grown, poverty is widespread; and there is a feeling that, if we want to succeed this time, several structural changes still have to take place in our societies.

At the heart of the problematic is the question of governance. In the past two decades, fourteen elected presidents in the region have failed to finish their constitutional terms, and six of their replacements, chosen according to their countries' constitutions, have suffered the same fate. In some of these cases, the failure to complete the term of office reflected impossible situations that were inherited by incumbents.

Democracy does not necessarily depend upon economic success, but it is always more difficult to govern when many citizens suffer the consequences of poverty and/or economic crisis. And these political crises have not been provoked by revolutions or military coups, as happened in the recent past. Social or political unrest has not been catalyzed by ideology, but rather by a pervasive discontent of common people at what they see as the inefficiency, the unfairness, the corruption of their governments. Ordinary citizens feel an unbridled rage over a situation that ordinary citizens cannot seem to control or change.

Some political analysts view these popular outbursts as a positive sign, as eruptions of participatory democracy or as a constructive expression of the common people. I do not believe this is the case. In most cases these movements do not present a political alternative. As President Hugo Chávez said when he took office in 1999, he is not a cause, he is a consequence; the consequence of misgovernment, of economic mismanagement, of uncertainty and fear, of a generalized disgust with the state of things.

"Que se vayan todos" ("Get rid of all of them," in a loose translation) is not a recipe for a positive outcome. It does not reflect a failure of democracy, but rather a failure of politics. Politics is meant to be not just a matter of ideas or values, but also, and very essentially, a matter of achieving results that are beneficial for the people. And this is precisely where some of our governments and our political elites have failed: they have created or exacerbated more problems than they have solved.

To illustrate my point, I reluctantly refer to an example from my own country, Chile. Before doing so, I must caution that it is not the only successful case in the hemisphere: several countries in the Caribbean, for example, have also developed good governance and high quality institutions. Recently other countries in the region, cases well documented in this volume, have also achieved significant economic growth thanks to improvements in the quality of public policies.

Chile is often referred to as a success story. But in understanding the Chilean case, insufficient attention has been paid to the one essential factor explaining its relative success. Unquestionably, the most relevant factor for the successes experienced by Chile over the past two decades is *politics*.

Without the quality of government that has prevailed in Chile throughout this period, without its dedication to building and strengthening democratic institutions and without the overriding consensus that has been built among political and social forces, including of course those among the opposition, many of Chile's achievements would not have been possible. Macroeconomic policies have been prudent; a very successful integration to the world economy has occurred; infrastructure has developed enormously; education and health benefits have been extended, many other achievements have been realized. But these achievements have been possible only because they rest upon the foundation of solid political institutions and a resulting political consensus.

Of course Chile still has many problems and its future is not a given. Poverty has not been eliminated; education is universal, but its quality is still very unequal; income distribution is sharply inequitable. But it still stands as the best case of successfully improving the condition of the people through democratic rule. It demonstrates unambiguously that successful governance plays a role.

The most urgent challenge for the stability of democratic governments in Latin America and the Caribbean today is to show that they can govern successfully and deliver to their citizens the benefits of democracy.

What are we referring to when we speak about providing good governance and delivering the benefits of democracy? Most of the attributes of effective governance are included in the Interamerican Democractic Charter, signed by all the member states of the OAS in 2001.

Governance has to do with more democracy and not with the limitation of democratic rights. Democratically elected governments should exercise power in a democratic way, extending freedom through inclusion, transparency, and participation. As Fareed Zakaria pointed out in his "The Rise of Illiberal Democracy" (Foreign Affairs, November 1997) there are several cases of governments in our times that are elected by a clear majority, but later suppress free speech, limit the freedom of the press and dissent, exclude minorities, promote or tolerate discrimination, and violate human rights. They may have been elected democratically, but they certainly do not govern democratically. Increasing democratic governance means increasing equal opportunity, participation, and freedom for all the people.

The same Latinobarómetro surveys we mentioned earlier suggest that, after recognizing democracy as the best form of government, many respondents still do not identify their own country as democratic or do not believe that democracy has reached them.

The countries of Latin America have advanced in these matters compared with the years of dictatorship, but we still have a long way to go. In general, governments are legitimately elected in Latin America, elections are clean, fraud is an exception, most people vote, and many times the opposition wins. These developments have a tremendous value, especially when compared to the political situations of a couple of decades ago. But as dictatorships become something of the past, people tend to make these comparisons less often. Abuse, inequality, discrimination, and racism still exist. The rule of law is not always equally enforced, and there are still too many poor and indigent. Improving these conditions is linked to democratic rule, and the demand for reform is indicative of a growing democracy.

Governments must be able to govern effectively. While democracy must always increase freedom and participation, a second condition of governance is creating the conditions for a stable government. A democratically elected government should have the capacity to rule the country effectively. This has to do with respect for the rule of law, but also with the strengthening of political institutions and adequate systems of representation.

Some may say that governments in the region are already too presidential. This is perhaps true, but at the same time their political regimes do not provide those presidents with congressional majorities that will allow them to govern effectively. The presidential systems by which authorities are elected sometimes do not provide requisite stable congressional majorities and, on the contrary, create unstable governing coalitions that last only as long as times are good.

The weakness of political parties and intermediate organizations further compounds the problem. As parties are not representative and lack internal discipline, majorities shift frequently and stable governing coalitions cannot be formed. A weak party system makes for a continuous power struggle, leaving little room for compromise and long-term decision making.

Strengthening governance entails creating political institutions that permit full participation and leave room for the formation of solid coalitions and government majorities. This, in turn, demands that political parties are able to play a role in the formation of those majorities and increase their capacity for political representation.

Successful democratic governance also requires building strong public institutions. This is probably one of the most intractable problems, not because many countries in the region lack the basic laws and institutions formally able to carry out public policies, but because these institutions many times are inefficient, too "politicized," or simply not respected. An independent judiciary, an empowered comptroller general, a fair and transparent tax system, and a non-corrupt and efficient police force usually exist on paper, but not in the daily life of many of our democracies, thereby deepening mistrust in government.

Beneath these institutional dimensions lies also the question of the size of government. One of the casualties of the reforms of the 1990s in many parts of the developing world was "big government," which was probably a welcome development, since most of these governments were responsible for productive activities that were costly, inefficient, and/or could be much better handled by the private sector.

However, "small government" became a matter of principle. Small government became a synonym for efficiency and transparency. Almost everything, it was argued, could be transferred to the private sector. This ideology soon crept into other domains of government activity, domains in which the government was in fact the best answer to the needs of most people, especially the poorest. Public education, health, housing, and pensions systems, which were previously big government programs, were reduced in size in response to this new ideology. Unfortunately, in many cases, these essential activities in service to the poor were, as a consequence, simply dropped.

In most developed and developing countries, the provision of public services in these and other areas of activity is a form of secondary income distribution which can be very competitive and efficient, as the European experience has demonstrated. The size of government, as Foxley argues in this volume, has little to do with transparency and competitiveness. Indeed, the most competitive countries according to the World Forum Index have relatively large-sized government sectors.

Many of the problems of good governance in Latin America are not the result of too much government, but rather of inadequate government capacity and resources to deal effectively with social problems in which citizens expect redress. This failure is perhaps the most important source of declining confidence in government.

Of course, appropriate social policies cannot fully make up for the consequences of inequitable economic policy, but they do point to an essential role of government in providing basic social services, with increased quality and efficiency.

Some have argued that small government leaves less room for corruption, but this has not been the experience of the last years in many countries of the hemisphere. On one hand, private business can be prone to corruption, as several corporate scandals have recently shown. On the other hand, though the role of government as a direct producer of goods and services may have diminished, this has been replaced by the authority to make concessions and allocations of resources to private business, a process even more exposed to the pressures of money and influence. If government activity is not fully transparent, this authority can result in a complex association between money and politics, making corruption a structural feature of the political system.

The many rules, laws, and procedures needed to fight corruption and increase transparency are widely known. They all point to the need to separate money from politics, and have concrete institutional expression in laws regulating lobbying activity: transparency and limits in campaign financing, coupled with public financing laws, declarations of wealth and interests of public servants, and transparent systems for the procurement of goods and services, among others.

Improving the conditions that enhance the prospects for successful democratic governance lies at the heart of the challenge that faces Latin American countries as we begin the twenty-first century. Efforts such as the ones undertaken by this valuable volume can make an important contribution toward achieving this end.

Index